# Byzantium in a Changing World

# Byzantium in a Changing World

JAMES HOWARD-JOHNSTON

OXFORD
UNIVERSITY PRESS

OXFORD
UNIVERSITY PRESS

Great Clarendon Street, Oxford, OX2 6DP,
United Kingdom

Oxford University Press is a department of the University of Oxford. It furthers the University's objective of excellence in research, scholarship, and education by publishing worldwide. Oxford is a registered trade mark of Oxford University Press in the UK and in certain other countries



Published in the United States of America by Oxford University Press
198 Madison Avenue, New York, NY 10016, United States of America

British Library Cataloguing in Publication Data
Data available

Library of Congress Control Number: 2025933684

ISBN 9780198897873 (hbk)
ISBN 9780198897897 (pbk)

DOI: 10.1093/9780191999093.001.0001

Printed and bound by
CPI Group (UK) Ltd, Croydon, CR0 4YY

MIX
Paper | Supporting responsible forestry
FSC® C013604

The manufacturer's authorised representative in the EU for product safety is Oxford University Press España S.A. of El Parque Empresarial San Fernando de Henares, Avenida de Castilla, 2 – 28830 Madrid (www.oup.es/en or product.safety@oup.com). OUP España S.A. also acts as importer into Spain of products made by the manufacturer.

*For my former pupils*

# Preface

This book has been written in response—a late, late response—to a commission received nearly thirty years ago. The Oxford University Press wanted a short history of Byzantium for inclusion in its OPUS series. It was to be accessible to a non-academic readership. I agreed and devised a structure modeled on Jonathan Israel's magnificent and massive history of the Dutch Republic in its golden age—the analytical parts being sandwiched between scene-setting narratives. The deadline, December 2000, passed. I continued to gather material and had every intention of writing the book, notwithstanding the proliferation of such works issued by other publishers. The OPUS book was one in a series of projected works, which, in the manner of Oblomov, I would take pleasure in contemplating from time to time, but which somehow did not materialize.

Then came *defunctitude*, entry into retirement, which for academics, as for actors and barons of industry and finance, is usually a continuation of the old life. With little or no teaching, there is more disposable time for the production of learned works, but, of course, that time is not unlimited. It will come to an end at a yet-to-be-defined time, when the mental powers fail or life itself slips away. It is *indefinity*, a precious phase of life, not to be wasted. *Oblomovka* must cease. Books must be either written or struck off. The latter was the fate of the OPUS book. It ceased to exist. Its vital organs, the analytical chapters, were removed, and reassigned to a separate work, *Byzantium: Economy, Society, Institutions 600–1100*. All that was left was a yet-to-be-written skeletal narrative framework.

*Byzantium in a Changing World* began to take shape during the first Covid-19 lockdown in 2020, a rather idyllic time, I am afraid to say, of glorious weather and happy family life. An introduction and two chapters (on Late Antiquity and the Dark Age) were written. It gathered momentum and began to break out of the bounds of a normal potted history, ranging deep into the ever-changing world surrounding Byzantium. Four more chapters, chronologically ordered, were written during the second lockdown, to complete a political, military, and diplomatic history of Byzantium. It is designed to complement the collection of analytical pieces, which is being published separately. Hence its character. It is not a rounded history, of structures as well as events, but one which is deliberately focused on the agitated surface of Byzantine history at home and abroad.

My gratitude to my undergraduate pupils and latterly to graduates taking Master's degrees knows no bounds. It is to them that I dedicate this book. Finally I thank Dan Gallaher for compiling the index.

JH-J

*Brighton, 2024*

# Contents

# List of Figures

# List of Maps

# List of Abbreviations

| | |
|---|---|
| BAR | British Archaeological Reports |
| *BCH* | *Bulletin de Correspondance Hellénique* |
| *BMGS* | *Byzantine and Modern Greek Studies* |
| *Byz.* | *Byzantion* |
| *BZ* | *Byzantinische Zeitschrift* |
| *CAH* | *Cambridge Ancient History* |
| CFHB | Corpus Fontium Historiae Byzantinae |
| *CMH* | *Cambridge Medieval History* |
| *DOP* | *Dumbarton Oaks Papers* |
| *EHR* | *English Historical Review* |
| *JHS* | *Journal of Hellenic Studies* |
| *PP* | *Past and Present* |
| *REB* | *Revue des Études Byzantines* |
| *TM* | *Travaux et Mémoires* |
| TTB | Translated Texts for Byzantinists |
| TTH | Translated Texts for Historians |

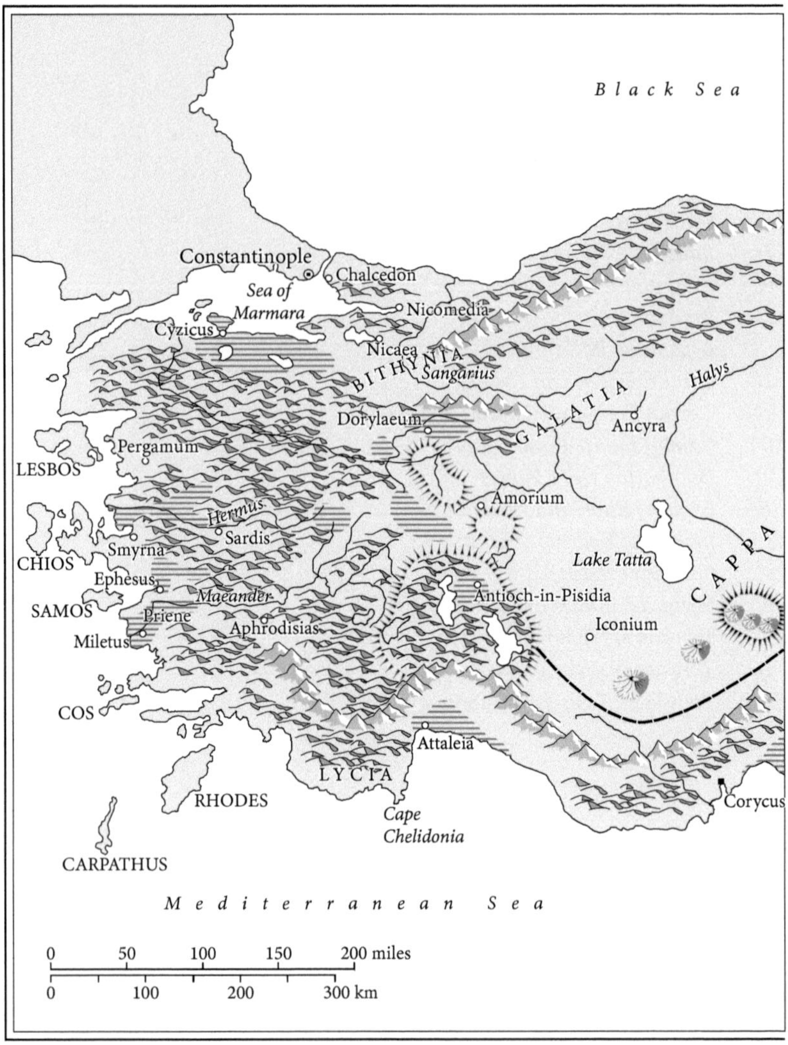


**Map 1** Asia Minor.

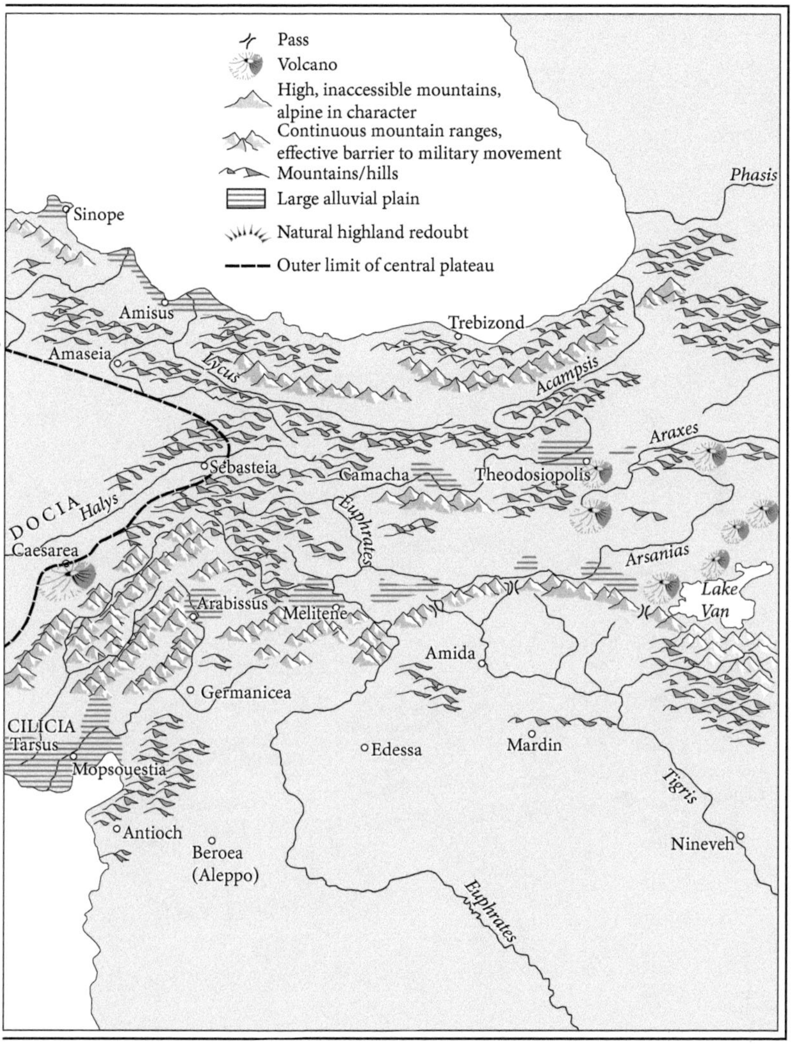


**Map 1** Continued.

**Map 2** Balkans and Aegean.

**Map 3** Late Roman empire *c.*390.

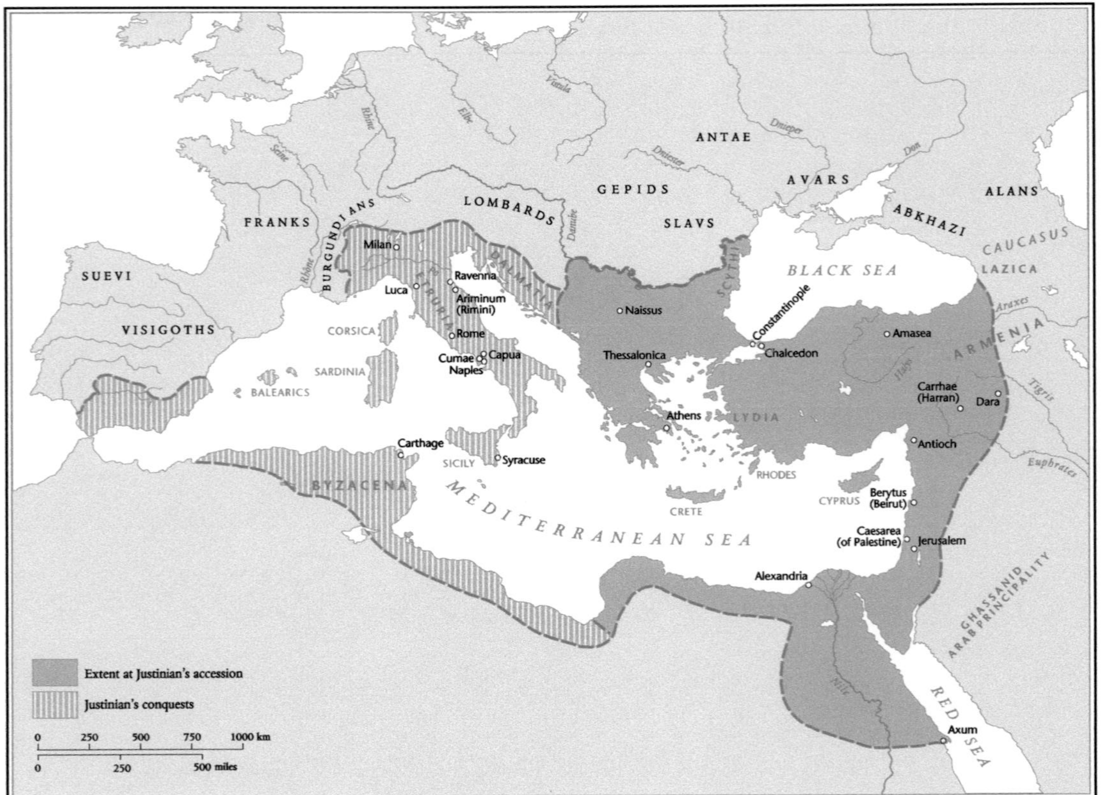


**Map 4** Justinian's empire in AD 565.

Map 5 Theme commands *c.*720.

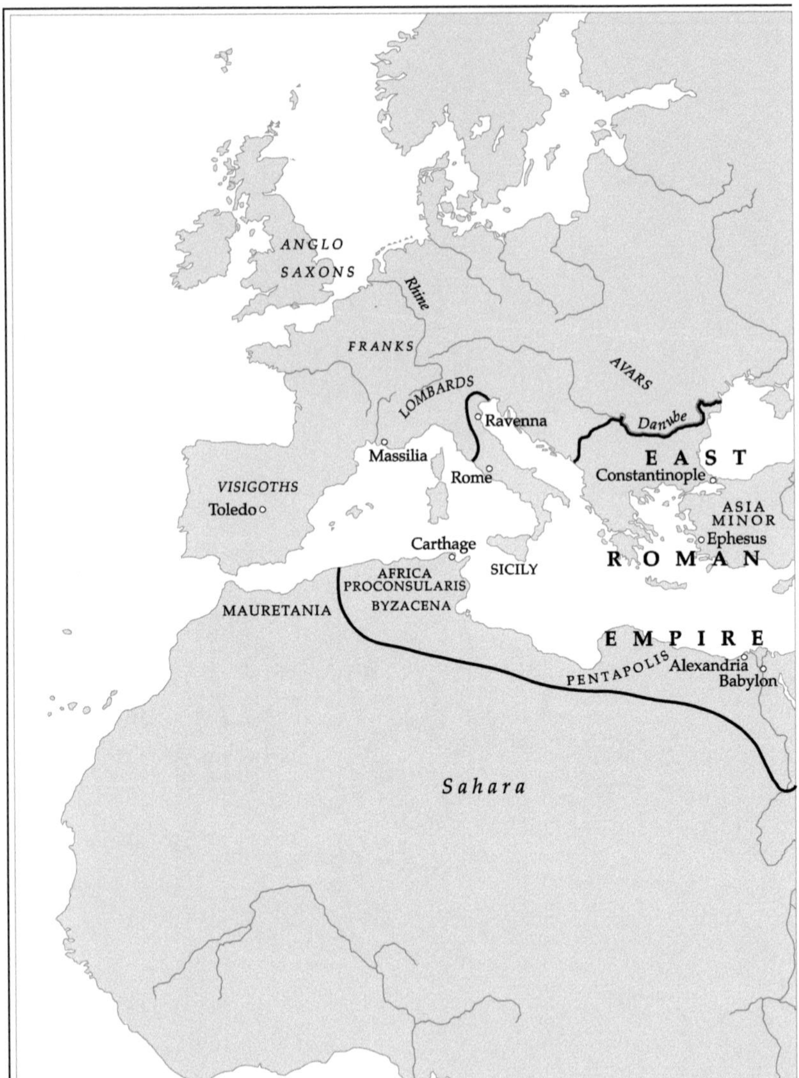


**Map 6** Eurasia on the eve of the Arab Conquest.

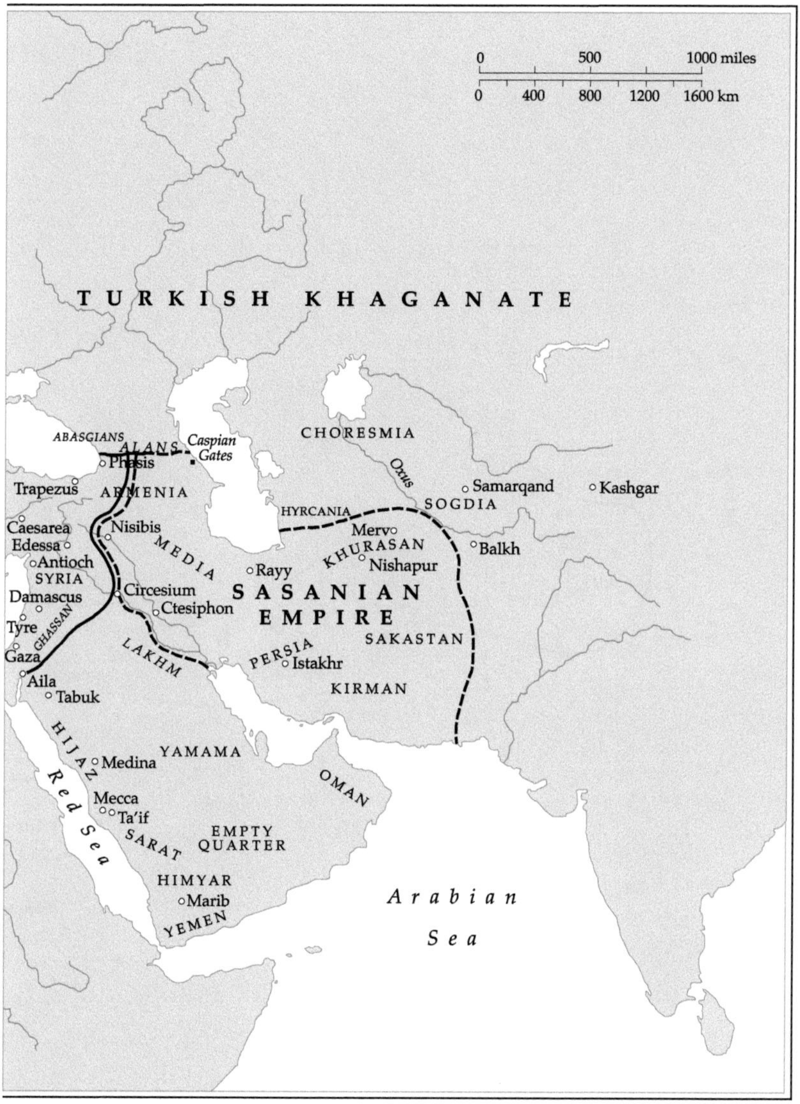


**Map 6** Continued.

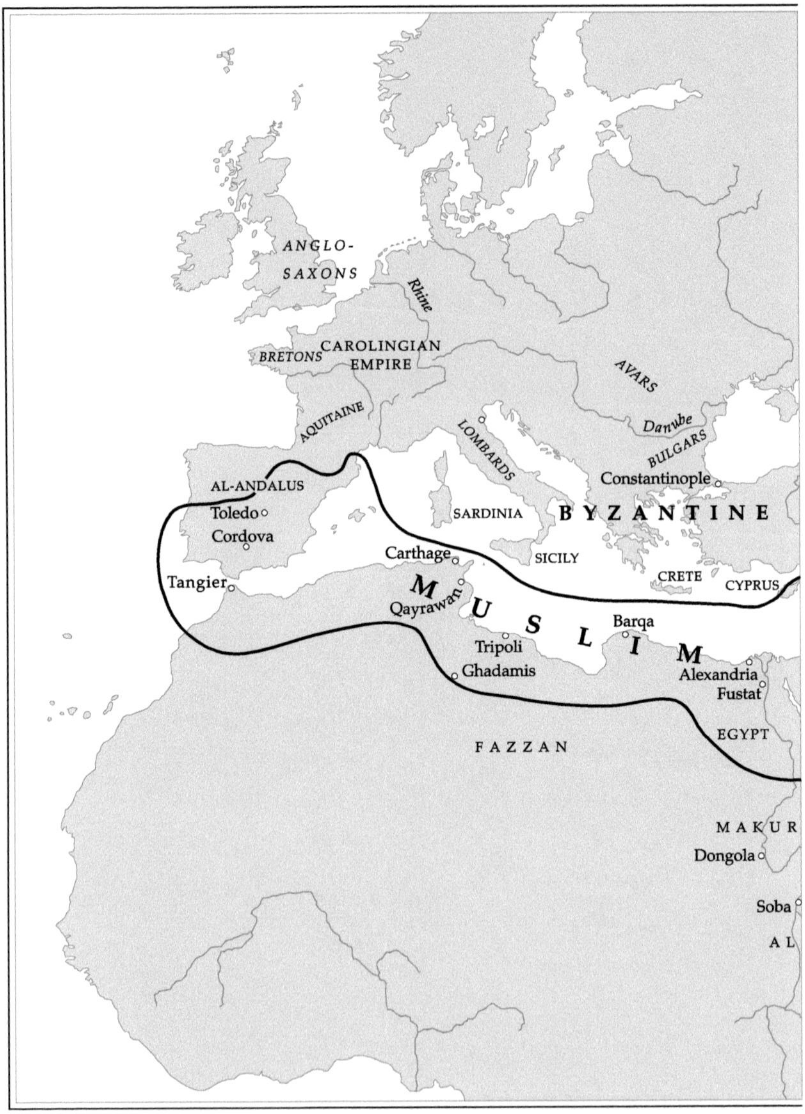


**Map 7** Limits of Muslim rule in 750.

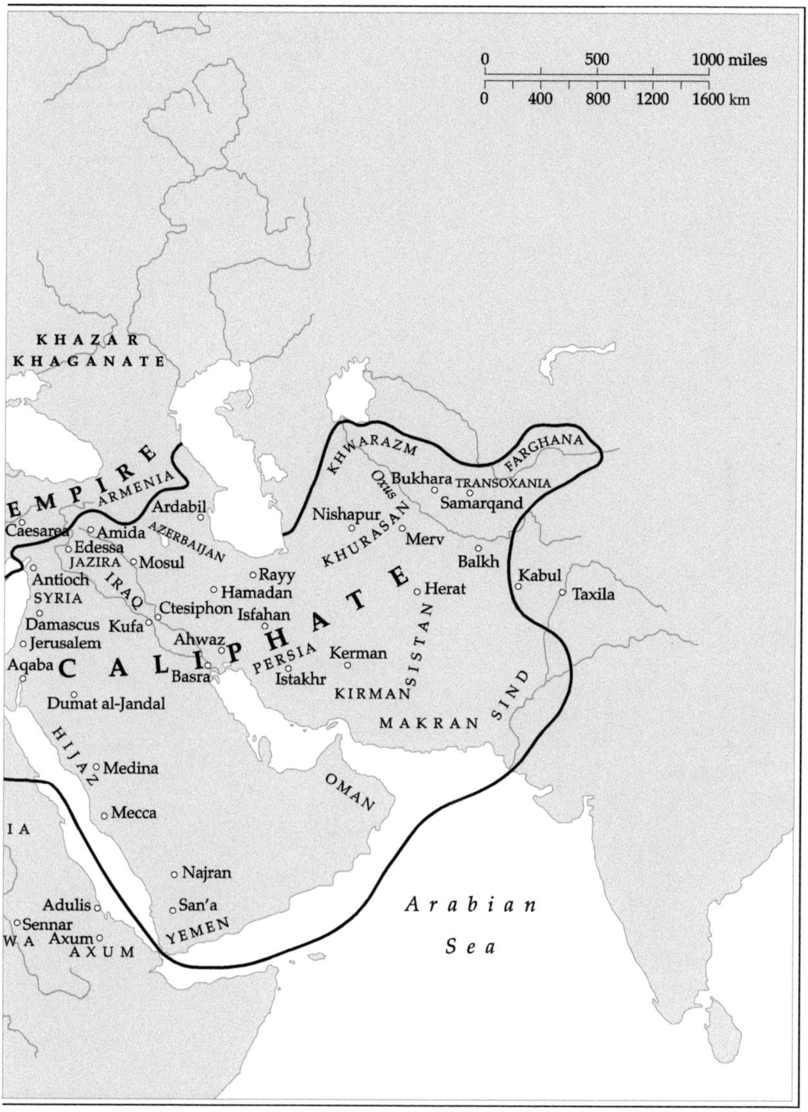


Map 7 Continued.

**Map 8** Northern neighbours, seventh to tenth centuries.

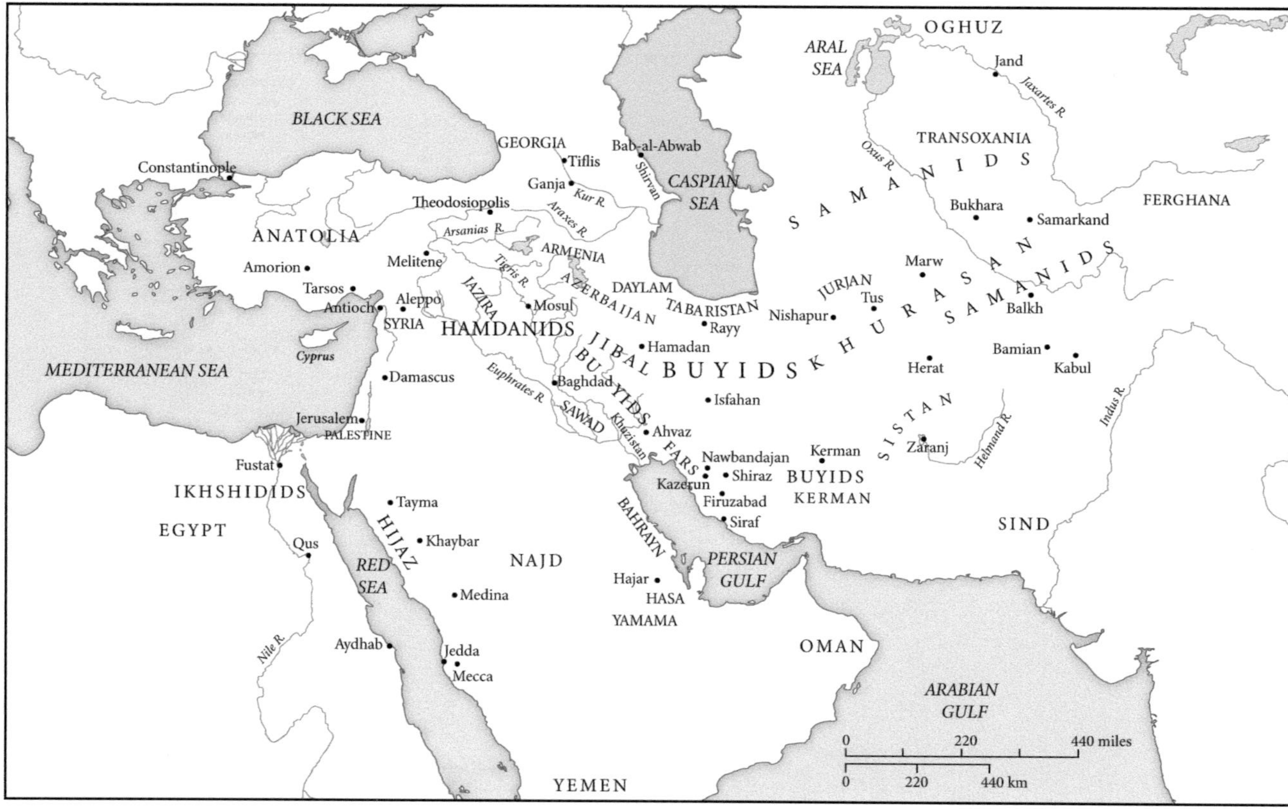


**Map 9** Islamic world in the tenth century.

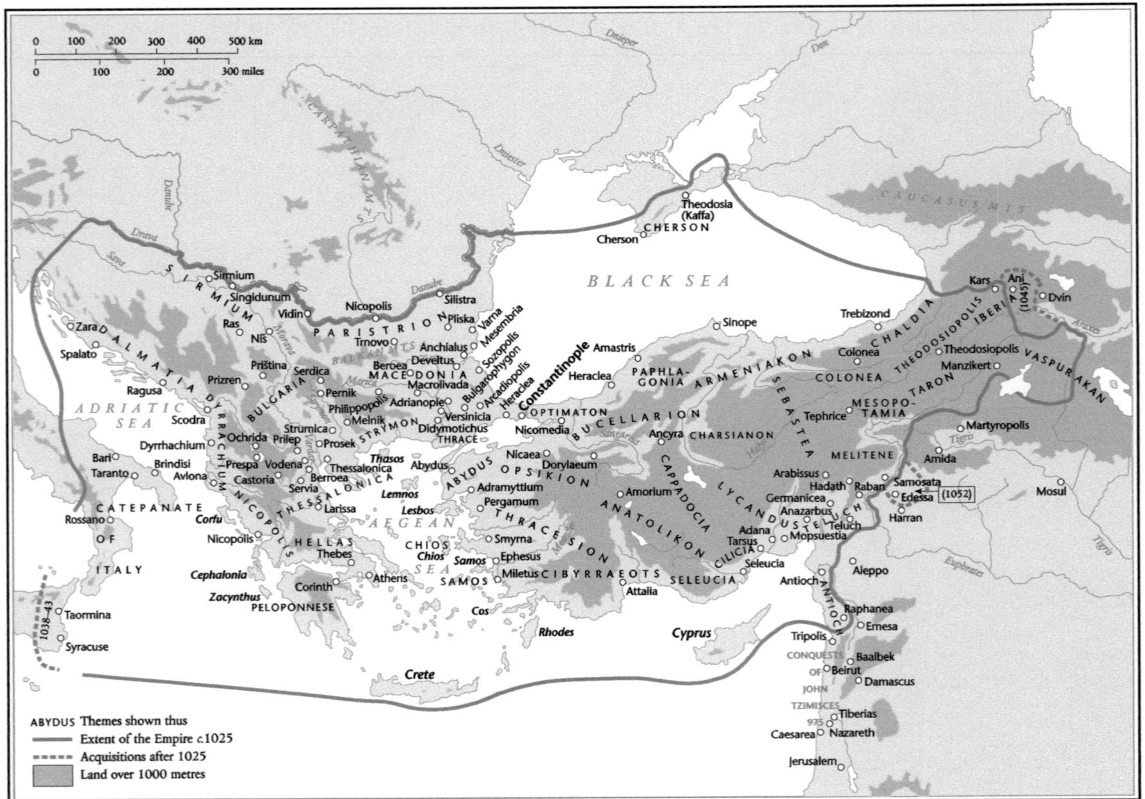


**Map 10** Byzantium in the middle of the eleventh century.

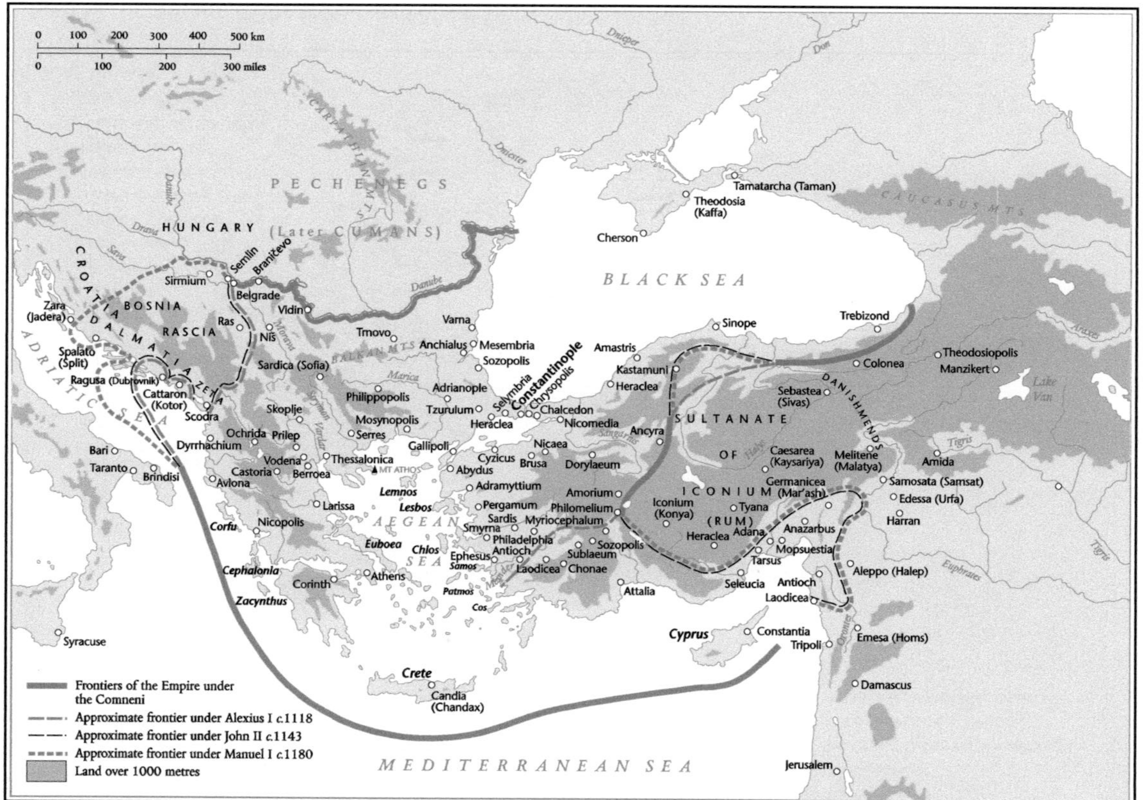


**Map 11** Komnenian Byzantium.

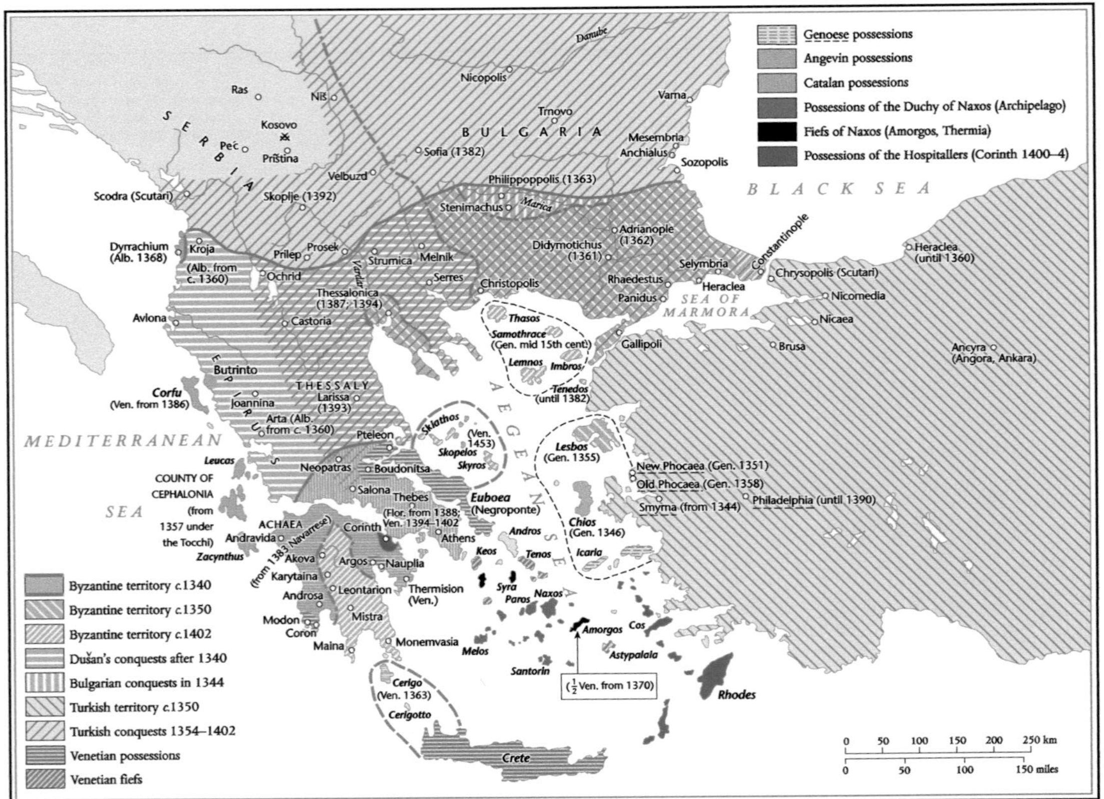


Map 12 Byzantium in the second half of the fourteenth century.

# Introduction

All of us who write history must think at times of the complexity and difficulty of the task. I view history as having *layers*. These are not geological strata since it is above all motion which characterizes the human past. Rather they are the various layers of water in a river, which itself changes course and width, sometimes speeding down narrows in a turbid flow, at other times flowing calmly and steadily in a broad channel, at others meandering slowly from side to side. There are three main layers, which interact with each other below the agitated surface of *politics* in all its forms, and generate a slower-moving flux in human affairs—*the economic, the social, and the institutional.* The physical constraints on the flow of water, the banks of the river, represent *the natural environment*, within which human economies, societies, and states develop. There is a final element, to my mind the most important, namely *the thoughts, intentions, ideas, etc. generated in human minds.* They may perhaps be envisaged as puffs of wind which ruffle the surface and bubbles which emerge from the depths. Given the impossibility of tracing the consequence of a single trivial event in the natural world—a breath of wind, a single wave, the leap of a predator, the cry of the prey—it is far, far beyond the capacity of man to gain a full understanding of a past shaped by a near-infinity of brain cells and trillions of limbs.

Byzantium is a small part of that past, straddling the end of antiquity and the Middle Ages, located towards the western end of Eurasia. Its territory comprised two substantial land masses, Asia Minor and the Balkans; islands, large and small, in the Aegean and Adriatic; and a small number of distant enclaves (notably Sardinia, Sicily, southern Italy and Crimea). These were the parts of the Roman empire over which emperors exercised authority from Constantinople, after the destruction of the classical world order by the Arabs in the seventh century. Byzantium, a neologism of the early modern period in Europe, was that remnant of the Roman empire which survived the Arab onslaught and remained as a standing affront to the new empire of the Muslim Arabs, flaunting its Christianity and claiming parity of imperial status.

Byzantium's history was shaped by its geography. There is nothing unusual in that. But, in Byzantium's case, geography aided its dour resistance over centuries to predatory outside powers. Asia Minor has good natural defences in the form of the Taurus and Anti-Taurus mountain ranges which mark it off from the north-west segment of the Fertile Crescent (the plains of Cilicia and northern Syria) and from western Transcaucasia. Where the mountains are fronted by the Euphrates, as it cuts its way south against the grain of the landscape, the defences are virtually impenetrable. Elsewhere a few passes lead up onto the interior plateau, but they had hazards, pinch-points which could be exploited by defenders.[1] The Balkans, by contrast, relied on a great river, the Danube, to hold off invaders. Mountains may dominate the interior—the Haemus range which delimits the Danube plain to the south and runs east from the Iron Gates to the Black Sea coast, the Rhodope mountains on the edge of Thrace, and the set of ranges which dominate the western Balkans and back onto the Adriatic. But they simply provided secure redoubts into which local populations could retreat. If the Danube line (heavily fortified in the late Roman period) were breached, invaders would find enticing settlement areas before them in the lowlands, either the large and continuous plains north and south of the Haemus mountains or the many fertile basins scattered across the uplands of the Macedonian heartland of the Balkans.[2] Most vulnerable of all—to attack by sea—were the islands and peninsulae protruding from the mainlands of Italy, Greece, and Ukraine. The same was true of the fertile Aegean and Marmara coastlands of Asia Minor.

The capital, Constantinople, was well placed for managing a Mediterranean-wide empire, once its centre of economic gravity had moved to the Middle East. But with the lopping off first of its western half, then of its rich provinces in the Levant and Egypt, Byzantium was extraordinarily exposed. Its two main resource-bases were separated by the Bosporus. Attacks could come from all points of the compass, by sea from north and south, by land from west and east. The governing elite had no choice but to adopt a *global* foreign policy, scanning the horizon of diplomatic vision around its full 360 degrees for potential danger, coordinating policies towards different neighbours, and establishing priorities (which would change with changing

[1] T. B. Mitford, *East of Asia Minor: Rome's Hidden Frontier*, 2 vols. (Oxford, 2018); M. Whittow, *The Making of Orthodox Byzantium, 600–1025* (London, 1996), 176–9.

[2] D. Obolensky, *The Byzantine Commonwealth: Eastern Europe 500–1453* (London, 1971), 5–24; N. G. L. Hammond, *A History of Macedonia*, 3 vols. (Oxford, 1972–88), I *Historical Geography and Prehistory*, 3–12.

circumstances). That was the first geographically determined trait of Byzantium. It was forced to rely more than ever on its wits, on accumulated knowledge of the surrounding world, and to react swiftly with an appropriate mix of force, diplomacy, and propaganda to perceived or anticipated threats from without.

Byzantine armies, lineal descendants of those which had conquered and managed the Roman empire, were, of course, adept at land warfare, and would, as in the past, resort to fighting to secure the frontiers of the reduced empire. What was new was the threat posed to the Aegean and its fringing lands (as well as to Constantinople) by naval powers which might emerge in nearer and more distant reaches of the Mediterranean and in the Black Sea. The Aegean, together with its northern antechamber the Sea of Marmara, was the central arena of Byzantine commerce. The coastal plains of northwest and western Asia Minor (together with Thrace) were the main grainlands, generating most of the agricultural surpluses from which Constantinople was provisioned. Security by sea was absolutely vital for Byzantium's prosperity and survival. Byzantium had no choice but to build up a large navy. Its new naval character was the second important aspect dictated by geography.

The material environment exercised influence over human life in numerous other ways. The interior plateau of Asia Minor, for example, receives reasonable but not abundant rainfall and has cold winters. It is in effect laid out by nature as a huge grazing land for large herds and flocks, easily cultivable arable land being concentrated in the *ovas*, depressions found along river valleys.[3] It was only in the course of the twentieth century that the whole plateau was ploughed up as the population of Turkey rocketed. Looking back to the Byzantine period, we should be watching out for the development of ranches by larger landowners, but only in times of peace. For the plateau was also a natural arena for mobile warfare. By contrast, we should expect to find a society of sturdy, independent peasants, a natural recruiting ground for fighting men, in the broken and wooded terrain of the mountains ranges which surround the plateau, a world away from the peasantry living easier lives in villages on the coastal plains.

The Aegean Sea, studded with islands, with numerous lines of communication criss-crossing the sea and linking it to the surrounding mainlands, was a nursery of sailors, fishermen, and traders. Hence its centrality—to

[3] Naval Intelligence Division, Geographical Handbook Series, *Turkey*, 2 vols. (Oxford, 1942), I, 19–28, 160–8, 216–17, 226.

judge by such scattered pieces of evidence of production and exchange as are available to us—alongside Constantinople, in the commercial life of Byzantium. In the Balkans, it was the forested mountains which played the most influential role in the early Middle Ages as zones where peoples ousted from the plains or, like Slav settlers, nervous of the plains, could lead independent lives. Thereafter, as security improved, the lowlands prospered and the upland plains of Macedonia developed into the nodal points of Byzantine provincial administration.

Nature could be less benign. Byzantium was prey to occasional earthquakes—it lay athwart a geological fault. From time to time herds of livestock were depleted by disease. The last bouts of bubonic plague (in the Mediterranean and Middle East from late 541) came in the first half of the seventh century.[4] Weather could cause problems, as always—floods, droughts, and bad winters (the worst came in 763–4 when icebergs floated down the Bosporus).[5] There must have been many instances of local crop failure, but there is only one attested instance of large-scale famine, in 928.[6] That famine undoubtedly exacerbated a tendency, already in evidence, for those with power to buy up properties belonging to those of lesser means. But the most striking single instance of natural intervention in human affairs came in 726, when there was a violent volcanic eruption in the southern Aegean near Thera. Within the belief system of the time, this could only be interpreted as violent manifestation of divine anger. Its location, in Byzantium's own inner sea, could not have made it clearer that it was Byzantine sins which were the cause. Once idolatry in the form of icon-veneration was identified as the chief sin, the authorities initiated a campaign to root it out. Within the history of events, it is, in my view, Byzantine iconoclasm which was most directly influenced by the material environment.[7]

We have learned over the last few generations to pay proper attention to thought-worlds, conceptual frameworks, *imaginaires*—namely half-articulated as well as properly formulated ideas about man, society, the

[4] L. K. Little, ed., *Plague and the End of Antiquity: The Pandemic of 541–750* (Cambridge, 2007).

[5] *Nicephori patriarchae Constantinopolitani breviarium historicum*, ed. & trans. C. Mango, CFHB 13 (Washington, DC, 1990), c.74; *Theophanis chronographia*, ed. C. de Boor (Leipzig, 1883), trans. C. Mango & R. Scott, *The Chronicle of Theophanes Confessor: Byzantine and Near Eastern History AD 284–813* (Oxford, 1997), 434.6–435.5.

[6] *Symeonis Magistri et Logothetae Chronicon*, ed. S. Wahlgren CFHB 44.1, (Berlin, 2006), 136.57, trans. S. Wahlgren, *The Chronicle of the Logothete*, TTB 7 (Liverpool, 2019).

[7] Nicephorus, cc.59–60; Theophanes, 404.18–405.2.

divine, and the cosmos, which are present in all human societies, from the apparently simplest of forest, pastoral, and agrarian peoples to hierarchically ordered states. Nothing about the performance of individuals and groups in the past can be understood properly if we do not pay attention to the intellectual, ideological, and religious context of their decisions and actions. Demus and Dodds, Baines and Brown have been the pathfinders in the history of *mentalités* in late antique and Byzantine studies.[8] No account of Byzantium, however short and impressionistic, should be denuded of the beliefs and ideas which animated emperors, court, apparatus of government, army, navy, and society at large, down to the level of the village.

Let us venture into these ethereal worlds in ascending order of importance. We can begin with collective memories of the classical past and with the inheritance from that past carried on into the middle ages. Byzantium was, in the first instance, a thoroughly *Hellenic* society. The name Hellene itself might have been devalued—it became a standard designation for pagans—but the heritage of classical Greek literature was treasured. Some early Christian thinkers rejected it as potentially infectious, suffused as it was with pagan ideas and myths, but the majority accepted it as an essential component in the education of Christians within the late Roman empire, to be completed with induction into scripture and Christian writings.[9] Secular writing continued to flourish under late Roman and Byzantine emperors, who, with a few striking exceptions, most notably Justinian I (527–65), set an example for the upper echelons of society with their patronage of literati. The medium used was classical Greek, the official language of government, well removed from everyday speech. This mandarin language remained a living language—indeed it was to do so until the very last years of Byzantium's existence.[10] Fine works of literature were written, reaching an early apogee in the poetry of George of Pisidia, protegé of patriarch (Sergius) and emperor (Heraclius).

In the course of two centuries of defensive warfare (from the middle of the seventh century to the middle of the ninth), there was a necessary retrenchment of culture, but a basic canon of classical Greek writers

[8] O. Demus, *Byzantine Mosaic Decoration: Aspects of Monumental Art in Byzantium* (London, 1948); E. R. Dodds, *Pagan and Christian in an Age of Anxiety: Some Aspects of Religious Experience from Marcus Aurelius to Constantine* (Cambridge, 1965); N. H. Baynes, *Byzantine Studies and Other Essays* (London, 1955); P. Brown, *The World of Late Antiquity: From Marcus Aurelius to Muhammad* (London, 1971).

[9] R. I. Marrou, *A History of Education in Antiquity* (London, 1956), 314–29, 340–2.

[10] R. Browning, *Medieval and Modern Greek* (London, 1969), 13–15, 60–1, 73, 76–9.

continued to be read, headed by Homer, the great Athenian playwrights, Demosthenes, and Aristotle.[11] It is true that many classical texts dangled by the thinnest of threads, being picked up by a single manuscript in the age of revival following this dark age, and that all too many others were lost (except for such fragments as were preserved in Egyptian papyri and later Byzantine texts). But it is undeniable that the Byzantine governing class and its intelligentsia were aware that they were the bearers of high classical culture. In addition to literature, their heritage included a wide range of historical, geographical, philosophical, and scientific texts. They could pull rank over their Arab counterparts, who had to rely on intermediaries to translate the corpus of Greek texts which conveyed the learning of the classical Mediterranean to later generations.[12] They were aware of their special status as representatives of the classical and Hellenistic intelligentsia in the contemporary world, above all because it was their language which they still used, and it was the genres defined in antiquity to which they tailored their writing.

The *Roman* past of Byzantium loomed rather larger than the Hellenic. Byzantium was Roman through and through, in both the political and social spheres. It had, in theory, an elective monarchy, inherited ultimately from the Principate established by Augustus. Hence the continuing importance of formal popular acclamation of new emperors, and of the divine *imprimatur* bestowed by the patriarch in the coronation ceremony. But, as in the Roman past, behind the constitutional façade it was brute power which secured the throne. Incumbent families with their hands on the levers of power could make the empire hereditary for a few generations, but faced the ever-present danger of military coups. It was normally the military, or those at the centre confident of the support of the military, who brought dynasties to an end. These pseudo-constitutional monarchs governed with the aid of a pseudo-Senate, long since transformed into a court of former and current senior postholders.[13] They ran an apparatus of

[11] N. G. Wilson, *Scholars of Byzantium* (London, 1983), 18–27.

[12] P. Lemerle, *Byzantine Humanism: The First Phase* (Canberra, 1986), 81–280; D. Gutas, *Greek Thought, Arab Culture: The Graeco-Arabic Translation Movement in Baghdad and Early Abbasid Society (2nd–4th/8th–10th Centuries)* (London, 1998); P. Magdalino, 'The Road to Baghdad in the Thought-World of Ninth-Century Byzantium', in L. Brubaker, ed., *Byzantium in the Ninth Century: Dead or Alive?* (Aldershot, 1998), 195–213, at 195–206.

[13] A. Omissi, *Emperors and Usurpers in the Later Roman Empire: Civil War, Panegyric, and the Construction of Legitimacy* (Oxford, 2018), 1–14; P. Heather, 'New Men for New Constantines? Creating an Imperial Elite in the Eastern Mediterranean', in P. Magdalino, ed., *New Constantines: The Rhythm of Imperial Renewal in Byzantium, 4th–13th Centuries* (Aldershot, 1994), 11–33, at 12–21.

government at the centre and in the provinces which had evolved continuously over the centuries from that of the Principate.

The whole social order too remained Roman in its fundamentals, governed by a legal system which had its origins in the deep Republican past. A high standard of law and order was to be enforced throughout Byzantine lands. While privilege was recognized as in the past (bringing exemption from treatment regarded as degrading), legal redress was open to all and there was no attempt to freeze the social order. While high birth was an advantage, it was talent above all which was meant to lead to preferment in the bureaucracy as in the officer corps.[14] It is striking that titles never became hereditary in Byzantium and that women continued to enjoy the unusually strong legal rights given by Roman law, in particular entitlement to equal shares of paternal estates.

Memory of an imperial past, of the centuries when the Mediterranean and its continental hinterlands had been united under the rule of Roman emperors, was of the utmost importance. It boosted the status of Byzantines in their own eyes, and gave them a useful diplomatic weapon in their dealings with the Germanic successor states established on former Roman territory in the west. Byzantium was regarded for several generations as a superordinate power, operating on a higher plane than mere kingship. As late as 812, the Emperor Michael I could use Byzantium's special status to extract tangible concessions from Charlemagne, when he agreed to abandon his claim on Venice in return for being granted the title of emperor.[15] The principal contribution of the Roman past, though, was to give a rationale for the continued existence against the odds of a reduced Roman state in the middle ages. It sustained Byzantine morale in dark days of apparently unending struggle, and energized the expansionist drive of the tenth and early eleventh centuries, construed as a drive to recover lost Roman provinces, as well as to improve security.

Most important of all, though, was faith. The church and the effective managerial structures which it had developed in late antiquity, modelled on those of the state, endured. The patriarch and his senior officials presided over a hierarchy of metropolitan bishops, archbishops, and bishops

[14] A. H. M. Jones, *The Later Roman Empire 284–602*, 3 vols. (Oxford, 1964), I, 519; D. R. Simon & D. R. Reinsch, *Die Peira: Ein juristisches Lehrbuch des 11. Jahrhunderts aus Konstantinopel—Text, Übersetzung, Kommentar, Glossar*, 2 vols. (Berlin, 2023), c.61; G. T. Dennis, ed. & trans., *The Taktika of Leo VI*, CFHB 49 (Washington, DC, 2010), 2.13–17.

[15] T. S. Brown, 'Byzantine Italy, c.680–c.876', in R. McKitterick, ed., *New Cambridge Medieval History*, II *c.700–c.900* (Cambridge, 1995), 320–48, at 338–40, and M. McCormick, 'Byzantium and the West, 700–900), in McKitterick, *op. cit.*, 349–80, at 367–8.

covering the whole territory of the empire. It is a pity that we know virtually nothing about ordinary priests, apart from their existence and their incidental appearance in historical narratives, but impressions of the impact of Christianity in the localities can be obtained from numerous lives of those monks and solitary ascetics who gained recognition as holy men.[16] The Christianizing of Asia Minor was not complete in the sixth century, but we may, I think, presume that the threat from Islam helped the dominant, officially sanctioned religion reach into the remotest highland recesses in the course of the seventh and eighth centuries. In the Balkans, by contrast, external pressure radically diminished Christianity's presence. Pagan Slavs migrated in large numbers into northern Thrace and the whole of Illyricum. They percolated south into Greece, some penetrating into the Peloponnese. The recession of Christianity from the north-east was made permanent once the Bulgars established a state there in the late seventh century.[17]

Still, in most of the territories subject to Byzantine rule, Christianity's grip tightened. This was true of the islands of the Aegean and Byzantium's distant possessions in the west and north-east. The role of faith in the lives of individuals and communities should not be underestimated. It can override rational calculations of self-interest, as has been demonstrated on many, many occasions in the past—as for example at Omdurman, in great rebellions against British rule in east Africa in the late nineteenth century; in the suicide missions of medieval Assassins and their modern Sunni heirs; above all in the victorious progress of the Arabs over the Levant, Iran, north Africa and central Asia in the seventh and eighth centuries. Faith did not just strengthen secular motive forces, devotion to comrades and leaders, patriotism, etc. (which by themselves could and did propel millions to their deaths in the twentieth century). It acted as a supercharger—powering extraordinary Christian as well as Muslim ventures in the Middle Ages.

The submission of the faithful to an awesome, all-powerful, all-knowing divinity may have been unique to Islam, but, within early medieval Christendom, it was probably the faith inculcated by the Orthodox church which gave the strongest boost to the élan of soldiers and sailors and to the commitment of society at large to war against non-Christians.[18] Confidence

[16] R. Morris, *Monks and Laymen in Byzantium, 843–1118* (Cambridge, 1995), 31–63; B. Moulet, *Évêques, pouvoir et société à Byzance (VIII–XIe siècle)* (Paris, 2011).

[17] North-east: M. Jankowiak, '*Notitia* I and the Impact of the Arab Invasions on Asia Minor', in C. Zuckerman, ed., *Constructing the Seventh Century, TM* (2015), 435–59, at 442–8, 450–2, 457–8.

[18] J. Howard-Johnston, *Byzantium: Economy, Society, Institutions 600–1100* (Oxford, 2024), 45–52.

came from knowledge that there were supernatural auxiliaries who could be called upon to help, through the intercession of saints. The failure of two concerted iconoclast campaigns, in the eighth century and the first half of the ninth, suggests that private devotion to personal icons of saints was deeply entrenched by the late seventh century. The faith of individuals was also enhanced by two particular features of Orthodoxy: Byzantines found themselves in another world, untroubled by human threats, when they entered a church, a sacred space which was viewed as a microscosm, a human-scale replica, of the cosmos; and in the course of the annual liturgical cycle, the Gospel story was not simply remembered but *re-enacted* in the present, thereby impressing itself more strongly on the mind of the worshipper.[19]

Its Christian faith was a key characteristic of Byzantium as a political entity, in combination with its Roman identity. As the chief champion in the Middle East of the monotheist religion which Islam claimed to have superseded, the Christian Roman empire was the Caliphate's chief ideological rival. That ideology, in its early medieval form, imparted real tensile strength to the body politic. The emperor was pictured as God's vicegerent upon earth, thus as the most privileged and best protected of rulers. The claims to universal rule of late Roman emperors were tempered by grim reality. In place of an authority extensible over the known world, it was its *quality*, its unique strength, which was picked out in an era of retrenchment. The role of Byzantium in a hostile world was, in the course of the seventh century, equated with that of Israel in the Old Testament. The Byzantines were a Special, Chosen People, under God's direct protection. Defeat, like the eruption in the southern Aegean, was a consequence of God's anger with his people. If the sin which had provoked his wrath could be identified and purged, then Byzantium's fortunes would improve.[20] This notion of divine judgement and punishment (theodicy) was taken over from the Old Testament, along with confidence that ultimately God would never desert the New Israel. Knowledge that Byzantium's survival was guaranteed and that Byzantium's role, in theory, was that of divinely sanctioned arbiter of earthly affairs, was of immeasurable importance in sustaining Byzantium's will to fight on, after a single, fleeting moment of doubt in 654.

[19] Demus, *Byzantine Mosaic Decoration*, 10–16; J. K. Campbell, *Honour, Family, and Patronage: A Study of Institutions and Moral Values in a Greek Mountain Community* (Oxford, 1964), 347–48.

[20] M. T. G. Humphreys, *Law, Power, and Imperial Ideology in the Iconoclast Era c.680–850* (Oxford, 2015), 37–80.

Armoured with this triple heritage—Hellenic, Roman, and Christian—Byzantium was able to hold its own in a hostile world. It was a middle-ranking power, one of two on the western and north-western flanks of the Caliphate, in the early middle ages. It was ideas as much as efficient use of material resources which ensured its survival, and which then inspired its revival between the middle of the ninth century and the middle of the eleventh. The extraordinary resilience shown after the battle of Manzikert (1071) and the loss of much of Asia Minor to Turks and Turkmen testifies to the continuing vitality of the Byzantine conception of earthly affairs, to its grip on both Byzantine and western minds. How else was Byzantium able to rouse up a spirit of holy war in Latin Christendom and to direct it against its principal Turkish enemies in the Middle East? How else was Byzantium able to prevent the cultural antipathies growing up in the course of the First Crusade from souring all aspects of relations with the western powers? Above all, how was it that Byzantium, as a political entity, survived the catastrophe of the Fourth Crusade and the loss of Constantinople, and managed over the following half-century to reconstitute itself?

In essence, Byzantium was a constellation of ideas derived ultimately from the late antique world. This became clearer in the last centuries, when the medium-sized power of the early middle ages was squeezed and broken up by the pressure from without. It was now that the Hellenic character of Byzantium came to the fore, its intelligentsia pulling rank for the final time over the nascent humanism centred in the thriving cities of Italy.[21]

Fleeting glimpses have been caught of the flow of events through time in the foregoing account of the roles of the material environment and of ideas in the history of Byzantium. The Arabs have conquered the Levant, Egypt, and north Africa, in effect stripping the east Roman empire of its empire. The 726 volcanic explosion has galvanized the elite of church and state into instituting a campaign against icons and icon-veneration. A long defensive war has been fought to hold the Taurus and Anti-Taurus mountain frontiers against Islam. Slavs have inundated the northern Balkans, while Bulgars have established a small but powerful nomadic state in the north-east. There has been a political and cultural revival which ended in disaster at Manzikert, followed by a century-long attempt to orchestrate the affairs of Christendom which also ended in disaster. Finally, we have seen something of the last, sad centuries of steady dismemberment, offset by intellectual and artistic achievements.

[21] H. Ahrweiler, *L'idéologie politique de l'empire byzantin* (Paris, 1975), 60–4.

The history of events is too often disregarded these days, the attention of serious scholars being turned to the analysis of structures and the tracing of systems of ideas. But events matter and mattered. They impinged continuously on inherited structures, and could not but affect patterns of thought. It is events too which attracted the attention of contemporary historians and so fill most of the pages of the historical texts which have come down to us. So, as well as probing key aspects of the economic, social, and institutional history of Byzantium, it is vital to get a sense of Byzantium's trajectory through time.

First, something should be said about the background in late antiquity, about the pan-Mediterranean empire from which Byzantium emerged. The history of Byzantium proper can then be broken down into three distinct phases: first, a dark age of two centuries, from the middle of the seventh to the middle of the ninth century, when war and the demands of war shaped almost every aspect of life in Byzantium; then what seemed to be a new dawn from the middle of the ninth century, when the demands of war eased, allowing Byzantium to take initiatives abroad and releasing hitherto repressed social and cultural forces; and finally from the middle decades of the eleventh century the long decline of Byzantium, punctuated by two short periods of recovery after the catastrophic defeat by the Turks at Manzikert (1071) and the fall of Constantinople to the Fourth Crusade (1204).

Given that the Byzantines, and to a lesser extent the Romans from the third century, were not masters of their destiny, each section of the historical overview begins with a survey of peoples within the radius of Byzantium's diplomatic vision, homing in on potential enemies capable of doing serious damage. War against these principal adversaries looms large, both because it was a prime concern of successive imperial regimes (the prestige which could be won or lost was a vital political asset) and because of the demands which it put on state, society, and economy. So too does the effort put into managing the upper echelons of the political class, and maintaining church unity. These aspects of late Roman and Byzantine history provide a context within which to view developments in the organization of the state (whether willed from above or *ad hoc* responses on the ground) and slower-paced changes in the economy and social order.

*Byzantium in a Changing World*. James Howard-Johnston, Oxford University Press.
 DOI: 10.1093/9780191999093.003.0001

# 1
# Late Antiquity

*Late antiquity*, like *Byzantium*, is a term of art. Thanks above all to a fine Irish historian, with extraordinary imagination and command of language, it has achieved wide currency over the last sixty years.[1] It designates, for most us, the last four centuries of classical history (300–700 AD). Rather than seeing a slow decline of a once-great civilization, we now view them as a period of cultural innovation and political achievement, worthy of study in its own right. The driving force in the sphere of ideas was the spread of Christianity within and beyond the Roman empire and its strengthening grip on individual minds. The individual intelligences on which it impinged were responsible for a whole series of original intellectual schemes, theologies which strove to express the doctrines of the new faith in Greek philosophical terms.[2] In the material world, it stimulated the authorities, local notables, and bishops into endowing cities with large, sumptuously decorated temples for the new faith, staffed by a new priesthood kept quite distinct from existing local elites.[3]

A second phenomenon which distinguished the later period of Roman history from its earlier phases, the Republic, the Principate, and the Antonine Empire, was its place in the wider world. Instead of being the acknowledged paramount power in western Eurasia, the centre of the known world, projecting its power and radiating its influence over surrounding peoples, the Christian Roman empire was *embattled*. The two main types of barbarian—the eastern, supposedly effete and wallowing in luxury; and the northern, supposedly governed by swirls of emotion, fierce and eager for gain—ceased to be malleable creatures on the margins of the

[1] Peter Brown, 'The World of Late Antiquity Revisited', with comments by G. W. Bowersock et al., *Symbolae Osloenses*, 72 (1997), 5–90.

[2] See pp. 27–30 below.

[3] B. Ward-Perkins, *From Classical Antiquity to the Middle Ages: Urban Public Building in Northern and Central Italy AD 300–850* (Oxford, 1984), 65–84; K. Hattersley-Smith, *Byzantine Public Architecture between the Fourth and Early Eleventh Centuries AD, with Special Reference to the Towns of Byzantine Macedonia* (Thessaloniki, 1996), 39–170; J. H. W. G. Liebeschuetz, *The Decline and Fall of the Roman City* (Oxford, 2001), 30–63; C. Rapp, *Holy Bishops in Late Antiquity: The Nature of Christian Leadership in an Age of Transition* (Berkeley, Los Angeles, 2005), 7–8, 220–3, 236–9, 288–9.

civilized world.[4] They took the form respectively of the Sasanian empire, a highly militarized state straddling Mesopotamia and Iran, and a plethora of Germanic peoples in an early stage of state formation. Both attacked and savaged the Roman empire in the third century, and posed a constant, serious threat thereafter.[5]

The Romans were forced to adapt, principally by strengthening the sinews of the state. The imperial authorities tightened their hold on the localities, by reducing the size of administrative units (doubling the number of provinces) and by encroaching on the traditional prerogatives of cities. They improved their ability to tap the resources of the country with a complete overhaul of the fiscal system. The organs of central government accordingly grew dramatically in size.[6] The army doubled to some 500,000 men, all told—a *standing* army, it should be stressed, not a *host* mobilizable on occasion.[7] There can be no doubting the organizational capability of the embattled empire. Its most spectacular manifestation was the construction of St Sophia in Constantinople, after the Nika Riot nearly overthrew Justinian in 532. From the first design stage and the organization of brick production to the completion of the building and its decoration, this great domed church, innovative in its overall design and construction technology (see Figure 1.1), was completed in *five and a half years*. It was an astonishing feat of engineering and organization.[8]

A third distinguishing feature of this late-antique phase of Roman history was the shift of the political centre from west to east, with Constantine's decision to transform the old city of Byzantium on the Bosporus into his capital.[9] It was a belated recognition that the economic and cultural centre of gravity of the empire lay in the east, where cities, dating back to deep antiquity, congregated closer together than in the west (outside Italy) and where the city rather than the rural villa was the place of residence of the aristocracy.[10] It was in the east too, in Egypt and the Levant, that industrial

[4] E. Hall, *Inventing the Barbarian: Greek Self-Definition through Tragedy* (Oxford, 1991); Y. A. Dauge, *Le barbare: recherches sur la conception romaine de la barbarie et de la civilisation* (Brussels, 1981).

[5] See pp. 14–16, 19–20 below. [6] See p. 27 below.

[7] Jones, *Later Roman Empire*, I, 42–6, 61–6, II, 732–4; H. Elton, 'Military Forces', in P. Salin, H. Van Wees, & M. Whitby, eds, *The Cambridge History of Greek and Roman Warfare*, 2 vols. (Cambridge, 2007), II, 270–309, at 284–6.

[8] R. J. Mainstone, *Hagia Sophia: Architecture, Structure and Liturgy of Justinian's Great Church* (London, 1988).

[9] C. Mango, *Le développement urbain de Constantinople (IVe–VIIe siècles)* (Paris, 1985).

[10] Jones, *Later Roman Empire*, II, 715–18; A. Marzano & G. P. R. Métraux, eds, *The Roman Villa in the Mediterranean Basin: Late Republic to Late Empire* (Cambridge, 2018).

**Figure 1.1** Hagia Sophia, as depicted in a watercolour by Turner. The construction of the grand new church, with its huge dome, demonstrated the organizational capability of the east Roman state. It took no more than five and a half years (532–7) from the initial stages of design, procurement of building materials and assembly of workforce to completion.
*Source*: Bridgeman.

production was concentrated and demand for manufactured products and natural produce was at its highest.[11]

A chasm of political turbulence and invasion from without, from east and north, separated the late-antique phase of Roman history from the heyday of the empire in the second century. It was a grave crisis, which lasted some fifty years. Any account of the later Roman empire, however cursory, must consider the attacks from without and how they were contained, must note the political turmoil and how it was calmed, before venturing further.

## 1.1 Third-century crisis

The most dangerous of the foreign adversaries were those who attacked from the east. The relatively loose-limbed Parthian empire had not posed a

[11] Howard-Johnston, *Byzantium*, 110–20.

serious danger. In the south, in the Fertile Crescent, its posture had been purely defensive, while north of the Taurus it had merely striven to counter the advance of Roman influence in Transcaucasia through clients of its own.[12] But early in the third century roles were reversed, with the rise in Iran of a new dynasty, based like the Achaemenids in the south, in Persia proper. Ardashir I, founder of the Sasanian dynasty, built up his power incrementally, his authority increasing and his following growing with each successive military success. The traditional Zoroastrian faith also played a part, there being a close connection between the Sasanian family and the priesthood in Persia.

Ardashir's father, Pabag, made the first move, seizing power in Istakhr. He was a priest of the temple of Anahid there. In a little under twenty years (*c.*206–24), in a classic example of the dynamic growth of power, Ardashir first united central and eastern Iran under his rule, then imposed his authority on Media and eastern Transcaucasia, and finally took control of one of the two milch cows of the Middle East, Mesopotamia (the other being Roman Egypt). The war machine which was churning out the prestige he needed did not cease its work when he was crowned in the Parthian capital, Ctesiphon, in 226. He turned west against the Romans, whom he was able to face on equal terms.

In the reign of his son and successor, Shapur I (240–72), the balance swung decisively in the Persians' favour. Crushing victories were won over grand Roman invasion forces in 244 and 252. Persian forces attacked in turn in 252 and 260, sweeping over the Roman provinces south of the Taurus, capturing Antioch (252), and penetrating north into Cappadocia (260).[13] At this point there was a first stirring of Arab power, galvanized by the notables of Palmyra, the great commercial and political centre of northern Arabia. For more than a decade, the whole Levant and Egypt slipped out of effective Roman control.[14]

In Europe, too, the balance had begun to shift in those regions of inner northern Europe which were in close contact with the Romans. Goods percolating into these notionally barbarian lands tended to accumulate in the hands of elites, enhancing their prestige and gradually intensifying the authority of their leading members, some of whom proved all too ready to

[12] E. W. Gray, 'The Roman Eastern *Limes* from Constantine to Justinian: Perspectives and Problems', *Proceedings of the African Classical Associations*, 12 (1973), 24–40, at 28–9.

[13] T. Daryaee, *Sasanian Persia: The Rise and Fall of an Empire* (London, 2010), 2–8.

[14] F. W. Millar, *The Roman Near East: 31 BC—AD 337* (Cambridge, MA., 1993), 164–73.

take up arms. Individual tribes, partly perhaps because of increasing exchange but mainly in reaction to the military threat posed by the empire, began to coalesce into large federated groupings, Franks on the lower Rhine, Alamans on the upper Rhine and upper Danube. They spawned numerous warbands, which raided exposed frontier provinces from the 230s, causing widespread damage and gathering booty and prisoners in large quantities. The raids increased in range and frequency as the crisis in the east peaked. On the lower Rhine, the raiding culminated in coordinated attacks on a large scale on northern Gaul across the Rhine in 253 and 276, further east in deep-penetrating raids through Raetia and across the Alps into Italy (260, 268).

Outer regions of the northern world, beyond the immediate belt of tribes neighbouring the empire, were also affected by contact and exchange with Romans. It was the stronger leadership thereby engendered and the driving force of a heroic ethos which impelled Goths and a number of other peoples (Heruls, Taifali, Gepids, etc) to move south from Scandinavia in the second half of the second century and to oust the weakening Sarmatians as the hegemonic power in the steppes beyond the Danube. They first raided across the lower Danube in 238. A large force devastated the eastern Balkans north and south of the Haemus mountains in 250–1, capturing and looting Marcianopolis (the main Roman base in the north-east Balkans) and Philippopolis. The Emperor Decius was defeated and killed near Abritus. They also took to the sea from 255, attacking the east coast of the Black Sea, followed by raids on northern Asia Minor and Bithynia, some of which penetrated deep into the interior. In 259–60 a Gothic fleet entered the Aegean and marauded over the rich coastlands of Asia Minor. The climax came in 268, when Goths and Heruls sailed south, tested the defences of Marcianopolis and Byzantium, and then, dividing into separate marauding forces, attacked Macedonia, Greece as far south as the Peloponnese, western Asia Minor, and the large islands of the east Mediterranean. The Roman military response (269) was effective, and was followed up a few years later by a successful expedition north of the Danube.[15]

[15] J. Wilkes, 'Provinces and Frontiers', *Cambridge Ancient History*, XII *The Crisis of Empire, AD 193–337*, eds A. K. Bowman, P. Garnsey, & A. Cameron (Cambridge, 2005), 212–68, at 222–9; P. Heather, *Empires and Barbarians: Migration, Development and the Birth of Europe* (London, 2009), 36–150; M. Meier, *Geschichte der Völkerwanderung: Europa, Asien und Afrika vom 3. bis zum 8. Jahrhundert n.Chr.* (Munich, 2019), 125–48, 309–37, who believes that the process which led to the coalescence of Alemans and Franks only began in the third century.

The third ingredient in the crisis was political and domestic. There was a weakening of an anyway weak dynastic principle in the face of senatorial disgruntlement. The Senate itself was ceding *de facto* power to increasingly independent-minded regional armies. There were some eighty claimants to the throne and twenty changes of regime in the fifty years from the usurpation of Maximinus Thrax in 235. The veneer of constitutional rule was stripped away, as general succeeded general until the accession in 284 of one endowed with great political and strategic vision (Diocletian), who could build on the success of three competent predecessors (Claudius Gothicus [268–70], Aurelian [270–5], and Probus [276–82]).[16]

A fourth ingredient was inflation, initially induced by fiscal profligacy, subsequently accelerating to intolerably high levels in the middle of the century. This had serious consequences for the functioning of the state, and, in particular, for the logistics of equipping and provisioning the armed forces. The efficient medium of cash was no longer available for the extraction and distribution of resources.[17]

## 1.2 Foreign wars and domestic conflict, late third to late fifth centuries

The survival of the empire through these dark years and its revival under the regime of the Tetrarchate instituted by Diocletian (284–305) testify above all to the strength of the idea of empire and the commitment of its citizens to a common cause, despite all the internal commotion (see Figure 1.2). By the 280s the western and Balkan provinces had been cleared of raiders, Roman authority being re-extended to the old frontiers along the Rhine and Danube. In the Middle East Aurelian brought the Palmyrene era of hegemony to an end in 272 with a victory outside Antioch. Political tensions within the Sasanian empire enabled Romans to redress the balance and undertake offensive operations, penetrating deep into Mesopotamia in 283.[18]

Diocletian, brought to power by the eastern army in 284, set about improving Roman defences with a massive fortification programme, giving priority to a *limes* of strategic roads and forts extending from the Gulf of

[16] Omissi, *Emperors and Usurpers*, 9–21.

[17] M. Corbier, 'Coinage and Taxation: The State's Point of View, A.D. 193–337', *CAH* XII, 327–92, at 330–46.

[18] B. Dignas & E. Winter, *Rome and Persia in Late Antiquity: Neighbours and Rivals* (Cambridge, 2007), 25–6.

**Figure 1.2** Tetrarchs. Porphyry statues of Diocletian and his colleagues, originally attached to columns, brought to Venice after the sack of Constantinople in 1204.
*Source*: Wikimedia/Nino Barbieri.

Aqaba to the Euphrates, designed to shield the Roman Levant from the desert. His successors strengthened the defences of the principal cities between the Euphrates and the Taurus, so that they could double as major military bases in times of war.[19] The defences in this main theatre of war were thus brought up to the standard of the *limes* along the upper Euphrates constructed under the Principate.[20] There was a concomitant increase in troop numbers and in cavalry relative to infantry, and a reorganization of army commands (between the reign of Gallienus [254–68] and that of Constantine [306–37]). The development of a system of reserve armies,

[19] J. Howard-Johnston, 'Military Infrastructure in the Roman Provinces North and South of the Armenian Taurus in Late Antiquity', in A. Sarantis & N. Christie, eds, *War and Warfare in Late Antiquity*, 2 vols. (Leiden, 2013), II, 853–91, at 861–72.
[20] Mitford, *East of Asia Minor*.

kept well back from the frontiers, gave the empire much-needed strategic flexibility.[21]

Relations between the two great powers of the Middle East now entered a more stable phase. Wars were fought. Massive resources were committed by both sides. But the fruits of victory were meagre. The Romans annexed five smallish districts beyond the Tigris after the defeat in 297 of Narses, who had attacked in the hope of boosting his prestige after a contested accession. The Persians recovered those same districts together with the cities of Nisibis and Singara in 363, after the defeat of a massive invasion army led by the Emperor Julian in 363.[22] The peace agreed around 387 then held until 502. Both sides refrained from exploiting each other's troubles. It was not just that any possible gains were not worth the risk and expense of war. Both Romans and Persians were reacting to the sudden appearance in the west Eurasian steppes of the Huns (Xiongnu) who brought with them an organizational capability and statecraft developed over centuries of dialogue with the Han Chinese. They constituted a third great power, capable of taking on and defeating each of the established empires.[23]

The Germanic world north and north-east of the Roman empire was reconfigured by the Huns. Gothic hegemony in the Pontic steppes ended in the defeat, flight, and dispersal of both supra-tribal groupings of Teruingi and Greuthungi in the 370s. In the west, beyond the Danube and Rhine frontiers, familiar enemies, Franks and Alamans, from whom fourth-century emperors—notably Constantine, Constantius (337–61) and Julian, as Constantius' junior colleague in the west (355–9)—had continued to garner prestige, were brought within the Hunnic sphere. There they were joined by a whole gallery of other subordinated peoples, Germanic (Goths, Vandals, and Suebi among others), Turkic (Bulgars), and Caucasian (Alans). The Huns' reputation as pan-Germanic rulers reached the far north, where their memory lodged itself in the mythical early history of Scandinavia.[24]

Both halves of the Roman empire were well aware of Hunnic power, but the only concerted invasions took place late, in the reign of Attila between

[21] Elton, 'Military Forces', 272–8, 286–95.

[22] Dignas & Winter, *Rome and Persia*, 122–34.

[23] R. C. Blockley, *East Roman Foreign Policy: Formation and Conduct from Diocletian to Anastasius* (Leeds, 1992), 42–5; H. J. Kim, *The Huns* (London, 2016), 12–65; R. Payne, 'The Making of Turan: The Fall and Transformation of the Iranian East in Late Antiquity', *Journal of Late Antiquity*, 9 (2016), 4–41, at 7–9, 20–3.

[24] Kim, *Huns*, 66–77; Heather, *Empires and Barbarians*, 207–38; L. Hedeager, *Iron Age Myth and Materiality: An Archaeology of Scandinavia AD 400–1000* (London, 2011), 177–228.

441 and 453. The real damage was done by their subjects—in the east by those Goths who had taken refuge south of the Danube (they defeated and killed the Emperor Valens at the battle of Adrianople in 378), and in the west by Vandals, Alans, and Suebi. Driven across the Rhine in winter 406–7, they spread out over Gaul and Spain, and were joined in Gaul in 412 by Goths from the Balkans, now known as Visigoths. These last were led west by Alaric *via* Italy, where they sacked Rome in 410. It was only in the east that Roman forces were strong enough to contain Gothic and Hunnic forces (in the Balkans) and eventually to reimpose Roman authority up to the Danube.[25]

As in the third century, but to a much lesser extent, domestic political crises weakened the empire in the fourth century, and presented predatory neighbours, in particular Franks and Alamans, with opportunities to attack. Much about these conflicts has been obscured by successive broadcasts of political propaganda from the victorious sides, but the main storylines of the principal episodes can be caught. Constantine's rise to power, exhibiting boldness and patience, took place against a background of fighting between tetrarchs (Augusti and their junior colleagues, Caesars), of whom he was one (see Figure 1.3). Large-scale military action was needed to dispose of his two main rivals, Magnentius who was killed at the Battle of the Milvian Bridge outside Rome in 312, and Licinius, eastern Augustus, challenged in the Balkans in 316, defeated in the east in 324, and subsequently executed.[26]

Tensions rose between Constantine's three sons, Constantine II, Constans, and Constantius, after his death in 337. Constantine II was killed when he invaded Constans' territory in Italy in 340. Constans himself was caught and executed after a military coup d'état by Magnentius at Autun in 350. There followed a full-scale civil war (350–3) between Magnentius in the west and Constantius, Constantine's sole surviving son, in the east. Heavy losses were incurred by both sides in the war for the Balkans, won by Constantius' forces, at Mursa in 351. Two subsequent campaigns saw Constantius' forces push first into Italy (352) and then into Gaul (353), prompting Magnentius to commit suicide.[27] This prolonged crisis, unlike the wars of Constantine I, had serious repercussions on foreign relations. It was exploited by Franks

[25] Kim, *Huns*, 77–89; Heather, *Empires and Barbarians*, 151–206.
[26] Omissi, *Emperors and Usurpers*, 103–52.
[27] Omissi, *Emperors and Usurpers*, 154–92.

**Figure 1.3** Two imperial statues: (a) fragments from a colossal statue of Constantine the Great (306–37); (b) Colossus of Barletta, a bronze statue, probably of Leo I (457–74), taken from Constantinople after the Fourth Crusade and shipwrecked off the coast of Barletta.

*Source*: (a) Wikimedia/Bradley Weber; (b) Wikimedia/H. U. Schmitt.

and Alamans, the former being appeased with the cession of Toxandria, the latter subjected to sustained Roman counter-operations.[28]

Such internal conflicts did not cease with the accession of Theodosius I (379), a strong emperor, with solid power bases in both halves of the empire. They had deleterious consequences abroad, weakening the empire's hold over the Goths. There were two rounds of civil war in Theodosius's reign, against Magnus Maximus (387–8) and Eugenius (394). Political troubles multiplied after his death in 395, as successive strongmen sought to manage the courts of each of his sons, Honorius in the west and Arcadius in the east. The assassination of the western strongman, Stilicho, in 408, exacerbated a growing crisis triggered by the proclamation of pretenders in Britain, the third of whom, another Constantine, took control of Gaul in 407. This crisis compounded the problems caused by a mass crossing of the Rhine by Vandals, Alans, and Suebi in winter 406–7.[29]

Two further usurpations, those of Maximus (409–11) and Jovinus (411–13), and the arrival of the Visigoths in Gaul (412), amplified the troubles in the western half of the empire. Disorder spread from Gaul to Spain. There was a concerted attempt by the western imperial court to stabilize affairs in 418, by establishing client relations with Visigoths and Burgundians and allocating them defined regions of Gaul (Aquitaine in the south-west and Sapaudia on the edge of the Alps in the south-east). Later reliance was put on a generalissimo (Aetius, 433–54) and his mainly Hunnic army to manage affairs in Gaul. But there was a steady attenuation of Roman authority, as resources declined (the Vandal conquest of the rich north African provinces, 429–39, was a mortal blow), as the residual Roman forces shrank, and as the loyalty of provincial elites frayed. By 476, when the last nominal western emperor was deposed, the whole of the western empire, including Italy, had slipped out of Roman control.[30]

At roughly the same time, in the 460s and 470s, a similar combination of dangers threatened to destabilize the eastern half of the empire: rival Gothic groups manoeuvred against each other in the Balkans and angled for imperial support, while a new nexus of senior generals from the Isaurian highlands in south-east Asia Minor gained power in Constantinople, eventually placing one of their own, Zeno, on the throne (474–91). Isauria,

[28] Omissi, *Emperors and Usurpers*, 263–90.

[29] Omissi, *Emperors and Usurpers*, 263–90; P. Heather, *The Fall of Rome: A New History* (London,2005), 191–232.

[30] Omissi, *Emperors and Usurpers*; Heather, *Fall of Rome*, 233–99, 369–84, 407–30.

**Figure 1.4** Theodosian walls of Constantinople, built in 404–13.
*Source*: Bridgeman.

however, was but a single, albeit strategically placed, highland area in the Middle East and small by comparison with two other highland recruiting grounds, Illyricum and the Roman sector of Armenia. An Isaurian regime could not possibly sustain itself in the long run, without the consent of the wider Roman Middle East, and, even more important, that of the governing elite and population living in Constantinople. The Goths too were in a weak position, faced with the massive land walls of the city (built 405–13) (see Figure 1.4) and its outer defences, natural (the Haemus and Rhodope mountains) and man-made (above all a number of virtually impregnable small fortresses north of the Haemus and the Long Wall some 64 kilometres west of the city). There was nothing surprising in the decision of the victor in the intra-Gothic wars, Theoderic the Amal, encouraged by the Emperor Zeno, to move into Italy in 488.[31]

The survival of the eastern empire is not too hard to explain. It was richer than the west, thus better able to fund its armed forces. Those armed forces were relatively unscathed in the early fifth century, unlike the field armies of the west which suffered heavy losses between 395 and 420. Nor did the east have to face as many attacks by Germanic peoples, a sharp

[31] P. J. Heather, *Goths and Romans 332–489* (Oxford, 1991), 240–308.

contrast with the third century. Apart from the deterrent effect of superior defences, human and natural, there was, on at least one occasion before 488, a conscious policy of diverting a dangerous potential adversary, again Goths who had forced their way into the empire and were holed up in Epirus, to the west in 393. There, the all-weather roads with which the Romans had endowed the provinces conquered in the first century BC offered Alaric and his Goths, the Visigoths, and those other peoples who crossed the Rhine in winter 406–7, the opportunity of ranging far and wide over Gaul and Spain. Finally the ruling, opinion-forming classes were more numerous, more variegated, and more secure (given their residence in fortified cities rather than rural villas) in the east. As the notables of Balkan cities demonstrated in the late fourth century and again in the late fifth, they proved more resistant to the pressure to collaborate with Germanic intruders.[32]

## 1.3 Social, economic, and cultural developments

Despite its internal and external wars, the whole empire prospered in the fourth century, and the east continued to do so until the coming of bubonic plague in 541–2.[33] Apart from the testimony of texts, there is hard evidence from excavation of new buildings and refurbishment of existing monumental structures in cities (see Figure 1.5).[34] Most impressive of all was the massive project of creating an imperial capital out of the small city of Byzantium on the Bosporus. This involved a great deal of infrastructure work—levelling and terracing, harbour construction, creation of a network of aqueducts to tap distant water sources, excavation of large open-air cisterns—and construction of monumental plazas, colonnaded streets, government buildings, churches, aristocratic palaces, housing and markets…[35]

[32] P. Heather, *Fall of Rome*, 431–59; P. Sarris, *Empires of Faith: The Fall of Rome to the Rise of Islam, 500–700* (Oxford, 2011), 33–73; A. G. Poulter, 'The Transition to Late Antiquity', in A. G. Poulter, ed., *The Transition to Late Antiquity on the Danube and Beyond* (Oxford, 2007), 1–50, at 4–8, 15–23; J. H. W. G. Liebeschuetz, 'The Lower Danube Region under Pressure: From Valens to Heraclius', *op. cit.*, 101–34, at 101–10; J.-P. Sodini, 'The Transformation of Cities in Late Antiquity within the Provinces of Macedonia and Epirus', *op. cit.*, 311–36. Key text for Balkans: Malchus, fr. 2 & 20, ed. & trans. R. C. Blockley, *The Fragmentary Classicising Historians of the Later Roman Empire: Eunapius, Olympiodorus, Priscus and Malchus*, 2 vols. (Liverpool, 1981–3), II, 406–9, 434–51.

[33] See pp. 30–1 below. [34] Liebeschuetz, *Decline and Fall*, 30–74.

[35] J. Crow, 'The Infrastructure of a Great City: Earth, Walls and Water in Late Antique Constantinople', in L. Lavan, E. Zanini, & A. Sarantis, eds, *Technology in Transition AD 300–650* (Leiden, 2007), 251–85.

**Figure 1.5** Gerasa (Jerash) in its second-century heyday: (a) oval plaza and beginning of colonnaded Cardo; (b) propylaeum to Temple of Artemis. Gerasa flourished in late antiquity. At least fifteen churches were built in the city. An extraordinary boom, founded on intensive and extensive agriculture and inter-regional exchange, affected the whole of the Roman Levant. The city was destroyed by an earthquake in 749, having survived the Arab conquest without damage.

*Source*: author.

Cities remained the basic constituents of the empire, governmental (responsible for the collection of taxes from their territories), economic (as producers, consumers, and centres of exchange), social (as the places of residence of local landowners, great and middling), and cultural (manifest in their amenities and churches).[36] With the currency stabilized, from the issue of full-bodied gold solidi under Constantine, exchange of all sorts was facilitated and commerce boomed, local, inter-regional, and long distance.[37] The evidence is to be found in the durable artefacts distributed throughout the Mediterranean and deep into its hinterlands, notably glass vessels of many sorts and fine tableware made in north Africa and north-west Asia Minor, and in the containers (amphorae) used to transport goods in bulk, mainly wine, olive oil, and fish sauce, which can be traced back to different production centres by their shape and fabric.[38]

Naturally the establishment of non-Roman kingdoms in the west had a dampening effect on trans-Mediterranean commerce from the fifth century. So too did the sixth-century Persian commercial policy of squeezing out Roman merchants from the Indian Ocean, in retaliation for the Romans' refusal to agree a full, formal peace at the end of the first sixth-century war (502–5). There was no general dampening effect, though, on economic activity, as demand continued to grow from booming cities throughout the Roman Middle East. The inland sea continued to be an active zone of enterprise and commerce until the middle of the sixth century.[39]

The imperial government gained more of a grip on the cities as a result of Diocletian's reform programme. Provinces were roughly halved in size. Civil and military powers were separated. Tax reform, in particular the introduction of regular censuses and the calculation of liability in terms of artificial units of land (*iuga*) and labour, animal and human (*capita*),

[36] C. Wickham, *Framing the Middle Ages: Europe and the Mediterranean 400–800* (Oxford, 2005), 591–60, 602–4.

[37] J. Banaji, *Exploring the Economy of Late Antiquity: Selected Essays* (Cambridge, 2016), 1–6, 13–19, 61–88.

[38] D. Foy, 'An Overview of the Circulation of Glass in Antiquity', in A. Wilson & A. Bowman, eds., *Trade, Commerce, and the State in the Roman World* (Oxford, 2017), 265–99; M. Bonifay, 'The Distribution of African Pottery under the Roman Empire: Evidence versus Interpretation', *op. cit.*, 327–51; P. Reynolds, 'The Supply Networks of the Roman East and West: Interaction, Fragmentation, and the Origins of the Byzantine Economy,' *op. cit.*, 353–95.

[39] R. Hodges & D. Whitehouse, rev. C. Morrisson, J. Lefort, & J.-P. Sodini, *Mahomet, Charlemagne et les origines de l'Europe* (Paris, 1996), 29–55; Sarris, *Empires of Faith*, 73–82; J. Howard-Johnston, 'The India Trade in Late Antiquity', in E. W. Sauer, ed., *Sasanian Persia: Between Rome and the Steppes of Eurasia* (Edinburgh, 2017), 284–304, at 290–6; S. Kingsley & M. Decker, eds., *Economy and Exchange in the East Mediterranean during Late Antiquity* (Oxford, 2001).

contributed greatly to the efficiency of the fiscal system. The sums sought by the imperial government could also be more equitably distributed between regions, provinces, and city territories. This new more intrusive government, as well as the division of power between east and west, necessitated an increase in the staffing of the administration.[40]

At the highest level of *palatini* and officials of senatorial status, there was a massive expansion of personnel, from 250 to 3,000 in each half of the empire in the fourth century. This had consequences for the empire as a whole and for individual cities. A significant percentage of the best-educated and best-connected local notables, traditionally liable for local public duties and serving as members of the city councils (*curiae*), was siphoned off into the imperial administration, gaining entry at the apex of their careers into the court. An inevitable consequence was a relative empoverishment of city councils (their membership limited increasingly to middling rentiers) and a weakening of urban self-government, which became very apparent in the sixth century. But this was more than offset by the new cohesion given to the empire, by high-flying officials, who, especially after retirement as *honorati*, could act as links between the governing centre and the localities. They formed a vital new social stratum, below the level of magnates with supra-regional connections and large dispersed properties, and above that of landowners whose horizons did not extend beyond the province and those middling urban rentiers who served on city councils. The social order of the eastern empire was thus many-layered and wide-reaching in late antiquity.[41]

The principal development, though, was the spread of monotheist belief among all strata of the Roman population from 312 when Constantine announced that he was giving it his personal support (not that he would ever attend the liturgy or be baptized until just before he died). There was resistance, of course, most notably at the highest social level of the Roman Senate (in the fourth century) and in remoter recesses of the countryside (in the sixth century, if not later). Nor would polytheistic notions which explained the vagaries of life disappear without trace. The old gods remained active in the collective *imaginaire*, as demons fighting a guerrilla war against the new faith.[42]

[40] Jones, *Late Roman Empire*, 42–52, 61–8.

[41] Heather, 'New Men for New Constantines', 18–25; M. Whittow, 'Ruling the Late Roman and Early Byzantine City', *PP* 129 (1990), 3–29; Liebeschuetz, *Decline and Fall*, 104–24.

[42] S. Mitchell, *A History of the Later Roman Empire, AD 284–641* (Oxford, 2007), 225–300; P. Brown, *Power and Persuasion in Late Antiquity: Towards a Christian Europe* (Madison WI,

But the progress of Christianity accelerated with official backing. There was a single brief hiatus in the reign of Julian (361–3), an open champion of polytheism. Theodosius I (379–95) took the decisive step of imposing Christianity on his subjects, encouraging the closure of temples and banning blood sacrifice.[43] It helped that the new religion was structurally compatible with the Roman state: like its pagan predecessors, it had a priesthood and fixed places of worship; its local organization was hierarchical, and patterned on the provincial system. Church and empire were gradually integrated, a process which culminated in the merger of imperial and church ceremonial in the reign of Theodosius II (408–50). He was an emperor who committed himself publicly to worship, took part in religious processions, and made manifest his role both as God's vice-gerent on earth and the Romans' chief intercessor with God.[44]

There were three features of the new faith which were to prove, in combination, a source of trouble. First and foremost, it was not pure monotheism. *The godhead was triune*, comprising the creator of everything, outside time and space; the son, who was for a while immersed in the material world; and the holy spirit. The primary message of salvation, proffered through the voluntary self-sacrifice of the son, which was so enticing, whatever one's status in this world, was liable to become tangled in complex theological argumentation, once human reason was unleashed upon it. There was no question but that this would happen, given centuries of philosophical disputation and the advanced education available to the well-off. There was no lack of intellectuals ready to leap in.[45] Second, there was a consensus among churchmen that there should be *agreement about doctrine and rites*. The faithful should be bound together by a single faith and should follow a single liturgical tradition in worship.[46] This would endow the empire ruled over by God's vice-gerent with a new binding agent. Third, the emperor, who had played a leading role in the empire's religious practices in the pagan past, continued to do so. As supreme judicial authority, he

1992), 89–103, 146–52; P. Brown, *Authority and the Sacred: Aspects of the Christianisation of the Roman World* (Cambridge, 1995), 3–26.

[43] Mitchell, *History of the Later Roman Empire*, 245–51.

[44] N. McLynn, 'Imperial Piety in Action: The Theodosians in Church', in S. Destephen, B. Dumézil, & H. Inglebert, eds., *Le prince chrétien de Constantin aux royautés barbares (IVe-VIIIe siècles)*, *TM* 22.2 (2018), 315–39.

[45] J. Pelikan, *Christianity and Classical Culture: The Metamorphosis of Natural Theology in the Christian Encounter with Hellenism* (New Haven, CT, 1993).

[46] J. Meyendorff, *Imperial Unity and Christian Divisions: The Church 450–680 A.D.* (Crestwood, NY, 1989), 5–20.

was all too soon embroiled in property disputes between church factions. It was also natural that he should preside over meetings of senior churchmen from all over the empire, when they were convened to solve theological disputes or, at least, to come up with formulations which satisfied the parties involved. His authority was then called upon to aid the dissemination of what had been agreed, if necessary, with coercion.[47]

An insistence on precisely defined orthodoxy, as well as orthopraxy, in the naturally contrary world of highly educated and competitive churchmen generated disputes. They took place *within the framework of empire*, the opposing parties striving to win over the authorities to their side. Even in the late sixth century, after two and half centuries of disputation, confessional attachments did not undercut the loyalty of Romans to the empire. But the stridency of the disputants, their use of every intellectual and rhetorical device to best their opponents, and the growing entrenchment of opinion in each party undoubtedly weakened the cohesion of the empire and distracted emperors from affairs of state. There were phases of abatement and intensification in disputation, the theological focus of which moved about, but the empire was never at peace in this religious sphere.[48]

Roman history in late antiquity was punctuated by ecumenical councils summoned to resolve or defuse disputes: the first two, held at Nicaea in 325 and Constantinople in 381, were mainly concerned with devising a formula about the Trinity which could be adopted throughout Christendom; the next two, held at Ephesus in 431 and Chalcedon in 451, wrestled with the insoluble issue of Christ's *diune nature*—were his divinity and humanity, each fully formed, complete, perfect, *combined and inextricably conjoined or fused*? This was a dispute which was to carry on throughout the sixth century, and to mutate in the seventh into one about his *will* and the motive force or *energy* which communicated his will to his diune nature.[49]

Emperors were inevitably implicated: Constantius subsequently criticized for backing the Arians, a portmanteau term for those reluctant to assent to every detail of the Nicene formula; Zeno who attempted to broker a compromise when the Chalcedonian formula about Christ roused serious opposition; Justinian (527–65) who took a close interest in theological

[47] C. Humfress, *Orthodoxy and the Courts in Late Antiquity* (Oxford, 2007).

[48] Meyendorff, *Imperial Unity and Christian Divisions*, 251–92; M. Whitby, *The Emperor Maurice and His Historian: Theophylact Simocatta on Persian and Balkan Warfare* (Oxford, 1988), 213–15.

[49] Meyendorff, *Imperial Unity and Christian Divisions*, 165–206; B. E. Daley, *God Visible: Patristic Christology Reconsidered* (Oxford, 2018).

issues and succeeded in coercing Pope Vigilius into supporting a new compromise formula at the second council of Constantinople in 553; and finally Heraclius (610–41) who brokered a new monothelete formula (Christ's diune nature being fused at the level of the will) and was well on the way to winning over the dissident churches of Egypt, Syria, and Armenia when the familiar Christian world of the Middle East was overwhelmed by the Arabs.[50]

## 1.4 The last century and a half

Two figures tower over the final phase of Roman history (491–641)—the Emperor Justinian (527–65), renowned as law-maker and builder, who strove to recover large parts of the western empire; and Heraclius (610–41), a great war-leader who, by military strokes of extraordinary boldness, transformed imminent defeat at the hands of the Persians into victory.

The military aspect of Roman history, always prominent from the distant Republican past through the early to the late empire, came yet more to the fore. There may have been relatively few bouts of civil war—two in the reign of Anastasius (491–518), one which brought down the Emperor Phocas (602–610)—but there were many foreign wars. The world outside proved increasingly threatening as time passed. Towards the end of the sixth century, Roman forces, which included a high percentage of foreign troops, were engaged on four fronts—south and north of the Armenian Taurus in the east, in the Balkans, and in Italy—against Persians, Avars (successors of the Huns as the hegemonic power in eastern Europe), Slavs, and Lombards. In the early seventh century, the balance in the fighting, hitherto roughly even, swung decisively against the Romans on all four fronts. In the fourth decade the empire was destroyed, being stripped of its Middle Eastern provinces.

The story was a grim one from the Roman point of view. Two additional contributory factors lay outside human control. First there was a mysterious dimming of the sun and sharp drop in temperature, after massive volcanic eruptions far to the east in 536 and 539/40. This had a direct effect on harvests. Then, far worse, was the coming of bubonic plague from east Africa in late 541. From Egypt it spread swiftly round the Mediterranean and its

[50] Meyendorff, *Imperial Unity and Christian Divisions*, 207–50, 333–61; R. Price, P. Booth, & C. Cubitt, *The Acts of the Lateran Synod of 649*, TTH 61 (Liverpool, 2014), 5–17.

coastlands in 542, and onto Sasanian territory in 643. This marked a real caesura in economic history, bringing the late antique boom to a halt, save perhaps in the interior of Arabia and in highland Iran, well away from the sea. Its mortality may not have been as high as that of the Black Death, but the effect on Roman finances (as a year later on those of the Persians) was serious, as revenue dropped. There was, it seems, a general darkening of mood, most clearly expressed by the historian Procopius.[51]

Back in the 490s and early decades of the sixth century, hopes were high. A senior palace official, the *silentiarius* Anastasius, was jobbed in as Zeno's successor by the head of the Bedchamber, in the hope that he would reassert the primacy of the central bureaucracy in government. The new emperor proved more than competent, although there were two serious challenges to his rule. The first came from the Isaurian faction, when its two leading office-holders were purged in 491. The civil war lasted seven years, ending finally in 498 with imposition of effective Roman authority on their highlands in south-east Asia Minor. The second came from Vitalian, the general in command in Thrace, who advanced on the metropolitan region in 514 and 515, and then holed up in Anchialus until an amnesty in 518. Nonetheless Anastasius was able to introduce a series of reforms: (1) to boost the economy (abolition of the main tax on trade), (2) to improve the working of the fiscal system (notably the appointment of *vindices* to oversee tax collection at the level of the city), (3) to make management of crown lands more efficient, and (4) to improve the justice system.[52] He was reputed to have left the treasury with large reserves (320,000 pounds of gold) for his two immediate successors, Justin I (518–27), a palace guards commander from the Balkans who was elected by the Senate under considerable military pressure; and Justin's nephew, Justinian (527–65), see Figure 1.6.[53]

Justinian is much lauded for his sponsorship of a full codification of Roman law carried out by two editorial commissions in the opening years of his reign (528–34) and for the subsequent legislation which continued

[51] The ultimate origin is identified either as East Africa (P. Sarris, 'The Justinianic Plague: Origins and Effects', *Continuity and Change*, 17 (2002), 169–82) or as Central Asia (K. Harper, *The Fate of Rome: Climate, Disease and the End of an Empire* [Princeton, 2017], 201–2, 206–14, 217–35). Harper puts the death toll at 50% of the Black Death's (232–5, 263, 343), assuredly an overestimate. Temporary cooling: Harper's Late Antique Little Ice Age (*Fate of Rome*, 249–54).

[52] F. K. Haarer, *Anastasius I: Politics and Empire in the Late Roman World* (Leeds, 2006), 1–6, 22–8, 164–79, 193–9, 207–11, 222–3.

[53] Haarer, *Anastasius*, 246–9; P. Sarris, *Justinian: Emperor, Soldier, Saint* (Cambridge, 2023), 60–5.

**Figure 1.6** Justinian and entourage, San Vitale, Ravenna. The church was completed in 547, after the east Roman reconquest of Italy. The notables accompanying Justinian in the mosaic include Bishop Maximian (named), responsible for the final phase of work; the banker Julius Argentarius, who funded it; and the victorious generals, Belisarius and Narses.
*Source*: Bridgeman.

the work, begun by Anastasius, of improving the justice system and the efficiency of tax collection, not to mention the updating of family law and the introduction of numerous administrative changes.[54] Most of the projects in his building programme, remembered above all for the innovative designs of grand Constantinopolitan churches, continued Anastasius' programme of upgrading and extending deep systems of frontier defence.[55] His prime

[54] C. Humfress, 'Law and Legal Practice in the Age of Justinian', in M. Maas, ed., *Cambridge Companion to the Age of Justinian* (Cambridge, 2005), 161–84; P. Sarris, *Economy and Society in the Age of Justinian* (Cambridge, 2006), 208–17; D. Miller & P. Sarris, *The Novels of Justinian*, 2 vols. (Cambridge, 2018).

[55] Churches: Mainstone, *Hagia Sophia*; R. Ousterhout, 'Aesthetics and Politics in the Architecture of Justinian', in *Constantinople réelle et imaginaire: Autour de l'oeuvre de Gilbert Dagron*, *TM* 22.1 (2018), 103–20; Sarris, *Justinian*, 163–71. Defences: M. Whitby, 'Procopius and Roman Defences in Upper Mesopotamia', in P. Freeman & D. Kennedy, eds, *The Defence of the Roman and Byzantine East*, BAR Int. Ser. 297 (Oxford, 1986), 717–35, at 724–30; J. Howard-Johnston, 'Procopius, Roman Defences North of the Taurus and the New Fortress of Citharizon', in D. H. French & C. S. Lightfoot, eds, *The Eastern Frontier of the Roman*

concerns were those of a military man—defence, security in the interior (governors were assigned military as well as civil powers in provinces where disorder was prevalent), law and order. He was unusually devout—hence perhaps the urgency with which he pressed churchmen to agree a Christological formula. He showed little of the usual interest in patronizing intellectuals and writers.[56] There was more than a streak of ruthlessness in his character, as was shown in his handling of the Nika Riot in Constantinople when it threatened to get out of hand in January 532—the crowd was lured into the hippodrome which was turned into a killing ground. A figure of 30,000 for the dead comes from a reputable source. This resort to the use of brute force suggests that there may have been some truth in his portrayal as a demonic being in Procopius' *Secret History*.[57]

War, though, dominated the empire's history in the sixth century. The long period of almost entirely peaceful co-existence in the Middle East ended in autumn 502 with an unprovoked Persian attack, which netted a great prize, the city of Amida, in January 503. Kavad I, recently restored to the Sasanian throne by his nomad (Hephthalite) overlords, was plainly seeking to garner prestige from military success in the west. The war was to last some three years, and to involve possibly the largest number of troops ever deployed by the Romans in a single theatre of war (some 80,000 men in northern Mesopotamia in 504).[58] It ended with a return to the *status quo* (Amida was recovered by the Romans) and an uneasy armistice. The Romans invested large sums in military infrastructure, in preparation for a war of revenge. The Persians responded with an embargo on Roman shipping in the Indian Ocean.[59] The war of revenge broke out in 528 along the full length of the frontier, from the far north where Persian Iberia was the target of three field armies, to the far south where the Axumites invaded Himyar as Roman proxies. The outcome (save in the far south) was disastrous for the Romans, who thereafter remained on the defensive until they

*Empire*, BAR Int. Ser. 553 (Oxford, 1989), 203–29, repr. in J. Howard-Johnston, *East Rome, Sasanian Persia and the End of Antiquity: Historiographical and Historical Studies* (Aldershot, 2006), no. II; J. D. Alchermes, 'Art and Architecture in the Age of Justinian', in Maas, *Companion*, 343–75, at 355–66.

[56] P. T. R. Gray, ' The Legacy of Chalcedon: Christological Problems and Their Significance', Maas, *Companion*, 215–38, 16 227–35; Sarris, *Justinian*, 287–308; A. Cameron, *Procopius and the Sixth Century* (London, 1985), 19–23; C. Rapp, 'Literary Culture under Justinian', in Maas, *Companion*, 376–97, at 382–92.

[57] G. Greatrex, 'Nika Riot: A Reasssessment', *JHS* 117 (1997), 60–86; Procopius, *Anecdota*, 12.24–7, 18.1 & 36, 30.34, ed. & trans. H. B. Dewing (Cambridge, Mass., 1935).

[58] G. Greatrex, *Rome and Persia at War, 502–532* (Leeds, 1998), 73–119.

[59] Greatrex, *Rome and Persia*, 120–38; Howard-Johnston, 'India Trade', 293–6.

were able to negotiate peace with Kavad's son and successor Khusro I (531–79)—on humiliating terms (in 532).[60]

It is no wonder then that Justinian, his credentials also damaged by the Nika Riot, sought to emulate Kavad and recoup lost prestige by a western military venture, a naval and military expedition against Vandal Africa in 533. Victory over the Vandal army and the capture of Carthage led to the collapse of Vandal rule early in 534—something much trumpeted by the regime—and a long subsequent struggle by the Roman military authorities to impose their authority on the interior.[61] A gathering political crisis in the Ostrogoth regime in Italy in the 530s provided Justinian with an opportunity to recover more lost ground in the west. His policy was pragmatic, to seize an advantage when it was proffered, in the hope, it appears, of establishing a series of coastal enclaves from which to control the western basin of the Mediterranean. The last was acquired in 551 in Spain.[62] As happened in north Africa, the initial success of the campaigns in Sicily (535) and Italy (537–40) took time and effort to follow up, the difficulties being compounded by the effects of plague and competing demand for resources from the army in the east and in the Balkans. Final victory was only achieved in 552 (after which a Frankish invasion [553–4] had to be countered).[63]

In the east, Khusro took advantage of Justinian's preoccupation with the west in 540. He invaded northern Syria and gathered a rich haul of booty. Antioch, an even greater prize than Amida in 503, was captured. This highly successful campaign drew attention away from Lazica, which was occupied by Persian forces in 541. The Roman empire's standing and position in the Middle East was seriously weakened on the eve of the plague. This third round of fighting between the great powers was to last for nearly twenty years, but was limited to the Lazica front after 545.[64] There were also problems on the Danube frontier, not so much the raiding of nomad ('Hunnic') forces, reported in 539 and 544, as the infiltration into the Balkans of Slavs, a people unknown to the Romans before the sixth century and relatively

[60] Outbreak: *Ioannis Malalae chronographia*, ed. J. Thurn, CFHB 35 (Berlin, 2000), xviii. 4, 15, 26, trans. E. Jeffreys, M. Jeffreys & R. Scott, *The Chronicle of John Malalas*, Byzantina Australiensia 4 (Melbourne, 1986). Course from 529 and outcome: Greatrex, *Rome and Persia*, 160–3, 168–218.

[61] P. Heather, *Rome Resurgent: War and Empire in the Age of Justinian* (Oxford, 2018), 11–21, 135–46, 237–51.

[62] Heather, *Rome Resurgent*, 142, 147–57, 298.

[63] Heather, *Rome Resurgent*, 115, 164–79, 251–68.

[64] G. Greatrex & S. N. C. Lieu, eds, *The Roman Eastern Frontier and the Persian Wars, Part II AD 363–630: A Narrative Sourcebook* (London, 2002), 102–34.

untouched by Roman culture, a process encouraged from 545 by the principal regional power, the Germanic Gepids of the middle Danube.[65]

There was some relief in the late 550s and early 560s, partly because of Justinian's success in neutralizing the Gepids with Lombard help, but mainly because of revolutionary events at the far end of the Eurasian steppes. There the dominant nomads, the Rouran, were challenged and defeated by their Turk subjects in 552. The Turks then extended their authority westward with remarkable speed, in a re-enactment on a yet grander scale of Hunnic achievements. Their senior khaganate remained firmly rooted in the steppes fronting China while their power was projected to those fronting Iran, where in the early 560s, with the backing of the Sasanians, they destroyed the last Hunnic state, that of the Hephthalites, established north of the Hindu Kush.[66] Their expansion had an initially beneficial consequence for the Romans. Khusro I's regime became much more amenable and negotiated a full peace treaty in 561–2, relinquishing its claim to Lazica. But the knock-on effects were disastrous.[67]

Remnants of the Rouran, known in the west as Avars, fled from the Turks, eventually establishing a mini-empire centred on the Carpathian basin, where they constituted a more dangerous potential adversary than the Gepids. Their arrival there prompted the Lombards to migrate south in 568, across the Alps, to the relative security of the Po valley, where they came into conflict with the Roman authorities.[68] All too soon, Justinian's successor, Justin II (565–78) turned potential into actual enmity in the Balkans, by taking a haughty, intransigent line in negotiations with the Avars, and embarked on war in the Middle East in 573, tempted by an offer of alliance from the Turks.[69] An attack was launched on Nisibis, the main forward base in Persian Mesopotamia. It was brilliantly countered. The Roman expeditionary force was defeated and Dara was captured, in what turned out to be the opening episode of a fourth round of serious fighting

[65] A. Sarantis, *Justinian's Balkan Wars: Campaigning, Diplomacy and Development in Illyricum, Thrace and the Northern World A.D. 527–65* (Prenton, 2016), 65–82, 101–8, 240—88.

[66] Sarantis, *Justinian's Balkan Wars*, 312–20; M. R. Jackson Bonner, *Three Neglected Sources of Sasanian History in the Reign of Khusraw Anushirvan*, Studia Iranica, cahier 46 (Paris, 2011), 89–101.

[67] Greatrex & Lieu, *Roman Eastern Frontier* 130–4; J. Howard-Johnston, 'The Sasanians' Strategic Dilemma', in H. Börm & J. Wiesehöfer, eds, *Commutatio et contentio—Studies in the Late Roman, Sasanian and Early Islamic Near East: In Memory of Zeev Rubin* (Düsseldorf, 2010), 37–70, at 46–9.

[68] W. Pohl, *The Avars: A Steppe Empire in Europe, 567–822* (Ithaca, NY, 2018), 21–5, 33–8; N. Christie, *The Lombards: The Ancient Longobards* (Oxford, 1995).

[69] Pohl, *Avars*, 47–50, 53–62; Howard-Johnston, 'Strategic Dilemma', 49–52.

between the great powers (to 591). After biding their time, the Avars joined in from 578, orchestrating a large-scale movement of Slavs into the Balkans and undertaking raiding expeditions of their own.[70]

It was in the reign of Maurice (582–602), a former general, that the fighting rose to a crescendo on four fronts. The Lombards extended their authority in northern Italy. Slavs and Avars ranged relatively freely over the Balkan interior while the war in the east continued. It was a dour attritional struggle in the 580s, fought on both fronts, north and south of the Armenian Taurus. It was only after the renewal of peace with the Persians (on very favourable terms after the Romans restored Khusro II [590–628] to his throne) that Maurice could turn his attention to the Balkans. He strove to assert control over areas of Slav settlement and to pen the Avars back into the Carpathian basin. In Italy he could do little more than try to contain the Lombards in the north.[71] In 602 the strain of war finally proved too much. A mutiny of the Balkan army developed into a full-scale rebellion. Maurice was deposed and executed along with five of his six sons. This prompted Khusro II to declare war on the usurper, Phocas, who had killed his benefactor, beginning another round of warfare, the last of the five Roman–Persian wars fought from 502.[72]

This was the beginning of the end. Both great powers invested all their resources in the struggle. The fighting extended from Transcaucasia to Mesopotamia. Arabs, Armenians, Iberians, Albanians, and Laz were drawn in. So too were the nomad powers, the Turks who dominated western and eastern Eurasia and the Avars in central Europe. The movement of Slavs south started again. They colonized the mountainous spines of the Balkans and began to lap against the plains still controlled by Roman cities, as far south as the Peloponnese. In Italy, the Lombards took control of the whole length of the Apennines, confining Roman control to three separate substantial blocks of territory—around Ravenna, around Rome, and in the south.[73]

After an initial phase of attritional warfare, the Persians broke into the Roman interior beyond the inner defensive line on the Euphrates. They were helped by civil war. Rebel forces led by Heraclius, son of the Exarch of Africa, gained control of Egypt and broadcast anti-government propaganda

[70] Whitby, *Emperor Maurice*, 86–9, 254–75; Howard-Johnston, 'Strategic Dilemma', 51–7.
[71] Whitby, *Emperor Maurice*, 138–83, 276–304; Christie, *Lombards*, 84–91.
[72] J. Howard-Johnston, *The Last Great War of Antiquity* (Oxford, 2021), 12–22.
[73] Whitby, *Emperor Maurice*, 184–91; Christie, *Lombards*, 89–97.

throughout the Levant. The rebellion against Phocas' regime culminated in a naval attack on Constantinople in autumn 610. Five years later Khusro II took the fateful decision to destroy the Roman empire, when his forces were taking over the Levant and he could look forward to the conquest first of Egypt and then of Asia Minor. The climactic moment came in 626, when two Persian armies and a huge Avar host converged on Constantinople. Despite the efforts of Heraclius, a brilliant exponent of a new style of warfare, relying on speed of movement, superior intelligence, and deception, to surprise his opponents and take them on in detail, the Roman empire seemed to be doomed. Admittedly Constantinople held out thanks to the strength of its walls and successful efforts by the authorities to maintain morale. But there would be more Persian offensives, more of the Balkans would be overrun, and the Lombards would extend their sway in Italy.[74]

That was indeed the grim future awaiting Heraclius and his regime—but after a hiatus. It was not Persians but Arabs who reduced the Roman empire to the status of a medium-sized power in the Middle East and eastern Europe. For the Turks were drawn into the conflict on the Romans' side and, from 627, set about the conquest of the Persians' sector of Transcaucasia, thereby posing an increasing threat to the north-western regions of Iran proper (Adurbadagan and Mad [Media]). Romans and Turks coordinated their actions. The summit held by Heraclius and the supreme khagan outside Tiflis in autumn 627 demonstrated their commitment to the struggle. The boldest of all Heraclius' campaigns, a march across the Zagros mountains on the eve of winter and a thrust south against the metropolitan region, was the trigger for a *putsch* against Khusro. The unstable regimes which followed halted the fighting and sued for peace, eventually (630) being forced to disgorge all Khusro's gains.[75]

Much larger changes were already in train. The Eurasian hegemony of the Turks was brought to an abrupt end in 629 by well-timed and well-directed diplomatic and military strokes from the second Tang emperor of China.[76] In Arabia, the stark monotheist message of Muhammad, laced through with apocalyptic foreboding, proved astonishingly persuasive. Within two years of the compromise agreed at Hudaybiyya in 628 (the Prophet's offer to incorporate the pagan *hajj* within Islam secured an end to

[74] Howard-Johnston, *Last Great War*, 37–133, 191–292.

[75] Howard-Johnston, *Last Great War*, 293–359.

[76] J. Howard-Johnston, 'World War in Eurasia at the End of Antiquity', in R. Gyselen, ed., *Sasanian Persia and the Tabarestan Archive*, Res Orientales 27 (Bures-sur-Yvette, 2019), 9–28.

the blockade of the Muslim community in Medina), the Meccan exiles and their Medinan helpers were able to take control of Mecca. Thereafter the new faith, with its galvanic effect on the minds of the faithful, acting in combination with the organizational capability and statecraft of a highly developed city-state, was able to unite Arabia (force reinforcing prophetic charisma) and to divert internal tensions (whether between nomad tribes, or between nomads and sedentaries) outwards. Within two years of the Prophet's death in 632, Arab forces set about the dismemberment of the Roman empire in the Middle East (a victory inland from Gaza on 4 February 634 opened Palestine to attack). After two years of fighting, Roman forces withdrew from Palestine and Syria. In 636 Sasanian Mesopotamia was targeted and was firmly occupied after four years of hard fighting. In 640, it was the turn of Egypt to face surgical military strikes, and likewise, after two years' fighting and a ten-month armistice, to be evacuated by the Roman authorities (September 643). Finally the core Iranian component of the Sasanian empire was overrun in two swift campaigns (642–4 and 648–52).[77]

The urban notables who acknowledged the brute fact of Arab military power, who knew that continued resistance would only lead to the destruction of their valuable suburban properties, had every reason to expect that the Romans would return, as they had done at the end of the Persian war. Neither they nor the two parties competing for power in Constantinople after Heraclius' death in 641 could conceive of a world no longer managed by Romans. But that world was gone. The political and economic centre of gravity of western Eurasia was already moving east, away from the Mediterranean, in 644, when the Caliph ʻUmar I went down to the port of Jar to witness the arrival of the first convoy bringing the surplus grain of Egypt to the burgeoning cities of Medina and Mecca.[78]

*Byzantium in a Changing World*. James Howard-Johnston, Oxford University Press.
 DOI: 10.1093/9780191999093.003.0002

[77] J. Howard-Johnston, *Witnesses to a World Crisis: Historians and Histories of the Middle East in the Seventh Century* (Oxford, 2010), 445–73, supplemented by P. Booth, 'The Muslim Conquest of Egypt Reconsidered', in C. Zuckerman, ed., *Constructing the Seventh Century*, *TM* 17 (2013), 639–70 and J. Howard-Johnston, 'The Coming of the Arabs to Iran', *Sasanian Studies*, 1 (2021), 99–126.

[78] Howard-Johnston, *Witnesses*, 469–70, 475–6; F. Bessard, *Caliphs and Merchants: Cities and Economies of Power in the Near East (700–950)* (Oxford, 2020).

# 2
# Dark Age

The two centuries following Heraclius' death and the loss of the rich Middle Eastern provinces constituted a dark age for Byzantium, in two senses; it was a grim time, and little light is thrown on it by historical sources.

Byzantium, the rump of the Roman empire which had survived the initial Arab onslaught, was involved in a long, dour defensive war against the Caliphate in the east, and, later, in the ninth century, in the central Mediterranean. Danger also threatened on other fronts. A small, highly militarized and ideologically charged Bulgar state, secure behind the Haemus mountain range in the north-east Balkans, menaced Thrace and the Thracian approaches to Constantinople. The Byzantine enclaves in Italy were exposed to depredation by the Lombard kingdom in the Po valley and the dukedoms in the Apennines. There was also the rising power of the Franks beyond the Alps which might challenge Byzantium's preeminence within Christendom.

Unprecedented demands were put on Byzantium's diminished resources, immaterial as well as material. All manner of reforms had to be introduced, to improve the efficiency of the state machine and to maximize its military potential.[1] Every aspect of life was affected across the whole social order—in town and country, on the mainland and in the islands of Byzantium's own inner sea, the Aegean. The impact was felt by the whole population, from the most powerful to the humblest, from the imperial court in the fastness of Constantinople to the peasantry in the remotest recesses of the mountains which enclose the plateau of Asia Minor.

The political elite and the literate stratum of society serving in the apparatus of government had little time for the leisure pursuits of their late-antique predecessors. Writing of all sorts, artistic production, and intellectual activity were reduced to a subsistence level. The canon of classical writers who were still taught and read was much reduced.[2] In the sphere of history writing, very little was produced. A single, highly tendentious memoir, now lost,

[1] Howard-Johnston, *Byzantium*, 18–35, 41–52.
[2] Wilson, *Scholars of Byzantium*, 18–27.

written around 720 and traditionally ascribed to the Patrician Trajan, was the only indigenous Byzantine work to cover the fifty fraught years, from the middle of 669 to the time of writing. As such both extant historians of the period following the death of Heraclius fell upon it—the future Patriarch Nikephoros, who wrote a short classicizing history in the 780s; and the well-connected abbot Theophanes, at work some thirty years later. Most of the crucial reign of Constans II (641–69) lay outside Trajan's scope and was simply left out by Nikephoros. The patchwork of notices with which Theophanes filled the gap was taken mainly from a Syrian chronicle.

A second indigenous source (also lost), a chronicle which incorporated much official material and carried the story on for another fifty years (from the 720s to the 770s), provided the only coherent Byzantine account of that period for Nikephoros and Theophanes. Hence the large degree of overlap between their accounts, the principal difference being a strong streak of psogism in Theophanes'. The light finally brightens in the 780s, when Theophanes could draw on contemporary material.[3] Thereafter there tend to be at least two independent, fairly continuous streams of historical narrative on which the latter-day historian can draw.[4]

## 2.1 Threats from without: Arabs

The rise of Islam and the formation of an Arab empire infused with the new religion were the principal events of the seventh century. The geopolitics of western Eurasia were utterly transformed. Instead of a binary world order, a single superordinate power bestrode the Middle East and projected its authority far beyond.

The process of its expansion can be followed in outline, through the observations of outsiders and a few skeletal Arab chronicles put together within a generation or two of the events. Normal explanations for so extraordinary a historical phenomenon as the emergence of a durable world empire in a single generation (622–52) are hard, indeed virtually impossible, to find (see Figure 2.1). Contemporaries, both Arabs and their defeated adversaries, could not but think that God had intervened directly and decisively in human affairs. Fourteen hundred years later we can only point

[3] Howard-Johnston, *Witnesses*, 268–79.

[4] J. Howard-Johnston, *Historical Writing in Byzantium*, Kieler Felix-Jacoby Vorlesungen (Heidelberg, 2014), 19–33.

**Figure 2.1** Dome of the Rock: (a) exterior, (b) interior. It was built during the second Arab civil war and completed in 691/2. The building marked the site of Creation and would serve as the courtroom for the Last Judgement.

to that key moment, before the negotiations at Hudaybiyya in 628, when the Prophet realized that he must compromise, that he must accept the full array of rites associated with pilgrimage to the principal pagan sanctuary in Arabia (including animal sacrifices) if the faith was to spread outside the confines of the Meccan exiles and their local allies beleaguered in Medina. That was the point of ignition of a conflagration which spread with astonishing speed.[5]

The mechanisms of expansion—an ability to assemble and to provision armies numbered in the low thousands rather than low hundreds, to direct operations from a distance, to determine priorities, to target forces at vulnerable points, to disseminate propaganda, etc.—were not to be found in the core groups of Muhammad's followers (the *umma* or Muslim community) but in Mecca, which had exercised a loose hegemony over the other cities of the Hijaz and over the ambient nomad tribes.[6] But the driving force behind the conquests can only have been the new faith with its austere world view of a single awesome, uncircumscribed deity, infinitely remote, *aware of the thoughts, words, and deeds of all the myriad human beings on earth*; stern, requiring complete submission on the part of the believer, who was to be individually accountable at an *imminent* day of judgement. It is hard, but not impossible, to envisage the impact of this—because we are all too familiar with the pockets of the faithful driven to extremes and eager to die for Islam.[7]

If the impetus came originally from faith, if faith inspired extraordinary commitment from the faithful through successive stages of the conquests, it was itself boosted by a phenomenon remarked upon in antiquity and the Middle Ages, when a minor, local movement built up unstoppable momentum in a short time. Such a *dynamic* growth of power was evident in the early third century, when a small rebel movement on the edge of the southern Zagros developed into a military movement capable of taking over the Parthian empire.[8] It can be best observed many centuries later in the expansion of Norman power, first in France, then in England, southern Italy, and the Levant.[9] In these and other cases a virtuous circle was at work, success boosting prestige, increased prestige attracting more support, that accretion of support magnifying military power and generating further and greater success.

[5] Howard-Johnston, *Witnesses*, 408–18, 456–60.
[6] Howard-Johnston, *Witnesses*, 398–402, 451–2.
[7] Howard-Johnston, *Witnesses*, 462–4, 448–51.
[8] See pp. 14–15.
[9] J. Le Patourel, *The Norman Empire* (Oxford, 1976), 279–96.

A process of this sort can clearly be seen in the first few Arab campaigns: the first victory of note outside Arabia was won over a local Roman defensive force, and opened up the fertile coastlands of Palestine to raiding (February 634); within two years, Arab forces were capable of engaging and defeating a large Roman field army in southern Syria (probably late spring 636), invading Mesopotamia (later in 636), laying siege to Ctesiphon (637), making a fighting retreat to the edge of the desert in the face of a massive Sasanian counteroffensive (late 637), and defeating that victorious Sasanian field army in open, orthodox combat at Qadisiyya (6 January 638).[10]

Those early campaigns were not haphazard. A directing intelligence or intelligences can be seen at work. Forces might have been divided, as in 634 against Palestine and 640 against Egypt, but their operations were coordinated, so as to confuse the enemy into expecting the main blow in the wrong place (Palestine) or to divide the targeted region in two (Egypt).[11] There was a succession of prime targets—initially Palestine (634–5), followed by Syria (635–6), Mesopotamia (636–40), Egypt (640–2), and Iran (642–52). The clearest evidence of strategic direction is provided by a contemporary Armenian source, the *History of Khosrov* traditionally ascribed to Sebeos. After the final destruction of the Sasanian empire in 652, a general order was issued for the redeployment of all available forces in the west against Byzantium. It was obeyed in 653, and the next year the order was given to attack Asia Minor and Constantinople (of which more below).[12]

Belief that they were empowered by God greatly improved the combat effectiveness of the Arabs, morale mattering as much, if not more, than fighting skill and weaponry. Yet more striking was the resilience which faith imparted, when things went wrong on the battlefield. There can be no denying that the armies of conquest had extraordinary tensile strength, manifest also in their powers of endurance and speed of march.

This last quality was most evident in the conquest of western Iran, after a second major victory over massed Sasanian field forces at Nihawand in 642. Before the end of the year the whole of Media was occupied, and was

[10] Howard-Johnston, *Witnesses*, 464–8.

[11] Howard-Johnston, *Witnesses*, 465–6, 469–70, with corrections of Booth, 'Muslim Conquest of Egypt Reconsidered', 639–70.

[12] A. Marsham, 'Were there Strategic Considerations in the Seventh-Century Arabian Conquests?', Proceedings of 2017 Tübingen conference on the Battle of Yarmuk (forthcoming). Key text: G. V. Abgaryan, ed., *Patmut'iwn Sebeosi* (Erevan, 1979), 164.7–12, 169.18–23, 170.5–23, trans. R. W. Thomson, in R. W. Thomson & J. Howard-Johnston, *The Armenian History Attributed to Sebeos*, TTH 31 (Liverpool, 1999), with Historical Notes 68 & 75.

secured from attack along the southern edge of the plateau by seizure of the twin cities of Jay and Isfahan. A similar move, likewise designed to shield Media from attack from the east, netted Rayy (the predecessor of Tehran) on the northern edge of the plateau, and, further east, Qumis and Jurjan, possibly before the end of the 642 campaigning season. In 643 it was the turn of Adurbadagan (Iranian Azerbaijan) to be targeted, with a display of armed might which led to its formal submission. This was swiftly followed by the dispatch of three raiding forays which ranged over western Transcaucasia, from the northern edge of the Zagros in the south to Iberia and Albania in the north. By 644 Arab forces were ready to advance north to take Derbend at the eastern end of the Caucasus. The decisiveness and speed of Arab attacks magnified the shock given to Sasanian authority, which collapsed in the western half of the empire after a mere two years or so of Arab operations, to be followed, after a gap, by the conquest of the eastern half (648/9–651/2).[13]

Checks were imposed, very occasionally, on Arab military expansion by organized states, but in the long run it was distance and internal tensions which brought the process to a close in the early ninth century. Before then we watch as Arab forces operated over larger and larger geographical areas. They were subjected for the first hundred years or so to something akin to a grand strategy, with a series of distinct phases defined by the prime target or targets: eastern Iran (649–52); Byzantium and the Mediterranean (654, 662–82); Byzantium, North Africa, and Spain (692–716); and finally the longest and most impressive outward thrust, over Central Asia (705–51), which drove back the forces of Tang China.[14]

The dimensions of the Islamic empire thus built up by the Arabs, extending from the Atlantic to the Altai Mountains, exceeded those of any preceding land empire outside China, save for the relatively ephemeral Turk khaganate of the sixth and early seventh centuries. The Caliphate, in the sense of a territorial state, presided over by a single religio-political leader, was to endure as a great power for a century and a half from the early eighth century, before centrifugal forces led to its fragmentation.

This endurance is largely explicable in terms of two religious institutions, both imposing obligations on able-bodied Muslims—the external *jihad*,

[13] J. Howard-Johnston, 'The Coming of the Arabs to Iran', *Sasanian Studies*, 1 (2022), 99–126.

[14] H. Kennedy, *The Great Arab Conquests: How the Spread of Islam Changed the World We Live in* (London, 2007), 200–323.

participation in warfare against unbelievers, which led to a steady movement of fighters to the periphery; and the *hajj*, pilgrimage to the sacred centre of Islam, the Ka'ba at Mecca. The Caliphate remained a dynamic empire, bound together by these contrary internal thrusts, and by awareness, in the urban centres colonized by Arabs and converts, of their potential vulnerability in refractory regions.[15]

There were political and religious tensions within the Muslim community from the first. On three occasions in the first 120 years they burst out into open civil war, *fitna*. The first (656–61) involved four factions: (1) supporters of Muhammad's cousin and son-in-law 'Ali, who had seized power after the murder of 'Uthman in 656; (2) the Meccan (Qurayshi) elite among the early Muslims; (3) the Syrian army which backed the governor of Syria, Mu'awiya, son of the Meccan leader who had opposed Muhammad until Hudaybiyya; and (4) *khwarajis* (ultras, distant predecessors of contemporary Islamists). There were five factions at odds in the second civil war (682–92), two based in Syria, one each in the Hijaz and Iraq, and ultras. Third came the Abbasid revolution (746–50), in which the secularized Syrian–Arab leadership of the Caliphate was replaced by one backed by the army of Khurasan, more explicitly religious and ready to accept converts as equal members of the Islamic community. But, apart from Spain which remained loyal to the Umayyad dynasty after 750, there were no political secessions from the Caliphate before the ninth century, and the bouts of civil war merely created intermissions in the wars of expansion.[16]

The Caliphate, then, was the great power which threatened Byzantium's existence for two centuries. Its lowering presence in the Middle East, and the naval power which it rapidly developed in the Mediterranean, were the prime influences on the radical reforms to inherited institutions and the traditional social order of Byzantium.[17] The political history of dark-age Byzantium can be largely written within the framework of the war with Islam. Changes of regime in the critical years 695–717 were primarily motivated by the perceived need for effective military (and naval) leadership; and it was only during the breathing spaces afforded by pauses in Arab

[15] X. de Planhol, *Les fondements géographiques de l'histoire de l'Islam* (Paris, 1968), 59–68; M. Bonner, *Jihad in Islamic History: Doctrines and Practice* (Princeton, 2006); T. Bianquis, P. Guichard, & M. Tillier, eds, *Les débuts du monde musulman VIIe–Xe siècles: De Muhammad aux dynasties autonomes* (Paris, 2012), 263–6.

[16] H. Kennedy, *The Prophet and the Age of the Caliphates: The Islamic Near East from the Sixth to the Eleventh Century* (3rd edn, London, 2016), 62–71, 76–85, 107–10.

[17] Howard-Johnston, *Byzantium*, 18–35, 62–73, 77–96.

expansion that attention could be given to other sectors of the frontier, above all in the Balkans.

## 2.2 Threats from without: the west and the north

No other people in Europe was subjected to so radical a reconfiguration. The great power of Latin Christendom, Merovingian Francia, evolved relatively undisturbed. The populations living in outer Europe, east of Frankish Austrasia, were at an early stage in the development of supratribal institutions, while the Northmen of Scandinavia, like the small kingdoms of England, found themselves drawn into the Frankish orbit which embraced the North Sea.[18]

It seems likely that Byzantium lost touch with Francia after a phase of active diplomatic communication in the late sixth century, although such news of events north of the Alps as reached northern Italy probably continued to be relayed to Byzantium. Italy, by contrast, did not slip beyond the horizon of vision. For Byzantium retained six possessions there—(1) the refuge strongholds in the Venetian lagoon which constituted the province of Venetia; (2) a rump territory north of the Apennines around the administrative capital, Ravenna; (3) Rome and its territory bounded to the north by Tuscany and Umbria (in Lombard hands since the 620s), to the east and south by the Lombard duchy of Benevento; (4) Apulia; (5) Calabria; and (6) Sicily. There was no question, though, of the Lombards' posing a threat outside Italy, just of their wearing down the resistance of the authorities, notables, and senior clergy in the Byzantine enclaves.[19]

Finally, there was no direct Byzantine stake in Spain after the loss of the coastal enclave around Cartagena in the 620s. But Byzantium maintained its ties with Sardinia, which was a loyal satellite and useful vantage point for keeping track of changes in the west Mediterranean—in particular for giving early warning of the emergence of any naval power which might

[18] I. N. Wood, *The Merovingian North Sea* (Alingsås 1983); I. Wood, *Merovingian Kingdoms 450–751* (London, 1994), 159–324; P. Heather, *Empires and Barbarians: Migration, Development and the Birth of Europe* (London, 2009), 361–77.

[19] C. Wickham, *Early Medieval Italy: Central Power and Local Society, 400–1000* (London, 1981), 33–47, 74–9; S. Gasparri, 'The Formation of an Early Medieval Community: Venice between Provincial and Urban Identity', in V. West-Harling, ed., *Three Empires, Three Cities: Identity, Material Culture and Legitimacy in Venice, Ravenna and Rome, 750–1000* (Turnhout, 2015), 35–50.

threaten Byzantium.[20] The Arabs' crossing of the Straits of Gibraltar in 711, their swift subsequent subjection of most of Spain, and their penning back of Visigoths into a small northern enclave did not, for the moment, rouse concern.[21]

The Avar khaganate, its standing fatally damaged by failure before Constantinople in 626, faced rebellions within and interventions from without over the next generation. The first stirrings among its Slav subjects occurred as the great host mobilized against Constantinople in 626 began its long retreat—not unexpectedly, given the losses suffered by Slav troops sent on mass assaults by land and water.[22]

It is impossible to piece together a coherent story of the subsequent breakdown of Avar hegemony in eastern Europe. All we know is that Byzantium and Francia intervened, to back rebel movements. A late source, a historically enriched diplomatic handbook which reached its final form in the hands of the bookish tenth-century emperor Constantine Porphyrogenitus (913–59), picked up reports that two non-Slav peoples, Serbs and Croats, were invited to come from north of the Carpathians (where they had perhaps cast off Avar authority), cross the Danube and settle in Illyricum (in effect to take charge of Slav tribes established there). The initiative is attributed to Heraclius, and may perhaps be associated with the appearance of Samo, a Frankish merchant familiar with the Avar khaganate, who led a general rising of Moravian Slavs in the 620s.[23]

The disturbances spread to the Carpathian basin, where the Avar authorities faced a rebel movement led by Kouber, a Bulgar. A key component of his following was the tribe he had been appointed to lead, a sub-Roman tribe formed out of the descendants of Roman prisoners-of-war taken during Avar sweeps down the Danube valley in the 580s. The rebels were defeated and scattered, some taking refuge on Frankish and Lombard territory, some (including the sub-Romans) led by Kouber to

[20] S. Cosentino, 'Byzantine Sardinia between West and East: Features of a Regional Culture', *Millennium*, 1 (2004), 329–67.

[21] Kennedy, *Conquests*, 308–19.

[22] J. Howard-Johnston, 'The Siege of Constantinople in 626', in C. Mango & G. Dagron, eds., Constantinople and its Hinterland (Aldershot, 1995), 131–42, at 137–42, repr. in Howard-Johnston, *East Rome*, no. VII.

[23] Key texts: Constantinus Porphyrogenitus, *De administrando imperio*, ed. Gy. Moravcsik, trans. R. J. H. Jenkins, CFHB 1 (Washington, DC, 1967), cc.31.3–20, 32.2–12, & 16–27; J. M. Wallace-Hadrill, ed. & trans., *The Fourth Book of the Chronicle of Fredegar with its Continuations* (London, 1960), iv.48 (pp. 39–40).

the rich plain of Pelagonia in Macedonia, from where they made contact with Thessalonica.[24]

The Avars were able to reconstitute their khaganate but on very a reduced scale, confined to the Carpathian basin. They ceased to have a significant impact on Balkan affairs.[25]

They were replaced as Byzantium's main northern adversary by Bulgars from the trans-Danubian steppes. It is again impossible to establish a precise chronology. All we know is that civil war, on a far grander scale than that in the Avar heartland, broke out in the Turk khaganate after the defeat and capture of the supreme khagan by Tang forces in 629. In the east, the Turks eventually prevailed and established a stable, but much reduced khaganate in Mongolia. In the west, two leading peoples among their many nomadic and sedentary subjects, Khazars and Bulgars, fought for supremacy. The victors were the Khazars, whose authority north of the Caucasus (their future heartland) was acknowledged around 670. Their defeated Bulgar rivals were split between those who remained under Khazar control and moved, or were directed, north to the Volga–Kama confluence, and those who escaped west towards the Danube.[26]

These Danubian Bulgars set about securing their position as a fully independent but small nomad power. They may have incorporated the remnants of Kouber's Balkan Bulgars, before, a generation or so later, in the late 670s, pushing across the Danube with a view to seizing the Dobruja, the rich grasslands in the north-east Balkans, protected by the river to the north, the Black Sea to the east, and the Haemus mountains to the south and west. There, after repelling a major Byzantine counterstrike in 681, they established a small, remarkably stable nomad state, shielded to the south by two Slav tribal federations which were resettled along the wooded Haemus mountains, and strengthened by the co-option of

[24] Key texts: P. Lemerle, *Les plus anciens recueils des miracles de saint Démétrius*, 2 vols. (Paris, 1979–81), I *Le texte*, ii.5.284–90; Fredegar, iv.72 (pp. 60–61); L. Bethmann & G. Waitz, eds, *Pauli historia Langobardorum*, MGH, Scriptores rerum Langobardicarum et Italicarum saec. VI–IX (Hanover, 1878), 12–87, trans. F. Bougard, *Paul Diacre Histoire des Lombards* (Turnhout, 1994), v.29.

[25] Pohl, *Avars*, 335–97.

[26] P. B. Golden, 'The Peoples of the South Russian Steppes', in D. Sinor, ed., *Cambridge History of Early Inner Asia* (Cambridge, 1990), 261–5; C. Zuckerman, 'Khazars and Byzantium—The First Encounter', in P. B. Golden, H. Ben-Shammai, & A. Róna-Tas, eds., *The World of the Khazars: New Perspectives*, Handbook of Oriental Studies 17 (Leiden, 2007), 399–432, at 417–31.

sub-Romans as junior partners who could staff the chancellery and provide useful craft skills.[27]

## 2.3 Byzantium's response

The first of the periods of political disturbance which punctuated Byzantine history in the dark age followed the death of Heraclius (641). The main divisive issue was policy towards the Arabs. There were appeasers, ready to accept the loss of Egypt and the Levant, given the costs and risks of war. They backed Heraclius' widow (and niece) Martina against a more belligerent faction who lined up behind Heraclius' eldest son by his first marriage, Heraclius the New Constantine, and, when he died after a few months, his 14-year-old son, Constans II. The battle was fought in the Senate, which reasserted itself after many, many centuries of quiescent existence as little more than a court in Roman guise, and came down on the side of the hawks.

The new regime, acting in the name of Constans, seems to have made recovery of Egypt its top priority. An expeditionary force was dispatched in 646 to occupy Alexandria and raise up rebellion in the Delta, only to be swiftly and effectively countered and driven out. There were no serious repercussions while the caliphal authorities were preoccupied with campaigns in the east, campaigns which succeeded in destroying the Sasanian empire by 652. Arab offensive actions against Byzantium were modest—a first attack on north Africa in 647, raids on Armenia and Cappadocia in 648, and raids on Cyprus in 649 and 650.[28]

But as the war with Iran drew towards a close, the caliph 'Uthman was able transfer troops to the west and to prepare for a first grand assault on Byzantium and its organizing centre. That was the reality, but it appeared that Armenia was the target. A leading prince had been suborned and had induced his fellow princes to submit to the Arabs. This had its intended effect of drawing Byzantine attention away from Constantinople. Under pressure from the army, the young emperor Constans, now of an age to take command, marched east with the field army to reassert Byzantine authority. A warning not to intervene, delivered by Arab messengers, stiffened his

[27] Key text: Theoph., 358.11–359.21. *Cf.* F. Curta, *Southeastern Europe in the Middle Ages 500–1250* (Cambridge, 2006), 79–81; P. Sophoulis, *Byzantium and Bulgaria, 775–831* (Leiden, 2012), 65–79, 107–12.

[28] Howard-Johnston, *Witnesses*, 474–8.

resolve. After receiving the formal submission of many princes and nobles at Theodosiopolis, he dismissed most of his troops and continued east to Dvin, the chief city of Armenia, meaning to spend the winter of 653–4 there and to sort out the affairs of Transcaucasia. Whole regions—Iberia, Siwnikʿ, and Albania—had gone over to the Arabs.[29]

It was from there that he had to hurry back early in 654, once he realized what the Arab plans were. Fleets from Syria and Egypt sailed on Constantinople, after winning a victory off the coast of Lycia. The main Arab army, commanded by Muʿawiya, emir of Syria, advanced northwest, likewise without encountering resistance. *The inhabitants of the interior plateau, its peripheral mountains and coastlands all submitted.* Constantinople was left utterly exposed, as an armada of great ships, loaded with siege equipment and carrying troops, accompanied by lighter, more manoeuvrable vessels, took control of the waters around the city. The sea walls would be assaulted first from the great ships. The siege proper would begin when the land forces were ferried across the Bosporus and could attack the land walls. But all these plans were disrupted when a violent storm rose and mauled the fleet, forcing it to withdraw. For the Christian defenders, this was a self-evident miracle. God had come to the aid of his people.[30]

There followed an interlude which gave the Byzantine authorities time to improve their defences (notably by strengthening city fortifications in Asia Minor, see Figure 2.2, and building up the navy) and to imbue soldiers, sailors, and civilians with more fighting spirit. It became possible to begin the long process of structural reform so as to militarize the state (through the extension of military commands over the whole of its reduced territory) and to gear its institutions more than ever before to the demands of war. It was also the beginning of a fundamental remoulding of the social order, as the upper layer of landowners was forced to seek safety in the larger and better-defended cities, above all in Constantinople, where it was transformed into an aristocracy of service.[31]

Arab failure at sea before Constantinople was followed by (1) defeat of the army guarding Muʿawiya's communications through Cappadocia (654), (2) the start of an insurgency in north-west Iran (654–5), (3) failure of a punitive expedition into Iberia (655), and (4) defeat north of the Caspian

[29] Ps.Sebeos, 164–6, 168, with Hist.Com., nn.69, 71–2.
[30] Ps.Sebeos, 170.5–171.27, with Hist.Note 75. *Cf.* Howard-Johnston, *Witnesses*, 475–80.
[31] Howard-Johnston, *Byzantium*, 18–35, 41–52, 91–3.

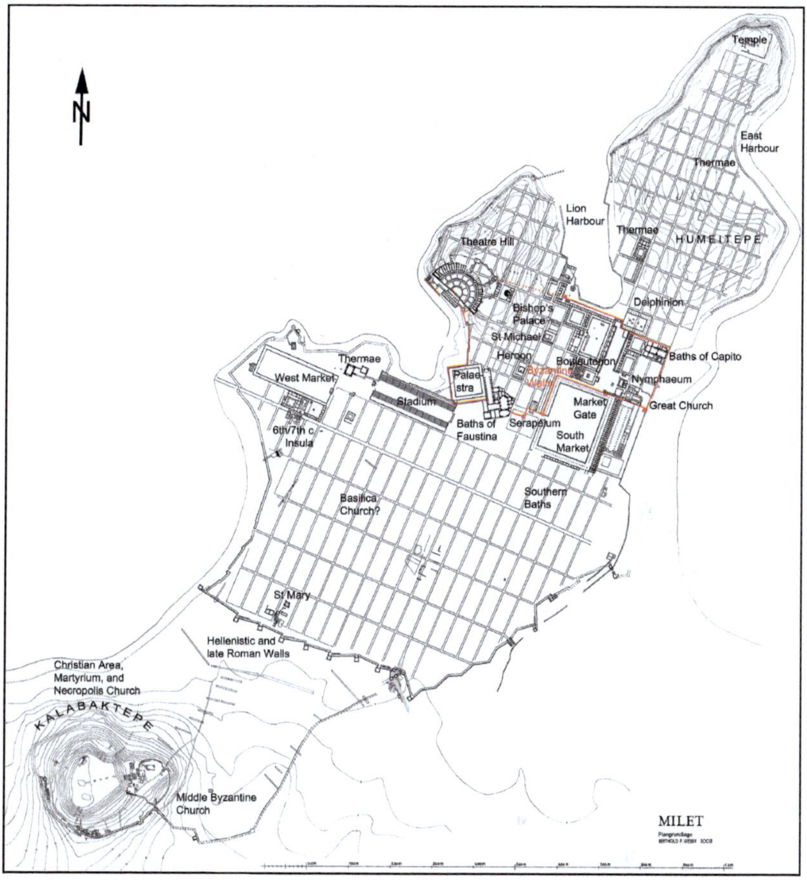


**Figure 2.2** Early medieval Miletus. The city was transformed into a hard-point fortress in the course of the seventh century, as Byzantium hunkered down for a long, defensive war. Its principal public monuments were turned into bastions in the reduced circuit walls.
*Source*: Philipp Niewöhner.

Gates (655). Doubts and divisions rose among the Arabs, leading to the assassination of the Caliph 'Uthman in 656 and the seizure of power by the Prophet's cousin and son-in-law 'Ali without authorization from a council of the leading Arabs. There followed five years of civil war (first *fitna*) which reached a climax after the assassination of 'Ali in 658. The four main regional armies formed up in opposing camps, Syria and Egypt against Iraq and Iran, the former prevailing when the army of Iran was won over by

Mu'awiya, and 'Ali's elder son, Hassan in Iraq, acknowledged defeat and withdrew into retirement in Medina.[32]

Towards the end of first *fitna*, Constans took action to strengthen Byzantium's position in Transcaucasia. He went on an imperial progress in 660–1. He received the formal submission of the leading princes of Armenia, Siwnik', and Albania. It looks as if he was planning to assemble a grand coalition of Christian rulers with which to pen the Arabs back behind the chain of mountains running from the Euphrates to the tangled mountains east of Lake Van and the northern Zagros. Next, in 662 he made an even more dramatic move, marching west through Thrace and Greece (he spent winter 662–3 in Athens) to Italy, his intention being to shore up the Byzantine position in Italy and then to establish a base of operations at Syracuse in eastern Sicily. From Syracuse he could mobilize naval and military forces for a renewed assault on Egypt from the rich north African provinces still in Byzantine hands.[33]

Meanwhile Mu'awiya renewed the war with Byzantium, dispatching raiding armies into Asia Minor. The last and largest in 668, commanded by his son Yazid, reached the Bosporus.[34] Clearly aware of Constans' activities in the distant west, he devised a brilliant counter-plan in consultation with a dissident faction in the Byzantine court and Juansher, the leading prince of Caucasian Albania. Juansher was well informed. He had met Constans twice during his stay in Transcaucasia. The plan had several interrelated parts: (1) the assassination of Constans himself (carried out on 15 July 669 in a bathhouse in Syracuse); (2) the rebellion of a high-ranking Armenian, Mzhezh belonging to the Gnuni noble family, backed by the army in Sicily (669); (3) Arab attacks by land and sea on north Africa (669)—apparently a strategic feint, since the campaign was closed down in 670 when Constans' successor Constantine IV sailed west with the main battle-fleet; and (4) a direct naval attack on Constantinople (670) followed by a blockade over the following winter while the main fleet was away.

Affairs in the west were sorted out by Constantine: north Africa was secured, except for the island of Jerba which remained under occupation; action was taken against the rebel forces in Sicily, Mzhezh himself being killed, but the rebellion, now led by his son, John, continued for a year or two. In the east, though, the pressure on Byzantium grew over the following

[32] Howard-Johnston, *Witnesses*, 480–3. [33] Howard-Johnston, *Witnesses*, 484–6.

[34] M. Jankowiak, 'The First Arab Siege of Constantinople', in Zuckerman, *Seventh Century*, 237–320, at 290–304.

few years in what looks like a strategy of piecemeal conquest. Winter and summer raids by land in 672–3 were followed by the seizure and garrisoning of Rhodes in 673, the occupation of Smyrna and strategic points on the coasts of Cilicia and Lycia over winter 673–4, and the landing of a large expeditionary force in Lycia in 674. It was not unreasonable to expect that Constantine IV's government would yield in the face of brute reality, exposed to attack by land from the south-east (Cilicia) and south (Lycia) and by sea.[35]

At which point the wheel of fortune turned. The Arab expeditionary force in Lycia was intercepted and defeated by three Byzantine armies. The fleet, after re-embarking the surviving troops, was annihilated in a naval engagement which saw the first use of Greek fire (ship-borne flame throwers). The Byzantines now embarked on a prolonged counteroffensive, which proved remarkably successful. Naval raids prepared the way for the landing of special forces (Mardaites) on the Syrian coast, with the objective of rousing the provincials against Arab rule. They succeeded in attracting large numbers of local activists and, over the next ten years, spread the insurgency from the Amanus range in the north to the Golan Heights in the south.

The Arab authorities feared for their position, especially after the outbreak of second *fitna*, two years after the death of Muʿawiya (680), between the Umayyad dynasty and its opponents in the Hijaz, Iraq, and Syria. Eventually the leader of the Umayyad faction, ʿAbd al-Malik b. Marwan, realized that he had to rid Syria, his power-base, of the Mardaites. This he achieved in 685 by negotiating a treaty with Constantine IV's son and successor, Justinian II (685–95, 705–11). The concessions he made were substantial: (1) payment of a little over five thousand pounds of gold as tribute every year together with 365 horses, (2) demilitarization of Cyprus, and (3) a free hand for Byzantium in Transcaucasia.

Byzantium's position may have deteriorated in the Balkans after the failure of Constantine's counterstrike in 681, but in the east, with the security provided by the agreement with ʿAbd al-Malik, it was able to project its authority well beyond its traditional sphere, to Media and Albania. For the princes and nobles of the whole former Sasanian north-west were under

[35] Howard-Johnston, *Witnesses*, 489–93, with corrections of V. Prigent, 'Des pères et des fils: Note de numismatique sicilienne pour servir à l'histoire du règne de Constantin IV', in O. Delouis, S. Métivier, & P. Pagès, eds., *Le saint, le moine et le paysan: Mélanges d'histoire byzantine offerts à Michel Kaplan* (Paris, 2016), 589–616, at 593–602.

threat from without and in need of protection by a great power. The Khazars who had consolidated their position in the steppes north of the Caucasus in the 670s showed an interest in extending their influence south of the mountains. An invasion in force, which caused widespread devastation in 685, made the danger very clear, while, at the same time, the fighting in the south, between Umayyads and Zubayrids, the two main parties in the civil war, spilled over into Armenia when the latter intervened between 687 and 689.[36]

Justinian II evidently saw himself as the restorer of Byzantium as an imperial power which could and should challenge Arab hegemony in the Middle East. As second *fitna* was drawing to a close in 691 with 'Abd al-Malik's campaign into Iraq, Justinian prepared the Byzantines for a renewal of war, reconvening the sixth ecumenical council of the church (680–1) in autumn 691, to bring about a moral cleansing of Christianity and to harness the intercessory power of clergy and monks to the Byzantine cause.[37] 'Abd al-Malik, for his part, provoked the Byzantines by presenting the tribute for 691 in a new type of gold coin, on which the cross was stripped of its arms and a brief declaration of faith was put in the margin of the reverse. Justinian issued a new type of his own, which asserted his role as Christ's vice-gerent on earth (see Figure 2.3a). He also resettled some Cypriots on the Cyzicus peninsula (in contravention of the 685 treaty, according to the Arabs), and mobilized his forces in the north.[38]

Justinian's aggressive stance proved disastrous. The field army suffered a crushing defeat in Lazica in 692 and the Arabs were able to reassert their authority over Transcaucasia step by step over the following five years. Justinian was deposed and mutilated in a *putsch* in 695, before the worst blow came in 697, with a final, successful Arab push into the inner core of Byzantine North Africa (Byzacena). Carthage was captured and a Byzantine naval counterattack was repelled in 698. Nonetheless Justinian and his successors, Leontius (695–8), leader of the *putsch*, and Apsimar, the admiral sent to Carthage who ousted Leontius on his return and assumed the name Tiberius (698–705), exchanged blows as equals with 'Abd al-Malik. Their

[36] Howard-Johnston, *Witnesses*, 494–9, with corrections of S. J. Forrest. *Destroying the 'Brazen Wall': Byzantium and the Umayyad Caliphate in the First Reign of Justinian II, 685–695* (MPhil, Oxford, 2018).

[37] Humphreys, *Law, Power and Imperial Ideology*, 46–57, 62–73, 77–80.

[38] L. Treadwell, 'Byzantium and Islam in the Late 7th Century: A "Numismatic War of Images"', in T. Goodwin, ed., *Arab–Byzantine Coinage and History* (London, 2012), 145–55.

**Figure 2.3** Two dark-age coins: (a) Solidus of Justinian II (685–95, 705–11), with image of Christ Pantokrator on the obverse. Both Byzantines and Arabs were reaffirming their religious identities in the 690s. (b) Miliaresion of Leo III (717–41). This new silver coin competed with the Arab dirham, being thin and large, with a religious inscription around the cross on one side and the name of the emperor on the other. This example was struck over a dirham.
*Source*: reproduced courtesy of the Barber Institute.

targets were northern Syria (699), Cilicia (703), and Armenia where Arab forces were engaged in putting down an uprising (703).[39]

The war abated somewhat after the death of ʿAbd al-Malik in 705 (his son Walid's priorities lay in Central Asia [Sogdia was the target 705–15] and in the far west [Arab forces crossed into Spain in 711]). In Byzantium, Justinian

[39] Howard-Johnston, *Witnesses*, 499–501, 507–8.

II, who staged a countercoup with Bulgar backing in 705, was preoccupied with cracking down on political opponents. But from 709, local Arab forces renewed the pressure on Asia Minor, seizing and garrisoning strongholds as they advanced step by step from 711 to 714. They were not effectively opposed either by Philippicus, the usurper who finally disposed of Justinian II in 711, or by Anastasius II, who ousted Philippicus in 713.

Byzantium's position was precarious in 716. Constantinople was designated the ultimate objective of major offensive operations, under the command of Maslama, brother of al-Walid (caliph 705–15) and his successor Sulayman (715–17). The land forces were aided by a massive naval force, comprising fleets from Syria, Egypt, and North Africa. Troops were ferried across the Bosporus to besiege the city by land, while it was blockaded by sea. Divine intervention this time took the form of severe winter weather, with human aid coming from Bulgars who harried the besiegers in Thrace and Byzantine naval squadrons which launched fire attacks on the Arab fleets at anchor. In August 718, after more than a year, Maslama had no choice but to withdraw, a move which damaged his reputation as a general and did much to undermine the prestige of Sulayman's successor, the short-lived Caliph 'Umar II.[40]

For three generations after the initial Arab conquests, successive regimes in Byzantium were thus preoccupied with the war in the east. The emperors fought as *emperors*, as heirs of those who had united the Mediterranean world under Roman rule in the distant past, against the upstart Arab Muslim power which had usurped their position in the Middle East. When the fighting subsided, whether because of commitments elsewhere as between 643 and 653 or because of civil war, measures could be introduced to strengthen the fixed defences of Byzantium, to reorganize and revitalize the army, to build up a navy, and to streamline the apparatus of government at the centre and in the provinces. They were the years when reforms of many sorts were forced on Byzantium, when the economy was put on a war footing, and when the inherited social order underwent near-revolutionary change. That is why the turbid surface of events has been described in considerable detail.[41]

The anxieties engendered manifested themselves in disputation over an abstruse theological issue, the precise mechanisms by which union of the divine and the human was achieved in the person of Christ—two or one

[40] Howard-Johnston, *Witnesses*, 508–10.
[41] Howard-Johnston, *Byzantium*, 18–35, 41–59, 62–73, 84–96.

activating force, two or one will? The singularity thesis was devised during the later stages of the Persian–Roman war as a compromise to bring together the Chalcedonian and Miaphysite confessions. Heraclius was well on the way to achieving a grand reunion of churches in the Middle East when the Arab attacks began.[42] At which the hardliners in both camps took heart. Chalcedonians, inspired by two great churchmen—Sophronius, Patriarch of Jerusalem, and Maximus, monk and brilliant theologian—insisted on duality. A council of bishops and monks, including many refugees from the Middle East, met at the Lateran in 649, roundly to condemn singularity (monotheletism). Both Pope Martin, who presided, and Maximus, the intellectual driving force behind the council, were arrested and taken to Constantinople. Both were given show-trials and condemned to exile and, in addition in Maximus' case, to amputation of hands.[43] While each side blamed the other for bringing disaster on the Roman empire, there is no evidence that the theological dispute undermined the war effort against the common, non-Christian foe before or after Chalcedonian orthodoxy was accepted at the sixth ecumenical council of 680–1.[44]

The Arabs, as we have seen, were not only able to fend off Byzantine counterattacks and to end the dangerous Mardaite-led insurgency (at the cost of temporary concessions), but greatly extended their sphere of control in the west and in central Asia. They consolidated their hegemonic position in the Mediterranean and were plainly the rising power in central Asia, where they would go on to defeat a Chinese force on the Talas river in 751, a defeat fraught with consequences for the Tang empire.[45] The only setback, but one of considerable ideological moment, was failure before Constantinople in 717–18. Its effect was mitigated by a propaganda campaign which succeeded in transforming 'Umar II, the caliph responsible, into the very type of pious, reformist ruler. Maslama, the general in charge, was eventually rehabilitated by success against the Khazars.[46]

[42] Howard-Johnston, *Last Great War*, 373–7; P. Allen, *Sophronius of Jerusalem and Seventh Century Heresy* (Oxford, 2009).

[43] P. Allen & B. Neil, *Maximus Confessor and his Companions: Documents from Exile* (Oxford, 2002); *Acts of the Lateran Synod*.

[44] M. Jankowiak, *Essai d'histoire politique du monothélisme à partir de la correspondance entre les empereurs byzantins, les patriarches de Constantinople et les papes* (PhD, Paris–Warsaw, 2009).

[45] D. Twitchett, 'Hsüan-tsung (reign 712–56)', in D. Twitchett, ed., *Cambridge History of China*, III *Sui and T'ang China* (Cambridge, 1979), 333–463, at 443–61.

[46] A. Borrut, *Entre mémoire et pouvoir: L'espace syrien sous les derniers Omeyyades et les premiers Abbassides* (Leiden, 2011), 229–320.

As for policy, Byzantium ceased to be a prime target. The main Arab history of the period, the *Annals* of al-Tabari, devotes most of its coverage of foreign affairs over the next quarter of a century to campaigning in the east, where the successes achieved by Walid in Sogdia were consolidated and extended. The Khazar khaganate, the hegemonic power of the west Eurasian steppes, which had twice raided Transcaucasia (in 662 and 685), also had to be contained in the north, both by strengthening the Caucasus defences and by counterstrikes to the north.[47] Brief notices, normally placed at the end of year-entries, record annual raids on Asia Minor, some by sea, the majority by land. Most were directed at the frontier zone, where key strongholds were targeted. From the 720s a pattern developed of summer raiding, which often involved two distinct forces and was occasionally accompanied by a sea raid.[48]

## 2.4 Byzantium beleaguered

Leo III, a general whose prevarication managed to delay the attack on Constantinople by a year from 716 to 717 (his offer to defect was followed by long negotiations) and who took power on the eve of the siege, was the first emperor to acknowledge the brute fact that the empire had been lost (see Figure 2.3b). There is indirect but convincing evidence that it was he who changed the whole approach of the armed forces to war, abandoning the age-old commitment of Romans to orthodox methods in favour of all the wiles and devices of guerrilla warfare.[49]

At the same time, the new realism showed itself in the sphere of ideas. While it was never obliterated, the imperial ideology of Romans was overlaid by one which conformed much better to reality—that of the Byzantines as a chosen people, a new Israel, under God's special protection as long as they did not arouse his anger by sinning. Justinian II's project of summoning a church council to institute a general moral upgrading of church and society in 691–2, on the eve of a renewal of war with the Arabs, was

[47] *Annales quos scripsit Abu Djafar Mohammed ibn Djarir at-Tabari*, II.3, ed. I. Guidi, D. H. Müller, & M. J. de Goeje (Leiden, 1885–9), 1418 (AH 102)–1718 (AH 123), trans. K. Y. Blankinship, *The History of al-Tabari*, 24 *The Empire in Transition* (Albany, NY).

[48] R.-J. Lilie, *Die byzantinische Reaktion auf die Ausbreitung der Araber*, Miscellanea Byzantina Monacensia 22 (Munich, 1976), 143–55, 158–62.

[49] See below.

undoubtedly motivated in part by such a world-view. It is made explicit in the preface to the practical handbook of law issued to the courts by Leo in 741—a good justice system was essential if God's favour was to be retained and Byzantium was to fare well in war. Apposite quotations and citations came in much larger numbers from the Old than from the New Testament.[50]

Coverage of the fighting between Byzantine and Arabs in the 720s, 730s, and early 740s (after which the Abbasid revolution introduced a long interlude) is patchy, the two extant Byzantine sources homing in on Byzantine successes, the Arab ones restricted to pithy notices.[51] Glimpses, though, can be obtained of the new Byzantine strategy. In the first place, there were no more offensive strikes into the Arab borderlands. Second, it looks as if increased reliance was placed on fixed defences (see Figure 2.4a and b). Indeed this is made explicit in the summary of an official news release about a general order issued in 779, to fall back on strongholds and limit operations to shadowing the enemy.[52] Third, there were occasions when units detached from the main raiding force were intercepted and defeated—this happened to a foray in 723–4, to a unit from Antioch in 727–8, and to one commanded by al-Battal in 731–2.[53]

These were key elements of a guerrilla strategy of defence, which, in its final, fully developed form, was described in a military handbook commissioned by the Emperor Nikephoros II Phokas (963–9), for the benefit of future generations.[54] As in other times and places where resort has been had to guerrilla methods, it relied on a strong and pervasive sense of common interest in the population at large and on the wholehearted cooperation of soldiers and civilians.[55] The ultimate object was to conserve as much as possible of Byzantium's resources—human, animal, and material—with a minimum of risk. The population and its livestock in districts threatened by enemy attack were to be evacuated to nearby strongholds, either man-made (i.e. cities with good defences) or natural (i.e. highland redoubts to be found in the mountains circling the Anatolian plateau and a few isolated ranges within), while stores of grain were concealed in underground silos. Civilians were expected to respond immediately once alerted to the danger of attack. Soldiers were to be ready to fight to the last to block the

[50] Humphreys, *Law*, 93–105. [51] See n. 48 above. [52] Theoph., 452.6–12.
[53] Tab., II.3, 1462.6–7 (trans. Powers), 1495.9–10, 1559.16–1560.7 (trans. Blankinship).
[54] H. Dagron & H. Mihăescu, ed. & trans., *Le traité sur la guérilla (De velitatione) de l'empereur Nicéphore Phocas (963–969)* (Paris, 1986).
[55] Howard-Johnston, *Byzantium*, 38–59.

**Figure 2.4** Kotyaion and Loulon. (a) Kotyaion (Kütahya), one of many shrunken cities in western Asia Minor. The fortifications of the town, with close-spaced towers, were probably built in the seventh century. (b) Loulon, a small castle overlooking the northern outlet of the Cilician Gates. In the ninth century it was the first in a line of nine beacons stretching from the frontier to the capital, which could send warnings of Arab attacks.

*Source*: author.

routes to refuges within natural strongholds if they were threatened with direct attack.[56]

Once the countryside was cleared, the prime task of local defensive forces was to harry the raiders, primarily by targeting forays sent out to forage and widen the swathe of destruction. Surprise attacks on such forays, if successful (as they were likely to be), would both dispirit the raiders and limit their foraging, forcing them to withdraw sooner rather than later for lack of provisions. The decisive engagement was postponed to the final stage of withdrawal as the raiders were crossing the frontier mountains, encumbered with booty and prisoners and eager to be home. Advantages of surprise and terrain would normally ensure that ambush by infantry stationed at a narrow passage in the mountain pass would destroy the raiding army as a fighting force, with many casualties and the loss of its plunder.[57]

There were two periods of regular Arab raiding expeditions into Asia Minor in the eighth century. The first culminated in a large-scale invasion by three army corps in May 740. Their targets were Tyana (commanding the northern outlet from the main, Cilician Gates pass across the Taurus), Akroinion (modern Afyon Karahisar, on the western edge of the plateau), and the Aegean coastlands. The Byzantines defeated a 20,000-strong corps as it besieged Akroinion, killing al-Battal, one of its two commanders.[58] The second began after the new Abbasid regime had consolidated its hold on the Caliphate, shifting the political centre to Iraq and building a new capital at Baghdad (750–75).[59] Byzantium's guerrilla strategy of defence proved its effectiveness against a series of attacks (776–82) which were on a larger scale than before: in 779 one of two raiding armies was forced to abandon its siege of Dorylaion after 15 days for lack of provisions; in 780 a foray was intercepted and defeated in the Aegean coastlands; and finally the operations of a massive invasion army (numbering well over 90,000 men) under the nominal command of the young Harun al-Rashid nearly ended in disaster in 782. Harun and the advance corps were trapped in Bithynia by a force of Byzantine guards shipped across the Sea of Marmara which seized the passes leading south and east. It was only by breaking the rules of diplomacy and taking hostage the three high-ranking Byzantine emissaries sent

[56] *Traité sur la guérilla*, cc.1–3, 17.1–4, 22.1 (pp. 36–41, 96–9, 120–1).

[57] *Traité sur la guérilla*, cc.4, 6–10, 13–18, 22–5 (pp. 44–73, 78–107, 120–35).

[58] Theoph., 411.14–26; Tab., II.3, 1716.14–15, trans. C. Hillenbrand, *History of al-Tabari*, 26 *The Waning of the Umayyad Caliphate* (Albany, NY, 1989) simply notes al-Battal's death.

[59] Kennedy, *Caliphates*, 110–18.

to negotiate with Harun that the Arabs managed to secure safe passage home and tribute from the Byzantines.[60]

As for the intervening period, the long intermission in Arab raiding occasioned by the Abbasid revolution, Leo III's son, Constantine V (741–75), who had to fight his cousin Artabasdos for the throne in 742–3, took advantage of his increased freedom of manoeuvre to move onto the offensive in the Middle East and the Balkans (at the expense of neglect of Italy). He made several improvements to Byzantium's fighting capability. Two long-standing regiments of largely ornamental court guards (Scholai and Excubitores) were transformed into crack cavalry units (*tagmata*), to form the nucleus of a more offensive-minded field army. Logistics were improved by the creation of a specialized support regiment (Optimatoi).[61] The mobilization of provincial armies (*themata*) was systematized, a number of assembly points being designated where individual themes would join the field army and where provisions would be stockpiled.[62] Finally, he developed an amphibious capability, which was of particular value for operations in the north, against Bulgaria.

First, as the Umayyad regime was increasingly distracted in the 740s, Constantine made two successful thrusts into the Arab borderlands, capturing Germanikeia and Doulichia in 744/5 (Arab Maraş and Duluk), Theodosiopolis and Melitene in 750/1. Their populations were transferred to Thrace.[63] Then he turned his attention to the Balkans and set about impressing Byzantine authority on the Bulgars. He signalled his intentions by resettling the prisoners taken from the Arab marches in purpose-built fortified townships in northern Thrace, in effect a new militarized zone close to the Bulgar frontier. When the Bulgars demanded compensation, he refused, regarding it as tantamount to a demand for tribute (*pakta*). The predictable attack which followed (in 756) was repulsed.[64] A few years later he opened offensive operations by land and sea on a very large scale. The most notable campaigns picked out by the Byzantine sources took place (1) *c.*760 when ship-borne troops raided the interior of Bulgaria from the

[60] J. Howard-Johnston, 'Theophanes on the Recent Past: The Crisis of 782 and its Antecedents', in M. Jankowiak & F. Montinaro, eds., *Studies in Theophanes, TM* 19 (Paris, 2015), 473–90.

[61] L. Brubaker & J. Haldon, *Byzantium in the Iconoclast Era, c.680–850: A History* (Cambridge, 2011), 156–61.

[62] J. F. Haldon, ed. & trans., *Constantini Porphyrogeniti tres tractatus de expeditionibus militaribus imperatoris*, CFHB 28 (Vienna, 1990), 80–93.

[63] Theoph., 422.11–18, 427.14–16, 429.19–22.

[64] Nik., c.73.1–11; Theoph., 429.19–22, 25–30. *Cf.* Sophoulis,*Byzantium and Bulgaria*, 92.

Danube and the land forces had mixed success; (2) in 763 when a decisive Byzantine victory at Anchialus triggered a serious crisis at the apex of the Bulgar government; (3) in 766 when the fleet suffered serious storm damage and the attack was called off; and (4) in 774, the only time when Constantine sailed with the fleet.[65]

Byzantium, it seems, was never reconciled to the establishment of an independent state south of the Danube. But the Haemus range provided the Bulgars with formidable natural defences, which proved even more effective than the Taurus and Anti-Taurus were for the Byzantines. It was only when the higher coordinating authority (Bulgar) was weakened, at a time of intense political crisis in 765, that a small Byzantine raiding force was able to surprise the Slav defenders of the passes and raid the steppe heartland of the Bulgar state.[66] But the military balance had been altered when Constantine introduced specialized horse-transports into the Byzantine navy. Cavalry forces capable of independent operations could be shipped north, bypassing the Haemus defences, and landed at any number of points on the Black Sea coast and up the Danube.[67] Including, as it probably did, an infantry component carried in requisitioned merchant ships, the raiding army would be able to range far and wide over the inner land of Bulgaria, the Dobruja, with relative impunity, while much of the Bulgar army was detained in the south to stiffen the Haemus defences against the main Byzantine field army. Combined operations on this grand scale were carried out successfully on three occasions—*c.*760, 763, and 774. Without a fleet, the Bulgars were all too vulnerable to such attacks, and had little choice but to sue for peace, as they did in 774.[68]

## 2.5 Iconoclasm

Leo III and Constantine V were capable military commanders and presided over the final stage in the militarizing of Byzantium. They were both successful, Leo III in overseeing the defence of Asia Minor, Constantine V in

[65] First grand attack (*c.*760): Nik., c.73.11–18; Theoph., 431.6–11 (focused on a Byzantine reverse). Anchialos victory 763: Nik., cc.76–7; Theoph., 432.29–433.22. Naval expedition aborted 766: Nik., c.82; Theoph., 437.19–25. 774 campaign: Theoph., 446.27–447.9. *Cf.* Sophoulis, *Byzantium and Bulgaria*, 92–5.

[66] Nik., c.79; Theoph., 436.8–24. *Cf.* Sophoulis, *Byzantium and Bulgaria*, 99–103.

[67] Specific references to horse-transports: Nik., c.76.7–11, Theoph., 432.29–433.1 (763); Theoph., 447.29–448.1 (774).

[68] Nik., c.82.5–11 (766); Theoph., 446.17–447.2 (774).

moving on to the offensive in the east and in the Balkans. Both also took measures to assuage God's anger, by cutting out from the body politic the great sin which had caused it, after a literal explosion of divine fury in Byzantium's inner sea, the Aegean, taking the form of a volcanic eruption in the sea between Thera and Therasia in 726.[69] The sin, a great sin, was readily identifiable. It had been repeatedly denounced by the irascible God of the Old Testament, who loomed large in the thoughts of Byzantines, from the top to the bottom of society. The new Israel must turn away from *idolatry*, from the veneration of images of the divine and of the holy deceased which had spread through eastern Christendom in late antiquity.[70]

The first reported move was made by Constantine Bishop of Nakoleia in Asia Minor, whose doubts are likely to have been shared by many in the church.[71] Christological considerations (first fully articulated at the iconoclast church council of Hieria in 754) surely played some part in their thinking, in particular the difficulty of reconciling pictorial representation of Christ's body with the doctrine of intertwined but distinct humanity (visible) and divinity (invisible).[72] It is hard to imagine that, after nearly three centuries of debate about the nature(s) of Christ, which had continued up to the eve of the siege of Constantinople, such issues were not still playing upon the minds of the churchmen who first voiced iconoclast opinions.

The leading role, though, in the campaign to root out icon-veneration was taken by the secular authorities. It was, after all, the body politic which was threatened with annihilation. The first public declaration of iconoclasm was made in 730 by the Emperor Leo III to a gathering of senior courtiers and churchmen at a *silention*, presumably after a great deal of private discussion, persuasion, and arm-twisting. At this the elderly Patriarch Germanos resigned (he would not accept the new doctrine without the backing of a church council) and was replaced by a more compliant figure.[73]

In a centralized autocracy such as Byzantium's, the authorities were in a position to implement the new policy without delay, although it was prudent to proceed cautiously. We should probably envisage its imposition in

[69] Nik., cc.59.1–60.6; Theoph., 404.18–405.4.

[70] P. R. L. Brown, 'A Dark-Age Crisis: Aspects of the Iconoclast Controversy', *EHR* 346 (1973), 1–34, repr. in P. Brown, *Society and the Holy in Late Antiquity* (London, 1982), 251–301, esp. 284–8.

[71] *Cf.* Brubaker & Haldon, *Iconoclast Era*, 94–8.

[72] Brubaker & Haldon, *Iconoclast Era*, 189–97.

[73] Brubaker & Haldon, *Iconoclast Era*, 119–27.

stages—initially the removal of prominent images in public places; subsequently that of all images which were likely to attract veneration; and finally the pressurizing of laity, clergy, and monks into destroying private images. It is the opposition roused in this last stage which is registered in the sources. One of the leaders, a well-known holy man, was executed in 765, for his moral denunciation of the emperor as well as his involvement in a high-level conspiracy. The most intransigent opponents of iconoclasm, to be found as one might expect in monastic circles, were also targeted, those in Constantinople (in 765) and Thrakesion (in 771) being subjected to public derision in ceremonies laid on to cow them into conformity (see Figure 2.5a).[74]

Iconoclasm was undoubtedly divisive, but not to the extent of creating deep social or political divisions—whether between regions, or between elite and society at large, or between town and country. *There is no evidence whatsoever that it undermined the war effort.* Strong feelings were aroused, but as far as can be seen they were usually internalized—for a simple reason: all but extremists were both iconoclasts and iconophiles, both points of view jostling for primacy within them. They could not but acknowledge that God's wrath was aroused by icon-veneration, the idolatry of the latter-day chosen people, hence that the authorities were right to crack down on the practice, but, on the other hand, they were habituated to using icons in their private devotions, to directing their prayers to a saint pictured in the household's or their personal icon. The confrontation was between reason and emotion.

There was nothing surprising then in the gradual acceptance of iconoclasm in the course of the reigns of Leo III and Constantine V, especially after it was given the *imprimatur* of a church council in 754, nor in the subsequent swing back to iconophilism carefully orchestrated from above by the Empress Eirene and her young son Constantine VI, once it was backed by a carefully scripted iconophile council held in Nikaia in 787. Conformism was simply allowing first one, then the other internal side to prevail, as remained the case in the ninth century when there was a reversion to iconoclasm in 813–15, at a time of military difficulty (readily attributable to divine displeasure after the restoration of icons), and a final and definitive restoration of icons in 843.[75]

[74] Brubaker & Haldon, *Iconoclast Era*, 234–43.
[75] Brubaker & Haldon, *Iconoclast Era*, 260–80, 366–85, 447–52.

**Figure 2.5** Miniatures from a manuscript of the chronicle of John Skylitzes, illustrated in southern Italy in the late twelfth century: (a) persecution of iconophile monks; (b) battle against Arabs.
*Source*: Madrid National Library.

## 2.6 Threats from without around 800

In many ways, Byzantium's external position worsened in the late eighth and early ninth centuries. The Bulgars could not be expected to remain submissive, without occasional demonstrations of Byzantine military power. In the east, Harun al-Rashid set about strengthening the Caliphate's hold on the borderlands fronting the Taurus and Anti-Taurus. He fortified Cilicia and its hinterland to the east with a network of military bases (the most important being Tarsos, Adana, Mopsouestia, Anazarbos, Adata, and Haruniya), and militarized the rear areas in northern Syria and south-western Armenia, to deepen the zone of defence and to provide reinforcement and supplies for the forward bases.[76]

This programme shifted the balance of power on the frontier in the Arabs' favour. It both improved the security of the Caliphate and provided platforms for regular raiding expeditions into Asia Minor and for occasional larger caliphal attacks (see Figure 2.5b). The flow of volunteers for the *jihad* against Byzantium was likely to grow, given the availability of free board and lodging in the three main forward bases—Tarsos, Melitene, and Theodosiopolis. The spirit of *jihad* also showed itself in the Mediterranean. The danger of massed naval attack on the metropolitan area around Constantinople had receded with the shift of the Caliphal capital to Iraq, but the spread of Islam among coastal communities in north Africa and Spain led, in time, to the formation of raiding fleets and a steady extension in the range of their operations. By the late 820s the Africans were targeting Sicily, while a force of Andalucians, driven first out of Spain, then out of Alexandria, took over Crete in 828. Despite the advantage of inner lines, Byzantium's naval resources were increasingly stretched.[77]

Further afield there were other ominous developments. Under a new dynasty the Franks were extending their control beyond their heartlands in the Rhineland and France, as well as tightening their administrative grip across their territories. Pippin (741–68) and Charlemagne (768–814), the second and third Carolingian rulers, directed campaigns of conquest south-west into Aquitaine (759–69), south into Italy (755–6, 773–4), south-east into the Carpathian basin (791, 796), and east into Saxony (772–804). The king's authority was enhanced with each conquest, being sustained in the interim by the annual processes of mobilization at a designated assembly place, marching, and fighting.[78]

By the late 790s there was no question but that Charlemagne was presiding over an empire, a dynamic political entity dedicated to spreading the

[76] A. A. Vasiliev, *Byzance et les Arabes*, I *La dynastie d'Amorium (820–867)*, rev. H. Grégoire & M. Canard (Brussels, 1935), 94–7 (cited henceforth as *BA* I); J. F. Haldon & H. Kennedy, 'The Arab Byzantine Frontier in the Eighth and Ninth Centuries: Military Organization and Society in the Borderlands', *Zbornik Radova Viz. Inst.*, 19 (1980), 79–116.

[77] *BA* I, 54–61, 64–9, 71–84, 86–8.

[78] M. Costambeys, M. Innes, & S. MacLean, *The Carolingian World* (Cambridge, 2011), 51–79.

Christian faith over pagan peoples (Saxons in the first instance), with a top-down governmental structure, much modified but ultimately inherited from the Roman empire. Pressure from the papacy (and the lure of the Roman past) turned Charlemagne's attention away from Scandinavia and Britain (with baleful consequences in the long term), and led ultimately to his coronation as emperor by Pope Leo III on Christmas Day 800. Byzantium was thus directly challenged in the ideological sphere, as well as finding a potential adversary close to its south Italian provinces and lowering over the Balkans from central Europe.[79]

There was a second stirring of the social and political order in the far north. Scandinavia had been enriched by two to three centuries of commercial development in the North Sea and the Baltic and was increasingly aware of distant worlds where prestige and wealth might be harvested. Northmen, known as Rus, ventured south-east and established a first trading station by Lake Ladoga in the middle of the eighth century. Over the following generations, they established other trading stations in the upper catchment area of the Volga, gained control of the courses of the Volga and Don to the north of the Khazar khaganate, and established a forward base at Kiev on the middle Dniepr.[80] The Khazars responded to this growing threat from the north with a programme of fortress construction and the sort of ethnic re-engineering to which great nomad powers might resort to improve security. In this case Hungarians, who had hitherto been guarding the eastern approaches to the khaganate beyond the Volga, were relocated to the steppes of Ukraine, on either side of the Dniepr. There they were reorganized into seven artificial tribes, were put under the command of an eighth Khazar tribe, and were designated Turks (which they were not). They were replaced between the Volga and Ural rivers by the Pechenegs, another re-engineered grouping of nomads, organized in eight divisions.[81] Rus, Turks (aka Hungarians), and Pechenegs would all impinge on Byzantium before too long.

A countervailing development, however, greatly eased the pressure in the second and third decades of the ninth century—the crisis which gripped the Caliphate after the death of Harun al-Rashid in 809. An increasingly acrimonious dispute between the new Caliph, al-Amin, in Baghdad and his

[79] Costambeys, Innes, & MacLean, *Carolingian World*, 160–94.

[80] S. Franklin & J. Shepard, *The Emergence of Rus 750–1200* (London, 1996), 3–27, 42–50, 65–70, 91–111.

[81] J. Howard-Johnston, 'Byzantine Sources for Khazar History', in Golden, Ben-Shammai, & Róna-Tas, *World of the Khazars*, 163–93, at 174–5.

brother al-Maʿmun in Khurasan developed, after two years, into full-scale civil war, in effect a fourth *fitna*, which ended with the capture of Baghdad after a year-long siege by al-Maʿmun's forces and the death of al-Amin in 813.

The delicate system of checks and balances and dynamic ideological links between centre and peripheries broke down during the six years which followed. Al-Maʿmun's authority was attenuated by distance (he only arrived in Baghdad from Merv, his interim capital in eastern Khurasan, in 819). There was virtual anarchy in Iraq and Egypt as local interest groups, tribal, military, and religious, struggled for power. The once-privileged Arab tribes of Syria sought to regain the status lost at the time of the Abbasid revolution. North Africa seceded under its Aghlabid rulers, while a rising of indigenous highlanders, the Khurramiyya, under a local, non-Muslim leader in Persian Azerbaijan (816–37), a region of intensive Arab colonization, proved hard to suppress.[82] Many years of negotiation and military action were required before order was restored and the fractious regions of the bloated Muslim empire were reunited.[83]

At first, troubles came upon Byzantium from all sides. There were Arab raids which had to be fielded in the 780s and 790s, two (in 797 and 798) on a large scale and transecting Anatolia. Their prime purpose was probably to mask ongoing building work in the frontier zone.[84] Regular raiding resumed from 803, preparing the way for a massive attack through the Cilician Gates, led by the Caliph Harun in person in 806. His aim seems to have been to establish a permanent Arab base on the Anatolian plateau at Tyana, inside the mountain rim, and to weaken Byzantine defences in the frontier province of Cappadocia, by taking out strongholds and causing extensive devastation.[85] It was a moment of acute danger, but the campaign was not followed up, presumably because of a crisis in Central Asia which drew Harun east to Khurasan in 808. Regular raiding continued but petered out after 811.[86]

In the Balkans an expedition to Corinth and Patras in 783 reinforced Byzantine prestige in Greece. Action was also taken to uphold Byzantium's

[82] P. Crone, *The Nativist Prophets of Early Islamic Iran: Rural Revolt and Local Zoroastrianism* (Cambridge, 2012), 59–76.

[83] Kennedy, *Caliphates*, 128–35.

[84] W. Treadgold, *The Byzantine Revival 780–842* (Stanford, 1988), 78–9, 91, 93–5, 89, 102–3, 104–5, 107–8, 111–13.

[85] M. Canard, 'La prise de Heraclée', *Byz.* 32 (1962), 345–79; Treadgold, *Revival*, 131–5, 138–40, 144–6.

[86] Treadgold, *Revival*, 147–8, 155, 157, 168–9.

position vis-à-vis the Bulgars—an imperial progress through Thrace in 784 (inaugurating a three-year fortification programme), threatening military moves in 791, 792 (resulting in defeat at Markellai), and 796.[87]

Further afield, an approach was made to Charlemagne in 781, broaching the idea of an imperial marriage between his young daughter, Rotrud, and Constantine VI, son of the Empress Irene (780–91, 797–802). Nothing came of it—Charlemagne backtracked in 787—and relations deteriorated later when Venice, very much within the traditional Byzantine sphere of influence, toyed with submission to the Franks and did so on two occasions, voluntarily in 806, coerced in 808–9. On each occasion Byzantium responded swiftly by sending powerful fleets to reassert its authority over Dalmatia and Venice. It required a significant ideological concession in the subsequent negotiations, Byzantine recognition of Charlemagne's imperial title, to secure the independence of Venice under Byzantine oversight in 812.[88]

By then Byzantium was facing growing problems in the Balkans from a revanchist regime in Bulgaria. The predictable response of the Emperor Nikephoros I (802–11), without distractions in the east and confident of Byzantium's military superiority, was to attack in force in 811. He managed to cross the Haemus (possibly because the Bulgars made less effort than usual to hold the passes). He raided the Bulgar heartland and sacked the capital Pliska, only to find that he was trapped on the wrong side of the mountains. A surprise attack by Bulgars and Slavs destroyed his army as a fighting force. Nikephoros was among the large number killed.

It was now the Bulgars' turn to lord it over the eastern Balkans, prompting a mass exodus from the Byzantine towns. The important strongholds of Mesembria and Adrianople fell, and Constantinople itself was threatened. It was only the death of Khan Krum, on the eve of a new campaign in 814, which brought the phase of fierce Bulgar aggression to a close, and made it possible, two years later, for the two sides to negotiate a durable peace.[89]

## 2.7 Byzantium in the ninth century

From 816, a strange, unfamiliar quiet descended upon Byzantium, thanks to the agreements reached with Carolingians and Bulgars, and the implosion

[87] Sophoulis, *Byzantium and Bulgaria*, 159–72.

[88] Treadgold, *Byzantine Revival*, 70–1, 89, 130, 143–4, 147, 155, 159, 166–7, 178–9, 182–3; E. Kislinger, 'Byzantinische Flotten in der venezianischen Lagune 806–810/811: Zu chronologisch-inhaltlicher Manipulation in der Annales regni Francorum', *Millenium*, 17 (2020), 303–22.

[89] Sophoulis, *Byzantium and Bulgaria*, 184–216, 221–45, 249–70, 275–86.

of the Caliphate. Domestic politics assumed an even larger place than normal in both extant histories of the reigns of Staurakios (Nikephoros' son, deposed October 811), Michael I (abdicated 813), Leo V the Armenian (assassinated in a palatine chapel on Christmas Day 820), and Michael II (820–9, founder of the Amorian dynasty).[90] The court was the main arena for political action and posturing. It was there that leading figures and their followings pursued their rival interests, and that the emperor played them off against each other and made important political and religious declarations. While there was a blunting of harsh punishment, above all execution, in the dark age (a delayed effect of faith on justice), the losers might still be mutilated (as were four of the five sons of Constantine V after a conspiracy in 792) or blinded (as was Nikephoros, the eldest of those sons, in 792 on the orders of Constantine VI, and then Constantine himself on the orders of his mother Irene in 797).[91]

The assassination of Leo V was unusual, as was the trouble which it generated, a full-blown but short-lived Byzantine civil war—the first since Artabasdos had challenged the succession of his cousin Constantine V in 742–3. It seems to have originated in the rivalry between three senior army officers, who, as young men, had served together on the staff of a certain Bardanes, when he was supreme commander of the armies of Asia Minor in 802–3. The murder of one of them, Leo the Armenian, by another, Michael of Amorion, so angered the third, Thomas, at the time commander of the Foideratoi (an elite military formation in Anatolikon), that he rebelled and had himself acclaimed emperor by the army of Anatolikon.

With the support of most of the armed forces in Asia Minor (only Opsikion and Armeniakon backed Michael) and a large fleet, Thomas was able to cross over to Europe, take control of Thrace and Macedonia and lay siege to Constantinople in 821 and again in 822. Michael survived, thanks to the loyalty of soldiers and civilians in Constantinople; the intervention of the Omurtag, the Bulgar khan, on his side; two victories over Thomas' fleet in 822; and the defeat of Thomas' land forces in Thrace in 823. Thomas himself was captured and executed when Arkadiopolis, one of four towns in which his troops had taken refuge, fell in October 823.[92]

[90] Treadgold, *Byzantine Revival*, 174–7, 186–9, 223–5.

[91] Treadgold, *Byzantine Revival*, 101, 108–9.

[92] Treadgold, *Byzantine Revival*, 225–30, 232–44; *cf.* also the detailed commentary of J. Signes Codoñer, *The Emperor Theophilos and the East, 829–842: Court and Frontier in Byzantium during the Last Phase of Iconoclasm* (Farnham, 2014), 40–59, 183–208, who makes new suggestions on dating, prosopography, and the role of the Arabs.

Domestic politics now entered a stable phase. There was doubtless much covert opposition to the official policy of iconoclasm, but almost all courtiers and office-holders seem to have been ready to conform—as they did after the final restoration of icons by the Empress Theodora in 843 (but they were careful not to replace the innocuous image of cross on steps with those of saints for another three or four generations).[93] The leading figures might be at odds, but there was no resort to bloodshed until the 860s.

There is clear evidence of economic growth from the 820s and of the gradual emergence of something akin to an aristocratic caste (manifest in the spread of surnames) in the higher echelons of the governing apparatus and the senior officer corps.[94] The more egalitarian society of the dark age—when the peasant village was acknowledged to be the vital, basic element in the social order, and the social elite was largely confined to the servants of the state—was giving way to something closer to the historical norm, as officers and officials invested in landed estates. Town life was gradually reviving in the provinces, as insecurity diminished and economic activity increased.[95]

The chief problem remained that of Islam, threatening Byzantium's heartland in Asia Minor by land and its outlying islands by sea, Sicily (where the Aghlabids steadily gained ground after the initial attack in 827), and the Aegean (from Crete, conquered in 828 by the Andalucians, after their expulsion from Alexandria). The arrival of several thousand refugee Khurramiyya in two stages (833 and 837) provided a timely reinforcement for local theme armies.[96]

Two major assaults were mounted, a systematic effort to break through the Taurus defences in the last years of al-Ma'mun (830–3), and an exchange of offensive blows in 837–8 between Theophilos and al-Ma'mun's successor al-M'utasim. Thereafter the war reverted to one of raiding expeditions from forward *jihad* bases.[97] The resulting proliferation in attacks complicated the task of defence. This was stretched to breaking point in the *annus nefastus*

[93] I. Koltsida-Makre, 'The Representation of the Cross on Byzantine Lead Seals', *Studies in Byzantine Sigillography*, 4 (1995), 43–51.

[94] A. E. Laiou & C. Morrisson, *The Byzantine Economy* (Cambridge, 2007), 45–9, 74–6, 87–9; J.-C. Cheynet, 'L'aristocratie byzantine (VIIIe-XIIIe siècle)', *Journal des Savants* (July–December 2000), 281–322, at 284–98.

[95] Howard-Johnston, *Byzantium*, 93–5.

[96] Treadgold, *Revival*, 248–57, 282–3, 285–6; J.-C. Cheynet, 'Théophile, Théophobe et les Perses', in *He Byzantine Mikra Asia* (Athens, 1998), 39–50; Crone, *Nativist Prophets*, 41–2; Signes Codoñer, *Theophilos*, 145–9, 321–4.

[97] *BA* I, 98–127, 137–75.

of 860, when a truce for the exchange of prisoners was followed by three Muslim raids, two by land from Melitene and Tarsos, one by sea which captured the citadel of Attaleia (capital of the Kibyrraiot theme), and also a separate attack from Tephrike, a stronghold in the wild country north of Melitene where dualist Paulicians had established themselves (with the encouragement of the Arab authorities). An attack in force by a Rus fleet on Constantinople compounded the difficulties, forcing the Emperor Michael III to abort his march east.[98]

Nonetheless, it was plain that the Arab threat was abating. Byzantium had survived all the assaults launched against it. There might be other years when raiding forces ranged deep into Asia Minor, other Rus attacks, and large-scale warfare against the Bulgars in the Balkans, but the existence of a Christian, Hellenic, Roman state would no longer be imperilled. A bold naval attack on Damietta (853) heralded a new era.[99]

It is unfashionable to call the period extending from the middle of the seventh century to the middle of the ninth a *dark age*. But it *was* dark, both in terms of a dearth of contemporary sources of information and because of the grim life of successive generations of infantry and cavalry soldiers, sailors and marines, peasants, townsmen, and officials, great and small, in a long era of unremitting warfare. The offensives against Asia Minor directed by Harun in 803–6 and al-Maʿmun in 830–3 were the final spasms of serious aggression from the Caliphate as a whole. Both were inaugurating strategies of piecemeal conquest, beginning with the construction of a large military base at Tyana. But those strategies had to be aborted, because of the problems generated by an overlarge political entity (trouble in central Asia from 806, and al-Mʿutasim's need to deal with domestic troubles after al-Maʿmun's death on 7 August 833).[100] The raids which were to continue into the 950s were much less threatening, and could be contained by the strategy of guerrilla defence developed in the dark age.

A new era of revival opened in the 860s.

*Byzantium in a Changing World*. James Howard-Johnston, Oxford University Press.
 DOI: 10.1093/9780191999093.003.0003

[98] *BA* I, 240–7. [99] *BA* I, 214–18. [100] *BA* I, 124–7.

# 3
# Age of Revival

Byzantium lived in the shadow of Islam, its existence threatened first by Arabs, later by Turks. But there were interludes when the shadow lightened.[1] One such interlude began in the second half of the ninth century. It was a side-effect of the slow dissolution of the Caliphate into a number of independent regional states. It lasted much longer than the earlier intermissions occasioned by four bouts of civil war over the succession. There was, however, no near-complete halt in the fighting as there had been during each *fitna*, but simply a decline in the military resources available for striking at Byzantium. Individual raiding cities on the frontiers and regional powers in their hinterlands could not pose a threat as great as the Umayyad and Abbasid Caliphates in their heydays. There was a discernible shift in the balance of power, which allowed Byzantium to take more and more of the initiative.

With more freedom of manoeuvre than before, successive emperors could alter foreign policy priorities. It was, as it still is, a natural inclination of any new regime to review the policies of its predecessor and to seek to make a mark by deliberate changes. Once the pressures on Byzantium from without eased, such changes could be made where they would be most noticeable, namely in relations with foreign powers, non-Islamic as well as Islamic. Byzantine history in the century or so following the terrible year 860 can be divided up into distinct phases, corresponding to successive reigns and distinguished from one another by the degree of the regime's concentration on a single sector of the surrounding world, by its choice of sector or sectors, and by the mix of soft and hard power deployed. From the 970s there were more constraints than before, because of the rise of expansionist regional powers within the Islamic *oikoumene*, to the south and east of Byzantium, but Byzantium remained a major force in international relations.

[1] The heyday of Byzantium is covered in rather more detail than the preceding or following periods, in this and the following chapter, with more citation of primary sources on issues of particular importance.

Military success, territorial expansion, and renewed confidence in its divinely appointed imperial mission were fundamental features of Byzantium in its two-century heyday, from the 860s to the 1060s. Whole regions of the surrounding world were conquered, roughly doubling Byzantium's size. In response to the dual threat of Muslim sea raiders and Carolingian land forces, Byzantine expeditions were dispatched to southern Italy and managed, by the beginning of the tenth century, to gain control of all Apulia and Calabria. In the east by 950, the no-man's land fronting Asia Minor—namely the looming mass of the Taurus mountains (separating Cappadocia from Cilicia) and the ridges of the Anti-Taurus which splay out from the Taurus north-east towards the Euphrates—was annexed, together with western Armenia beyond the Euphrates. Naval hegemony in the east Mediterranean was secured with the recovery of Crete and Cyprus in the 960s. In the Levant, Byzantine armies pushed south and east, to create, by the 970s, a large Christian bridgehead in Muslim Syria, with Antioch as its capital. In the north, the authority of the emperors was extended once again, after a gap of nearly four centuries, to the Danube, with the occupation of the core territory of the Bulgar state. Some fifty years later, after a long war against Bulgar insurgents in Macedonia and Dalmatia, the whole of the Balkans was incorporated into the renascent empire. Finally, the Syrian bridgehead was extended and large swathes of territory in central Armenia were annexed in the eleventh century.

Major reforms were undertaken to adapt the highly centralized administrative system of the dark-age guerrilla state to the scale of the tasks now confronting the authorities. The ubiquitous presence of the army in the interior provinces came to an end, with the military confined to the outer, frontier zones. There was therefore a greater divide than before between civilian and military authorities, and, within the military, a clear distinction between frontier forces under the command of theme *strategoi* and regional field armies under the command of dukes or katepans. More special agents were required to keep an eye on the localities, and, in particular, on the tax authorities.[2]

A series of other developments can be discerned: (1) sustained economic growth, increasing prosperity, and an associated revival of towns;[3] (2) a growing self-confidence in the aristocracy which ceased to be an aristocracy of service, almost entirely dependent on imperial authority, and invested on

[2] Howard-Johnston, *Byzantium*, 219–40, 263–7.

[3] Howard-Johnston, *op. cit.*, 247–51.

an increasingly large scale in land; (3) an increasingly fraught confrontation between crown and aristocracy, which culminated in two dangerous Anatolian rebellions, but which was ultimately and not unexpectedly resolved in favour of the crown;[4] and (4) an efflorescence of literature, art, architecture, and learning, exemplified best in church building and decoration (which made manifest the thought-world of Byzantines).[5]

It was no accident that this was a period of exceptional dynastic stability, in which a single dynasty, the so-called Macedonian dynasty founded by Basil I who seized power in a bloody coup in 867, established its legitimacy in the minds of the citizens and continued in power until the death of its last member, Theodora daughter of Constantine VIII, in 1056.

## 3.1 Fragmentation of the Caliphate

The Caliphate had been extended far beyond the normal bounds of a single political entity in the initial faith-driven phase of conquests. The creation of a single market on an unprecedented scale and the continuing dynamic forces linking centre and periphery (the outward thrust of *jihad* and the inward pull of *hajj*) held it together for the first Abbasid century—with the two exceptions of Spain which seceded at the outset under a remnant of the Umayyad dynasty and Ifriqiya which achieved *de jure* independence under the Aghlabids from 800.[6] But geographical realities—the thousands of kilometres separating Baghdad from the frontier regions in central Asia and the far west, the formidable ranges of mountains impeding communications, the heterogeneity of habitats and peoples contained within the *dar al-Islam*—did eventually weaken the ties of religion and erode the authority of the centre. The chief component parts of what was, in human terms, an Arab empire—Ifriqiya, Egypt, Syria, Iraq, Iran, and Transoxiana—had distinct political identities and distinct cultures, shaped by centuries of pre-Islamic existence. These did, with time, reassert themselves, aided by the factional and political rivalries inherent in so huge a political structure.

The crisis following the death of Harun al-Rashid in 809 provided an earnest of what was to happen within a generation or two. The two main pillars of the Abbasid regime, Khurasan which provided its elite forces, and

[4] Howard-Johnston, *op. cit.*, 162–80. [5] Howard-Johnston, *op. cit.*, 244–7.

[6] H. Kennedy, *Muslim Spain and Portugal: A Political History of al-Andalus* (London, 2014); M. Brett, *The Fatimid Empire* (Edinburgh, 2017), 26–7.

Iraq, the governing centre, were set against each other. There was a consequential loosening of their hold on the rest of the empire, in particular on Egypt and Iran, both sidelined under the early Abbasids. A further loosening followed in the 860s, when elite Turkish troops, recruited in larger and larger numbers from the steppes and funnelled from Khurasan to the centre, divided into factions and fought each other in the huge palace-city of Samarra. Although their status was that of indentured military retainers, they became for six years the arbiters of the Caliphate. A rapid succession of caliphs and a temporary retraction of military power fatally weakened the authority of the centre over the periphery, a weakness compounded when the centre itself faced a major rebellion, that of the Zanj, African slave labourers in southern Iraq.[7]

The first region to break away was Sistan, in the far south-east, where caliphal authority was attenuated by distance and order was disturbed by dissident Kharijis. The commander of one of several local militias which had sprung up in response, Ya'qub b. Layth, known as the Coppersmith (al-Saffar), rebelled and rapidly built up his power. After seizing the provincial capital, Zaranj, and gaining control of the whole province, he extended his power north-east over Khurasan, east to Ghazna, Kabul, and Bamyan, and west over Kirman into Fars and the lowlands across the Zagros (between 861 and 875). It was a provincial rebellion on the grandest possible scale which ended with defeat before Baghdad in 876, shortly followed by Ya'qub's death. Not quite as serious was the contemporary *de facto* secession of Egypt, which, like Iran, had a deep-embedded culture quite distinct from that of the Arabs. The governor from 868 to 884, Ibn Tulun, a senior Turkish general, took advantage of the Caliphate's troubles to withhold much of the massive fiscal contribution made by Egypt to the centre from 872, and to confront and repel the forces sent against him by the centre.[8]

Within Iran Ya'qub's rebellion had the effect of loosening ties with the centre and opening the way for the rise of the Samanids in Transoxiana (controlled from 873) and Khurasan (conquered after victory over Ya'qub's brother Amr in 900). Their position was greatly strengthened by a massive flow of silver from mines in the Panjshir valley, and their privileged position at the crossroads of north–south and east–west trade routes on the

[7] Kennedy, *Age of the Caliphates*, 147–50, 154–5; M. S. Gordon, *The Breaking of a Thousand Swords: A History of the Turkish Military of Samarra (A.H. 200–275/815–889 C.E.)* (Albany, NY, 2001), 75–149; A. Popović, *The Revolt of the African Slaves in Iraq in the 3rd/9th Century* (Princeton, NJ, 1999).

[8] Kennedy, *Age of the Caliphates*, 152–4, 205–7.

eastern edge of the Islamic single market. They strengthened their position by calling up memories of the pre-Islamic Iranian past and sponsoring a revival of Persian as a practical and literary language. They were also committed Sunnis who sought to propagate the faith among the nomadic Turks in the neighbouring steppes. Sufism developed into a significant movement.[9]

The primary drive behind other movements which weakened the Caliphate were religious—as was only to be expected in what was a political structure founded on faith. Their aim was not merely secession but destruction of the Abbasid regime. From the 870s charismatic preachers were at work spreading the Ismaeli version of Shi'ism among the Beduin of north Arabia, in Iran and in north Africa. The Kutama Berbers of the highlands of Kabylia were galvanized into military action to spread the faith. Stronghold after stronghold fell in the years 902–7, and in 909 they were able to take the provincial capital Qayrawan and to invite the Fatimid Mahdi to take charge of Ifriqiya. Egypt, which had been brought back under caliphal control in 905, was now under threat from a militant Shi'i neighbour.[10] The same was true of Iraq, under threat from the Qarmatis of north Arabia, a threat which reached its climax in the 920s.[11]

There was a steady diminution in the flow of revenue to the centre, leading to financial crisis in the 920s, compounded by political infighting. By the middle 930s, the last effective fighting force under caliphal control dissolved after the execution of its commander Munis.[12] The central lands of the Caliphate were carved up, between the Hamdanid emirate of Mosul and military adventurers, three Buyid brothers from the highlands of Daylam who, from a first success in Fars in 934, took control of Iran. The Buyids won the battle for Baghdad in 942–4, forcing the Hamdanids to turn their attention to northern Syria where a second junior emirate was established at Aleppo. It was in the same period that a second general of Turkish origin, Ibn Tughj, known, from his honorific title, as the *Ikshid*, took over Egypt and much of Syria.[13]

The same process of fragmentation can be seen to have taken place in Transcaucasia. After the crushing of a general Armenian rebellion in the 850s with the aid of Ashot, the leading Bagratid prince, this complex region with a multitude of local principalities and emirates remained peaceful, its

[9] L. Treadwell, 'The Samanids: The First Islamic Dynasty of Central Asia', in E. Herzig & S. Stewart, eds, *Early Islamic Iran*, The Idea of Iran 5 (London, 2012), 3–15.

[10] Brett, *Fatimid Empire*, 20–40.

[11] Kennedy, *Age of Caliphates*, 166–7, 245–50.

[12] Kennedy, *Age of Caliphates*, 161–8.

[13] Kennedy, *Age of Caliphates*, 182–6, 229–34, 236–7, 267–9.

cities flourishing as the single market boomed. There were two higher authorities—Ashot who, as the chief Arab client in Transcaucasia, was given the governorship of Armenia, and al-Afshin, the Sajid emir of Azerbaijan, the main area of Arab settlement in Transcaucasia. Al-Afshin and his son Yusuf, who succeeded him in 901, were formidable military commanders of Turkish extraction like Ibn Tulun and Ibn Tugjh. Their task was to watch over the Bagratids and the whole panoply of Muslim and non-Muslim local rulers. They controlled a large army (upon which the central authorities might call) which they used to extract the resources needed to maintain it. There were several tiers of subordinated rulers, headed by the emirs of Manzikert and Melitene, the Artsruni princes of Vaspurakan and branches of the Bagratids in Iberia and west Armenia, and ranging down to those controlling restricted territories (like the Paulicians at Tephrike) or single cities (such as Qaliqala [Theodosiopolis], Šimšat [Arsamosata], and Ardanuj)

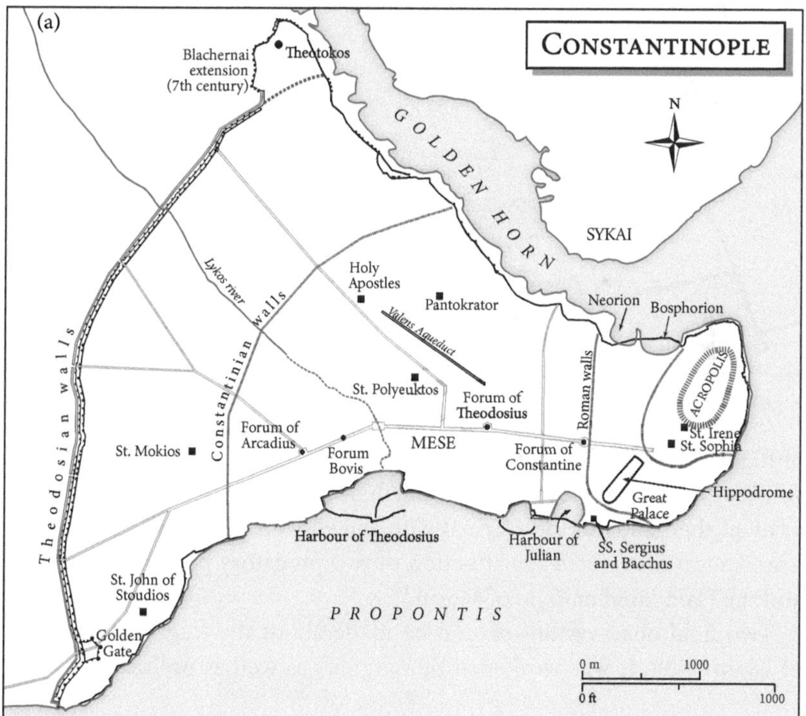


**Figure 3.1** The power centre in Byzantium's heyday: (a) Plan of Constantinople; (b) Plan of the Great Palace.

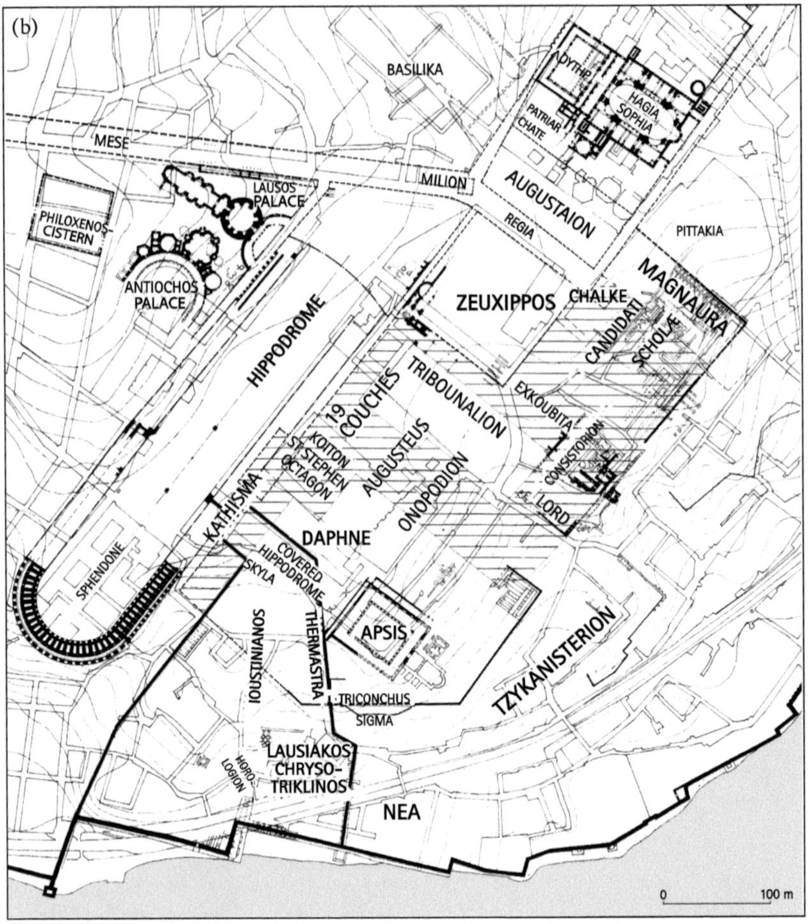


**Figure 3.1** Continued.

or highland redoubts (as in Siwnik', the east Caucasus, and the Elburz). The whole system fell to pieces after the death of Yusuf and the destruction of his army at the hands of the Qarmatis on the edge of Iraq in 927. Thereafter Transcaucasia attracted the attention of two predatory powers, Byzantium and the Hamdanid emirate of Mosul.[14]

Two final observations should be made about the fragmenting world of Islam. First, it was weakened by religious as well as political division.

[14] B. Martin-Hisard, 'Constantinople et les archontes du monde caucasien dans le *Livre des cérémonies*, II, 48', *TM* 13 (2000), 359–530, at 361–4; A. & J.-P. Mahé, *Histoire de l'Arménie des origines à nos jours* (Paris, 2012), 122–49.

This was manifest not only in the rise of a sectarian Ismaili state in north Africa, and the raids of Qarmatis on Iraq, Syria, and the *hajj* routes in Arabia, but also in the proliferation of Sunni legal schools and the presence in many Islamic lands, particularly on their desert and mountain margins, of pools of heterodox belief—for example, Zaydis in Yemen and the mountains fronting the Caspian, Twelver and Sevener Shi'ites in Iran, and Khariji statelets in the Sahara oases.[15] The sects were not rebelling against higher earthly authority, since it had ceased to exist once the religious authority of the caliphs was challenged and destroyed by the accumulated weight of religious scholarship deployed by the *'ulama* in the middle decades of the ninth century. It was their critical compendia of *hadith* about the Prophet's words and deeds which, together with the text of the Qur'an, formed the *sunna*, the material from which a handful of great scholars developed their divergent legal systems.[16] The Shi'a minority *did* acknowledge higher authority, since it believed that divine inspiration continued to be channelled to humanity through descendants of the Prophet, but uncertainty about the precise identity of the divinely empowered descendant encouraged the proliferation of sects, distinguished from one another by their choice of Mahdi, earthly vice-gerent of God.

Second, these many divisions did not destroy a shared world-view. There remained a sharp distinction between the world of Islam and an outside, infidel world, which reinforced a sense of community. So too did a general commitment to *hajj* and *jihad*. The *dar al-Islam* was a single ideological space, within which new religious movements, inspired by charismatic preachers, could spread with surprising speed. The work of the Ismaili agent who roused up and united the Kabylia Berbers in support of his Mahdi was continued by Fatimid missionaries dispatched to widely separated regions of the Islamic world. The ability of words to galvanize whole peoples was shown again in striking fashion in the late eleventh century, in the far west where the Sanhaja nomads of the Sahara were united and transformed into holy warriors, who went on to conquer Morocco and Spain, and in the Middle East where a heterodox Ismaili preacher from Rayy, Hasan-i Sabbah, succeeded in spreading Ismailism into the mountain fastnesses of Iran and Syria and in inspiring his followers with extraordinary determination.[17]

[15] Brett, *Fatimid Empire*, 26–9, 68–72.

[16] Kennedy, *Age of the Caliphates*, 140–2; J. P. Turner, *Inquisition in Early Islam: The Competition for Political and Religious Authority in the Abbasid Empire* (London, 2013).

[17] Brett, *Fatimid Empire*, 73–4, 116–20, 144–6, 191–2, 227–30, 248–51.

For infidel aggressors against Islam, even in its weakened state, there remained a perennial danger that charismatic preachers, whatever their religious stripe, might rouse up the faithful from near and far away and might conjure up whole armies of *jihad*-fighters to march to defend a threatened frontier region.

## 3.2 Byzantine world-view

Byzantium's location at the junction between Asia and Europe and between northern and southern seas had exposed it to attack by land and sea from all points of the compass in the dark age. Increasingly from the later ninth century it turned into an advantage, with Byzantium enjoying diplomatic inner lines. The southern arc of territories fronting the Mediterranean from Syria to Spain was by the 940s broken up into four independent and mutually hostile states, with two more (Buyid and Samanid) lurking in the background. They formed half of the concert of powers with which Byzantium dealt. They could be played off against each other, or kept quiescent while Byzantium chose one as its prime target. The wiles of a long-established polity in command of all the devices of diplomacy would enable Byzantium steadily to expand its territory and sphere of influence at the expense of Islam.

The same was true in the northern arc of territories stretching from one great power in the east, the Khazar khaganate north of the Caucasus, to another, the leading Germanic state with imperial pretensions, in the west. The Khazar khaganate's hold over its chief clients—Oghuz, Pechenegs, Hungarians, Alans, and Rus—may have been weakening, but it remained the prime mover in the nomadic world of western Eurasia in the 940s. Three of those clients (Pechenegs, Hungarians, and Rus) impinged on Byzantium, but again, in the case of Pechenegs and Rus, could be played off against each other.[18] The Hungarians, after their forced migration into the Carpathian basin in the 890s, entered a phase of heightened militarism, raiding far and wide, but Byzantium was relatively unharmed since it was

[18] Golden, Ben-Shammai, & Róna-Tas, *World of the Khazars*, 7–57 (P. B. Golden, 'Khazar Studies: Achievements and Perspectives'), 163–93 (Howard-Johnston, 'Byzantine Sources'), 373–86 (D. J. Wasserstein, 'The Khazars and the World of Islam'), & 399–432 (Zuckerman, 'The Khazars and Byzantium').

shielded by the Balkan Bulgar state.[19] The Bulgars, Byzantium's main northern adversary in the past, entered a quiescent phase, with their conversion to Christianity in 864 under intense political pressure from Byzantium. They were enlarging their territorial base, by colonizing Macedonia and pushing west towards the Adriatic in the decades following the end of Krum's war of revenge in 817.[20] In the far north-west, the Carolingian world was fragmenting, as central, top-down authority finally yielded to locally rooted lordship, while the role of a higher, divinely favoured rule was taken up by the most powerful of east German peoples, the Saxons.[21]

Six Muslim and six non-Muslim states thus constituted the concert of powers among which Byzantium manoeuvred in the 940s and 950s. That was the world contemplated in two works commissioned by the bookish emperor Constantine VII Porphyrogenitus (913–959). The first is a diplomatic handbook, misleadingly known as *De administrando imperio*, about those of Byzantium's neighbours who were regarded as being susceptible to Byzantine allures, who might be useful as allies or clients. It provided information, including a fair amount taken from documentary sources, about the selected peoples, their territories, their institutions, and their histories. Rather than treating the outer world as alien, inferior, populated by barbarians, Constantine and his contemporaries saw a patchwork of *nations*, defined very much as we would define them.[22] Byzantium had a special role as a superordinate state, raised above all others by its special relationship with God. The court, as he explained in another of his commissions, *De cerimoniis aulae Byzantinae*, was a microcosm of the heavenly court, its carefully choreographed ceremonies mimicking the movements of heavenly bodies.[23]

The *De cerimoniis* is the second text to cast light on the Byzantine worldview. Two chapters preserve sets of protocols for addressing foreign rulers

[19] K. Bakay, 'Hungary', in T. Reuter, ed., *New CMH* III *c.900–c.1024* (Cambridge, 1999), 536–52, at 536–44.

[20] J. Shepard, 'Slavs and Bulgars', in R. McKitterick, ed., *New CMH* II *c.700–c.900* (Cambridge, 1995), 228–48, at 237–48.

[21] J. L. Nelson, 'The Frankish Kingdoms, 814–898: The West' and J. Fried, 'The Frankish Kingdoms, 817–911: The East and Middle Kingdoms', *New CMH* II, 110–41, at 136–41, and 142–68, at 155–68; J. L. Nelson, 'Rulers and Government' and E. Müller-Mertens, 'The Ottonians as Kings and Emperors', *New CMH* III, 95–129, at 95–112, and 233–66, at 233–54.

[22] *DAI*, II Commentary, ed. R. J. H. Jenkins (London, 1962); Russian commentary in Konstantin Bagrjanorodny, *Ob Uprovlenii Imperij*, ed. G. G. Litavrin & A. P. Novosel'tsev (Moscow, 1989).

[23] Constantin VII Porphyrogénète, *Le livre des cérémonies*, ed. & trans. G. Dagron, B. Flusin, D. Feissel, & M. Stavrou, 5 vols. (Paris, 2020), I, proem, 3.5–10, 4.33–7.

in writing and their ambassadors in audiences. They date from the time of writing, that is, the joint rule of Constantine and his young son Romanos II (945–59).[24] Distinguished Byzantinists have characterized the picture which can be pieced together as a *hierarchy* of earthly rulers or a *family* of princes, centred on the Byzantine emperor, the implication being that there was an international *order*, foreign rulers being viewed as occupying carefully graded positions like the servants of the crown within Byzantium.[25] But this is surely to misunderstand two fundamental principles of diplomacy—(1) the need for flexibility so as to take account of the ups and downs in the fortunes and the relative strengths of diplomatic partners, and (2) the importance of avoiding disputes over precedence, which might antagonize one or both of the parties involved. The overarching aim was to flatter foreign rulers, to entice them into useful relationships. So they were to be given no more than a *vague* sense of their position in Byzantine eyes. The various elements in the protocols—weight of golden bull attached to a diplomatic letter, spiritual relationship with the emperor, honorific epithets, and title—were deliberately not harmonized with each other, and would indicate no more than the general standing of a people in Byzantine eyes.

It is possible to gain a sense from the protocols of the political configuration of Europe, the north, Transcaucasia, and the Middle East as seen from Byzantium. Spiritual leaders were singled out at the beginning of the list—the pope, the only potentate to be addressed as spiritual father; the patriarchs of Alexandria, Antioch, and Jerusalem; and the caliph, who, unlike the patriarchs, all of whom receive 3-solidus bulls, but like the pope receives a 4-solidus bull.[26] Secular rulers, except for the last three in the list, are grouped in geographical clusters—first Transcaucasia, then the West, the Mediterranean, and the north (Balkans and steppes).[27] The leading position of some is clearly acknowledged—thus the rival Bagratid and Artsruni princes in Armenia are each designated 'most famed', receive a 3-solidus golden bull, and are given a high ranking, either as 'Premier of Greater Armenia' and spiritual son (the Bagratid) or as 'Prince of Princes' (the traditional designation of the presiding prince, now held by the Artsruni).[28] The lower status of ten other princes in Armenia is marked by the plain 'commands' which they receive, simply addressed to them as ruler of their

[24] *Livre des cérémonies*, III *Livre II*, ed. & trans. G. Dagron, cc.47–8 (pp. 346–75).

[25] G. Ostrogorsky, 'The Byzantine Emperor and the Hierarchical World Order', *Slavonic and East European Review*, 35 (1956–7), 1–14.

[26] *De cer.*, ii, c.48.2–19.

[27] *De cer.*, ii, c.48.20–63, 73–128.

[28] *De cer.*, ii, c.48.20–9.

locality.[29] The same distinction between higher- and lower-level rulers is made in other parts of Transcaucasia (the 'most renowned' Curopalate of Iberia, the Exousiokrator of Alania who is spiritual son, and the 'famed' Exousiastes of Abasgia being singled out, all of whom receive 2-solidus golden bulls) and the steppe world where the status of the hegemonic power is marked by the weight of the bull (3 solidi) and the honorific 'most noble and most famed' used in correspondence with the khagan of Khazaria.[30]

These protocols provide some insight, as I have said, into Byzantium's imperial outlook. The emperor was ready to lay on the flattery when dealing with powerful Muslim powers—the Fatimid Caliph in Africa is addressed as 'most renowned and most noble Exousiastes of the Muslims', the Ikshidid emir of Egypt as 'our beloved friend, the most noble emir of Egypt' who, as such, received a 4- rather than 2-solidus bull.[31] The radius of Byzantium's active diplomacy is impressively large, reaching France (but not Britain or Ireland) in the west, the Rus in the north, Khurasan in the east, and 'India' and 'Blessed Arabia' in the south.[32] A lingering affinity with the Latin west is signalled by the designation of each of the kings of Saxony, Bavaria, France, and Germany as 'sought-after spiritual brother'.[33]

What is plain above all is the central role assumed by Byzantium in the affairs of western Eurasia. The *idea* of empire, their empire, was projected outward. Its status rested partly on memories of a past when the Roman empire had in reality dominated the civilized world within its reach, partly on the modest territorial gains it was making, above all upon the most successful exercise of gesture politics in human history. Byzantium was an empire because it willed itself to be an empire and took every opportunity to enhance its status—as in the triumphal ceremonies staged to celebrate the arrival in Constantinople of the most charged of Christian relics, those connected with the Passion of Christ, captured in the course of carefully controlled military forays in the Middle East.[34]

## 3.3 Sources of information

The later ninth, tenth, and eleventh centuries witnessed a great increase in literary and artistic output, which was paralleled in the sphere of

[29] *De cer.*, ii, c.48.30–7.
[30] *De cer.*, ii, c.48.38–40, 46–53, 109–13.
[31] *De cer.*, ii, c.48.83–92.
[32] *De cer.*, ii, cc.47.91–105, 48.74, 114–16, 129–34, 139–42.
[33] *De cer.*, ii., c.48.73–9.
[34] M. McCormick, *Eternal Victory: Triumphal Rulership in Late Antiquity, Byzantium and the Early Medieval West* (Cambridge, 1986), 152–78.

government by the production of several humdrum, practical texts. The latter included imperial commissions like *De administrando imperio*, a handbook of foreign policy intended for Constantine Porphyrogenitus' young son, Romanos II, and *De cerimoniis* which presented detailed protocols for the conduct of court ceremonies through the year, including seating-plans for imperial banquets in the Christmas and Easter seasons. No less important were the massive compendium of Roman law, the *Basilica*, and a compilation of classical and late-antique military advice, the *Tactica*, both completed in the reign of Leo VI (886–912).[35]

It was an age of taking stock, gathering useful information together, and putting together practical handbooks. Official lists of government posts and episcopal sees were produced, to establish an agreed order of precedence. There were tactical manuals and instructions for siege warfare (intended for what was presumably a literate officer corps), a guide to fiscal technicalities (intended presumably for trainee clerks), an introduction to the workings of the guild system of Constantinople (for incoming eparchs of the city?), and a collection of texts of imperial enactments which formed a growing appendix to the alphabetically ordered legal handbook in common use (for practising lawyers).[36] Collections were also made of classical treatises which retained practical value—such as the *Geoponica* (written, it seems, for gentry farmers) and the *Hippiatrica* (useful for the army and for better-off civilians who owned horses).[37] These can be supplemented by other private collections of material offered for the edification of contemporary and future readers—for example the oddball book of advice for different walks of life written by Kekaumenos in the late eleventh century, and numerous collections of letters, official and private, of named individuals, which acted as both durable memorials to their authors and examples of good writing.[38]

[35] *Basilicorum libri LX*, ed. H. J. Scheltema, D. Holwerda, & N. Van der Wal, 17 vols. (Groningen, 1945–88) - digital ed. B. H. Stolte & T. E. van Bochow (Leiden, 2017); *Leonis VI Tactica*, ed. & trans. G.T. Dennis, *The Taktika of Leo VI*, CFHB 49 (Washington, D.C., 2010).

[36] Philotheus, *Cletorologium*, ed. & trans. N. Oikonomidès, *Les listes de préséance byzantines des IXe et Xe siècles* (Paris, 1972); *Das Eparchenbuch Leons des Weisen*, ed. & trans. J. Koder, CFHB 33 (Vienna, 1991); N. Svoronos, ed., *Les novelles des empereurs macédoniens concernant la terre et les stratiotes* (Athens, 1994), trans. E. McGeer, *The Land Legislation of the Macedonian Emperors* (Toronto, 2000), with N. G. Svoronos, *La Synopsis Major des Basiliques et ses appendices: Recherches sur la tradition juridique à Byzance* (Paris, 1964).

[37] *L'agricoltura antica. I 'Geoponica' di Cassiano Basso*, ed. & trans. E. Lelli *et al.* (2010), with J. Teall, 'The Byzantine Agricultural Tradition', *DOP* 25 (1971), 33–59; A. McCabe, *A Byzantine Encyclopaedia of Horse Medicine: The Sources, Compilation, and Transmission of the* Hippiatrica (Oxford, 2007).

[38] G. G. Litavrin, ed., *Sovety i rasskazy Kekavmena: sochinenie vizantijskogo polkovodtsa XI v.* (Moscow, 1972); M. Mullett, 'Epistolography', in E. Jeffreys, J. Haldon, & R. Cormack, eds., *The Oxford Handbook of Byzantine Studies* (Oxford, 2008), 882–93, especially 886.

The bulk of the documents which provide evidence about underlying structures lurk within these compilations and handbooks, the majority of which date from the tenth century. There are others, preserved in their original form, in monastic archives, a few dating from the tenth century, many more from the eleventh and later centuries. The most valuable of all have survived independently—(1) a fragmentary document from the late eleventh century listing land holdings in the vicinity of Thebes, their owners, and their tax liabilities; and (2) a work put together by a legal clerk devoted to the memory of a great judge of the early eleventh century which summarizes many of the cases he heard, his judgments and his reasoning.[39]

There are extant traces of many thousands of other documents, most of them probably letters. Because they were made of *lead* (a peculiar choice of late Roman and Byzantine officialdom) rather than clay or wax, the seals which secured and authenticated archived documents and correspondence, private and official, have survived in large numbers—some 80,000 at the latest count—whether buried in landfill or left in abandoned archives or thrown into the sea. An important category has legends giving the name, post held, and rank of individuals serving in the governing apparatus. These *personal office seals* (required presumably to ensure individual accountability—one of several indications of the intensely bureaucratic character of the Byzantine state) constitute roughly a third of the total of extant seals, but a minuscule proportion of those originally in existence, since the great majority of seals attached to letters were recycled for reuse by the recipients. While individual seals provide mere droplets of information, studied in aggregate these personal office seals—which can be dated to a limited period of twenty or twenty-five years—have transformed our knowledge of the evolution of Byzantine state institutions, especially in the age of revival, and have provided the basic prosopographical materials for a deeper understanding of politics and the social order.[40]

There are narrative snippets in some of these documentary and semi-documentary sources, but they throw very little light on the history of events, from the development of policy to the actions of individual players at specific times and in specific places. For this we must turn to overtly historical sources. It is paradoxical that a culture as conscious of its past as

[39] N. G. Svoronos, 'Recherches sur le cadastre byzantin et la fiscalité aux XIe et XIIe siècles: le cadastre de Thèbes', *BCH* 83 (1959), 1–145, 805–25; D.R. Simon & D.R. Reinsch, *Η ΠΕΙΡΑ: Die Peira, ein juristisches Lehrbuch des 11. Jahrhunderts aus Konstantinopel – Text, Übersetzung, Kommentar, Glossar*, 2 vols. (Berlin, 2023).

[40] J.-C. Cheynet, *La société byzantine: L'apport des sceaux*, 2 vols. (Paris, 2008), 1–82.

Byzantium should have produced so few histories of the recent past, before the intellectual revival really gathered way in the eleventh century. There were but two continuous narrative accounts of the ninth century from 813 where Theophanes' coverage stopped. Neither was written within living memory of even the latest events reported. The so-called continuation of Theophanes was commissioned by the Emperor Constantine Porphyrogenitus soon after his seizure of power in January 945, with a clear political purpose—to burnish the image of the Macedonian dynasty founded by his grandfather Basil I (867–86), after a period of occlusion when his father-in-law, Romanos I Lekapenos, governed alone (919–944). There were two parts: (1) a history in four books of Basil's predecessors (Leo V [813–20], Michael II [820–9], Theophilus [829–42], and Michael III [842–67]), the last of whom was subjected to severe criticism; and (2) a highly classicizing and laudatory Life of Basil I, which may well have been modelled, like Einhard's Life of Charlemagne, on a biography of Augustus (in this case Plutarch's lost life).[41]

The second history, attributed to a logothete Symeon (possibly Symeon Metaphrastes), was written a generation later. It was a universal history of mankind, reaching back to the beginning of time (on the third day of Creation) and coming down to the middle of the tenth century. There is nothing unusual about its coverage of the deep past (recycled from earlier universal histories), but the recent past is viewed through jaundiced eyes. It can best be described as an *anti-history* of the Macedonian dynasty. All available pieces of political and personal abuse were picked up and thrown at the four members of the dynasty whose reigns were covered—Basil I (867–86) who was subjected to the most vitriolic attack, Leo VI (886–912), Alexander (912–13), and Constantine VII (913–59) who was relatively unscathed, mainly because the account halted after only four years of his personal rule (945–8).[42] This polemical colouring to a history was not unprecedented—it was much in evidence in late-antique church histories, in the political memoirs of the Patrician Trajan, and in ninth-century accounts of iconoclasm (those of Theophanes and the even more

[41] *Chronographiae quae Theophanis continuati nomine fertur Libri I-IV*, eds. & trans. M. Featherstone & J. Signes Codoñer, CFHB 53 (Berlin, 2013); *Chronographiae quae Theophanis Continuati nomine fertur liber quo Vita Basilii Imperatoris amplectitur*, ed. & trans. I. Ševčenko, CFHB 42 (Berlin, 2011). *Cf.* R. J. H. Jenkins, 'The Classical Background to the *Scriptores post Theophanem*', DOP 8 (1954), 11–30.

[42] *Symeonis magistri et logothetae Chronicon*, ed. S. Wahlgren, CFHB 44.1 (Berlin, 2006), trans. S. Wahlgren, *The Chronicle of the Logothete*, TTB 7 (Liverpool 2019), cited henceforth as Sym.Log.

intemperate George the Monk).[43] If there was a political motive behind the composition of the last, polemical part of the text (entertainment of the reader should not be discounted as an aim), its sponsorship should probably be attributed to aristocratic circles in Anatolia at the time of the great rebellions of the 970s and 980s against Constantine's grandson, Basil II (976–1025).[44]

Neither of these two works presented contemporary history. While it is possible that the author of the anti-history (henceforth the Logothete) knew people who had been alive in the 930s and 940s, there is no indication in the text that he drew on oral sources. Both texts should be viewed as amalgams of antecedent written materials of various types. We may speculate that memoirs and sponsored biographies were written by or for distinguished figures; that other individuals may have written down accounts of particular episodes of interest to them (battles, say, or unusual natural phenomena); and that provincial aristocratic families, like those of Sasanian Iran, may have sponsored heroic accounts of the family's deeds through time. But the only evidence we have, through the traces left in the extant histories, is of three types of basic written source: *encomia*, available in the numerous laudatory speeches delivered to the court; *psogoi*, almost certainly picked up from clandestine pamphlets; and, most useful of all, official communiqués on which the imperial government relied to keep the official classes, in Constantinople and in the provinces, informed about current events.[45]

The eleventh century is better covered. There are two extant contemporary histories written by well-educated and well-connected figures. Michael Psellos, the most celebrated intellectual of his day, wrote vividly about court politics as an eyewitness and was very ready with his opinions (his notion of cool, objective history was of a chequer-board of psogism and laudation); Michael Attaleiates, a successful lawyer, could also draw on personal experience, having accompanied the Emperor Romanos IV Diogenes on campaign as army judge.[46] Two other works were written: a historical

[43] Patrician Trajan: Howard-Johnston, *Witnesses*, 256–60, 306–307. Theophanes and George the Monk: L. Brubaker & J. Haldon, *Byzantium in the Iconoclast Era (ca.680–850): The Sources—An Annotated Survey* (Aldershot, 2001), 168–71, 172–73.

[44] C. Holmes, *Basil II and the Governance of Empire (976–1025)* (Oxford, 2005), 240–98.

[45] Howard-Johnston, *Historical Writing*, 43–53.

[46] *Michaeli Pselli Chronographia*, ed. D. R. Reinsch, Millennium-Studien 51 (Berlin, 2014), trans. E. R. A. Sewter, *Fourteen Byzantine Rulers: The Chronographia of Michael Psellos* (Harmondsworth, 1966), with Ja. N. Ljubarskij, *Mikhail Psell: Lichnost' i tvorchestvo* (Moscow, 1978); I. Pérez Martín, ed., *Miguel Attaleiates, Historia* (Madrid, 2002), trans. A. Kaldellis &

compendium reaching back to 813 (so another continuation of Theophanes), put together by John Skylitzes, a senior judge in the late eleventh century, with an eye on material likely to interest the great and the good of his own day; and a draft history of the decade 1071–81, written 50 to 60 years later by Nikephoros Bryennios, who had a rare ability to bring characters to life and to draw the reader into his tales of derring-do and political intrigue.[47]

By contrast, the tenth century, when the imperially sponsored revival of classicism was underway, is scantily covered. For the flow of information is reduced to a thin stream for two long periods: the only connected account for the period from Leo VI's accession in 886 to the start of Constantine's personal rule in 945 is the biased history retailed by the Logothete, while any modern account of the ups and downs of Basil II's reign (976–1025) has to be extracted from the patchy coverage of Skylitzes, supplemented by the short overview with which Psellos prefaced his history.[48] The intervening period (945–976) is better covered, since Skylitzes' potted history can be fleshed out (1) with an annexe to Theophanes Continuatus covering the period from Constantine Porphyrogenitus' seizure of power (945) to the death of Romanos II (963), and (2) with the classicizing history of the reigns of Nikephoros Phokas (963–9) and John Tzimiskes (969–76) written by the Leo the Deacon, who had a good vantage point at court under Basil II.[49]

It is fortunate that indigenous Byzantine histories for the later ninth, tenth, and early eleventh centuries can be filled out with material provided by foreign observers and recorded in the works of Arab, Armenian, and western historians. Otherwise foreign affairs would only be covered rather thinly, with void patches. Useful additional material can also be culled from extant letter collections (which include extensive diplomatic correspondence at the time of greatest antagonism between Byzantium and Bulgaria,

D. Krallis, *The History: Michael Attaleiates* (Cambridge, Mass., 2012), with D. Krallis, *Michael Attaleiates and the Politics of Imperial Decline in Eleventh-Century Byzantium* (Tempe, Arizona, 2012).

[47] H. Thurn, ed., *Ioannis Scylitzae Synopsis historiarum*, CFHB 5 (Berlin, 1973), trans. B. Flusin & J.-C. Cheynet, *Jean Skylitzès, Empereurs de Constantinople* (Paris, 2003); P. Gautier, ed. & trans., *Nicephori Bryennii historiarum libri quattuor*, CFHB 9 (Brussels, 1975), with L. Neville, *Heroes and Romans in Twelfth-century Byzantium: The* Material for History *of Nikephoros Bryennios* (Cambridge, 2012).

[48] Sym.Log., 133–6; Skyl., 314–69 (trans., 263–306); Psellos, *Chron.*, i.

[49] Skyl., 233–47 (trans., 197–261); I. Bekker, ed., Theophanes continuatus (Bonn, 1836), 436–9; C.B. Hase, ed., *Leonis Diaconi Caloënsis Historiae libri decem* (Bonn, 1828), trans. A.-M. Talbot & D. F. Sullivan, *The* History *of Leo the Deacon: Byzantine Military Expansion in the Tenth Century* (Washington, DC, 2005).

890s–927)[50] and from references to current events in several biographies of noted holy men.[51] Even more important has been the contribution of sigillographic evidence now that it has been subjected to close scrutiny. It not only casts light on institutional developments but also provides a prosopographical base for a deeper exploration of politics—much can be learned about the background of individual families, about the social nexuses formed in the course of bureaucratic and military careers, and about the domestic challenges faced by successive regimes.[52] Finally, there is, of course, material evidence. Appreciation of physical geography—mountain ranges and the passages through them; plains, larger and smaller, where settlements were concentrated; anchorages, harbours, and sea-routes—and direct knowledge of town and country provided by a multitude of excavations and surveys, along with the thousands of coins, gold, silver and copper, issued over two centuries, immeasurably enhance our general understanding of the functioning of the Byzantine state and of its performance in war and peace.[53]

The historian of Byzantium thus has a reasonably complete set of sources for the whole age of revival, but must, at all times, be aware of the limitations imposed by extant indigenous histories. He/she is unable to see the fine grain of events, for lack of the wealth of detailed sources available to historians of Europe from the high Middle Ages and to Islamic historians from the tenth century. History has to be written from above with only the most celebrated or vilified individuals coming into focus. There is also the problem of bias. One must be on guard, at all times, watching out for progic and laudatory material lurking below the surface, and also for the spin inevitably put on officially released information.

Take, for example, the two extant accounts of the seizure of power by Basil I, founder of the Macedonian dynasty. A great deal of circumstantial detail is packed into the Logothete's account of a carefully planned and

[50] G. Kolias, ed. & trans., *Léon Choerosphaktès, magistre, proconsul et patrice; biographie-correspondance* (Athens, 1939); R. J. H. Jenkins & L. G. Westerink, ed. & trans., *Nicolai I Constantinopolitani Patriarchae epistolae*, CFHB 6 (Washington, DC, 1973), *epp.* 3–31; J. Darrouzès & L. G. Westerink, ed. & trans., *Théodore Daphnopatès, Correspondance* (Paris, 1978), *epp.* 5–7.

[51] J. Howard-Johnston & P. A. Hayward, eds., *The Cult of Saints in Late Antiquity and the Early Middle Ages: Essays on the Contribution of Peter Brown* (Oxford, 1999), Introduction, 1–24, at 21–3.

[52] J.-C. Cheynet, *Pouvoir et contestations à Byzance (963–1210)* (Paris, 1990).

[53] *Oxford Handbook of Byz. Studies*, 219–31 (M. Whittow), 295–308 (K. Belke), 317–95 (H. Saradi, A. Harvey, J. Bardill, R. Ousterhout, C. Bakirtzis, R. Cormack); Laiou-Morrisson, *Byzantine Economy*, 8–17, 70–89.

efficiently executed *putsch*. First there was the murder of the Emperor Michael, whom Basil had put to bed in the imperial bedchamber, after tampering with the lock: the actions of each of the conspirators involved, four of whom were Basil's relatives, were noted—the five who stood guard outside the door, while Basil and four others forced their way in; the identities of those who cut off the emperor's hand, delivered the lethal sword thrust, and dispatched the emperor's new favourite, Basiliskianos asleep on a couch. Next came the elaborate subterfuge to distance the conspirators from the crime: their slipping out of the palace; the house where they regrouped across the Golden Horn; and their admission into the palace by a Khurramite, once he had been told (in Persian) that the emperor had been killed. By contrast, the histories commissioned by Constantine Porphyrogenitus are studiously vague about what happened. The murder is attributed to chamberlains and dated to the night of 23–4 September 867 at the end of Theophanes Continuatus, iv, while the Life of Basil simply recycles the official account issued by the new regime: Michael had exhausted the treasury in fourteen years and was planning a purge of the governing class, killing those purged and appropriating their estates; so the senior members of the government and the Senatorial elite had him killed through soldiers on duty in the palace. Basil was then proclaimed emperor by the Senate, the lower ranks, the army, and the people.[54]

The Logothete is undoubtedly right to attribute direct responsibility to Basil, co-emperor but under increasing suspicion at the time. The names of those involved on the night probably represent those known to be close to Basil and his relatives. But it is impossible to be sure of anything else, given that classical and ancient writers knew that an accumulation of detail aided verisimilitude.[55]

## 3.4 Foreign policy, 860–927

We must backtrack a few years to pick out the episode which demonstrated clearly that the balance of power between Byzantium and the Caliphate was shifting in Byzantium's favour. The raiding army of Melitene invaded northern Asia Minor in summer 863. The theme of Armeniakon was ravaged. The city of Amisos was sacked. Meanwhile there was a general mobilization

[54] Sym.Log., 131.48–54; Theoph.Cont., iv.44.45–55; *Vita.Bas.*, cc.27–8.

[55] *Cf.* S. Mitchell, 'The Life of St. Theodatus of Ancyra', *Anatolian Studies*, 32 (1982), 93–113.

of Byzantine forces—the imperial *tagmata*, two themes from the Balkans (Thrace and Macedonia), and all themes and frontier commands of Asia Minor. Petronas, Strategos of Thrakesion and brother-in-law of the emperor, was given the supreme command, normally the prerogative of the Domestic of the Scholai. He succeeded in intercepting and surprising the raiders on their return march, at a carefully chosen spot, a water meadow in rugged country. Petronas deployed his forces in three corps, north, south, and west of the Arabs' encampment. All attempts by the Arabs to break out were repulsed. The encircling forces held firm and proceeded to annihilate the raiding army. The emir himself was killed. Never again would Melitene pose a serious threat to Byzantium. Tarsos was left as the sole major *jihad* base on the edge of Byzantine territory. Neither Arab-held Qaliqala (Theodosiopolis) nor Paulician Tephrike could match the military strength of Melitene in its heyday.[56]

Michael's regime had a second significant foreign policy success in 864. Taking advantage of a famine in Bulgaria, he forced the ruler (Boris) and the governing class to convert by threatening to attack by land and sea. This inaugurated a period of peace as was only to be expected between two fraternal Christian powers.[57] Two years on, when Ragusa on the coast of Dalmatia came under attack from the Arabs of Bari, the prompt and efficient response of Byzantium—the organization of an expeditionary force to relieve the siege of the city—should almost certainly be credited to Michael before his murder.[58] It is indeed worth noting that amid all the abuse flung at Michael, there is no criticism of his conduct of foreign affairs.

The usurper Basil inaugurated a new era in Byzantine foreign policy, as indeed he did in domestic affairs. Renewal was the watchword of the regime—renewal meaning a deliberate attempt to reconnect with the late-antique past and a drive to improve different facets of government, notably the functioning of the justice system. Abroad, Byzantium was moving on to the offensive. The east was the priority for him and his successors, save when crises flared up elsewhere. The underlying aim was to probe Arab defences and to exploit weak points, beginning a slow but steady push back into formerly Roman territory in the Levant. Clearly the peace with Christianized Bulgaria made it more difficult to adopt a similar policy in the Balkans, but there is every indication that Byzantium had never reconciled itself to the loss of much of the interior. Even if it was no more than a

[56] Theoph.Cont., iv.25; Sym.Log., 131.26 (pp.243.224–244.231). *Cf. BA*, I, 249–56.

[57] Shepard, 'Slavs and Bulgars', 239–48.

[58] *BA*, II.1, 11–13.

pipe dream at times, there remained a hope that the Bulgars might be incorporated into what was in essence a polyethnic state and that once again the frontier might follow the course of the Danube.

First, though, Basil had to deal with the crisis in the Adriatic. It was vital to keep open the sea-lanes to Venice, Byzantium's principal client in Italy, and to prevent the Arabs from establishing a bridgehead in the Balkans. The naval expeditionary force mobilized by the previous regime was duly dispatched, to relieve Ragusa and drive the Arabs back to Bari (early in 868). That main objective was achieved, after which the expedition's role became more political—to show a watching world, both Christian and Muslim, that Byzantium was determined to reassert its naval hegemony in the central Mediterranean and that it was ready to act in concert with western powers. Troops were landed in Sicily to reinforce the local forces defending the Byzantine sector of the island against the advancing Aghlabids, and in 869 the fleet supported the Frankish army of Louis II which was besieging Bari.[59] Two years were then spent making preparations for offensive operations in the east, to be commanded by the emperor in person.

The targets lay in the Arab frontier zone, behind the Taurus and Anti-Taurus mountains which constituted a broad no-man's land with widely spaced castles under the control of local lords. The weakest raiding base, Tephrike held by the Paulician clients of the Arabs, was the first to be attacked (in 871). The object seems to have been to weaken, rather than to destroy, the mini-state. There was extensive raiding, the fortress-town itself was besieged and, during the withdrawal, outlier castles were attacked.[60] The main effect was to provoke the Paulicians into launching an attack of their own in the following year, which penetrated as far west as Ankyra. It ended in a second striking Byzantine victory over a raiding army as it withdrew, and the death of Chrysocheir, the Paulician leader. Tephrike ceased to be a threat, and was eventually abandoned some twenty years later.[61]

The second target (in 873) was Melitene, a great city instead of a large fortress, which, though weakened, was more than capable of defending itself.[62] The direct approach along the northern edge of the Anti-Taurus was

[59] V. von Falkenhausen, *Untersuchungen über die byzantinische Herrschaft in Süditalien vom 9. bis ins 11. Jahrhundert* (Wiesbaden, 1967), 18; *BA*, II, 13–22.

[60] *Vita Bas.*, c.37. *Cf. BA*, II.1, 32–3.

[61] *Vita Bas.*, cc.41–3. *Cf. BA*, II.1, 35–8; P. Lemerle, 'L'histoire des Pauliciens d'Asie Mineure d'après les sources grecques', *TM* 5 (1973), 1–144, at 96–104. I put the abandonment of Tephrike twenty years later than Canard, fifteen than Lemerle.

[62] For Melitene and its environs, see Mitford, *East of Asia Minor*, I, 149–92.

opened up when Taranta (modern Darende on the upper course of the Tohma river) came over in 872.[63] Again, the object was to cause damage rather than capture the city. There was extensive raiding by forays, one capturing Sozopetra at the north-east end of the important pass running west-south-west to Germanikeia and the broad corridor linking northern Syria to Cilicia. Another foray ranged much further afield, reaching and supposedly sacking Samosata, south of the Euphrates gorges (i.e. probably destroying extramural suburbs), before raiding across the river. In a second phase, the main force advanced from its camp near Arka (on the north-west edge of the Melitene plain), bridged the Euphrates, captured a castle on the east bank, and dispatched another foray to raid the canton of Anzitene which formed the eastern part of Melitene's territory (several more castles were taken). There was not much more than a token siege of Melitene, after an engagement before the walls. The campaign ended with a circuitous withdrawal through Paulician territory where four castles were captured and destroyed. The emperor celebrated the campaign with a formal triumph in Constantinople.[64]

Five years then passed without any action on a large scale, but Byzantium's strategic position was improved by the acquisition of three frontier strongholds.[65] It may have been that Basil was satisfied with the improved security gained for eastern Anatolia, and was biding his time until a new opportunity arose for a renewed thrust, when his eldest son, Constantine, would be old enough to take part and share the military glory. But a purely diplomatic initiative was taken vis-à-vis Armenia. Any hopes of regaining substantial amounts of territory in the Middle East would require the active collaboration of the Christian rulers of Armenia. This was acknowledged by Michael III, under whom the Patriarch Photios made overtures to the church authorities in Armenia, with a view to bringing about a union of the two churches. That initiative lapsed with his deposition at Basil's accession and, when renewed after his reappointment in 877, was firmly rebuffed.[66] Instead, there was an attempt to give Basil a claim to authority over Armenia. He was endowed with royal Armenian ancestry, reaching back to the Arsacid kings who had ruled Greater Armenia, until the imposition of Sasanian direct rule and the abolition of the monarchy in

[63] *Vita Bas.*, c.38. *Cf. BA*, II.1, 35.

[64] *Vita Bas.*, cc.39–40. *Cf. BA*, II.1, 43–7; Lemerle, 'L'histoire des Pauliciens', 104–8.

[65] *Vita Bas.*, c.46.

[66] T. Greenwood, 'Failure of a Mission? Photius and the Armenian Church', *Le Muséon*, 119 (2006), 123–67.

428 AD. It was an artificial genealogy, devised by Photios who was returning to favour. An implicit claim was being advanced to suzerainty over all the princes of Armenia, great and small. This was made explicit when Basil formally asked the Prince of Princes Ashot Bagratid for a crown, the Bagratids being the traditional coronants of the Arsacids.[67]

Good intelligence was a prerequisite for a successful foreign policy. It seems that Byzantium's antennae were good at picking up what was happening in the near abroad (the Balkans, the Pontic steppes, and the Levant). Mercantile networks undoubtedly played a key part in the swift dissemination of news, itself a valuable commodity. A striking example is provided by Byzantium's swift response to the 878 crisis in the Levant occasioned by the caliph's failed attempt to oust Ibn Tulun, governor of Egypt, and the ensuing advance of Egyptian forces into Syria and their siege of Antioch in the autumn.[68] The field army was mobilized. Basil, together with his son Constantine, took charge. The first target was the secluded plain in the central Anti-Taurus. Two castles were captured, one capitulated, as the army advanced along the old Roman road from Kaisareia to Melitene via Kokusos (some clearance was necessary beyond Kokusos). The army then struck south across the formidable southern ridges of the Anti-Taurus, probably using a Roman branch road through the gorges of the river Pyramos (modern Ceyhan), to devastate the plain of Germanikeia and advance north-east to besiege Adata, at the south-west end of the diagonal pass from Melitene.[69] A foray was sent south to raid the territories of Kaisun, Raban, and Ardil. Adata held out (as was probably expected), but valuable allies were acquired—Sim al-Tawil, Abbasid governor of Antioch (so the city had probably fallen) and an important border lord with his castles. This campaign, together with a successful raid by theme forces on Paulician territory and Cilicia, more than merited the celebration of a triumph by Basil and his son.[70]

The triumph was staged in May/June 879, and helped mask grim news from the west where Syracuse had fallen in May 878, despite the arrival of Byzantine reinforcements. This prompted the regime to switch its attention

[67] *Vita Bas.*, cc.2–3; ps.Symeon Magister (in *Theophanes Continuatus*, ed. I. Bekker [Bonn, 1838]), 689.5–690.3.

[68] Kennedy, *Age of the Caliphates*, 265–6.

[69] Evidence of a branch road (abutments and pier of a Roman bridge) was found near the southern outlet of the gorges by D. G. Hogarth and J. A. R. Munro, 'Modern and Ancient Roads in Eastern Asia Minor', *Royal Geographical Society, Supplementary Papers*, 3 (1893), 643–739, at 665–7.

[70] *Vita Bas.*, cc.46–9. *Cf. BA*, II.1, 87–94 (dating the campaign to 879).

back to the west, where the threat from Sicily had prompted many to seek Byzantine protection.[71] A new expedition was dispatched in 880, which bolstered the position in southern Italy, *inter alia* putting an end to the emirate of Taranto in 880. The arrival in 885 of troops from frontier commands in Asia Minor (Cappadocia and Charsianon) under the command of a capable general (the first of the Phokas family to gain high command) gave added impetus to the campaign, leading to a steady expansion of the territory under direct Byzantine control to cover all of Calabria and Apulia and the foundation of a new theme of Longibardia in 891.[72] In the east, policy became purely reactive and less successful—two attempts to instal a Byzantine client in Iberia failed, as did an attack by the full field army on Tarsos in 883 in reprisal for raids in 879 and 881/2.[73]

It is possible to give this relatively full account of the initiatives and campaigns of the first Macedonian regime, because much was made of them in the Life of Basil. We must, of course, beware of exaggeration in a laudatory work, but the details given probably derive from campaign reports written at the time and are, to my mind, trustworthy. They will, I hope, help to induct the reader into the intricacies of diplomacy and warfare in the late ninth and tenth centuries and to give an example of what could be achieved if resources and personal prestige were committed to campaigns with clear, limited objectives, within a realistic grand strategy. The lesson was reinforced by the disastrous outcome of the premature attack on Tarsos. What had been the great disadvantage of Byzantium in the past, its central position, could now be exploited to its advantage. The priority might lie in the east, but resources could be transferred speedily, thanks to inner lines, to other fronts if the need arose, as it did in 879. The overriding principle, though, was that of concentration of force, to be maintained as long as practicable against a prime target.

Basil was succeeded by his second son, Leo VI, after the untimely death of Constantine in 879. They were temperamentally at odds—Basil being very much the bold adventurer in politics and war, physically strong, decisive, and, when necessary, ruthless; Leo by contrast a man of intellect and genuine piety, who took charge of the legal reform programme and, as

[71] Notably the prince of Benevento (873), the notables of Bari (876), and Pope John VIII (877). *Cf.* von Falkenhausen, *Süditalien*, 18–19; *Cf. BA*, II.1, 70–9.

[72] Von Falkenhausen, *Süditalien*, 19–23; *BA*, II.1, 95–9, 109–14.

[73] *Vita Bas.*, c.50 (disguising the failure); Sym.Log., 132.25. *Cf. BA*, II.1, 99–105.

emperor, took on the role of priest-king, giving homilies to his court.[74] It is no surprise to find that Leo's foreign policy diverged from his father's. He did, it is true, sustain the momentum of conquest in southern Italy, while losing ground in Sicily, where the last Byzantine stronghold, Taormina, was captured in 902. But he provoked crises in the Balkans and Armenia without just cause. The consequences were disastrous. Even more dramatic was the capture of Thessalonike by the raiding fleet of Leo of Tripoli in 904.[75]

His behaviour towards newly Christianized Bulgaria was indefensible. He was tempted in 893 by an offer from the Hungarians to attack Bulgaria, after their successful involvement with a grand coalition of Franks, Alamans, and Bavarians in the campaign which destroyed the Moravian state in 892. A manufactured trade dispute provoked the Bulgars into taking military action (a raid towards Constantinople), providing the Byzantines with the excuse they needed. The following year (864), a Byzantine army under the command of the victorious general from southern Italy advanced across Thrace, drawing Bulgar forces south to defend the Haemus frontier. This opened the way for the Hungarians to invade and devastate the Bulgarian interior, with a Byzantine fleet on hand to ferry them to and fro across the Danube. This was but the preamble to a grand land offensive in 895, intended presumably to force the Haemus defences and take out the twin Bulgar capitals, Pliska and Preslav. It was a disastrous move. The full field army was caught by surprise as it marched north across Thrace and suffered a crushing defeat. Apart from the loss of prestige, there were two serious consequences. First, the Bulgars could take their revenge on the Hungarians with impunity, as they did in 896 when they staged a successful pincer attack in conjunction with the Pechenegs, which prompted the Hungarians to migrate into the natural redoubt of the Carpathian basin. Second, Byzantine policy-makers had to take account of Bulgar resentment at the actions of a supposedly fraternal Christian power for at least a generation. The freedom enjoyed for a generation to concentrate on the east or the west without regard to the Balkan front was gone.[76]

Leo's mistake in Armenia was to become too supportive of the Bagratids, rather than maintaining Basil's stance of benign, theoretical overlordship. Instead of restraining Smbat who had succeeded Ashot as Prince of Princes

[74] M. L. D. Riedel, *Leo VI and the Transformation of Byzantine Christian Identiy: Writings of an Unexpected Emperor* (Cambridge, 2018).

[75] Sym.Log., 133.40; *BA*, II.1, 134–7, 142–8, 152–81.

[76] J. Howard-Johnston, 'Byzantium, Bulgaria and the Peoples of Ukraine in the 890s', in *Materialy po Arkheologii i Etnografii Tavrii*, 7 (Simferopol, 2008), 342–56.

in 890 and had been crowned a little later by al-Afshin, emir of Azerbaijan, on behalf of the caliph, he seems to have encouraged him to assert himself vis-à-vis the Arab authorities. When the caliph demanded that he pay tax to al-Afshin, in effect retracting the gubernatorial powers granted to Ashot, Smbat refused. He attacked the two Arab brothers who had seized Dvin (during the early unsettled months of his reign), and, when the city fell, sent them in chains to Leo. He reaffirmed his father's hegemony elsewhere, confident of Byzantine support. But these initiatives came to nought when al-Afshin took advantage of a devastating earthquake in December 893 to advance into the plain of Ayrarat and, after a battle, to extract the tax owed to the caliphate. Then, in 895 Ahmad, Shaybanid emir of Ałjnik, rebelled, annexed Taron, and, with Artsruni help, drove off Smbat. At this point al-Afshin returned to the attack, lopping off the regions conquered by Ashot in Siwnikʿ and Iberia and occupying Kars. Worse was to come after his death and the succession of Yusuf b. Abu'l Sadj in 901. The three Kaysite emirs who dominated southern Armenia from Manzikert rebelled in 902, withholding their tribute, and routed Smbat when he marched against them. This time, though, the Artsrunis, neighbours of the Kaysites, came to his aid and helped him extract the tribute. In 903, by a swift circuitous thrust into the heart of Armenia, Yusuf forced Smbat formally to submit, thereby damaging his standing in Transcaucasia and encouraging his enemies, Abasgians in the north and Artsrunis in the south, to extend their territory. The kingdom was increasingly beleaguered until, in spring 909, Yusuf attacked in force with the Artsrunis; overran Siwnikʿ, central Armenia, and Iberia; and left the Artsrunis to destroy the last Bagratid fighting force in 910. Two years later, Smbat gave himself up and was executed by Yusuf at Dvin.[77]

Leo did what he could to minimize the damage. He made peace on humiliating terms with the Bulgars, agreeing to make annual cash payments which amounted to tribute. In Armenia, apart from limited military activity across the frontier and cultivation of the restored principality of Taron, he could only watch as Bagratid power was unravelled and Yusuf turned on his Artsruni allies. As for the main Anti-Taurus and Taurus frontiers, he did not renew Basil's aggressive campaigning, but merely strove to limit the damage caused by the raiding armies of Tarsos. This sensible restraint was probably advised by his senior general and military adviser, Nikephoros Phokas the elder who had directed the successful campaigns in southern Italy. He was also probably responsible for the interest shown by Leo in the mechanisms

[77] Mahé, *Histoire de l'Arménie* 131–7.

of *jihad* and in replicating some of them in Byzantium.[78] After the sacking of Thessalonike, the priority had to be a reassertion of Byzantine naval hegemony in the Aegean and a reprisal attack on a major Arab coastal city—successfully carried out in 910 against Laodikeia. Finally, again probably on the advice of senior officials in the Dromos (the foreign ministry), he reached out north to the Rus, to draw them into the Byzantine sphere of influence, by offering them substantial trade concessions in 907. They might be useful in future in helping to mitigate the disastrous effects of Leo's foreign policy. Their ability to move swiftly by water brought both Transcaucasia, in particular the Kura plains (in Azerbaijan), and Bulgaria within striking range.[79]

Leo died in 912, at the peak of the Armenian crisis. Only after much arm-twisting and a change of patriarch had his fourth marriage been recognized by the church in 907, thereby legitimizing the child of the marriage, Constantine, known as Porphyrogenitus (born in the porphyry chamber in the palace) to emphasize his imperial origin.[80] After the short reign of his uncle Alexander (11 May 912–6 June 913), power was exercised by a regency council, and then, after a bloodless coup, by the admiral of the imperial fleet, Romanos Lekapenos, appointed Caesar in September 919 when his daughter Helen was married to Constantine, and crowned emperor in December 920.[81] From the middle 920s, Romanos was to return to Basil's carefully targeted, cautious, step-by-step strategy of expansion in the east, but with a new guerrilla twist. First, though, he had to cope with the consequences of the anti-Bulgar policies of Alexander and the regency council.

Alexander's single foreign policy decision was to go to war with Bulgaria. His refusal to hand over the tribute due in autumn 912 was tantamount to a declaration of war, and led to the mobilization of both sides. His death on 6 June 913 and the attempted coup three days later of the Domestic of the Scholai, Constantine Doukas, disrupted Byzantine preparations, leaving the way open for the Bulgar ruler Symeon to march on Constantinople.[82] At

[78] J.-C. Cheynet, 'La guerre sainte à Byzance au Moyen Âge: un malentendu', in D. Baloup & P. Josserand, eds., *Regards croisés sur la guerre sainte: guerre, religion et idéologie dans l'espace méditerranéen latin (XI-XIIIe siècle)* (Toulouse, 2020), 13–32, at 23–4.

[79] Mas'udi, cc.458–60.

[80] S. Runciman, *The Emperor Romanus Lecapenus and his Reign: A Study of Tenth-Century Byzantium* (Cambridge, 1963), 40–3.

[81] Runciman, *Romanus Lecapenus*, 52–62, who follows Sym.Log., 136.11 in misplacing Romanus' coronation in 919.

[82] Sym.Log., 135.3–10. *Cf.* Runciman, *Romanus Lecapenus*, 45–51.

a summit meeting with the Patriarch Nicholas Mystikos, a member of the regency council, he was refused the imperial title he sought (Emperor of Bulgaria) but was persuaded to withdraw by the prospect of marrying a daughter to the young emperor when he came of age in 919. The regency council then compounded the problem by going to war, without due cause, in 917. A large expeditionary force, including Asia Minor as well as Balkan theme armies, was mobilized along with the fleet. The plan was for the fleet to ferry a Pecheneg army across the Danube to take the Bulgars in the rear while Byzantine land forces attacked in the south (as in 894 with the Hungarians). Instead it ended in a second disastrous defeat when the Pechenegs, suborned by the Bulgars, refused to cross the Danube and the Byzantine army was attacked and routed at Acheloos, well to the south of the Haemus.[83]

There was very little that could be done to redress the balance over the following years, beyond harassing Bulgar raiding forces, encouraging opposition in the Balkans (from the Serbs, apprehensive of rising Bulgar power), and speaking menacingly of attack by a grand coalition of steppe peoples. Political infighting in Byzantium did not improve matters, the chief protagonists being Leo Phokas, dismissed from his command after the battle of Acheloos, and a coterie around the young emperor. The beneficiary was Romanos Lekapenos, who had not been punished after being court-martialled. He staged a bloodless coup in 919, securing his position by marrying his daughter Helen instead of Symeon's to Constantine. That, of course, infuriated Symeon, who now demanded the abdication of Constantine and his own installation as emperor. There was no change, though, in the brute reality of a continuing military impasse on the ground.[84]

Romanos' first great success was achieved by words; by the long, wheedling letters sent on his behalf by the Patriarch Nicholas. Symeon was softened enough to enter into negotiations after a vain two-month siege of Constantinople in autumn 923. He realized that he could not take the city and that some sort of settlement must be reached if the fighting were ever to end. An additional factor was the hostile attitude of the Croats, after the

[83] Sym.Log., 135.10–11, 18–21. *Cf.* J. D. Howard-Johnston, 'A Short Piece of Narrative History: War and Diplomacy in the Balkans, winter 921/2–spring 924', in E. M. Jeffreys, ed., *Byzantine Style, Religion and Civilization: In Honour of Sir Steven Runciman* (Cambridge, 2006), 340–60, at 341–6.

[84] Sym.Log., 135.22–136.7, 136.11–14, 17, 19–20, 23–4, 27. *Cf.* Runciman, *Romanus Lecapenus*, 56–62, 86–7.

Serbs had been forced to submit. A summit was arranged at which he would meet Romanos—shunned hitherto because of his daughter's marriage to Constantine. The significance of the event was marked by the full dating given by the Logothete: the two rulers met on Wednesday 19 November 923 at the fifth hour of the day, on a specially constructed jetty outside the city. Symeon's demand to become emperor was neither accepted nor rejected—he was in effect licensed to style himself how he wished (it turned out to be 'Emperor of the Romans and the Bulgars'). A ceasefire was agreed, but Symeon was left free to take what action he saw fit against his Balkan adversaries.[85]

There was friction subsequently but the ceasefire held. Symeon turned his attention west against the Croats. That was a policy which ended in disaster. It was presumably from the broken country of Dalmatia that the Croats conducted their defence, until, in spring 927, they succeeded in destroying the invasion army. Symeon died in May soon after hearing the news. His death opened the way for a new era of peace in the Balkans.[86] Thenceforth, Romanos would be able to concentrate his attention on the east, and to resume the offensive initiated by Basil I against key Arab positions in the borderlands of western Armenia and the central Anti-Taurus.

On the whole Byzantium strengthened its position in this first phase of Macedonian foreign policy. An increase in available resources brought by the slow but steady economic growth discernible from the reign of Theophilos enabled this vestige of the Roman empire to take the initiative in its relations with the Muslim powers of the Middle East and to cope with the consequences of two misguided policies.[87] The first inroads were made into the borderlands to the south-east, a world of local lords and one major emirate. The situation in the central Mediterranean was stabilized, as the Adriatic was cleared of Arab privateers and Byzantine authority was gradually extended over Apulia and Calabria. A temporary loss of naval hegemony in the east Mediterranean following defeat in 898, which had allowed Arab forces to capture Demetrias (902) and Thessalonike (904), was brought to an end by victory at sea in 905 and a successful expedition against Laodikeia (910). Bulgaria was finally induced to make peace on mutually satisfactory terms after Symeon's death in 927.[88]

[85] Sym.Log., 136.29–37; *DAI*, c.32.104–28; Daphnopates, *ep.* 5.12–63. *Cf.* Howard-Johnston, 'Short Piece', 348–53.

[86] Howard-Johnston, 'Short Piece', 354.

[87] Howard-Johnston, *Byzantium*, 247–51.

[88] Howard-Johnston, 'Short Piece', 354–5.

Even in Armenia lost ground was recovered. Byzantium intervened in force, attacking Dvin, the Arab capital, in 915, in a very public show of political support for Smbat's heir, Ashot II. He had visited Constantinople in 914 and gained backing for a campaign to reconstitute the Bagratid principality. A second intervention in 922, this time by the full field army commanded by the young Domestic of the Scholai, John Kourkouas, signalled Byzantium's commitment to its fellow-Christians in Armenia. Dvin was again the target, but the main objective was probably diplomatic, to establish a nexus of alliances, beginning with the Artsrunis of Vaspurakan and several small principalities in central Armenia.[89]

Finally, Byzantium's diplomatic reach was extended north by a third initiative of Leo's. The Rus were drawn into an alliance by an offer of commercial concessions. This marked the beginning of a political and cultural liaison fraught with significance for the future. In the short term it gave Byzantium leverage vis-à-vis the Pechenegs in the Pontic steppe and the Khazar overlords of the Rus, and a means for attacking the Sajid emirate in Azerbaijan.

## 3.5 Foreign policy, 927–1025

It was in the reign of Romanos Lekapenos (920–44) that a new offensive strategy was developed. It was to prove remarkably successful in his hands and those of his successors down to Nikephoros Phokas (963–9).[90] During this second phase in the revival of Byzantium abroad the main forward zones of Arab defence, from Cilicia to western Armenia, were overrun, all three major *jihad* bases, Melitene, Theodosiopolis and Tarsos, being captured. By 970, Byzantium had annexed the whole of Cilicia, a large area in northern Syria, and Armenia as far as the Bingöl Dağ, and was poised to dominate the Middle East by land as well as by sea. After the last major raids dispatched from Tarsos by land and sea in 931, the only serious resistance had been put up by the Hamdanid emirate of Aleppo established by 'Ali (known by his honorific title of Sayf al-Dawla, 'Sword of the State'), younger brother of Nasir emir of Mosul. Sayf was a border warrior of rare talent, whose image as *jihad* leader was burnished and broadcast far and wide by writers at his court, in the first instance the great poet Mutannabi.

[89] Martin-Hisard, 'Les archontes', 371, 417–18; *BA*, II.1, 231–4, 249–50.
[90] See Howard-Johnston, *Byzantium*, 223–36.

He was able to assemble large forces, attracting many *jihad* volunteers to add to the Beduin and highlanders of the emirate. His armies could confront and defeat those of Byzantium in open combat. For fourteen years (947–60) he led the fight against the resurgent Christian power, launching raid after raid into Byzantine territory, slowing up but not halting Byzantium's advance.[91]

There were no serious, long-lasting distractions elsewhere. Bulgaria acted as a broad buffer between Byzantium and the Hungarians in their hyperactive raiding phase, except in 934 and 943 when predatory bands managed to penetrate as far as Thrace.[92] The struggle with the Arabs continued in the central Mediterranean, gaining in intensity after the Fatimid take-over of Ifriqiya in 910. Sicily was lost definitively. Several attacks on Calabria were fended off (918, 922, 924, 927–9) before peace was secured in return for tribute in 931–2.[93] Flamboyant forays by naval task forces, which helped take out the bases of Arab privateers at Garigliano in northern Calabria (915) and Fraxinetum in southern France (942), enhanced Byzantium's standing in Italy and in the wider Germanic world.[94] Within Italy there were good relations with the papacy. Campania was kept within the sphere of Byzantine influence (upheld by a show of force in 955). Clients were put to work on Byzantium's behalf, the most important of whom, leaving aside Venice, was Hugh of Arles (between 934/5 and 945).[95] There were two further outbreaks of fighting with the Fatimids by sea and land (in Calabria) in the 950s, both provoked by the Byzantines who concerted attacks in 951 and 956 with the Umayyads of Spain.[96]

There was, however, one year, 941, when offensive operations in the east had to be halted and the field army brought back to deal with a dangerous

[91] M. Canard, *Histoire de la dynastie des H'amdanides de Jazîra et de Syrie* (Paris, 1953), 755–804. *Cf.* A. Kaldellis, *Streams of Gold, Rivers of Blood: The Rise and Fall of Byzantium, 955 AD to the First Crusade* (New York, 2019).

[92] Sym.Log., 136.69, 77.

[93] *BA*, II.1, 244, 250, 255–6, 307–10. *Cf.* P. Prasad, *Diplomacy and Foreign Policy in the Personal Reign of Constantine VII Porphyrogennetos (945–959)* (DPhil, Oxford, 2015), 255–7, 263–4, 265–7. Prasad's thesis is accessible in digital form through the Bodleian Library, Oxford.

[94] *Liudprandi Antapodosis*, ii.51–4, v.9 & 16, ed. J. Becker, *Scriptores rerum Gemanicarum in usum scholarum* (Hanover-Leipzig, 1915). *Cf.* K. Leyser, 'Ends and Means in Liudprand of Cremona', in J. D. Howard-Johnston, ed., *Byzantium and the West c.850–c.1200, Byz.Forsch.* 13 (1988), 119–43, at 127–31.

[95] K. Leyser, 'The Tenth Century in Byzantine–Western Relationships', in D. Baker, ed., *Relations between East and West in the Middle Ages* (Edinburgh, 1973), 29–63, at 29–33, 36–41; G. Sergi, 'The Kingdom of Italy', *CMH* III, 346–71, at 351–5; Prasad, *Foreign Policy*, 264, 269–70, 273–4, 279–80.

[96] Brett, *Fatimid Empire*, 63, 74–5; Prasad, *Foreign Policy*, 154–61, 280–2.

enemy in the metropolitan area. Tensions had been growing with Khazars from the 920s, caused by Byzantine missionary work among the Alans of the north Caucasus (a core component of the khaganate) and anti-Jewish measures at home. They came to a head in 940, when Byzantium sponsored a Rus attack on the main Khazar base in the Sea of Azov. After repelling the attack, the Khazars forced the Rus to turn against Byzantium.[97] A large fleet attacked Constantinople in 941 and set about ravaging Bithynia. Although traditional guerrilla tactics could limit the damage, the field army was needed to drive off the Rus.[98]

With that single exception, the outward drive was sustained for over forty years. But when the Fatimids finally succeeded in taking over Egypt in 969, Byzantium found itself facing an equipollent Muslim power, which was ideologically charged with its Ismaili faith. When the following year a Fatimid expeditionary force pushed into Palestine and Syria and took the principal cities (Ramla, Tiberias, and Damascus), it became evident that the Fatimids would soon be taking action against the dominant infidel power in the east Mediterranean. This they did in 970–1, laying siege to Antioch for five months, until forced to withdraw so as to face a formidable coalition of Beduin and Ikshidid loyalists put together by the Qarmatis of Bahrayn on the desert margin of Syria.[99] This brought Byzantium's cautious, step-by-step and sustained outward drive to a halt. Thenceforth there would be occasional interventions, designed to impress Byzantine military power on potential adversaries and to deter them from aggression. Not that the ambition of bringing about a historic reversal of Christian–Muslim relations was abandoned either by John Tzimiskes (969–76) or by Basil II (976–1025). But both realized that the international context had changed and that Byzantium must revert to a reactive policy. Aggressive action would be countered in force. Opportunities, military or diplomatic, would be seized and Byzantine gains maximized.

Like the defensive strategy of the dark age, the offensive strategy in its final form (after an apparently short initial period of development) was described in writing, in two military handbooks dating from the second half of the tenth century: the *Praecepta* of Nikephoros Phokas included a pithy

[97] C. Zuckerman, 'On the Date of the Khazars' Conversion to Judaism and the Chronology of the Kings of Rus Oleg and Igor', *REB* 53 (1995), 237–70, at 256–7.

[98] Sym.Log., 136.71–5; Liudprand, *Antapodosis* v.15; *Povest'*, 33 (trans., 71–72).

[99] Brett, *Fatimid Empire*, 77–83; Howard-Johnston, *Byzantium*, 233.

summary of the main elements but was primarily concerned with a more orthodox mode of warfare appropriate for operations in open country south of the Taurus and Armenian Taurus; the second handbook dating from the reign of Basil II dealt in detail with the variation devised for counter-insurgency warfare in the Balkans. The guiding principles were: (1) concentration of force against a prime target; (2) patience—the deferral of a frontal assault on the target until it was so weakened as to be ripe for the taking; (3) destruction of its resource-base and demoralization of the defenders, by repeated raiding of its territory; (4) isolation of the target from cities to its rear, by wide-ranging raids; and (5) seizure or construction of one or more castles within striking range of the target, which could then act as secure bases for a localized war of attrition, carried on throughout the year.[100]

In its preference for the indirect approach, its deferral of open conflict to the optimum moment, and the key role of castles as raiding bases, this offensive strategy had a strong guerrilla character. It was this (and the caution implicit in it) which Nikephoros Phokas was concerned to shake off, once Byzantine forces had surmounted the frontier mountains and were operating to the south. Over the next generation or two Byzantine forces, operating in a conventional manner and relying on shock combat, established a clear psychological dominance over their Muslim adversaries.[101]

The story of Byzantium's expansion up to 969 can be told quite simply, as a set of campaigns directed at a series of urban targets in and beyond the borderlands. Taken in chronological order, the targets were (1) Melitene (926–34), the weakened *jihad* base, which commanded the routes east up the Arsanias valley into the heart of Armenia and south-west, past Sozopetra and Adata, to northern Syria and Cilicia; (2) the small emirate of Asmosaton (classical Arsamosata, Arab Šimšat—936–8), centred on a small plain in the Arsanias valley, upstream from Anzitene (which belonged to Melitene); (3) Theodosiopolis (938–49), the northern *jihad* base, occupying a key position below the Euphrates–Araxes watershed; (4) Adata (948-57) by the exit of the pass from Melitene; (5) Germanikeia (949-661/2), commanding the

[100] Nikephoros Phokas, *Praecepta militaria*, ed. & trans. E. McGeer, *Sowing the Dragon's Teeth: Byzantine Warfare in the Tenth Century*, DO Studies 33 (Washington, DC, 1995), 12–59; Nikephoros Ouranos, *Taktika*, cc.62–5, ed. & trans. McGeer, *op. cit.*, 134–63; Anon., *Taktika*, ed. & trans. G. T. Dennis, *Three Byzantine Military Treatises*, CFHB 25 (Washington, DC, 1985), 246–335.

[101] Theoph.Cont., ed. Bekker, 459.15–460.7 (Nikephoros Phokas from the later 950s). *Cf.* Skyl., 333.88–334.29 (Bardas Skleros' 3,000).

open country linking northern Syria to Cilicia; (6) Tarsos (962–5); and (7) Antioch (966–9).

The application of force was carefully correlated with diplomatic action, in order to enhance the effectiveness of both. As is demonstrated very clearly in the Armenian dossier of the *De administrando imperio*, Byzantium had refined diplomacy into a precision tool of client management. Inducements might be offered to one prince, in the hope of stimulating a competition for Byzantine favour from others—as happened in the case of Taron.[102] Persuasion was preferred to pressurizing, conciliation to command, flexibility to rigidity in negotiations. By refraining from insisting on legal rights (as when Romanos took a single castle, in lieu of half the principality of Taron which had been bequeathed to him) or from taking punitive action against an unreliable ally (e.g. the Magistros Bagrat, who insisted on the handover of Mastaton, an outlier of Theodosiopolis, after its capture by Kourkouas in 940, and promptly returned it to the Muslims), the Byzantines fostered good will among the Armenian princes and their peoples.[103] The publicly declared aim of Byzantium was to drive out the Muslims from Armenia and to develop a strong sense of Christian fellowship with Armenian princes. It may have taken many years—much longer than any individual military campaign—but in the long run the aim was achieved and Armenian regard was obtained (we know this in the cases of John Tzimiskes and Basil II).[104]

The offensive mode of guerrilla warfare proved extraordinarily effective, but there were, of course, setbacks, principally brought about by the Hamdanid ʿAli, the future Sayf al-Dawla, and his uncle Saʿid, when they intervened north of the Armenian Taurus. The first intervention, for example, by Saʿid in 931, had the effect of drawing out the strangulation of Melitene over the best part of a decade.[105]

Melitene was designated the first target in 926, when it was attacked by the field army under the command of John Kourkouas and an auxiliary force of Armenians led by Melias, a famous border warlord. The initial devastation of the large plain around the city was followed up by wider-ranging

[102] *DAI*, c.43.49–88.

[103] *DAI*, cc.43.163–86, 45.142–53.

[104] Tzimiskes: Stepʿanos Tarōnecʿi Asołik, *Patmutʿiwn tiezerakan*, ed. S. Malxaseancʿ (St Petersburg, 1885), 184 (iii.8), trans. T. Greenwood, *The Universal History of Stepʿanos Tarōnecʿi* (Oxford, 2017), 236. Basil II: J.-P. Mahé, 'Basile II et Byzance vus par Grigor Narekacʿi', *TM* 11 (1991), 555–73.

[105] Canard, *Dynastie des H'amdanides*, 478–87, 733–47.

campaigns against Dvin and Samosata (927) and the Qaysite emirate of Manzikert (928). These bold actions were designed mainly for show, to deter Muslims from coming to Melitene's aid and to cultivate Armenian support, particularly from the Bagratids, whose core territories abutted Dvin, and from the Artsrunis of Vaspurakan to the east of the Qaysite emirate. Melias kept up the direct pressure on Melitene, from the two castles he had built late in the reign of Leo VI—Lykandos in the central basin of the Anti-Taurus (see Figure 3.2a and b), and Tzamandos commanding the direct route down the Tohma valley. The strategy worked. The emir was forced to submit in 929 and to agree to contribute to the Byzantine war effort. However, the balance soon shifted. Melias' attack on Asmosaton, upstream from Melitene on the Arsanias, was repulsed in 930. The following year the Hamdanid Saʿid intervened, marched on Melitene, and forced the military commission installed by Byzantium to withdraw. It took several more years of direct guerrilla harassment and indirect action, notably a second expedition into Qaysite territory by Lake Van (931), before Kourkouas and Melias returned in force and laid siege to Melitene (934).[106]

After its capitulation, the city was occupied, Muslims who refused to convert were expelled, and the emirate's territory on the west bank of the Euphrates was divided between two themes (Melitene and Charpezikion to the north). All land abandoned by its owners was appropriated and organized into an imperial *curatoria*. That set a precedent for all subsequent annexations of Muslim territory.[107] Two years passed before this creeping offensive in western Armenia was resumed, the prime target now being Asmosaton. An initial attack south in 936, conventional in character and targeted on Samosata, was probably intended to mislead the Arabs about Byzantine intentions. The evidence is thin and patchy, but it seems that the application of direct pressure on Anzitene (Melitene's eastern dependency, adjoining Asmosaton) in 937 was delegated to the Banu Habib, traditional rivals of Hamdanids, who came over to Byzantium in two groups, the first in 935. The main field army operated in the hill country north of the Arsanias, engaged in the laborious task of bringing it under effective Byzantine control (and boxing in Asmosaton from the north). This was achieved by 938, the year when Romanos struck his generous deal with the Taronites, content to receive the castle of Oulnoutin, strategically placed to

[106] Sym.Log., 136.52–3; *DAI*, *c.*50.152–8; M. Canard, *BA* II.2 *Extraits des sources arabes* (Brussels, 1950), 151–2 (date of first submission). *Cf. BA*, II.1, 257–9, 264, 266–70.

[107] Howard-Johnston, *Byzantium*, 170–5.

**Figure 3.2** Lykandos: (a) general view; (b) detail of masonry. Melias, an Armenian warlord in Byzantine service from 908, built a castle on what remained of an old Roman fort, and used it as a base from which to control the interior basin of the Anti-Taurus. The multi-coloured masonry was probably later Danishmend work.

*Source*: Alexander Sarantis.

apply more pressure on Asmosaton from the north-east. It was also the year when 'Ali intervened to relieve the pressure on Asmosaton, with an attack on Anzitene in the autumn. By the end of the following winter, however, Asmosaton was in Byzantine hands, and the focus of operations shifted to the upper Euphrates valley.[108]

Theodosiopolis, the least active of the three *jihad* bases fronting Byzantium, had been under attack by local theme forces, led by Theophilos, Strategos of Chaldia, its territory subject to repeated devastation from 930. It now became the prime target and the search was on for secure bases closer at hand than Chaldia, from which to intensify the pressure. Havjij, on the route north-east from Oulnoutin to Theodosiopolis, on the west flank of the Bingöl Dağ, was occupied (probably in winter 938–9) and the Curopalate of Iberia (who had been invested as such in Constantinople in 923) was asked to allow Byzantine troops temporarily to take over Ketzeon, from where they could intercept caravans taking supplies to Theodosiopolis. The Curopalate's refusal and the forced evacuation of Havjij in late autumn 939 eased the pressure, so that the city was able to hold out in 940, when Kourkouas closed in and, refusing to be distracted by a wide-ranging counterstrike of 'Ali's, maintained the siege for seven months. It was only in 949 that the city finally submitted.[109]

There was a dramatic change in the character of the fighting over the two decades from 942 to 962. First came a sudden drop in the level of Muslim resistance, when the Hamdanids turned their attention to Baghdad and fought the Buyids for control of Iraq (942–4). Byzantine forces were able to roam over the Jazira and to extract the Mandylion, a highly prized relic of the Passion, from Edessa.[110] Second, the fighting power of the border marches was magnified when they were united (944–7) by 'Ali, now honoured as Sayf al-Dawla, after the failure of the Baghdad venture—save for one year (958) when Sayf was distracted by a Buyid attack on Mosul.[111] Sayf was committed to the *jihad* against Byzantium, unlike the Ikshidids of Egypt who had even signed a non-aggression pact in 938. He set about raiding the annexed borderlands and the interior of Anatolia. The new regime of Constantine Porphyrogenitus responded in kind. Battles were fought, some in open country (generally won by Sayf, until a change of command

[108] *DAI*, c.43.163–88. Howard-Johnston, *Byzantium*, 225–7.

[109] Theoph.Cont., 428.3–15; *DAI*, c.45.67–94. *BA*, II.1, 284 (Havjij). Howard-Johnston, *Byzantium*, 227–9.

[110] Prasad, *Foreign Policy*, 71–2.

[111] Canard, *Dynastie des H'amdanides*, 422–52, 579–626, 795–96.

on the Byzantine side in 955), others in passes (now under Byzantine control) where Sayf suffered several defeats, the worst in 960. But beneath the surface turbulence, Byzantine forces can be seen to have pursued the same strategy of picking out key targets—Adata and Germanikeia—with attacks by the full field army. Both were captured and partially dismantled, Adata in 948, Germanikeia in 949. Patience was again required—both were reconstructed after their initial capture—and resilience—the field army was badly mauled in 953 outside Germanikeia and 954 outside Adata. Both were eventually secured for good, Adata in 957 after being attacked and damaged two years earlier, Germanikeia in the course of a campaign directed at Aleppo itself in winter 961–2.[112]

The last two targets were Tarsos and Antioch, both great prizes, which were acquired in a short-lived phase (962–9) of dominance in Cilicia and northern Syria, when the Hamdanid regime was weakened and Sayf was dying. Those were years of victorious campaigning in open country by the field army under the command of Nikephoros Phokas and John Tzimiskes. The policy of cultivating the Christians of Transcaucasia bore fruit. It is reported that large numbers of Armenians and Iberians were serving in the army which conquered Cilicia. Transfers of power at the centre went smoothly, Constantine being succeeded by his son Romanos II (959–63), Romanos by his two small sons, Basil and Constantine, who, within a few months, came under the tutelage of Nikephoros Phokas after he was raised to the throne by the army and the people of Constantinople.[113]

Patience, raiding sweeps designed to diminish available foodstuffs, and seizure of a strategically placed base—those three key elements of the cautious offensive strategy pursued over the previous two decades—were all evident in the campaigns targeted on Tarsos (962–5) and Antioch (966–9). Anazarbos, captured early in 962, commanded the central plain of Cilicia and the two cities, Adana and Mopsouestia, controlling the bridges which gave access to the eastern and western plains. A year and a half later the field army reappeared, defeated the Tarsiot force sent to contest control of the central plain, and, apparently by its mere presence, caused the population of Adana to flee to Mopsouestia. Tarsos was now cut off from the rest of the Arab border marches, save for a few months in early 964 between the arrival of 5–6,000 *jihad* volunteers from Khurasan and their departure forced by

[112] Canard, *Dynastie des H'amdanides*, 761–2, 770–2, 775–7, 779–80, 793–4, 808; Prasad, *Foreign Policy*, 90–2, 98–124.

[113] Skyl., 248–61; Leo D., i.2, ii.10, iii.4–8.

dearth of supplies. When Mopsouestia fell on 15 July 965 after the second of two Byzantine sieges, Tarsos was doomed and, rather than resisting to the last, surrendered on terms (the Tarsiot *jihad*-fighters were allowed to leave with their weapons).[114]

There was only one sweeping campaign before Byzantine forces concentrated on Cilicia—a surprise attack on Aleppo in December 962. Sayf was forced to flee south. His suburban palace was ransacked and demolished. The city surrendered and was occupied (and looted) for seven days.[115] It was a dramatic demonstration of Byzantine military power, which prompted a charismatic preacher in Mayyafariqin to preach *jihad* and led to the formation of the Khurasani force which appeared in 964. In the case of Antioch, which could not be isolated like Tarsos, such sweeping campaigns assumed greater importance. One was carried out in 966, causing extensive damage in the Jazira to the east, a second in 968 to the south, up the Orontes valley. The castle of Bagras on the Amanus mountains to the west was then seized, refortified, and garrisoned, to keep up the pressure from the winter of 968–9, so successfully that its garrison was able to take Antioch on 28 October 969.[116]

With the fall of Antioch, the sustained outward drive in the Middle East came to an end. It has been analysed in some detail because it demonstrates the adaptability and subtlety of Byzantine statecraft in the sphere of war-making. The risks of failure were virtually eliminated. Expenditure of men and matériel was minimized. So too was the risk of igniting the ever-glowing embers of *jihad* in the Islamic world. By breaking the strategic offensive down into a series of limited campaigns, and by extending the operations of those campaigns over several years, the Byzantines limited the shock given to Muslims. The exception—the attack on Aleppo in 962—demonstrated all too clearly the danger of bold initiatives.

The seizure of power by Constantine Porphyrogenitus in December 944–January 945 did not lead to any alteration to Romanos' strategy in the Middle East, despite the natural inclination of Constantine to mark the beginning of his personal rule with new initiatives. He commissioned the two official histories of the ninth century which spotlit the achievements

[114] W. Garrood, 'The Byzantine Conquest of Cilicia and the Hamdanids of Aleppo, 959–965', *Anatolian Studies*, 58 (2008), 127–40, at 132–3, 135–8.

[115] Garrood, 'Conquest of Cilicia', 133–5.

[116] Howard-Johnston, *Byzantium*, 232–3.

of his grandfather Basil I.[117] In foreign affairs, he did not seek reparations for the Rus attack of 941, but renewed, on slightly different terms, the commercial treaty negotiated by his father, Leo VI. He took a softer line than Romanos with the Bulgars, investing Symeon's son Peter with the title Emperor of the Bulgars. Further afield he negotiated an understanding with the Umayyads of Spain, which led to the deployment of substantial forces in the central Mediterranean, for two joint attacks on the Fatimids in north Africa and subsequent defensive operations (951–2, 956–8). The only significant effect on policy in the Middle East was a reluctance to take major initiatives by sea until peace was signed with the Fatimids in 958. The exception—an expedition dispatched against Crete in 949 (which was defeated)—was more apparent than real. It was time-limited and intended to cause damage, not to conquer the island.[118]

By contrast, there was a major reorientation of policy after the assassination of Nikephoros Phokas by John Tzimiskes and his fellow-conspirators on the night of 10–11 December 969. Given that John was Nikephoros' nephew on his mother's side and his chosen successor as supreme commander in the Middle East, and given too that he was backed by senior military commanders like Michael Bourtzes and Isaac Brachamios, it is almost certain that the coup was occasioned by important policy differences as well as the growing unpopularity of Nikephoros' government. The fiscal demands of the war effort, a sharp rise in the price of bread, and his increasingly high-handed behaviour towards the governing elite all contributed to his unpopularity, but it was probably his move to take control over episcopal appointments and the transformation of the palace into a fortified citadel which roused most opposition.[119] The catalyst, though, for the violent coup was, I suspect, a fundamental disagreement over foreign policy.

Nikephoros discarded the caution ingrained in Romanos' offensive strategy. It was he who commanded the expedition to Aleppo in 962 which triggered *jihad* fever. Two years later, one of his first initiatives as emperor was to send off a large naval and military task force to Sicily, apparently to begin the process of expelling the Muslims. It ended in disaster, the land and naval forces being annihilated in turn. In the Middle East his stance was more aggressive, with attacks launched away from the main theatre of war in

[117] I. Ševčenko, 'Re-reading Constantine Porphyrogenitus', in J. Shepard & S. Franklin, eds., *Byzantine Diplomacy* (Aldershot, 1992), 167–95, at 172–4,184–8.

[118] Prasad, *Foreign Policy*, 92–8, 154–61, 231–3, 237–40, 287–93.

[119] Whittow, *Orthodox Byzantium*, 349–54. *Cf.* R. Morris, 'The two Faces of Nikephoros Phokas', *BMGS* 12 (1988), 83–115, at 87–8, 95–100, 108–15.

Cilicia and northern Syria—against Cyprus, to end the condominium with the Caliphate (965), and against Manzikert after the prince of Taron ceded his principality to Byzantium (966).[120] Finally—and this surely was the overambitious act which precipitated the political crisis—he stirred up the Balkans in 967, provoking the Bulgars to declare war and calling in the Rus to deal with them (as they did in late 968). Byzantium's position of growing strength in the Middle East had been transformed by the second half of 969 into one of extreme parlousness, with the Rus ensconced in Bulgaria, perilously close to Byzantium's home waters, and the principal expansionist power of Islam, the Fatimid imamate, in control of Egypt (taken over peacefully in the summer).[121]

The regimes which followed, those of John Tzimiskes (969–76), of Basil the Chamberlain on behalf of the young Basil II (976–85), and of Basil II himself (985–1025), reverted to a more conventional foreign policy. Its hallmarks were the concentration of resources—military, diplomatic, and propaganda—on one front at a time, and the use of force to press home a diplomatic point as much as to gain new ground. The restraint characteristic of Romanos' strategy was cast aside, now that Byzantium was a power more than capable of holding its own against regional rivals in the Middle East. It was only in the Balkans that the guerrilla mode of warfare was still used in what turned out to be a long counterinsurgency campaign against a recidivist Bulgar regime.

The priorities were not those of the dark age. It was the danger posed by a powerful Rus force based in the old Bulgar heartland of the north-east Balkans which had to be confronted first, as it was by John Tzimiskes in a hard-fought orthodox campaign in 971. Defeated in open battle and blockaded in Dristra on the Danube, the Rus leader, Svyatoslav, prince of Kiev, agreed, at a summit meeting, to abandon the venture and to return home. He was killed when the Rus were intercepted on the Dniepr by the Pechenegs.[122] The next task was to consolidate Byzantine gains in the Arab marches south of the Taurus and Anti-Taurus mountains, and to push out into the upper Tigris basin. Aleppo had been neutralized and turned into a protectorate immediately after Tzimiskes' coup, ceding territory in the west and north.[123] Three campaigns, two commanded by Tzimiskes in person

[120] Step'anos Taronec'i, 757.26–8, trans. Greenwood, 235.
[121] Franklin & Shepard, *Emergence of Rus*, 145–8; Brett, *Fatimid Empire*, 77–80.
[122] Franklin & Shepard, *Emergence of Rus*, 148–51.
[123] Canard, *H'amdanides*, 832–7.

(972, 974), one by the Domestic of the Scholai (973, a failure), made Byzantine designs on the Jazira very clear, and achieved their aim of deterring the Buyids from intervening. A whirlwind campaign south of Antioch in 975 served a similar deterrent purpose vis-à-vis the Fatimids, warning them that they should not encroach on the Byzantine bridgehead in northern Syria (as they had done in 970–1).[124]

Byzantium's military expansion in northern Syria and the Jazira was brought to a halt in 976 when a great rebellion broke out in eastern Anatolia, headed by a distinguished general, Bardas Skleros. Subsequent actions would be mainly defensive—as in 983 and 985 when Byzantine forces fended off Fatimid probes against Aleppo and Balanias on the Orontes.[125] The regime of Basil the Chamberlain took time to recover from a serious defeat at the hand of the rebel forces in 976 or 977 and had to resort to the exiled leader of a rival Anatolian aristocratic nexus, Bardas Phokas, and through him to the Curopalate of Iberia, to assemble an army capable of defeating the rebels (979).[126] The main thrust of Basil II's foreign policy became clear when his first important act after seizing power was to march into Bulgaria (see Figure 3.3). His priority lay in the Balkans, where a Bulgar insurgency had been spreading from its centre in Macedonia and had reached Serdike, on the edge of its old core territory in the north-east. Serdike was Basil's objective in 986. The crushing defeat which he suffered on the return march through the mountains hardened his resolve to concentrate on the Balkan enemy, but also confronted him with a second great Anatolian rebellion (987–9), led this time by Bardas Phokas, which was only defeated with the help of a large contingent of Rus.[127] When it was over, it took four years of successful Fatimid operations in northern Syria (991–4) before Basil could be drawn east to break the siege of Aleppo in May 995, returning in 999 to put on a show of force (a thrust south towards Baalbek) before negotiating a ten-year truce in 1001 (subsequently renewed in 1011 and 1023).[128]

North of the Taurus and Armenian Taurus mountains, Basil maintained the policy of cultivating the Christian princes of Transcaucasia, which had

[124] Canard, *H'amdanides*, 838–44; P. E. Walker, 'The "Crusade" of John Tzimisces in the Light of New Arabic Evidence', *Byz.* 47 (1977), 301–27; A. Kaldellis, 'Did Ioannes I Tzimiskes Campaign in the East in 974?', *Byzantion*, 84 (2014), 235–40, who answers no but leaves the year blank.

[125] Whittow, *Orthodox Byzantium*, 367–68; Brett, *Fatimid Empire*, 120–1.

[126] Holmes, *Basil II*, 450–7.

[127] Holmes, *Basil II*, 458–61, 491–3.

[128] Whittow, *Orthodox Byzantium*, 379–81; Brett, *Fatimid Empire*, 121–4, 126–7.

**Figure 3.3** Frontispiece of Psalter of Basil II.
*Source*: Bridgeman.

formed a key part of Romanos' wider strategy and which had been pungently expressed in the triumphal letter sent by John Tzimiskes to the Bagratid prince Ashot III, recounting the successes of his 975 campaign and his (fanciful) wish to have gone on to Jerusalem.[129] The high esteem in

[129] Matthew of Edessa, *Zhamanakagrut'iwn*, ed. M. Melik-Adamian & N. Ter-Mik'ayelian (Etchmiadzin, 1898), i.19–20, trans. A. E. Dostourian, *Armenia and the Crusades, Tenth to Twelfth Centuries: The Chronicle of Matthew of Edessa* (Lanham, Maryland, 1993).

which Basil was held in Armenia testifies to his success, as do the cessions of territory which he obtained on his two progresses in Transcaucasia—the territory in Tao of the Curoplate David (1000) and Vaspurakan (1021–2). Any military action by local forces continued to be targeted on Muslim enclaves—for example the Marwanid emirate of Van and the Diyar Bekr in 990.[130]

But the main military effort throughout his personal rule was directed against the Bulgars. Like other counterinsurgency wars, there were few notable engagements. Those picked up by the sources were fought in 997 (a victory won by Nikephoros Ouranos which halted a planned Bulgar invasion of Greece) and 1014 (a decisive victory in a pass north of Thessalonike). Of Basil's direct involvement after 986, we only know that he was in charge of operations for four years after his return from the Middle East (1001–4) when Thessaly, Serdike, and the key central zone extending from Berroia and Vodena in the south to Vidin on the Danube were recovered. It took another 14 years before the leaders of the local resistance were ready to submit, and Basil made a ceremonial progress through the Balkans.[131]

Finally Basil shifted his attention west, to the central Mediterranean. He was planning to send an expeditionary force to Sicily when he died in December 1025. His aims were probably to improve the security of Calabria and Apulia and to begin the long process of recovering the island, which controlled traffic between the western and eastern basins of the Mediterranean.[132] We may conjecture that he would then have turned back to the Middle East to resume the outward drive halted in 976. There were no natural features barring the way south-east into the Jazira, say to Edessa, or south towards Palestine. The southward percolation of Armenians into Cilicia, northern Syria, and the Jazira, encouraged by Byzantium and facilitated by the expulsion of resolute Muslims from conquered cities, was slowly shifting the demographic balance and eroding Muslim predominance. Armenian numbers were such by the second half of the eleventh century that they were able to establish an independent kingdom in Cilicia, to form a corps in the Egyptian army, and to provide five of the most effective and militarily competent vizirs for the Fatimid caliphs.[133]

Basil's great achievement was the effective subjection of the whole Balkan peninsula to Byzantine rule. A small number of strategically placed

[130] Whittow, *Orthodox Byzantium*, 382–6.
[131] Whittow, *Orthodox Byzantium*, 386–9. *Cf.* Holmes, *Basil II*, 493–501.
[132] Holmes, *Basil II*, 503–7.
[133] Brett, *Fatimid Empire*, 205–23, 228–31, 237–40, 251–2, 263–5, 267–74.

garrisons, at Skopje and along the Danube above the Iron Gates, secured control of the central third and provided the necessary force to back the authority of the emperor over the local clients left in place in Croatia, Dalmatia, and northern Serbia. The system of themes and higher-level ducal commands put in place in the old heartlands after the expulsion of the Rus was extended westward to the Morava–Vardar gap on the edge of Macedonia. Careful attention to local sensibilities was evident in the decision not to impose money taxes and to designate the see of Ochrid, the former rebel capital, an autocephalous metropolitanate.

Byzantium was once again indisputably a great power, equal if not superior to the Fatimid empire centred on Egypt. The future looked good. Its armies were feared in the Islamic world. The poet Firdawsi, writing for the Ghaznavid sultan, preferred discretion to truth when he erased the triumphs of a great Roman emperor, Heraclius, from the last part of his great epic poem. From the Ghaznavids in eastern Iran to the Ottonians in central Europe and the Norman colonists in north-west France, the world was aware of the resurgent Roman empire.

*Byzantium in a Changing World*. James Howard-Johnston, Oxford University Press.
 DOI: 10.1093/9780191999093.003.0004

# 4
# Byzantium at its Apogee

Byzantium could not shake off its past. The generations of combat with its great, predatory, ideologically charged neighbour exerted a strong gravitational pull on its culture as well as its institutions and social order. The pull of a remoter classical past was weaker but still sensible and was increasingly felt as the demands of war diminished from the 860s. The tension in the military sinews of the dark-age state began to ease. Private interest—inherent in most of humanity and rampant in late antiquity—began to compete with pursuit of the common good. Inherited culture which had been pared down to a bare minimum began to broaden and diversify. The service aristocracy of the dark age became more concerned with perpetuating itself, seeking to solidify its status by investing in land. The pressing issues of the present which had dominated minds began to yield ground to leisure pursuits. The consequent revitalization of art, architecture, literature, and learning was first clearly discernible in the reign of Theophilos (829–42). It gathered way under the new Macedonian dynasty, in the late ninth and tenth centuries, gaining extra impetus from the patronage of Leo VI and Constantine Porphyrogenitus. It was underpinned by steady growth in the economy, which, to judge by the monetary output of the state and the level of commercial exchange, reached its acme in the middle of the eleventh century.[1]

## 4.1 Governing class

Before turning to the various ways in which Byzantine culture expressed itself in its heyday, something should be said about the social milieux involved. The court remained the central arena of political life. The favour of the emperor and his immediate entourage played a determining part in the careers of individuals in government service, but family, family connections, and clientages were increasingly important. While talent was recognized and promoted, members of established families with distinguished

[1] Howard-Johnston, *Byzantium*, 146–51, 245, 247–94.

pedigrees reaching back, in some cases, to the late eighth or early ninth century, had expectations of preferment which could not be ignored. The increasing use of surnames, universal among the official classes by the middle of the eleventh century, signalled a solidification of status among those recognized as the 'powerful' in Byzantium, namely current or past office-holders, as well as the exceptional few who preferred to live quietly on their estates and those successful in trade, especially in Constantinople.[2]

Byzantine autocracy was thus moderated by the collective power of the aristocracy, which, at the same time, was building up its economic power at the expense of the peasantry, recognized since the Isaurian period as the fundamental social constituent of the state. The scene was set for a head-on confrontation between the crown and the 'powerful', in which the crown applied intense moral pressure as well as the force of Roman law on what were portrayed as voracious predators. That battle was won, to my mind, by the crown by the early eleventh century, with the additional help of Armenian princes and their followings resettled in eastern Asia Minor, where they acted as a counterbalance to the traditionally dominant indigenous military families.[3] But the whole complexion of the social order continued to change, not so much in relation to the peasantry, as within the governing elites themselves, powerful families weaving increasingly extensive webs of connections to create formidable nexuses of affinities, clientages, and allies. The response of the authorities was to make full use of their powers of patronage (i.e. freezing out the most dangerous nexuses), and to encourage intermarriage between the provincial, traditionally military families and those staffing the departments of state in Constantinople, thereby making it easier to apply pressure on the former. The result was an uneasy balance between emperor and magnate amalgams of civil and military lineages, all too evident in the third quarter of the eleventh century.[4]

Military success in the tenth century had the effect, not that paradoxical, of inaugurating a substantial demilitarization of Byzantium. Once again, as in the Roman past, military forces were concentrated in frontier zones under the command of regional dukes. The old heartland in Asia Minor, now distanced from potential theatres of war, reverted to a civil system of provincial government under magistrates, endowed with judicial as well as

[2] Cheynet, 'L'aristocratie byzantine', 282–98.

[3] Howard-Johnston, *Byzantium*, 162–214.

[4] J.-C. Cheynet, 'Transformations in Byzantine Society in the Eleventh Century, Particularly in Constantinople', in J. Howard-Johnston, ed., *Social Change in Town and Country in Eleventh-Century Byzantium* (Oxford, 2020), 16–43, at 20–5, 30–1.

administrative authority.[5] The office of provincial judge, with the influence and patronage which it brought, became a regular part of the *cursus honorum* of non-military families and contributed to the extension of nexuses of allies in the apparatus of government, as becomes abundantly plain from their correspondence. Judges and higher officialdom in general (and its clerical equivalent, the episcopate) loomed increasingly large in the life of Byzantium. The education which qualified young men for government service (and for the upper echelons of the church) equipped them with the literary skills and independence of mind characteristic of men of letters. They went on to exercise them away from their offices and to dominate the intellectual and literary life of Byzantium.[6]

Contemporary poetry and letters take us into the thought-world of this important segment of the governing class in the eleventh century, bound together by shared professional and literary interests. We find poets acknowledging presents from friends, commenting on unusual incidents (a procession which ended in a stampede, a crash in the hippodrome, a fire in a cemetery . . .), devising teasing riddles, writing joke psogic epigrams about friends, fawning to a greater or lesser extent on the reigning emperor. Banter and wordplay were key characteristics of this world, and were even more marked in the letters they exchanged.[7] But these high officials were serious too—praising noted intellectuals and holy men, writing obituaries of dead friends and colleagues, grieving over close relatives in long, affectionate poems, recording dedications to churches, and allowing their faith to show in poems about church feasts, saints, and doctrine.[8] Most remarkable of all are three poems decrying inequality and worldly ambition.[9]

[5] Howard-Johnston, *Byzantium*, 239–40, 263–7.

[6] F. Bernard, *Writing and Reading Byzantine Secular Poetry, 1025–1081* (Oxford, 2014), 155–6, 160–7, 175–92; J.-C. Cheynet, 'L'administration provinciale dans la correspondance de Michel Psellos', in M. D. Lauxtermann & M. Whittow, eds., *Byzantium in the Eleventh Century: Being in Between* (Abingdon, 2017), 45–59 ; M. Jeffreys & M. D. Lauxtermann, eds., *The Letters of Psellos: Cultural Networks and Historical Realities* (Oxford, 2017), 435–41 (M. Jeffreys, 'Psellos' Network of Non-Military Administrators').

[7] F. Bernard & C. Livanos, ed. & trans., *The Poems of Christopher of Mytilene and John Mauropous* (Cambridge, MA, 2018): presents—CM 45, 87–8, 110, 115, 117: incidents—CM 1, 6, 52, 82, 90, 136; riddles—CM 21, 35, 47, 56, 71, 111, JM 60; banter—CM 2, 4, 20, 31, 37, 84–5, 114, 132; fawning—CM 18, 24, 54–5, JM 54–5.

[8] Praise—CM 15, 27, 30, 61; funerary poems—CM 16, 44, 57–60, 72, 77, JM 36–9. John Mauropous includes many poems about icons, dedications and faith in his collection, but Christopher also allows his faith to show (3, 5, 25, 28 33–4, 41, 74, 80, 89, 93, 101, 106, 121, 123, 126, 128, 133, 139, 144).

[9] CM 13, JM 91–2.

In addition to these poems, the carefully composed, elaborate letters which well-educated officials sent to each other, and the many, brilliant turns which make up Psellos' contemporary history of the palace and high politics, bring the eleventh century alive. They also represent a revival of late antique modes of expression, and were symptomatic of a general desire to reach back to the pre-dark-age past.

## 4.2 Scholarship and writing

The dark age, though, continued to lower over Byzantium. It remained a strong state, those in its service dominating intellectual and cultural life. Historical writing, for example, was, with very few exceptions, the preserve of senior officials. This explains their use of a peculiar dating system—not linear from the beginning of an era, but the cyclical system of indictions used for the fiscal management of the state.[10] Literature too was mainly produced within the higher echelons of the apparatus of government, both lay and clerical. The shining lights of the eleventh century, who have already been cited, writers of literature in the purest form of poetry, were a high court judge (Christopher of Mytilene), a brilliant intellectual and government minister (Michael Psellos), and a metropolitan bishop (John Mauropous).[11] Scholarship was more the preserve of clerics—think of the role of high churchmen like John Grammatikos, Leo the Philosopher, Photios, and Arethas in initiating the recovery of ancient knowledge in the ninth century.[12] Until the twelfth century when a class of professional *littérateurs* emerged and survived on the patronage of fifty to sixty households, literature and scholarship were mandarin pursuits.[13]

A second peculiar feature of the Byzantine cultural world—not unique, it is true, but without parallel in contemporary Islam and Latin Christendom—was the concentration of literary and intellectual activity in Constantinople. Provincial cities, headed by Thessalonike, Ephesos, Trebizond, and Attaleia, were growing through the ninth, tenth, and eleventh centuries, but intellectuals and writers were drawn inexorably towards

[10] Howard-Johnston, *Historical Writing*, 33–5, 42.

[11] Bernard, *Writing and Reading*, 19–25.

[12] P. Lemerle, *Le premier humanisme byzantin: notes et remarques sur enseignement et culture à Byzance des origines au Xe siècle* (Paris, 1971), 135–241.

[13] P. Magdalino, *The Empire of Manuel I Komnenos, 1143–1180* (Cambridge, 1993), 336–56.

court and capital, in what had become, in the dark age, an extraordinarily centralized state.

A third feature, by no means odd in the contemporary context but in sharp contrast to the pluralism of the late antique empire, was the strength of Byzantium's Orthodox faith and its pervasive influence. Byzantines, all too conscious of their weakness and vulnerability, had relied on supernatural aid in the dark age. Knowing themselves to be a latter-day Israel, the favoured people of the sole, supreme deity who presided over the cosmos and all earthly affairs, they strove to obey God's commands and used all available means to gain and retain his favour. In some ways they were as submissive, as Muslims, to the divine will. With the restoration of icons and the reassertion of the intermediary role of supernatural personages (the Mother of God, archangels, martyrs, saints of all sorts), there were many more channels through which to invoke divine aid. It was in the tenth and eleventh centuries that the cult of military saints spread far and wide.[14] They might have specific local attachments, but they were mobile and could act as regional protectors. Another product of the dark age, the holy mountain, to which monks withdrew from the lay countryside, was put to use as a sort of intercessory loudspeaker, to send up the massed prayers of the holiest among Byzantines for divine help at times of serious crisis.[15]

The classical past still lurked in the Byzantine thought-world. Byzantines were Romans, heirs of a pan-Mediterranean empire (dimly remembered for the most part), and spoke and wrote the language of Greece. The past was impressed on the present by great public buildings—former temples like the Parthenon and that at Didymi turned into churches, the monumental buildings constituting the ceremonial centres of cities, massive circuit walls and towers, above all the masterpiece of church architecture built by Justinian (St Sophia) and the mass of large basilica churches built in late antiquity. In the cultural sphere, it was that last phase of the classical era which loomed largest, as the era in which the new faith had gained its hold on the empire, had accommodated itself to the ambient culture, and had been articulated by the church fathers into a coherent, philosophically secure system of belief and practice. But it was perhaps rivalry with the Abbasid court which did most to turn Byzantine minds to their classical

[14] C. Walter, *The Warrior Saints in Byzantine Art and Tradition* (Aldershot, 2003), 64–6, 125–34, 274–84.

[15] A. Lidov, *Holy Mountains in the Hierotopy and Iconography of the Christian World* (Moscow, 2017).

inheritance. For the Abbasids from the first sponsored a translation programme which, in due course, enabled Islam to ingest classical knowledge in the spheres of philosophy, mathematics, science, medicine, and geography from classical texts.[16] Theophilos and Michael III responded by including the leading intellectuals of their day in embassies to Baghdad. They were clearly riled by Arab predation of their cultural heritage. At any rate it was then and over the following few generations, under the first Macedonian emperors, that Byzantium can be seen to have engaged in a retrieval programme of its own.

The efforts of Byzantine scholars both parallelled and diverged from those of their counterparts in the Caliphate. They too delved into mathematical and scientific texts, extending their interest to philosophy in the late ninth century, but their prime concerns were literary, historical, and practical. Photios, the first Byzantine to deserve to be classified as a humanist, set about exploring libraries in Byzantium and Baghdad for works of ancient literature, summarizing their contents and giving pithy judgements of his own in his *Bibliotheca*, while a younger contemporary, Leo Kephalas, assembled a large collection of classical epigrams in the *Palatine Anthology*, which reached its final form half a century later.[17] These literary interests remained at the forefront of the Byzantine drive to recover something of the past and give a classical veneer to the present. They show up in the tenth century in the huge compendium of historical material, culled from classical and late antique texts and thematically arranged, which was commissioned by Constantine Porphyrogenitus, and the late tenth-century encyclopaedia of classical lore (mythical, historical, literary) entitled the *Souda*.[18] It looks, though, as if utility was the most important guiding force—hence Leo VI's sponsorship of the full retrieval of Justinianic law, rearranged and translated into Greek in the *Basilica*, and of a well-organized compilation of classical and late antique tactical manuals (his *Tactica*);[19] and Constantine's sponsorship of similar assemblages of classical texts about agriculture and horse-medicine.[20]

[16] Gutas, *Greek Thought, Arabic Culture.*

[17] A. Németh, *The* Excerpta Constantiniana *and the Byzantine Appropriation of the Past* (Cambridge, 2018), 199–204.

[18] Lemerle, *Premier humanisme*, 280–8, 297–300.

[19] T. Antonopoulou, 'Emperor Leo VI the Wise and the "First Byzantine Humanism": On the Quest for Renovation and Cultural Synthesis', in B. Flusin & J.-C. Cheynet, eds., *Autour du* Premier humanisme byzantin *& des* Cinq études sur le XIe siècles, *quarante ans après Paul Lemerle*, *TM* 21.2 (2017), 187–233, at 188, 192–3, 207–8, 225–6.

[20] See Chapter 3, n. 37.

Writers were more susceptible than artists or architects to the influence of the classical past, above all because of the extraordinary range of texts transmitted in manuscripts and their accessibility, the language of the educated classes being an ossified form of Attic Greek. The *Excerpta* of Constantine Porphyrogenitus supplied historians, at least those at work in court circles, with a huge body of classical historical material, for quarrying and emulation. Both histories commissioned by Constantine duly looked back to the classicizing tradition of late antiquity, using the rhetorical devices developed then to embellish their texts, allowing the principal protagonists to speak to the reader (literally if they larded narrative with speeches and letters), and giving fuller accounts of key episodes in war and peace.[21] This reclassicizing of history with a biographical focus, perhaps best exemplified in Psellos' history of eleventh-century emperors and court, was to have a long future up to and beyond the fall of Constantinople in 1453.[22] Poetry too was thoroughly imbued with classicism. While some poems, such as the didactic pieces written by Psellos, were written in a metre suited to the stress patterns of medieval Greek, poetry proper was thoroughly classicizing, expressed in classical language, sometimes extraordinarily recondite, incorporating classical expressions, and employing classical metres, principally iambics. So strong, though, was the pull of the past, so influential the giant figure presiding over classical literature, that poets found themselves drawn to writing Homeric hexameters, even though extraordinary ingenuity and linguistic contortion might be required to conform to the metre. John Geometres set a high standard in the late tenth century, which was emulated by his successors in the eleventh.[23]

## 4.3 Art and architecture

A classicising trend can also be observed in the visual arts, although much less had survived from the past to inspire mosaicists, painters, ivory-carvers, etc. because of the depredation of time and iconoclasts. It was quite natural, in a backward-looking age of revival, to turn to late antiquity for such models as could be found of what was properly and truly Roman. The basic

[21] Németh, Excerpta, 145–64.

[22] *Michaelis Pselli Chronographia*, ed. D. R. Reinsch, Millennium-Studien 51, 2 vols. (Berlin, 2014).

[23] E. M. van Opstall, ed. & trans., *Jean Géomètre, Poèmes en hexamètres et en distique élégiaques* (Leiden, 2008).

and most faithful act of retrieval was reproduction on a small scale. Illuminations as well as text were copied if the original manuscript was illustrated, as for example in the cases of the *Christian Topography* of Cosmas Indicopleustes and the *Theriaca* of Nicander.[24] The most classicizing of all manuscripts is the Joshua Roll, a meticulous copy of a late antique original (identifiable as a seventh-century cartoon for a historiated column celebrating the achievements of a latter-day Joshua), probably dating from the 970s or 980s after John Tzimiskes' 975 thrust into the Holy Land. The scenes flow into each other. Brief labels indicate what is happening. The action—fighting, marching, negotiating—is performed by elegant figures, classically armed and garbed, in naturalistic landscapes.[25] In a handful of original illustrated manuscripts, efforts were made to introduce a classical veneer by including deliberately classicizing motifs into the scenes—buildings, rocks and trees in the background, statuesque poses, realistic drapery, and personifications. The classicizing drive was perhaps most marked in ivory carving, in particular in caskets with reliefs of mythological scenes clearly derived from ancient models, but at several removes. Some of the elegance of the originals has been lost, resulting in Dionysiac scenes in which the dancers have become, in Cyril Mango's happy phrase, 'heavy-looking, obese, cavorting pygmies'.[26]

This late antique classicism, sponsored from above, was most evident in highly refined verse (hexameters) and the minor arts (Figure 4.1a and b). It was a fashion of the court and the intellectual elite, which did not have much effect on the wider world. Writers of letters and speeches were, it seems, encouraged to display erudition by enriching their language with recondite vocabulary and disguising their meaning in convoluted phrasing. They wrote as much to entertain and test their audiences as to convey information. But for the most part they continued to use the pared-down Attic Greek of the dark age both at work and at leisure. As for classical artistic motifs, there was some percolation into monumental art (particularly secular cycles in palaces), but their impact was, in general, limited, especially on schemes of church decoration. The influence of the past there was less

[24] M. Kominko, *The World of Kosmas: Illustrated Byzantine Codices of the Christian Topography* (Cambridge, 2013); K. Weitzmann, *Studies in Classical and Byzantine Manuscript Illumination* (Chicago, 1971), 176–223 ('The Character and Intellectual Origins of the Macedonian Renaissance'), at 184–6.

[25] S. H. Wander, *The Joshua Roll* (Wiesbaden, 2012).

[26] Weitzmann, *Studies*, 176–84,199–205, 208–12; R. Cormack, *Byzantine Art* (Oxford, 2000), 129–33, 140; T. F. Mathews, *The Art of Byzantium* (London, 1998), 83–6.

**Figure 4.1** Minor arts in the tenth century: (a) ivory plaque of Christ blessing Constantine VII Porphyrogenitus (913–59); (b) antique sardonyx cup made into a chalice for Romanos II (959–63).

*Source*: (a) Wikimedia; (b) Wikimedia/Dimitris Kamaras.

obtrusive but extensive. Figures were elongated and given substance by modelling of the face and realistic delineation of drapery. They gazed out at the viewer from largely void spaces, solemn, still presences, as in the sixth and seventh centuries. Gospel scenes were pictured, but very much as posed tableaux. No sculptures were made, not even of emperors. There was a growing penchant for shallow relief work with intricate incised carving, abstract patterns mattering more than, say, the mythical, stylized beasts depicted. Similarly abstract, decorative panels appeared more frequently in manuscripts.

It was in architecture, though, that the break with the classical past was most marked. Instead of the grand basilicas which were the focal points of late Roman towns, the more prestigious Byzantine churches, whether lay or monastic, urban or rural, were relatively small and centralized. The plan, where the founder could afford it, was a cross-in-square, surmounted by a dome, but many small churches in Byzantine towns were simpler basilical or small rectangular structures. Instead of size, architects concentrated on intricacy of exterior decoration—complex brick patterning, recessed blind arcades, niches, narrow arched windows . . .[27] While it may be argued that there was no need for Byzantines to compete with their contemporaries in Latin Christendom and Islam, given the endowment of magnificent churches inherited from antiquity, or that the episcopate in Byzantium did not have the resources of their western counterparts, a deliberate opting out from the endemic competition between courts in the sphere of religious architecture surely required some positive motivation. It was not as if Byzantines thought small or built small when it came to secular architecture. Fine palaces dotted the countryside, impressing the power and wealth of the great magnates on the surrounding world.[28] Nor was there a lack of patrons in towns, once notables re-emerged as an important social and political force in the eleventh century. But instead of banding together to fund the construction and decoration of large congregational churches,

[27] C. Mango, *Byzantine Architecture* (London, 1986), 108–40; P. Niewöhner, 'What Went Wrong? Decline and Ruralization in Eleventh-Century Anatolia: The Archaeological Record', in Howard-Johnston, *Social Change*, 98–132, at 99–115.

[28] No material remains have been found, but they are mentioned in historical texts. From the description of Digenes Akrites' country palace (*Digenis Akritis*, ed. & trans. E. Jeffreys [Cambridge, 1998], 204–9 [Grottaferrata version, vii. 42–108]), we may infer that they were grand versions of the rock-cut courtyard houses with reception halls, chapels, and stables still standing in Cappadocia (R. Ousterhout, *Visualizing Community: Art, Material Culture, and Settlement in Byzantine Cappadocia* [Washington, DC, 2017], 275–343, 349–59).

they preferred to act individually and found small, often tiny, neighbourhood churches.[29]

The reason must surely be sought in the Byzantine thought-world. Something had changed, almost certainly because icons assumed greater prominence in Orthodoxy after the end of the long battle over their legitimacy. Attendance at the liturgy lost some importance when the devout could send up efficacious prayers independently, channelling them through the myriad icons in their houses as well as those which increasingly filled the templon screens separating sanctuaries from naves. The liturgy was becoming a more esoteric rite conducted by clergy behind the iconastasis, performing a function analogous to the prayers of holy men, *on behalf of the laity*. Only on the great feasts of the Christian calendar would the mass of the faithful attend, crowding around as well as inside the church.[30]

Churches ceased to be grand works of man, part of this world, impressing themselves on onlookers by their size. Instead they became small, otherwordly arenas, microcosms of the universe, cut off from the temporal world (Figure 4.2.) A hierarchical scheme of decoration sacralized the interior—the presiding figures were Christ Pantokrator in the central dome and the Virgin Mother in the semi-dome of the sanctuary apse, with an array of saints standing and gazing at the onlooker from the bottom register. They were all *real presences* within the fabric of the church, witnesses to the rites being performed and the living beings taking part. The upper register was filled with Gospel scenes, tableaux placed within the church itself, without illusionistic backgrounds. The action caught in the tableaux was taking place there and then. The Gospel story was not being recalled from the past, it was being *re-enacted within a sacred space outside time*, just as it was in the liturgy.[31]

The small churches of Constantinople, Asia Minor, Greece, and the islands should be viewed as centres of spiritual power scattered across the townscapes and landscapes of Byzantium, a set of sacred spaces linking earth and heaven, foci of faith and of God's regard for his special people. They

[29] Notables: M. Angold, *Byzantium 1025–1081: A Political History* (2nd edn, London), 90–1. Small churches of Kastoria: A. J. Wharton, *Art of Empire—Painting and Architecture on the Byzantine Periphery: A Comparative Study of Four Provinces* (Pennsylvania, 1988), 98–101, 112–16, 120–3, 125–6.

[30] Templon screen: Cormack, *Byzantine Art*, 150–6. Liturgy: H. Wybrew, *Orthodox Liturgy: The Development of the Eucharistic Liturgy in the Byzantine Rite* (London, 1989), 129–44, especially 133–4 & 143–4.

[31] Demus, *Byzantine Mosaic Decoration*; Mathews, *Art of Byzantium*, 111–32.

**Figure 4.2** Katholikon of Hosios Loukas: (a) interior, general; (b) interior, detail. The church was built, probably in the first half of the eleventh century, as donations poured in from pilgrims to the miraculous tomb of St Luke. It is sumptuously decorated with mosaics, carved marble, marble revetment, and stucco.
*Source*: author.

were performing the same function as had the sacred fires of Sasanian Iran in late antiquity, carefully insulated from the secular world but irradiating the world with protective divine power. They were playing a crucial part in securing the survival and prosperity of Byzantium and the salvation of its citizens, great and small. Byzantium was profoundly Christian, and remained so, for all the froth of a phase of free-thinking in the eleventh century.

## 4.4 Threats from without

The great Christian power of the Middle East was reduced to a bloodied, battered, and enfeebled state in the course of the eleventh century. Its decline, manifest both in debasement of the gold coinage and loss of territory, accelerated after 1050, dramatically so in the 1070s.[32] The chief agents

[32] C. Morrison, 'Revisiter le XIe siècle quarante ans après: expansion et crise', in Flusin-Cheynet, *Autour*, *TM* 21/2 (Paris, 2017), 611–25.

of change were not policy-makers at home. There were, it is true, more frequent changes of regime than in the tenth century, but the main lines of foreign policy, in terms of both aims and methods (an amalgam of propaganda, diplomacy, and armed force), remained the same. At home there was no easing of the legal pressure on predatory landowners and no general disregard of the financial needs of the state, and in particular of defence funding. It was rather the threats from without—from north, west, and east—which put increasing strain on Byzantine resources, until they precipitated political crisis and near-collapse in the 1070s.

One threat, that posed by the Pechenegs from across the Danube, was familiar. The strengths and weaknesses of nomad federations were well known, from centuries of experience following the entry of the Huns into the Roman field of vision in the fourth century. The Pechenegs themselves, of great potential diplomatic value to Byzantium because of their strategic position, had been closely observed from their first appearance on the Pontic steppes in the 890s. Intelligence doubtless continued to be gathered (after the composition of the *De administrando imperio* in the middle of the tenth century) about general conditions in the steppes, where the Oghuz Turks were applying growing pressure on the Pechenegs from the east. The evolution of the artificial tribal system imposed by the Khazars on the Pechenegs would also have been of particular interest, because of the internal stresses which might be generated.[33] Both resulting phenomena, insecurity and instability, probably lay behind a new aggressive stance discernible soon after the death of Basil II. A first raiding expedition targeted Bulgaria in 1027 (effectively countered), to be followed by a bout of sustained raiding deeper into the interior (to Macedonia and Thrace) between 1033 and 1036. The response of the Byzantine authorities was sensible: it was to prepare for an influx of Pechenegs and their subsequent containment in designated settlement areas, by strengthening the fortresses on the Danube, by concentrating the provincials in major fortified centres, and by promoting trade at *emporia* on the Danube. There were several subsequent crises, involving large-scale fighting, but the policy proved effective in the long run.[34]

The second threat from without was both novel and recognizable. Byzantium was aware of the fierce fighting capability of Vikings, having had to withstand two attacks in force by the Rus on the metropolitan area (860 and 941). But the transfer of those qualities to purely land warfare, achieved

[33] *DAI*, c. 37, with Howard-Johnston, 'Byzantine Sources for Khazar History', 186–91.

[34] P. Stephenson, *Byzantium's Balkan Frontier: A Political Study of the Northern Balkans, 900–1204* (Cambridge, 2000), 82–9.

in Normandy, was unknown until the early eleventh century. Then something extraordinary happened. Bands of Norman fighting-men began appearing in larger and larger numbers in southern Italy. There was no swooping attack by the equivalent of a large raiding fleet, but rather infiltration by notional crews of individual warships. Warbands, at most a few hundred strong, made their way south, led by exiled nobles and adventurers aware of the glory and material gains to be made in a politically fragmented region. As their numbers grew, the Normans came to constitute a new military elite, acknowledged as such after demonstrating their striking power against Arab raiders (possibly as early as 999 at Salerno), against rival Lombard principalities (namely Salerno, Capua, and Naples, 1024–38) and against the Byzantine authorities (from 1017–18 when they supported the second rebellion of Meles).[35]

This migration over long distances from northern Europe to the southern extremities of Italy was a distant precursor of the Crusades. As in the case of the Crusades, an agent was needed to mobilize a warrior culture and ready it for a distant venture. The agent was almost certainly the same. For the papal states had suffered badly at the hands of Arab sea-raiders in the ninth century and remained wary of Arab (now Fatimid) naval power through the tenth and into the eleventh. The principal justification for enticing the Normans south was, almost certainly, the defence of Christendom, but there were subsidiary motives, above all assertion of papal authority over the churches of the Byzantine provinces and over the refractory Lombard duchy of Benevento.[36] Once their numbers had built up, the Normans were able to turn the fortunes of war in favour first of one side, then of another in Campania and to push step by step into Byzantine territory. They relied on strongholds, built from scratch or captured and strengthened, to project authority over the surrounding countryside. The methods used by the Byzantines on the Arab marches in the tenth century were now put to work against them in southern Italy. They were to prove all too effective.[37]

The Oghuz Turks were the third and most dangerous enemy to come into view from the 1040s. They were as familiar as Pechenegs *qua* northern steppe nomads, but more numerous and less organized than the great

[35] G.A. Loud, *The Age of Robert Guiscard: Southern Italy and the Norman Conquest* (London, 2000), 60–8, 72–6, 83–91; G. Noyé, New Light on the Society of Byzantine Italy', in J. Howard-Johnston, ed., *Social Change in Town and Country in Eleventh-Century Byzantium* (Oxford, 2020), 157–95, at 186–7.

[36] Loud, *Robert Guiscard*, 62–3.

[37] Loud, *Robert Guiscard*, 124, 126; Noyé, 'New Light', 159, 192–3.

federations which had dominated the eastern approaches to Iran in the past. When the caliphal embassy on which Ibn Fadlan served crossed the steppes separating Khwarezm (the fertile region south of the Aral Sea) from the Volga in 922, the Oghuz were the most numerous and widely scattered of the nomads they encountered. It looks as if their supreme leader, the *yabghu*, exercised no more than a loose authority over them.[38] When they came into contact with Byzantium over a century later, they brought to bear the raw energy of nomad warbands. They are conventionally called Turkmen. They came in large numbers, unimpeded by natural barriers, like the Danube delimiting the Pontic steppes or the continuous mountain rampart to the north of the Fertile Crescent which the Arabs had had to cross to reach Armenia and Asia Minor. They brought the fighting prowess of the northern nomad, with which Byzantines were all too familiar. The mounted warrior, armed with a reflex bow, operating in small units (the cavalry equivalent of a legionary maniple), and with impressive stamina, endowed larger and smaller Turkish forces with firepower, tactical flexibility, and strategic mobility which it was hard for any Byzantine army to match. Freed of the need for secure lines of communications, they could bypass the fixed defences held by Byzantine troops in Iberia and Armenia and flow on westward into Asia Minor.[39]

There was a second distinct element to the Turkish threat, besides that of the Turkmen warbands—a ruling *dynasty* which was able to project more effective authority than had *yabghus* in the past. The founder, Seljuk, had direct experience of organized states. He had served as a military commander in the Khazar khaganate, and played a part in its destruction at the hands of the Rus in the 960s. He then withdrew with his followers to Khwarezm where he converted to Islam and seems to have challenged the authority of the *yabghu*. He left and served as a client of the Samanids in their war against the Qarakhanids of Central Asia. He and his following, growing in size as he drew more and more Turks into his service, were granted summer and winter pastures in Transoxiana.[40] The mutually reinforcing processes of building up prestige and attracting larger numbers of followers were well underway. They would continue for many decades to come, as the Turks were pushed westward in the 1020s and 1030s into Iran

[38] *Risalat ibn Fadlan*, ed. S. Dahhan (Damascus, 1959), 91–103, trans. P. Lunde & C. Stone, *Ibn Fadlan and the Land of Darkness: Arab Travellers in the Far North* (London, 2012), 11–16.
[39] A. C. S. Peacock, *The Great Seljuk Empire* (Edinburgh, 2015), 22–4.
[40] Peacock, *Great Seljuk Empire*, 3, 24–7.

by the Ghaznavids, after they gained control of Transoxiana.[41] The Seljuk leaders, designated sultans, gathered a large, organized body of Turks around them and acted as the directing intelligences among the relatively amorphous mass of Turkmen. Then as the dynasty itself fractured, those cousins who challenged the sultan would build up their own followings and exercise a loose directing role over rival Turkmen groupings. Dynastic rivalry would impart an additional dynamic to Turkish/Turkmen expansion.[42]

## 4.5 Domestic and foreign affairs, 1025–55

Such were the three principal threats to Byzantium in the eleventh century. There were, of course, other potential adversaries—first and foremost Fatimid Egypt, Byzantium's chief rival in the Mediterranean and Levant; but also the Rus if ever they were to prefer raiding to trading; the German empire; and, within the Balkans, Bulgars, Serbs, and Croats, only recently subjected to Byzantine rule. The prime task of maintaining the empire's security was a far from easy one. Many skills, managerial, diplomatic, and military, would be needed by eleventh-century emperors, who owed their elevation more to the choices made by Basil II's nieces, Zoe and Theodora, and to the vagaries of court politics, than to their talents. Their collective performance, nonetheless, was more than commendable.

Basil II, who never married, was succeeded by his brother Constantine VIII (1025–8), who chose as his successor Romanos III Argyros (1028–34), member of a distinguished Anatolian military family who had made his own career in the law. Marriage to Constantine's elder daughter, Zoe, sealed his position. His reign is notable for the abrogation of the one piece of social legislation by Basil II which went too far and used the fiscal system to penalize the *powerful*, and for a vain attempt to garner prestige from a military venture in the Levant. In 1030 Romanos took personal command of an expedition against the satellite emirate of Aleppo, with the aim of imposing direct rule. It was a fiasco, and concerted pressure by frontier dukes was needed to reassert Byzantine authority in 1031 and to extract the annual tribute payment due from Aleppo. Seizure of Edessa a year later by a fine general, George Maniakes, Strategos of Telouch, showed the wider world that Byzantium was still bent on expansion.[43]

[41] Peacock, *Great Seljuk Empire*, 28–39.

[42] Peacock, *Great Seljuk Empire*, 40–3, 44–6, 50–4.

[43] Angold, *Byzantine Empire*, 31–2. Sources: Psellos, iii.4, 7–11; Skyl., 375, 379–83, 384–5, 387 (trans., 311, 315–21).

Romanos died shortly before Easter 1034. The hexameter poem about his death written by Christopher of Mytilene hints at something untoward, noting how suddenly he died and how quickly he was forgotten, after Zoe organized his funeral and married a second husband, Michael IV (1034–41). Clearly Zoe was not an entirely free agent. Michael was the brother of John the Orphanotrophos, the dominant figure in the civil administration, who had been held in high esteem by Basil II. The new regime, involving John, Michael, and two other brothers, is praised by Christopher for reaching out in all four directions of the compass and for managing several aspects of government (military, sporting, educational, and charitable).[44] It was responsible for a new foreign policy initiative, the resumption of Basil II's last project, the reconquest of Sicily.

Maniakes was put in charge and achieved considerable success over the two years of his command from 1038, winning an important victory in 1040 after which he captured Syracuse and took control of the eastern part of the island. Things then went wrong. The Norman contingent pulled out of the expeditionary force. Maniakes was recalled and replaced by incompetent commanders. There were risings against Byzantine rule in Taranto and Bari, the latter led by Meles' son Argyros. Then, in early March 1041, the Norman troops from Sicily, reinforced with Normans and Lombards from Campania and Benevento, reappeared on the frontier between the principality of Salerno and Apulia. They seized the key stronghold of Melfi and three nearby towns, and went on to inflict three defeats on Byzantine forces, despite the recall of troops from Sicily. Those left in Sicily were defeated. All Maniakes' gains were lost except for Messina. Apulia too was temporarily lost as the principal towns on the coast gave up resistance and submitted.[45] A grim situation was made worse when trouble erupted in Bulgaria, resentment at the imposition of money taxes triggering a revolt (1040–1) led by a supposed affine of the Bulgar royal house, Peter Deljan.[46]

This was the first occasion in the eleventh century when there was a convergence of crises. They were capped by political instability at the centre, after the death of Michael IV (10 December 1041). His designated successor, his nephew Michael V, who had been adopted by the Empress Zoe, proved hot-headed and overambitious. He sought to free himself of encumbrances (John the Orphanotrophos, the power behind the throne; Zoe, the symbol

[44] Cheynet, *Pouvoir et contestations*, 264–5, 273–4. Sources: CM, 8, 18–19; Psellos, *Chron.*, iii.26; Skyl., 390–2 (trans., 323–5).

[45] Loud, *Robert Guiscard*, 77–80, 92–4.

[46] Stephenson, *Byzantium's Balkan Frontier*, 130–1. Sources: Psellos, *Chron.*, iv.39–44; Skyl., 409–12 (trans., 338–41).

of dynastic continuity; and the Patriarch Alexios Stoudites) and turned for support to the people of Constantinople. It was a serious miscalculation. The Macedonian dynasty, which had achieved so much, inspired strong loyalty, especially among the inhabitants of the capital. At the announcement of Zoe's exile, they rose up and attacked the palace. Michael fled to the Stoudios monastery, where he was dragged from the church and blinded (21 April 1042). Zoe and her sister Theodora, at odds and backed by different factions, took personal charge of the government for a few weeks, until Zoe chose a third husband and had him made emperor (12 June 1042). He was a distinguished senator, Constantine Monomachos, who was related to two of the great Anatolian magnate families, the Argyroi and Skleroi (Figure 4.3).[47] As Constantine IX (1042–55) he was to prove a competent emperor, who

**Figure 4.3** Hagia Sophia, mosaic of Zoe and Constantine IX Monomachos (1042–55).
*Source*: Wikimedia/Myrabella.

[47] Angold, *Byzantine Empire*, 56–8; Cheynet, *Contestations et pouvoir*, 192–3, 267, 269, 273–4. Sources: Psellos, *Chron.*, v; Skyl., 416–23 (trans., 345–52).

managed to fend off the first serious attacks by Turks and Pechenegs and to launch a political and military counteroffensive against the Normans in southern Italy. First, though, he had to surmount two new crises—the rebellion of Maniakes who had been reappointed to his Italian command, and a Rus attack on Constantinople.

The Balkan rebellion had already been dealt with in 1041. A genuine royal affine, the Patrician Alousianos, escaped from Constantinople (surely with the connivance of the imperial authorities), joined Peter Deljan, siphoned off a large proportion of the rebel troops for a siege of Thessalonike, allowed them to be defeated by a surprise sally of the defenders, and then disposed of Deljan, luring him into a trap and blinding him. While Alousianos was rewarded with the rank of Magistros, the Emperor Michael reimposed imperial authority throughout the Balkans, save for the mountainous fastness of Diokleia in Dalmatia.[48] A similar policy seems to have been adopted in southern Italy. Atenulf, brother of the prince of Benevento, who had been elected leader of the invaders after their initial successes, defected, going back to Benevento with a large sum of ransom money. Argyros was elected in his place in February 1042, not long before a Byzantine counteroffensive led by Maniakes, who had been reinstated by Michael V. Maniakes consolidated Byzantium's position in the south around Taranto, and advanced north. At his approach in August, Argyros, who had clearly been suborned by Byzantine agents, changed sides, bringing with him the cities which had submitted in 1042. Like Alousianos, he was rewarded subsequently with the title of Magistros.[49]

It was Maniakes' loyalty which was now frayed, at the news that the Skleros nexus of families, with which he was at odds, was in favour. He came out in open revolt and was acclaimed emperor by his troops before the end of 1042. He then crossed the Adriatic and marched east along the Via Egnatia. The rebellion ended a few months later when he was killed in battle against the imperial forces guarding the approach to Thessalonike.[50] The Rus were already on their way, having decided, after seventy years of peace, to take advantage of Byzantium's troubles. The naval attack on Constantinople (July 1043) and the countermeasures, personally overseen by Constantine Monomachos, drew the attention of historians at the time

[48] Stephenson, *Byzantium's Balkan Frontier*, 131–5. Sources: Psellos, *Chron.*, iv.45–49; Skyl., 413–15 (trans., 341–3).

[49] Loud, *Robert Guiscard*, 94–7.

[50] Angold, *Byzantine Empire*, 59. Sources: CM, 65; Psellos, *Chron.*, vi.1.76–86; Skyl., 427–8 (trans., 355–6).

and subsequently.[51] But it was probably a feint, disguising the main Rus operation in which troops were landed on the Bulgarian coast, in what looks like a deliberate attempt to revive Svyatoslav's project of gaining a bridgehead in the Balkans and opening up the Danube as a commercial route into the heart of Germanic Europe. In the event imperial forces in Bulgaria, under the command of Katakalon Kekaumenos (a general who had distinguished himself in Sicily), resisted successfully and drove them off.[52]

Michael Psellos was one of many intellectuals who flourished under the new regime. He began his rise to the top of the government machine. But in his court-centred, gossipy history of the eleventh century which centres on the reign of Constantine Monomachos (it takes up roughly two fifths of the text), he mixed criticisms—serious ones—of Constantine's policies with praise of aspects of his character (and a great deal of self-praise). He has Constantine complete the ruin of the empire's finances, his prime concern being to extract enjoyment from his position. It is a grossly unfair judgement—for which Psellos apologized (citing the historian's obligation to truth!).[53] It took no account of the major problems confronting the emperor, which came from abroad, from Pechenegs and Turks. Psellos was only concerned with episodes when the capital was targeted (by Maniakes, the Rus, and Leo Tornikios who led a rebellion of the western armies in 1047).[54] In reality, Constantine's regime successfully defended Byzantium, when the Pechenegs crossed the frozen Danube *en masse* in winter 1046–7 (disease [dysentery] and two renegade Pecheneg tribes assisted the western armies), and fought a long and difficult war after the refusal of a 15,000-strong force of Pechenegs to march east and bolster the forces facing the Turks in 1048. For that was the year of the first serious Turkish incursion into Byzantine-ruled Armenia by Ibrahim Yınal, one of two restive nephews of the Sultan Tughrıl. The worst damage was suffered when Artze, a flourishing trade centre outside Theodosiopolis, was sacked. But, even without the Pechenegs, the two regional armies were able to prevent the main Turkish force from advancing down the upper Euphrates and pushed it back over the Euphrates–Araxes watershed.[55]

[51] Franklin & Shepard, *Emergence of Rus*, 215–17; Angold, *Byzantine Empire*, 35–7. Sources: Psellos, *Chron.*, vi.1.90–5; Skyl., 430–3 (trans., 357–60); *Povest'*, 103–4 (trans., 138–9).

[52] Skyl., 433 (trans. 360).

[53] Psellos, *Chron.*, vi.1.22–35, 47–9, 161–9, vii.1.55.

[54] Psellos, *Chron.*, vi.1.76–123. For Tornikios, see also Skyl., 438–42 (trans., 365–8).

[55] Angold, *Byzantine Empire*, 38–40; Stephenson, *Byzantium's Balkan Frontier*, 89–91; A. D. Beihammer, *Byzantium and the Emergence of Muslim–Turkish Anatolia, ca.1040–1130* (London, 2017), 77–80 (campaign), 33–6 (Arab and Turkish sources). Byzantine and Armenian sources: Skyl., 449–54, 455–61 (trans., 373–76, 377–82); Aristakes, 65–82 (trans. 57–72), a highly emotional account. Ibrahim Yınal: Peacock, *Great Seljuk Empire*, 44–7, 50–1.

Constantine's regime continued to cope, even though the external threats were beginning to mount up and converge. The Pecheneg war only ended in 1053 after a successful Byzantine campaign. Instead of the three separate upland plains in the Balkan interior which they were assigned in 1047–8, they were allowed to settle in the heartland of the old Bulgar state between the Haemus mountains and the Danube—an arrangement which in general held good into the 1070s.[56] The last phase of the reign coincided with a concerted effort to break the power of the Normans in southern Italy, masterminded by Argyros who had spent five years in Constantinople. He returned as Katepan in March 1051 with fresh troops and, using the large sum of money he brought with him, negotiated an alliance with Pope Leo IX, outraged at Norman depredations in Apulia. However, the planned joint attack on the Normans went disastrously wrong, as first the Byzantine army was defeated near Siponto in 1052 and then the mainly Lombard forces serving the pope were shattered at Civitate in 1053, the pope himself being captured.[57] The Byzantine position was irretrievably weakened. The Norman ascendancy was not in doubt, especially after the papal investiture of the new Norman leader, Robert Guiscard, with rule over Apulia, Calabria, and Sicily at Melfi in 1059. Calabria was overrun between 1055 and 1060, after which Norman forces began their final push into Apulia, first extending their enclave around Melfi to Troia and Acerenza (1060–1), then moving up from the south (taking Oria, Taranto, Matera, and Montepeloso, 1062–4). The Normans were adept at exploiting factional divisions among local notables, advancing step by step, stronghold by stronghold, towards the inner lands of Apulia around Bari. Bari fell after a long siege (1068–71).[58] Meanwhile, in the east, Byzantine defences held firm against Turks and Turkmen as late as 1054 when an attack by the Sultan Tughrıl on Manzikert was repulsed.[59]

## 4.6 Domestic and foreign affairs, 1055–81

After Constantine's death in January 1055, Byzantium's position began to deteriorate. The agreement with the Pechenegs might have been holding in

[56] Stephenson, *Byzantium's Balkan Frontier*, 91–3. Source: Skyl., 465–73 (trans., 384–90).
[57] Loud, *Robert Guiscard*, 114–20.
[58] Loud, *Robert Guiscard*, 121–37; Noyé, 'New Light', 165–6, 184–6, 189–93.
[59] Beihammer, *Muslim–Turkish Anatolia*, 80–3. Christian sources: Skylitzes, 462–4 (trans., 382–4); Aristakes, 84–94 (trans., 75–87).

the Balkans, but there was very little that the central authorities could do to stem the Norman advance in southern Italy beyond stirring up and funding a short-lived revolt (winter 1067–8).[60] In the east, the Turkmen who had taken over the rich grazing lands of Azerbaijan began to push west into the eastern fringes of Anatolia where they sacked Melitene in 1057 and Sebasteia in 1059. In the course of the 1060s they secured the southern route through Armenia (down the Arsanias valley) and pushed across the Euphrates by Melitene, reaching and sacking Kaisareia in 1067. In the south-east, other Turkmen were establishing themselves as a significant military and political presence in the upper Tigris basin (Marwanid emirate) and Aleppo region (Mirdasid emirate), all too close to Byzantine territory.[61]

On two occasions over those fifteen years, the balance in the civilian–military complex governing Byzantium shifted in favour of the military, when the government of the day was judged to be failing. For two and a half years after the death of Constantine IX Monomachos in January 1055, the empire was ruled by the last surviving member of the Macedonian dynasty, the aged Theodora (to August 1056) and her nominated successor, Michael Bringas, a former Logothete of the Stratiotikon. The high command made its move after the spring distribution of honours and salaries in 1057. The leading eastern generals—Isaac Komnenos, Constantine and John Doukas, Michael Bourtzes, Katakalon Kekaumenos—were thoroughly dissatisfied at their treatment, and prepared to launch a coup. At Kekaumenos' insistence, Isaac was their candidate for the throne. He was acclaimed in Paphlagonia and marched on the capital, defeating a force sent against him. Negotiations with a deputation from the emperor were superseded, when Michael, facing opposition in Constantinople itself, decided to abdicate.[62]

Isaac did what he could in his short reign (from September 1057) to improve the empire's finances, but managed in the process to antagonize the church and much of the apparatus of government. There was no improvement to the situation on the ground in Asia Minor, his only venture into the field being a short campaign to the Danube early in 1059, to remind the Pechenegs of Byzantine power. By autumn 1059, his unpopularity was such that he decided to follow Michael's example and abdicate, in favour of his fellow general Constantine Doukas. Psellos, a senior figure in the

[60] Loud, *Robert Guiscard*, 133–4.

[61] Beihammer, *Muslim–Turkish Anatolia*, 104–11, 115–24.

[62] Angold, *Byzantine Empire*, 71–3; Cheynet, *Pouvoir et contestations*, 339–44. Sources: Psellos, *Chron.*, vii.1.1–37; Skyl., 483, 486–500 (trans., 398–9, 401–11).

government, claimed to have played a key part in persuading him to go.[63] But the position continued to deteriorate in the east. Ani was sacked in 1064 in the course of the new Sultan Alp Arslan's expedition north to extend Turkish authority to the Kura river. As noted above, Kaisareia in Cappadocia fell to a Turkmen raiding band in 1067.[64] Like Isaac, Constantine's one success was his Pecheneg policy, in his case a conciliatory policy, which accepted the brute fact of Pecheneg control of Paradounavon, the whole Balkan north-east.[65] When he died in May 1067, there was once again rising demand for an emperor of proven military ability. The choice of Constantine's widow, Eudokia Makrembolitissa, fell on Romanos Diogenes, like Isaac and Constantine a member of a powerful Anatolian family. Unlike them he prepared to take to the field against the Turkmen.[66]

Turkmen raiding forces moved fast. A key component of the dark age strategy of defence, guerrilla harassment on the Anatolian plateau, was not an option against them. Instead they had to be intercepted on their way in or their way out. Romanos' strategy was to rely on the garrisons of cities (Sebasteia and Melitene) commanding the two main invasion routes from Armenia to block their inward passage, backed up by the field army in an advanced position further south—the enclosed basin of Lykandos in 1068, Kaisareia/Larissa in 1069, Kaisareia in 1070 and 1071—from which they could oversee the invasion routes across the Anti-Taurus and Taurus.[67] The field army's main task, though, was to intercept the raiders on their return march (once good intelligence was obtained) and, at the very least, to pursue them so hard as to force them to abandon their booty. To this defensive strategy Romanos added an offensive element—a push into the buffer zones annexed in the tenth century, northern Syria (1068), the westernmost part of Armenia on both flanks of the Mouzouron mountain range (modern Munzur Dağ) (1069), and the next section of Armenia running from the headwaters of the Euphrates to those of the Arsanias on either side of the Bingöl Dağ (1071).[68]

[63] Angold, *Byzantine Empire*, 73–6; Stephenson, *Byzantium's Balkan Frontier*, 94–5.

[64] Beihammer, *Muslim–Turkish Anatolia*, 111–15, 121–2.

[65] Angold, *Byzantine Empire*, 39–40; Peacock, *Great Seljuk Empire*, 53–4; Stephenson, *Byzantium's Balkan Frontier*, 96–8.

[66] Angold, *Byzantine Empire*, 77–8, 115; Cheynet, *Pouvoir et contestations*, 345–7. Sources: Psellos, *Chron.*, vii.3.1–10; Att., 16.8–14.

[67] Att., 105, 125, 139, 146–7 (trans., 193, 229, 253–5, 267–9).

[68] Att., 107–22, 131–5, 148–50 (trans., 195–223, 239–47, 271–5). *Cf.* Beihammer, *Muslim–Turkish Anatolia*, 137–55 for the campaigns of 1068, 1069, and 1070, making full use of Muslim sources.

Despite some criticism of the fighting qualities of the units assembled in Asia Minor, once they were assembled, smartened up, and reinforced with new recruits (units transferred from the Balkans and Pechenegs), Romanos was able to staunch Turkmen raiding.[69] The warband which raided Neokaisareia in 1068 was intercepted by Romanos near Sebasteia. It was pursued over rugged terrain behind Tephrike, caught and defeated. In 1069 the field army defeated one raiding force which was using the Melitene route and drove it back over the Euphrates, and, in the last operation of the campaign, blocked access to the Cilician Gates, forcing the Turkmen who had raided Ikonion to return across the rough country of eastern Isauria where they were harried by Armenians and lost almost all their booty.[70] Despite two successful raids targeting Amorion (1068) and Chonai (1070)—the first unopposed by the units garrisoning Melitene and the powerful fortress of Tzamandos (Figure 4.4a and b), the second defeating the army sent to block the Sebasteia invasion route—the dangers they were now facing acted as a serious deterrent.[71] Had Romanos' fourth campaign been equally successful, they would have found the hazards greatly increased, with Byzantine interception forces installed in the recently refurbished defences of Theodosiopolis (at the head of the northern Euphrates invasion route) and in the two strongholds commanding access to the southern, Arsanias invasion route, Manzikert and Chliat, once they were recovered from the Turkmen.

In the event the 1071 campaign went disastrously wrong, when Alp Arslan unexpectedly appeared with a crack force of cavalry, drove off the large detachment besieging Chliat, and defeated Romanos outside Manzikert.[72] Worse followed when Romanos, having reached an agreement with Alp Arslan, was released and found that the crown had been seized back by the Doukas family, Constantine's son, Michael VII (1071–8) being placed on the throne in a coup organized by his uncle, the Caesar John. This opened a short but fatal civil war, in the course of which the Turkmen were able to resume their raiding operations across Asia Minor, reaching its north-western extremities.[73] A small band, 200-strong, attacked Isaac and Alexios

[69] Att., 103–4 (trans., 189–93). *Cf.* Beihammer, *Muslim–Turkish Anatolia*, 138–40, 146–7, 151 for a more pessimistic view.

[70] Att., 105–6, 125–8, 131, 136–8 (trans., 193–5, 229–33, 239, 249–51).

[71] Att., 121–2, 139–41 (trans., 221–3, 255–7).

[72] C. Hillenbrand, *Turkish Myth and Muslim Symbol: The Battle of Manzikert* (Edinburgh, 2007); Peacock, *Great Seljuk Empire*, 54–6; Beihammer, *Muslim–Turkish Anatolia*, 155–7.

[73] Angold, *Byzantine Empire*, 46, 116–20; Cheynet, *Pouvoir et contestation*, 348–9; Beihammer, *Muslim–Turkish Anatolia*, 157–61.

**Figure 4.4** Tzamandos: (a) position; (b) general view. Tzamandos was a new castle built by Melias, probably in the 920s. Like Lykandos, it was later used by the Danishmends. It commanded the main route leading from Melitene to Kaisareia as it approached the Anatolian plateau.

*Source*: (a) author; (b) Alexander Sarantis.

Komnenos in Bithynia in 1073. Turkmen were there in larger numbers in 1074, and were percolating into Paphlagonia by 1075.[74] It was perhaps the threat presented by fortified centres of population in the plateau region which drove them to penetrate ever deeper into Byzantine territory—*the pinball machine phenomenon*, which can be cited to explain the swift percolation of Slavs into the central and southern Balkans in the late sixth century.[75]

The two principal Byzantine sources, the histories of Michael Attaleiates and Nikephoros Bryennios, preoccupied with overt political threats to the centre, pay only intermittent attention to affairs in Asia Minor in the 1070s. The receding of Byzantine authority and its replacement by that of Turkmen warlords and regional leaders is hard to trace, save from what is reported about individual cities. All that can be discerned are the main stages in this process. (1) The empire appeared to be intact, at least notionally, in 1072: Theodosiopolis and Koloneia in the north, Cilicia and the duchy of Antioch in the south were in Byzantine hands, when Romanos fought in vain to regain his throne.[76] (2) A year later, when the last recorded campaign of the field army in eastern Asia Minor took place (the two Komnenoi brothers, Isaac [23] and Alexios [16], were in command) and Roussel of Bailleul and his Normans rebelled, the Byzantines still controlled the cities guarding access to the interior plateau of Asia Minor—Sebasteia, Melitene, Kaisareia, and Ikonion.[77] (3) But very soon (it was during Roussel's rebellion in 1074–5) it looks as if the Turkmen established their ascendancy over the eastern half of the plateau. For it was only in the west that Roussel extended his authority from Armeniakon, first south over Galatia and Lykaonia, then north over Pontos.[78] The only city notables to feature in our sources were those of Ankyra and nearby towns (they raised the money to ransom Isaac Komnenos who had been defeated and captured) and Amaseia (Alexios Komnenos appealed there for the money owed to the Turks for handing over Roussel).[79]

By 1077–8, when a new round of rebellions broke out in Asia Minor and the Balkans, the Turkmen had become an important military and political force in western Asia Minor. The most important leader was Sulayman, one

[74] Beihammer, *Muslim–Turkish Anatolia*, 208, 210, 214.
[75] Whitby, *The Emperor Maurice*, 75–9, 80–3.
[76] Att., 167–75 (trans., 305–19). *Cf.* Beihammer, *Muslim–Turkish Anatolia*, 157–61.
[77] Att., 183–4 (trans., 333–5); Bryennios, ii.3–5 (pp. 144–51).
[78] Bryennios, ii.14 (p.167.3–6), 19 (p.183.2–5).
[79] Bryennios, ii.8 (p.157-5-15), 22 (pp.188–91).

of four sons of Kutlumush, a cousin of Tughrıl Beg, killed in late 1063 after rebelling against the new sultan Alp Arslan. The prestige Sulayman enjoyed as a member of the Seljuk clan, and the following of Nawakiyya Turkmen, whom he had brought from Syria after their defeat in 1075 by the officially recognized leader of the Syrian Turkmen, ensured his predominance.[80] Just as they had done in the Levant, the Turks (as they should be called, now that they were under Seljuk leadership) were able to play off rival Byzantine political factions against each other. Late in 1077 Sulayman backed the rebel general Nikephoros Botaneiates against the Doukas regime, and was well rewarded, when Botaneiates, aided by the opposition in Constantinople, entered the city and was crowned emperor on 3 April 1078.

Despite the abdication and tonsure of Michael VII and Botaneiates' marriage to Michael's wife Maria of Alania, the regime was vulnerable. There were two Balkan rivals, Nikephoros Bryennios and Nikephoros Basilakios, whom Alexios Komnenos defeated in the first few months with the aid of a contingent of Turks.[81] Two years later (towards the end of 1080), a new opportunity arose to consolidate the Turkish position in Asia Minor, when Nikephoros Melissenos challenged the rule of Botaneiates from his base on the island of Cos. In return for his support, Sulayman was allowed to install garrisons in all the towns which Melissenos, escorted by a group of Turkish nobles and soldiers, visited on a progress through western Asia Minor (Asia, Phrygia, and Galatia). A year later Sulayman gained control of Bithynia and its chief city Nikaia, when Melissenos abandoned his rebellion and went over to the new Komnenian regime in Constantinople.[82]

The Byzantine empire was in a parlous state. It had always been a modest empire, only meriting such a designation because of the geographical dispersal of its lands and the aura surrounding the descendants of the Romans. By 1081, it had been stripped of its Anatolian heartland. Undoubtedly there was a strong residual loyalty in the population of cities, towns, and villages in Asia Minor. There were surely more pockets of resistance in the highlands fringing the interior plateau, than those we hear of in Pontos (where Theodore Gabras established a principality) and the south-east, where Philaretos Brachamios had taken over the mountain country from Isauria

[80] Beihammer, *Muslim–Turkish Anatolia*, 183–8, 204–7.

[81] Angold, *Byzantine Empire*, 123–4; Cheynet, *Pouvoir et contestations*, 351–3; Beihammer, *Muslim–Turkish Anatolia*, 215–21.

[82] Cheynet, *Pouvoir et contestations*, 355–6; Beihammer, *Muslim–Turkish Anatolia*, 221–4. Melissenos' progress: Bryennios, iv.31 (p.301.1–12).

to the Anti-Taurus in 1078.[83] If a Byzantine army were to reappear and to prove a match for Turkish forces, it would be welcomed and aided by city notables. But there was little prospect of that in 1081, because of troubles elsewhere.

Byzantine authority was being openly challenged in the Balkans. An insurrection followed the withdrawal in 1072 of the customary subsidies for the Pechenegs settled in the north-east. They gained the backing of the Danube cities and of the governor, Nestor, sent out by Nikephoritzes, the hard man of the Doukas regime, to restore order. Nestor's failure to extract concessions with a demonstration of force outside Constantinople led to the *de facto* secession of Paradounavon. The danger grew towards the end of the 1070s, when the Pechenegs raided Thrace and established links with the Paulician colony near Philippopolis. In Macedonia, a Bulgar rebellion—again triggered by the financial demands of Nikephoritzes—broke out around the same time, headed by Constantine Bodin, son of Michael prince of Diokleia. Several military bases were taken—Skupi, Naissos, and Ochrid—but the garrison of Kastoria and a field army had little difficulty in crushing the rebels. There were threats from without—a Hungarian attack on Belgrade at some point in the 1070s, and a menacing extension of papal influence in the west to expansionist Croatia (1075) and restive Diokleia (1077). Finally, two bids for the throne were made in 1077–8 by successive dukes of Dyrrachion, Nikephoros Bryennios who had the backing of the powerful military families of Adrianople and attacked Constantinople, and Basilakios who gained hold of Thessalonike. Both were put down by Botaneiates' chief general (Domestic of the Scholai), Alexios Komnenos. It was plain that such loyalties as had been nurtured among the Bulgars and Slavs of the northern and central Balkans during two to three generations of Byzantine rule were being eroded.[84]

In Italy all had been lost in 1071. The Normans' military grip was secure. There was no prospect whatsoever of a Byzantine recovery, given that there had long been a latent antagonism which manifested itself from time to time in open rebellion and in the factional politics of cities. The danger rather was of Norman intervention in the Balkans. The Adriatic connected rather than divided Italy from Dalmatia. Robert Guiscard also had good grounds for going to war, as the betrothal of his daughter to Michael VII's

[83] Angold, *Byzantine Empire*, 118–19, 123.

[84] Cheynet, *Pouvoir et contestations*, 351–3; Angold, *Byzantine Empire*, 124–5; Stephenson, *Byzantium's Balkan Frontier*, 98–101, 141–5.

young son Constantine had been broken by Botaneiates' coup. News of political turbulence in Byzantium during Botaneiates' short reign encouraged him to make preparations for a large-scale naval and military expedition with the object of tearing the Balkans from Byzantine rule.[85]

These were the grim circumstances in which Alexios Komnenos staged a coup d'état on 1 April 1081. He had slipped out of the city some weeks earlier for fear of court intrigues against him, his mother and female relatives taking shelter in St Sophia. Apart from military support he had the invaluable backing of Caesar John Doukas, whose granddaughter Eirene he had married, and of the Empress Maria Alania, who had adopted him. The Caesar helped open the way into the city and won over the Patriarch Kosmas, who persuaded Botaneiates to abdicate.[86] A powerful aristocratic nexus thus placed a candidate on the throne who was to prove remarkably able and, as his daughter put it, was to steer the ship of state safely, like a latter-day Odysseus, as it was buffeted by winds and waves. As important was his founding of a new ruling dynasty, which gave Byzantium much-needed political stability and imparted tensile strength to the refurbished system of government.

*Byzantium in a Changing World*. James Howard-Johnston, Oxford University Press.
 DOI: 10.1093/9780191999093.003.0005

[85] Noyé, 'New Light', 162–6, 184–9; Loud, *Age of Robert Guiscard*, 209–17.
[86] Cheynet, *Pouvoir et contestations*, 354–7; Angold, *Byzantine Empire*, 124–7.

# 5
# Komnenian Age

Battered and mutilated, the Byzantium, which was taken over by the 33-year-old Alexios Komnenos in a bloodless coup in 1081, was the lineal descendant of the rump east Roman empire which had fought off Arabs, Bulgars, and Rus and had re-established itself as one of the two great powers of the Middle East in the tenth and eleventh centuries. The governing elite retained the notion that theirs was a special, elect earthly power, singled out for divine favour. Their role was to preside over a nearby concert of nations and to deal with the greatest polities of the contemporary world on equal terms. However delusional their ideas of empire, they believed in them and made them real in the *imaginaire* of their times.

The Byzantines were Greek through and through, although it was only from the twelfth century that they began to advertise their descent from the Greeks of classical antiquity and to call themselves *Hellenes*.[1] The Greek they spoke and wrote, in both its clear, mandarin and ornate, rhetorical forms, was a lineal descendant of the Greek of Homer, Aeschylus, Herodotus, Plato, and the fathers of the church. As in their political heyday in the tenth and early eleventh centuries, they immersed themselves in texts transmitted from classical Greece and the long silver age which extended through the Hellenistic and Roman periods to late antiquity. Their faith derived from the final phase of that silver age, in terms of both doctrine and practice, and was deeply embedded in society, vivified by the regular performance of the liturgy and the re-enactment of the Gospel story through the annual cycle of church feasts. The dark-age struggle for survival, in the course of which the icon was accepted as a legitimate conduit for prayer, *fixed* Orthodoxy, which acted thenceforth as a key marker of identity, differentiating the Byzantines from most of the Christians living under Islam, from the majority of Armenians, and, with fateful consequences, from Latin Christendom.

The governmental system, for all the structural changes introduced in the dark age (centralization of departments of state, consolidation of

[1] P. Magdalino, *Tradition and Transformation in Medieval Byzantium* (Aldershot, 1991), no. XIV ('Hellenism and Nationalism in Byzantium'), 10–18.

provincial government into regional units [themes]) and the subsequent adaptation of institutions to the enlargement of the state, remained in essentials that of the late Roman empire. Authority over all secular affairs was vested in the emperor. He headed the administration and the justice system. Extensive powers were delegated to heads of central departments, army commanders, and provincial governors, but they were all ultimately accountable to the emperor. It was a top-down system, with extensive outreach over the state's territory and downreach to the level of the village. The fiscal system, a modified version of the late Roman empire's, best exemplified this downreach, enabling the authorities to tap individual households for resources.[2] What was left of the inherited system of government had dissolved in the late ninth and tenth centuries in post-Carolingian Europe, to be replaced eventually by a system built up from the bottom and founded on local lordship.[3] Byzantium was not immune to centrifugal pulls, but the start of the process of drawing power down to the localities was delayed until the late twelfth century.

The social order too had evolved from that documented in the reign of Justinian. The peasantry was recognized as the bedrock of the state in the dark age. Such members of the old aristocracy as had survived were transformed into an aristocracy of service, tighter-knit than in the past because of the intertwining of careers. Their power was enhanced in the tenth and eleventh centuries by investment in land (monitored and to some extent limited by imperial legislation) and by development of extensive networks of kin (through intermarriage) and of patronage.[4] But they could not develop the locally rooted power of lords, great and small, which characterized the West in the twelfth century. There were countervailing forces in the localities, villages of peasants, who retained their legal freedom and remained a significant social formation, and notables in the reviving towns.[5] Honours, which contributed much to a family's status, remained in the emperor's gift. They were personal, not heritable. Surnames (and outward displays of wealth) were the markers of inherited status, not titles. Roman law continued to ensure that great fortunes were broken up at the death of the holder and divided equally between the children of the deceased, female as well as male. This partible system of inheritance, together with marriage

[2] Howard-Johnston, *Byzantium*, 21–4.

[3] T. N. Bisson, 'The Feudal Revolution', *Past and Present*, 142 (1994), 6–42.

[4] Cheynet, 'L'aristocratie byzantine', repr. In *idem*, *The Byzantine Aristocracy and its Military Function* (Aldershot, 2006), no. I.

[5] Howard-Johnston, *Byzantium*, 62–5, 67–71, 166–7, 252–60.

law, led to a steady growth in the size of affinities (very evident in the twelfth century), which, without primogeniture, would prove increasingly fractious.[6]

Byzantium was still Byzantium, in terms of culture and structures. But its relations to the surrounding world were utterly changed, now that rival Turkish powers were lording it over Anatolia, predators (Pechenegs, with assistance from Paulicians) were raiding the Balkans, and the Normans of southern Italy were preparing to invade Dalmatia. Rather than directing the affairs of Europe and the Mediterranean, jointly with the German empire and Fatimid Egypt, Byzantium was once again forced onto the defensive. Alexios and *all* his successors would have to react to threats from abroad, with diminishing resources. It was a sad and increasingly depressing tale.

Before embarking on this story of a steady rise (1081–1180) and vertiginous fall (1180–1204), we should conduct a survey of the surrounding world. It was extraneous events which determined the fortunes of Byzantium. Pressure was exerted by hostile powers in the Middle East and Europe (chiefly Turks and Normans), and from the 1180s by peoples incorporated into the empire but retaining distinct identities (Serbs and Bulgars in the Balkans).

There can be no doubt as to which of the neighbouring powers had caused the greatest damage by the end of the eleventh century. The Kutlumush branch of the Seljuk family had extended its authority over Asia Minor, reaching Bithynia on the Sea of Marmara in the north-west. Theirs, however, was only a light, attenuated authority, exerted by city-based Turkish forces and roaming Turkmen. Time and effort would be needed to transform it into effective rule. Initially they did not pose a serious threat to such Byzantine enclaves as were left, or indeed to the rival Turkish principalities which established themselves to the north, south-east, and west. For the main targets of the offensive thrusts made by the first two sultans of Rum, as the rulers of the Anatolian Seljuks styled themselves, lay in the south-east in northern Syria. In the medium term, the Seljuks and their chief regional rivals, the Danishmends of Armeniakon and Paphlagonia, were forced onto the defensive and lost territory.[7] In the long run, though,

[6] N. Oikonomidès, *Les listes de préséance byzantines des IXe et Xe siècles* (Paris, 1972), 281–90; J.-C. Cheynet, 'L'anthroponymie aristocratique à Byzance', in M. Bourin, J.-M. Martin, & F. Menant, eds., *L'anthroponymie document de l'histoire sociale des mondes méditerranéens médiévaux*, Collection de l'École française de Rome 226 (1996), 267–94, at 291–4; J. Howard-Johnston, 'Partitive Inheritance in Principle and Practice in Eleventh-Century Byzantium', in B. Caseau & S. R. Huebner, eds., *Inheritance, Law and Religions in the Ancient and Medieval Worlds* (Paris, 2014), 259–71.

[7] Beihammer, *Muslim–Turkish Anatolia*, 226–34, 265–85, 338–47, 358–60.

the westward advance of the Turks resumed, driven by a steady flow of Turkmen into Asia Minor from Transcaucasia.

Hostility between Normans and Byzantines was programmed in by events in the recent past. Normans were the most predatory of contemporary Germanic peoples. Once they had consolidated their hold over their core territory in northern France, they launched bold expeditions in the manner of Goths in late antiquity and Vikings in the early middle ages. Success in war and the prestige and wealth which it brought underpinned leadership, increased military followings, and added momentum to the extension of Norman authority.[8] This dynamic growth of power was nowhere better exemplified than in Byzantine southern Italy. With the conquest of Calabria completed in 1060, the Normans gained a reasonably secure platform for further ventures by land (renewed attacks on Apulia, culminating in the capture of Bari in 1071) and by sea against two conveniently close targets, Sicily (conquered piecemeal between 1061 and 1091) and Dalmatia. The deposition of Michael VII, who had been hoping to secure the services of the Normans against the Turks, and the appeal of a pretender who appeared in southern Italy provided the pretext for going to war against Byzantium.[9] The invasion of 1081, targeted on Dyrrachion, the terminus of the Via Egnatia, opened two centuries of antagonism between Byzantium and the rulers who controlled the central Mediterranean, the Normans and their Angevin successors. The danger to Byzantium peaked in 1282, but it was a key factor in Byzantine–western relations throughout the twelfth and thirteenth centuries.[10] Relations with the other western maritime powers, Venice, Pisa, and Genoa, fluctuated but were more amicable in general. The same was true of the major powers in contact with Byzantium—Hungary and the German empire.[11]

The third long-lasting threat came from within the Balkans. Non-Greek-speaking peoples had been incorporated into the Byzantine empire by the end of Basil II's reign (1025). Three generations on, their pre-Byzantine

[8] Le Patourel, *Norman Empire.* [9] Loud, *Age of Robert Guiscard*, 146–72, 209–14.

[10] E. Tounta, 'Political and Cultural Encounters between Byzantium and the Normans, 11th–12th Centuries', in N. Drocourt & S. Kolditz, eds., *A Companion to Byzantium and the West, 900–1204* (Leiden, 2022), 247–69; D. Abulafia, *The Western Mediterranean Kingdoms 1200–1500: The Struggle for Dominion* (London, 1997), 14–27, 57–81.

[11] R.-J. Lilie, *Handel und Politik zwischen dem byzantinischen Reich und den italienischen Kommunen Venedig, Pisa und Genua in der Epoche der Komnenen und der Angeloi (1081–1204)* (Amsterdam, 1984); N. Berend, 'Hungary in the Eleventh and Twelfth Centuries', in D. Luscombe & J. Riley-Smith, eds., *New CMH*, IV *c.1024–c.1198*, pt. 2 (Cambridge, 2004), 304–16; L. Exarchos, 'Komnenoi and Staufer: Ambition and Confrontation', in *Byzantium and the West, 900–1204*, 215–46.

pasts had not been erased from their collective memories. Rebellions at times of Byzantine weakness revealed their desire to escape from the mini-Greek empire's political and cultural embrace. Bulgars, after all, had held out against all the forces directed against them by Byzantium and had gone on to extend their authority over much of the Balkan interior in the ninth century. It was only the invasion of the Viking Rus in 968–9 which had broken their hold on their heartland in the north-east Balkans. It then took forty years of counter-insurgency warfare before the Byzantines were able to break the resistance of the successor state centred on Macedonia. Of the other Balkan peoples absorbed by Byzantium, Serbs, Croats and, Albanians, it was the Serbs who were most refractory, partly perhaps because they remembered their successful resistance in the early tenth century to one of the great Bulgar rulers, Symeon, partly because they could fall back on the highland redoubts of Duklija and Raška in northern Dalmatia, partly because provincial administration seems to have been left in the hands of local leaders.[12]

It was during the years of political conflict at the centre following the death of Manuel Komnenos in 1180 that both Bulgars and Serbs first asserted their independence. Inspiration was perhaps taken from the knowledge that in the north two powerful Slav kingdoms, Bohemia and Poland, had been established on the margins of the German empire. The trouble started in the Haemus mountains, where, facing high tax demands in 1185, Vlach transhumants, with Bulgar backing, rose up. Despite an initial defeat in 1187, the rebellion spread, drawing in increasing numbers of Bulgars. At the same time, the Grand Zhupan of the Serbs, Stefan Nemanja, began to push out south and south-east from his highland redoubts. The Serbs were to prove formidable rivals to the resurgent Byzantine state after the recovery of Constantinople in 1261. They were destined to establish a new hybrid Serb–Greek empire in the Balkans in the course of the thirteenth century. The Bulgars were more successful initially, recreating, by the beginning of the thirteenth century, an independent Bulgar state, now thoroughly slavicized, in their old heartlands of the Dobruja, lower Danube plains, and Haemus mountains. That was the stage at which it was evident to a watching world that Byzantium was seriously weakened, with its hold on large parts of its remaining substantial resource-base prised loose.[13]

[12] Obolensky, *Byzantine Commonwealth*, 219–23.

[13] P. Stephenson, 'Balkan Borderlands (1018–1204)' and A. Ducellier, 'Balkan Powers: Albania, Serbia and Bulgaria (1200–1300)', in J. Shepard, ed., *Cambridge History of the Byzantine Empire, c. 500–1492* (Cambridge, 2008), 664–91, 779–802.

## 5.1 Alexios Komnenos

As in the past, from the beginning of Byzantium's dark age, we have to extract a narrative of events from a relatively thin historical tradition. It is only in the last century or so when the disarticulated polity was at the mercy of outside powers that several accounts of the same events with different points of view and differing attitudes can be played off against each other.[14] The leading historians—from Anna Komnene writing in the middle of the twelfth century to Laonikos Chalkokondyles, one of four to cover the final siege and fall of Constantinople—strove as much as ever to write well in a classicizing style. History for them remained a branch of literature. Whatever the sources of information—principally personal recollections and documentary material, especially the news releases on which all governments relied to maintain their standing with the public—their object was to dress it up in fine prose, to bring scenes to life and to embellish narrative with classical tags, speeches, anecdotes, and turns on the exotic and antiquarian.[15] This literary bent was taken to an extreme by Constantine Manasses, who was commissioned by the great literary patron of the twelfth century, the Sebastokratorissa Eirene, to write a world history, from Creation to 1081, in 15-syllable verse. It was virtually worthless as history but elegant, entertaining, and deservedly popular.[16]

Manasses belonged to the minority who were primarily interested in retelling the story of humanity for their own generation and paid cursory attention to the recent past. There was the customary variety of genres in history writing—universal history (five examples besides Manasses), church history (one), and local history (five), in addition to the main sequence of high-style, classicising works.[17] Lay officialdom and the clergy remained prominent among historians. There was also one judge (Zonaras), three scholars who lived by teaching and writing (Manasses, Nikephoros Gregoras, and Chalkokondyles), one soldier (Nikephoros Bryennios), and two members of ruling dynasties (Anna Komnene and Andronikos VI

[14] Howard-Johnston, *Historical Writing*, 30–3; N. Necipoğlu, *Byzantium between the Ottomans and the Latins: Politics and Society in the Late Empire* (Cambridge, 2009), 8–15.

[15] L. Neville, *Guide to Byzantine Historical Writing* (Cambridge, 2018), 169–318. Classicism: see, for example, A. Simpson, *Niketas Choniates: A Historiographical Study* (Oxford, 2013), 229–79.

[16] *Constantini Manassis Breviarium chronicum*, ed. O. Lampsides, CFHB 36, 2 vols. (Athens, 1996), trans. L Yuretich, *The Chronicle of Constantine Manasses*, TTB 6 (Liverpool, 2018).

[17] Universal: Zonaras, Manasses, Glykas, Joel, Skoutariotes, Ephraim. Church: Xanthopoulos. Local: *Chronicle of Morea*; Panaretos; *Chronicle of Ioannina*; *Chronicle of Tocco*; Machairas.

Kantakouzenos). Most of the writers of full-blown histories of the recent past deviated from the example of their classical predecessors by being ready to intrude into their texts (Kantakouzenos' can be classified as a political memoir) and by allowing their own opinions to colour what they wrote. Contemporary ephemera, speeches and letters, and non-Byzantine histories have to be used as controls, and, occasionally where it exists, a Byzantine history with a contrary bias.[18]

The finest of all Byzantine histories was the *Alexiad* written by Anna Komnene. It is an extraordinary work, focused on her father, adulatory and exculpatory. It was written at the centre, by a princess with unprecedented access to the inner workings of the palace, but, to our astonishment, has relatively little to say about the imperial family, the court, Constantinople, and high politics. It looks instead to the periphery and is mainly concerned with warfare. Its core consists of a set of campaign narratives, organized by theatre of war, together with a detailed account of Byzantine dealings with the First Crusade. The closest analogy is Procopius' history of Justinian's wars, which is likewise organized by theatre. Unlike Procopius and her immediate predecessors, though, Anna gives relatively little background information about the adversaries and has difficulty sorting out her abundant military and diplomatic materials into coherent, chronologically ordered history. The impression of editorial skill oscillating between competence (evident in individual campaign narratives) and incompetence (evident in some of their arrangement), surely reflects the process of its gestation by a team of two, Anna and her husband, Nikephoros Bryennios, and its completion by Anna after Nikephoros' death in 1138.[19]

Their subject, Alexios I Komnenos (1081–1118), stands out among late Byzantine emperors as author of a remarkable revival in the fortunes of the state as well as the founder of a new dynasty. His marriage to Eirene Doukaina sealed an alliance between two of the three great aristocratic houses which had dominated the government from 1057—Komnenoi and Doukai. This effective fusion of two hitherto rival imperial families was

[18] See, for example, M. C. G. Lau, *The Emperor John II Komnenos: Rebuilding New Rome 1118–1143* (Oxford, 2023), 9–25.

[19] J. Howard-Johnston, 'Anna Komnene and the *Alexiad*', in M. Mullett & D. Smythe, eds., *Alexios I Komnenos* (Belfast, 1996), 260–302; T. Gouma-Peterson, ed., *Anna Komnene and her Times* (New York, 2000); E. M. Jeffreys, 'Nikephoros Brennios Reconsidered', in V. N. Vlysidou, ed., *The Empire in Crisis? Byzantium in the Eleventh Century (1025–1081)* (Athens, 2003), 201–14; J. Howard-Johnston, 'Bilingual Reading, the *Alexiad* and the *Gesta Roberti Wiscardi*', in T. Shawcross & I. Toth, eds, *Reading in the Byzantine Empire and Beyond* (Cambridge, 2021), 467–98.

overseen by Caesar John Doukas, the *eminence grise* of the 1070s. Their position was consolidated by other strategic marriages, in the first instance, with Melissenoi and Palaiologoi. Alexios needed all the support he could get because so much went wrong in the first years of his reign. Honours previously sold on a large scale to the upwardly mobile became valueless, as the annuities associated with them were cut. That did not make the new regime popular in the capital with successful merchants and craftsmen. Looting by Alexios' troops after his entry into the city caused outrage. So too did his appropriation of church plate in order to raise the funds for fighting the deadly threat posed by the Normans. His decision to leave government in the hands of his mother, Anna Dalassena, when he left Constantinople on campaign, was resented. But he had to take command in the field. There was no question of his appointing another commander, as a late Roman emperor might have done.[20]

He began mobilizing his forces soon after his seizure of power on 1 April 1081. A Norman expeditionary force was being assembled by Robert Guiscard at Otranto, and would, before the end of May, establish a bridgehead on the Dalmatian coast at Butrint. The initial objective was Dyrrachion, commanding as it did the western end of the Via Egnatia running east to Macedonia, from which Thessalonike or Thessaly could be attacked. By 17 June Robert was able to lay siege to the city by land and sea. It was a long siege, which the Venetians attempted to break by sea and Alexios by land. Alexios suffered a crushing defeat on 18 October. The city finally fell in February 1082. Reverse followed reverse for Alexios. He managed to deter the Normans from marching west along the Via Egnatia, by garrisoning Ochrid, on the far side of the Pindus range, but Robert pushed up the Devoli valley and captured Kastoria. When in April 1082 he had to return to Italy in response to an appeal for help from Pope Gregory VII (the German Emperor Henry IV had been urged to attack by Alexios), his son Bohemond took over the command, inflicting two more defeats on Alexios outside Ioannina (already in Norman hands) and Ochrid which was then captured, except for the citadel. In 1083, Bohemond renewed the offensive, now targeting Thessaly. Trikalla fell, Larissa was besieged, but the guerrilla tactics and sustained campaign of subversion to which Alexios resorted were increasingly effective, forcing Bohemond to withdraw first to the coast

[20] Angold, *Byzantine Empire*, 124–9, 137; Cheynet, 'Transformations in Byzantine Society', 37–42.

and then, after the recapture of Dyrrachion by the Venetians and of Kastoria by Alexios, to Apulia.[21]

Alexios remained preoccupied with Balkan affairs over the following years, accepting the *status quo* in the east. He observed the treaty he had signed in 1081 with Sulayman at Nikaia and received valuable military aid from him.[22] Robert Guiscard, accompanied by his heir Roger Borsa, attacked again late in 1084. A series of naval engagements with a Venetian fleet off Corfu ended in victory, opening up a maritime route of attack on Greece. After a difficult winter at Vonitsa on the mainland, the Normans sailed south and took control of Kephalonia, well-placed to act as the forward base for naval operations in Greek waters. But the threat evaporated with Robert's death in spring 1085 and Roger Borsa's hasty return to Italy to secure his inheritance.[23]

Alexios then turned his attention to the eastern Balkans, where Pechenegs, settled north of the Haemus mountains, were becoming increasingly restive. Renegade Paulicians were stirring them up. A first victorious thrust south of the Haemus in 1086 was followed up by an invasion in 1087 of a coalition of Pechenegs, Cumans from across the Danube, and Hungarians, who caused widespread devastation in Thrace. Byzantine success was limited to a successful ambush on the return march. An armistice was then negotiated. After its expiry, Alexios planned a riposte on the grand scale and in the manner of Constantine V, that is a co-ordinated attack by land and river on the Pechenegs' heartland in the Dobruja and the great fortress of Dristra on the edge of the Danube delta. But the campaign (to be dated probably to 1090) went disastrously wrong (Alexios suffering another decisive defeat), opening the way for a renewed invasion of Thrace late in 1090. It required all the wiles of Byzantine military science and the aid of the Cumans to defeat the Pechenegs (at the battle of Lebounion in 1091) and render them thenceforth amenable to Byzantine authority.[24] The last serious attack on

[21] Loud, *Robert Guiscard*, 211–19. [22] Angold, *Byzantine Empire*, 134.

[23] Loud, *Robert Guiscard*, 222–3; Howard-Johnston, 'Bilingual Reading', 480–95.

[24] General account: Stephenson, *Byzantium's Balkan Frontier*, 100–3. Detailed analysis: P. Doimi de Frankopan Šubić, *The Foreign Policy of the Emperor Alexios I Komnenos (1081–c.1100)* (DPhil, Oxford, 1998), 178–256. Anna Komnene, our principal source, presents the campaigns in chronological order: first invasion of Thrace (vi.14); Tzelgu invasion (vii.1); Alexios' expedition (vii.2.1–3, 5, 7, vii.3–4); autumn 1090 operations (vii.9–11); Lebounion campaign (viii.3.4–6.5) The only contrary indication is her notice about a solar eclipse, foreseen and used by the Byzantine side in negotiations with a large Pecheneg delegation (vii.2.8), which is placed immediately before the 1090 Byzantine campaign. Frankopan identifies it as the near-total eclipse of 16 February 1086, and redates the campaign to 1086. It is, however, extremely unlikely that an army would have pushed north of the Haemus and a fleet sailed up

the eastern Balkans came in spring 1095, this time from Cumans who crossed the Danube, broke through the fortified Haemus passes, and spread over the plains of Thrace. Traditional guerrilla tactics proved their worth and the Cumans were pushed back over the Haemus.[25]

All this time the Turks were left in control of Asia Minor. Their authority was doubtless still fragile, and potentially vulnerable to any serious Byzantine counterthrust. This was frustrating for Anatolian aristocrats whose power was rooted in the coastlands and interior plateau. The only Byzantine action was defensive, against the emir Tzachas, based in Smyrna, who had built a fleet and was targeting the two closest islands, Lesbos and Chios.[26] Otherwise Alexios' attention remained fixed on the Balkans, trained in the 1090s on northern Dalmatia and the refractory Serbs, targets of an expedition in 1094 and another the following year.[27] This was evidently too much for many Anatolian aristocrats, who looked to Nikephoros Diogenes, son of Romanos IV Diogenes, to take a lead. He had been given, probably in 1085 on obtaining his majority, the emoluments of the governorship of Crete, but was serving in the field army. He was a dangerous focus for disaffection, as he had a high reputation and a ramified following in the officer corps. It was Alexios who brought the crisis to a head after two failed assassination attempts on the long march towards north Dalmatia, at a time (late June 1094) and place (near Serres) of his choosing. Diogenes was arrested and tortured, until he confessed. Alexios then staged a confrontation with the officer corps in the imperial pavilion. Flanked by relatives and bodyguards, he explained what had happened and pacified them with a general amnesty.[28]

That was the most dangerous challenge to his rule, brought about by what seemed a deliberate policy to break the power of the Anatolian aristocracy, especially the nexus of Cappadocian magnates, while the Komnenos–Doukas union continued to consolidate its position. This it did by expanding its affinity through judicious intermarriage with powerful aristocratic families mainly from the capital and Thrace, and by extending its hold on the apparatus of government, as well as the armed forces. Its dominant

the Black Sea to the Danube in *winter 1085–6*. I suspect that Anna has misplaced a free-floating anecdote about a purely diplomatic episode which had occurred four years earlier.

25 Stephenson, *Byzantium's Balkan Frontier*, 103–5.

26 Beihammer, *Muslim–Turkish Anatolia*, 272–4.

27 Stephenson, *Byzantium's Balkan Frontier*, 147–50.

28 Cheynet, *Pouvoir et contestations*, 98–9, 365–6. The assassination attempts and final confrontation of Alexios and the officer corps are described in a series of vivid scenes at *Alexias*, ix.5–9 (full reference in n. 36 below).

position was made manifest through a reform of the honours system, the title *sebastos* being bestowed on senior members of the ruling family.[29] At the same time the financial foundations of the state were strengthened. The first and most fundamental reform was to the frayed monetary system: a new three-tiered currency was introduced in 1092 alongside the old debased coinage, comprising a gold nomisma or hyperpyron of 20.5 carats, a silver-gold alloy worth one third of a hyperpyron, and a billon (base alloy) coin worth 1/48th. The financial ministries were then brought together in 1094 under the control of a new supremo, the Grand Logariast of the Sekreta (to be joined in 1099 by the Grand Logariast of charitable foundations). Finally, in 1109, the tax system could be reformed, the register being brought up to date and care taken to adjust what was owned to what was owed in tax.[30]

## 5.2 First Crusade

Alexios' most striking initiative, taken in the 1090s, transformed the geopolitical position of Byzantium. In the short run it greatly boosted Byzantine power; in the long run it jeopardized the existence of a Byzantine state. It introduced a fourth important factor—the West—of which Byzantine foreign policy had to take account, in addition to the Turkish, Norman, and Balkan factors.

Alexios turned to Latin Christendom, fragmented politically, seething with local conflicts and highly militarized, for help against his eastern adversaries. Official appeals were buttressed by the arrival of news from many quarters about the deteriorating position of Byzantium. There can be little doubt that he aimed to tap the virtually inexhaustible manpower of Italy, Germany, France, and England for the supplementary armed forces which would enable him to take back control of the old Anatolian heartland of the empire. In the first instance he looked to the papacy, to organize what would have to be a collective effort by greater and lesser lordships. It was surely the superordinate religious authority of a pope which could best rouse enthusiasm for what could be construed as a religious war against Muslims.[31]

[29] Cheynet, *Pouvoir et contestations*, 369–73.

[30] Angold, *Byzantine Empire*, 153–5.

[31] J. Shepard, 'Aspects of Byzantine Attitudes and Policy towards the West in the Tenth and Eleventh Centuries', in Howard-Johnston, *Byzantium and the West*, 67–118, at 102–16; C. Tyerman, *A New History of the Crusades* (London, 2007), 4–10, 13–20; P. Frankopan, *The First Crusade: The Call from the East* (London, 2012), 60–1, 87–100.

The timing of the First Crusade, in the late 1090s, was, I believe, attributable to the call from Byzantium, itself timed to take advantage of a period of disarray among the Muslim powers of the Middle East following the deaths of the Seljuk Sultan Malik Shah (1092) and Badr al-Jamali, the powerful Armenian ruler of Fatimid Egypt (1094).[32] But the response which it evoked is explicable largely by reference to conditions in Latin Christendom. There was a plethora of fighting men, ready for adventure and eager for the spoils and glory obtainable on the battlefield. The antipathy between faith and fighting had been overcome in the deep past, in late antiquity, with the development of the notion of just war. While the struggle of Christians was primarily conducted in the spiritual sphere, the use of force in earthly affairs had been legitimized. War had even been *sanctified* from time to time, as in the age of Charlemagne. Armed men had been co-opted into the church's service, as protectors of Christian peace. Popes had proved ready to take the lead in sanctifying specific campaigns and offering absolution from sins for those who fought for them, as Gregory VII did for Robert Guiscard's attack on Dalmatia in 1081. There was nothing untoward then in Alexios' resort to the pope as potential instigator of war.[33]

The key question, though, concerns *the origin of the idea of a crusade, the conception of a plan to move very large numbers of armed men over huge distances, from one end of the known world to the other, to fight a war sanctified by the Christian church.* It could, of course, have come from the papacy itself, given the distant horizons of vision of the pre-eminent patriarch among the five patriarchs inherited from antiquity, which ran from the British Isles and Scandinavia to Russia, Byzantium, and the Middle East. Indeed the first articulation of something approximating to a crusade came in 1074 from the great reforming pope Gregory VII (before he turned against Byzantium). He issued several calls, two general, two addressed to individual rulers, for the Christians of the west to go east, to help the beleaguered eastern church. He even expressed the hope that he might lead the expedition. It is hard, though, to know how serious he was and how realistic was his plan. Given the circumstances, an escalating crisis in relations with the German empire, one suspects that his prime purpose was political, to assert his authority in Christendom—in effect an early example of gesture politics. In the event nothing came of it.[34]

[32] Beihammer *Muslim–Turkish Anatolia*, 251–60; Brett, *Fatimid Empire*, 228–32.

[33] Tyerman, *New History*, 28–49.

[34] Tyerman, *New History*, 49–51.

It is surely more likely that the idea with real pull came from Byzantium, which had, after all, had all too much experience of Islamic *jihad*. Leo VI had even tried to encourage voluntary enlistment and voluntary donations to the war effort from civilians, in emulation of Islamic practice. He was envious and admiring of the sanctification of war in Islam, where a charismatic preacher, who issued a call for *jihad*, might mobilize many thousands from near and distant parts of the Caliphate.[35] Alexios, I submit, was the prime progenitor of the idea of the crusade. This was the greatest of his foreign policy achievements. He identified Latin Christendom as a reservoir of fighting men far larger than that on which Muslims could draw. He knew that a call, issued from the right quarter, might evoke a massive response from a turbulent society suffused with Christian faith. He showed that he understood the *mores* of the western world, in his affability to the crusade leaders when they reached Constantinople and his use of homage to secure their loyalty.[36] It was he, in this scenario, who picked out Jerusalem as the prime objective of a Christian *jihad*, aware as he was of the pull it exercised on Latin Christendom, evident in the many western pilgrims who made the perilous journey. Above all, it was he who conceived of the pope as a peripatetic *jihad* preacher, with the task of mobilizing the faithful in region after region. Some of the devices used to enhance the solemnity of the occasions—elaborate ceremonial, the presence of holy relics, use of the symbol of the cross—may also have been partly inspired by Byzantium.[37]

Nothing should be read into Anna Komnene's silence about the origin of the Crusade. She has little to say about contemporary affairs in the wider world, beyond the arenas of combat (e.g. virtually no background information about the Turks, nothing at all about the Rus), perhaps because she found the task beyond her without the help of materials left behind by her husband, perhaps in the western case out of discretion.[38] There are signs, though, in the preparations Alexios was making in the 1090s, that he expected the pope's preaching to inspire very large numbers to come east.

[35] G. Dagron, 'Byzance et le modèle islamique au Xe siècle. À propos des Constitutions tactiques de l'empereur Léon VI', *Comptes rendus de l'Académie des Inscriptions et Belles-Lettres*, 127.2 (1983), 219–43. A notable case was that of the Khurasani volunteers who responded to the call of a charismatic Mayyafariqin preacher and marched to the rescue of Tarsos in 964 (see pp. 111–12 above).

[36] *Annae Comnenae Alexias*, ed. D. R. Reinsch & A. Kambylis, CFHB 40, 2 vols. (Berlin, 2001), x.9.2, 10.5–7, 11.1–2, 5, xi.3.1–2, trans. E. R. A. Sewter, rev. P. Frankopan, *The Alexiad* (London, 2009).

[37] Tyerman, *New History*, 62–72; J. France, *Victory in the East: A Military History of the First Crusade* (Cambridge, 1994), 100.

[38] Howard-Johnston, 'Anna Komnene', 296–300.

He strengthened the traditional alliance with Venice by offering generous trading terms in 1092. He made overtures to the Normans of southern Italy and Sicily, attested by grants of the title *protonobilissimus* to senior bureaucrats serving in the comital administration of Sicily. Relations certainly improved in the 1090s, as is shown in the conciliatory tone of the official Norman account of Robert Guiscard's reign, William of Apulia's *Gesta Roberti Wiscardi*, finished between 1097 and 1099.[39] Finally the Pechenegs, subjected to effective Byzantine rule by the middle 1090s, were ready to be deployed to marshal and police crusading forces as they made their way across the Balkans.[40]

The key moment of ignition can be dated precisely—to the council held by Pope Urban II at Piacenza in March 1095, when a formal appeal for help was brought by Byzantine ambassadors. After careful preparations, he set off to preach holy war in southern and central France, on a tour which began in Provence in July and lasted for fourteen months. The climactic event was the Council of Clermont (November 1095), attended by clergy from Italy, Austria, and the Anglo-Norman realms as well as France, plus some lay magnates (see Figure 5.1). Numerous decrees were issued on church matters, but the most important was a formal papal decree authorizing the crusade, a holy war targeted on the holy city of Jerusalem, a holy war which would reward all who took part with remission from their sins. This emphasis on penitence was the chief papal gloss on Byzantine ideas of holy war, explicable in the context of the general preoccupation of the western church with the Crucifixion rather than the Resurrection as opening a laborious way to salvation. The date for the assembly of forces and their departure was set for the feast of the Assumption of the Virgin (15 August 1096).[41]

There were other *jihad* preachers on the move in the north, principally in northern France and the Rhineland. Their leader, Peter the Hermit, spoke in a more down-to-earth revivalist way, bringing in visions and

[39] P. Frankopan, 'Byzantine Trade Privileges to Venice in the Eleventh Century: The Chrysobull of 1092', *Journal of Medieval History*, 30 (2004), 135–60; Howard-Johnston, 'Bilingual Reading', 470–1, 496–7; J. Johns, *Arabic Administration in Norman Sicily: The Royal Diwan* (Cambridge, 2002), 65–74—the known honorands were (1) Bonos, protonotary and senior judge, a close relative of Roger I's chaplain, Scholarios, attested with the title in in January 1110; (2) Nicholas, another protonotary and senior judge (in his case of all Calabria), attested with the title in August 1099; and (3) Christodoulos, as emir in charge of the whole comital administration between *c.*1107 and *c.*1120, who was granted the title in April 1109.

[40] France, *Victory in the East*, 102–7.

[41] Tyerman, *New History*, 61–8, 71–6; Mathews, *Art of Byzantium.*

**Figure 5.1** Pope Urban II (1088–99) preaching at Clermont in 1095 (Jean Fouquet, *c.*1420–81).
*Source*: Alamy.

stories of atrocities, and roused enthusiasm wherever he went. In the event it was Peter and his two chief deputies who succeeded in mustering the first hosts by Easter 1096 (13 April), totalling, it seems, up to 30,000 men. They were, it appears, more enthused with religious ardour (all too eager to attack the principal Jewish communities in Rhineland cities), but worse organized than the hosts raised by church authorities in France and Italy. They did not fare well. Three of the four forces which set off to cross Hungary did not reach Byzantine territory. The exception was the largest, led by Peter and preceded by an advance force. They were shipped over to a camp on the southern shore of the Gulf of Nikomedia, where, rather than waiting for the arrival of the papal forces, they launched a premature and disastrous attack on Nikaia.[42] The second, better organized, and larger wave of crusaders (some 50,000 all told) involved four armies from France, Lorraine, and Flanders under the command of powerful regional figures, and a smallish Norman force from southern Italy led Byzantium's old adversary, Bohemond. They made their way by land and sea to the Balkans, and were shepherded, with some friction, through to the metropolitan area, where they arrived between November 1096 and May 1097. Alexios succeeded in extracting oaths of fealty from their leaders and in transferring them one by one to the Asian shore of the Bosporus.[43]

The Byzantine plan to which the Crusade leaders agreed was for them to hand over whatever traditional Byzantine lands they recovered on their march to the Holy Land, in return for Byzantine military and logistic support and advice (to be provided by a senior general with a small staff who would accompany them). Without that advice, it is unlikely that the Crusade leaders would have cooperated so willingly and effectively with the Armenian diaspora in Cilicia and northern Syria, or, at an earlier stage, would have been able to march largely unscathed across the Anatolian plateau. Apart from direct help (troops, boats, and technical advice) for the siege of Nikaia, the chief Byzantine contributions were the shipping of supplies once the Crusaders gained control of Cilicia and the territory of Antioch, and the dispatch of two expeditionary forces in 1098, one into the Aegean coastlands of Asia Minor, the other commanded by the emperor across the plateau to join the Crusaders for operations in northern Syria and Palestine. The key figure who was to act as Byzantium's agent among the Crusade leaders was Bohemond, now reconciled with Alexios.

[42] Tyerman, *New History*, 78–81, 94–106; France, *Victory in the East*, 88–93.
[43] Tyerman, *New History*, 106–22.

Bohemond went so far as to ask for a formal appointment as Domestic of the East (a request refused for the moment).[44]

Things went according to plan in 1097: Nikaia surrendered after a siege of a month and a half; Turkish attacks were repelled, one as the siege was beginning, another afterwards as the Crusaders were advancing towards Dorylaion on the first stage of their march across Asia Minor; they then continued their difficult march in the heat of summer across the plateau; at Herakleia they divided, two forays invading Cilicia by the Cilician Gates, the main army following the old Roman road past Kaisareia to the enclosed basin within the Anti-Taurus, where it turned right (the road used by Basil I to attack Maraş in 878); the Crusaders reached Antioch on 21 October 1097. Antioch was their prime objective that year, as had almost certainly been agreed with the Byzantines. It was well placed to act as the base for future operations against the fractious emirates of Syria and Palestine, and was now isolated, the Crusaders being in control of Cilicia to the west, of the mountains to the north, and of Edessa to the east.[45]

The siege of Antioch lasted over seven months. At first it went well. An English fleet, acting perhaps on Byzantine instructions, had seized Laodikeia on 19 August. Other fleets, from Genoa, Pisa, and Venice, seized other ports. Supplies could be shipped in from Cyprus. But the decision, taken early on, to institute a tight siege of the city, rather than adopt the Byzantine strategy of maintaining pressure on the city and its territory from nearby strongholds, was unwise. Instead of relative comfort and security, the Crusaders were exposed to bitter winter weather and to attack by relieving armies. After a first such attack by the ruler of Damascus, which halted a large-scale foraging expedition inland (late December 1097), supplies ran low and the horses, needed for forays, died in large numbers. By the beginning of February morale had sunk and desertions were beginning. The chief Byzantine adviser, the general Tatikios, left to find supplies and bring reinforcements. A few days later the besiegers faced an attack by a strong relieving force from Aleppo, which was defeated in a hard-fought battle. Despite the easing of the supply problems from March (with arrival of a second English fleet) and a tightening of the blockade, the siege dragged on to a dramatic *dénouement*. Intelligence was received (on 29 May) of an imminent attack by a third army, more powerful than its predecessors, assembled by Karbuqa, *atabeg* of Mosul. Bohemond intensified his

44 Tyerman, *New History*, 120–2; France, *Victory in the East*, 110–21, 122–4, 143–5.
45 Tyerman, *New History*, 124, 129–34; France, *Victory in the East*, 160–96.

negotiations with a Turkish commander in Antioch and agreed a plan for the city's betrayal on the night of 2/3 June. The first units of Karbuqa's army arrived before the city on the 4th. The Crusaders had not been caught outside the city, but they still faced a double threat—from Karbuqa's army outside, and from the garrison of Antioch which had withdrawn to the citadel.[46]

The whole future of the Crusade now hung in the balance. Byzantium meanwhile had profited greatly, regaining, with little effort, important cities like Nikaia and Dorylaion and a whole strategic region on the edge of the Middle East (Cilicia), all handed over as agreed. Byzantine forces only entered the field in large numbers in 1098, with two objectives—(1) to consolidate and extend the territorial gains made in 1097, and (2) to back up the Crusaders as they moved south from Antioch. While one army prised loose the Turkish grip on the rich Aegean coastlands of Asia Minor and the Maeander valley, recovering Smyrna, Ephesos, Sardis, Philadelphia, and Laodikeia, along with the cult site of Choma and Botaneiates' home town of Lampe, a second under Alexios' personal command marched south on the inner, eastern side of the western hills to Philomelion where the two armies were to meet. The only serious resistance encountered and overcome was outside Ephesos and at Polybotos, near Philomelion. It was at Philomelion, on or about 20 June, that intelligence came about the arrival of the large army of Karbuqa at Antioch. It was brought by one of the Crusade leaders, Stephen of Blois, who had slipped away on 3 June, fearing the worst. Alexios naturally decided to halt his march. The Crusaders were obviously doomed, and the march would be fraught with danger both on the plateau and during the crossing of mountains beyond. There was little to be gained and a great deal to be lost if he pressed on. The Byzantine approach to war was rational, scientific, calculating, leaving as little as possible to chance. Not for them the rush of emotion and determination to seek glory, which was characteristic of Germanic peoples.[47]

The Crusaders, contrary to all rational expectation, escaped their doom. Displaying the solidarity and courage noted centuries before by Byzantine observers, they sallied out on 28 June under the command of Bohemond. They moved swiftly in several divisions to engage forward elements of

[46] Beihammer, *Muslim–Turkish Anatolia*, 253–9; Tyerman, *New History*, 135–47; France, *Victory in the East*, 206–96.

[47] France, *Victory in the East*, 299–302; Beihammer, *Muslim–Turkish Anatolia*, 315–18. Key text: *Alexias*, xi.5.1–6.5. *Mauricii Strategicon*, xi.3, ed. G. T .Dennis, CFHB 17 (Vienna, 1981), trans. G. T. Dennis, *Maurice's Strategikon: Handbook of Byzantine Military Strategy* (Philadelphia, 1984), 119–20.

Karbuqa's army at close quarters. This was the shock combat at which westerners excelled. The Muslims fought hard, but eventually broke as Karbuqa was bringing up the main army, which turned and fled.[48] It was a famous victory, after which the Crusaders halted for several months to consolidate their gains (and to squabble). The divisions among the leaders were serious. It was primarily pressure from below that pushed the leaders into action. First (in December) Raymond of Toulouse marched south to Ma'arrat al-Numan (captured) and Arqah (besieged for four months). At Arqah he was eventually (14 March) joined by the other leaders, except for Bohemond who stayed at Antioch. Finally (13 May), the united forces broke off the siege of Arqah and marched to Tripoli, thence swiftly down the coast to Arsuf before turning inland and reaching Jerusalem (7 June). With the aid of siege towers constructed by Genoese engineers out of large timbers cannibalized from their ships, the Crusaders stormed the city on 15 June 1099 (see Figure 5.2), after which there was uncontrolled carnage and plundering. More dissension between the leaders was then cut short by the approach of a large Fatimid army. The Crusaders' victory after a swift march and surprise attack sealed their hold on Jerusalem and their domination of Palestine.[49]

Alexios' failure to come to the aid of the Crusaders at Antioch, coupled with the earlier departure of Tatikios, poisoned relations. Suspicion, borne of differences of temperament between Byzantines and Latins, already plain as increasing numbers of the latter went east in the eleventh century, was immeasurably increased. Intelligence and cunning in warfare were all too easily construed as cowardice. Bohemond, the Crusade leader favoured by Alexios, was transformed into Byzantium's most intransigent foe.[50] He became the chief purveyor of anti-Byzantine propaganda in the west. In the short term he laid claim to Antioch in his own right, thus casting aside the commitment to return it to Alexios. Later, back in the west, he would launch a second Norman invasion of Dalmatia (1107–8).[51] Despite the best efforts of Alexios and his successors as well as westerners who were well disposed to Byzantium, there would be no ending of the estrangement between east and west. A latent antagonism undoubtedly helps explain the intransigence of both sides. It was to stymie successive imperial efforts to achieve

[48] France, *Victory in the East*, 280–96. [49] Tyerman, *New History*, 147–61.

[50] J. Shepard, When Greek Meets Greek: Alexios Komnenos and Bohemond in 1097–98', *BMGS* 12 (1988), 185–277.

[51] Tyerman, *New History*, 120, 147–8; Harris, *Byzantium and the Crusades*, 82–4, 93–7 (full reference in n. 71 below).

**Figure 5.2** Storming of Jerusalem by the First Crusade, 1099 (tapestry, Flemish school, 15th century).
*Source*: Bridgeman.

compromise over relatively trivial divergences of practice and doctrine between the churches. This in turn deepened the political rift.[52]

## 5.3 Komnenian foreign policy I (1099–1143)

Byzantium survived fierce Arab attacks from the seventh to the ninth century, above all because the natural defences of Asia Minor in the east were held. Arab armies could, if large and bold enough, break through those defences and march on to the Aegean and Marmara coastlands, or, if smaller, raid the interior plateau. But their few attempts to establish a permanent forward base on the inner side of the frontier mountains all failed. Two lines of defences thus secured the fertile lowlands in the west and north-west, an inner line of mountains backing on to the coastlands, and a forward line on the frontier, running from Cilicia to the Euphrates (Taurus

[52] Angold, *Byzantine Empire*, 166–7, 211–14.

and Anti-Taurus). In between lay the Anatolian plateau which served as the principal arena of combat as well as an important resource-base. Asia Minor—coastal lowlands, encircling highlands, and raised plateau—constituted the heartland of Byzantium through its long dark age and the age of revival. Its loss to the Turks in the second half of the eleventh century greatly diminished the state's resources and security. The Balkans, even after the incorporation of Bulgar lands in the north and west, were an inadequate substitute, partly because much of the west and north was lightly governed, forming something akin to a *terre d'insolence* (to use the French colonial term), but mainly because it was exposed to attack across the Adriatic from Italy and in the north from Hungary and steppe nomad peoples.

Alexios may have delayed his counter-offensive against the Turks in Asia Minor, because of one beneficial effect of their presence—the weakening of the great magnate families of the Anatolian plateau, who were potential rivals of the Komnenos–Doukas nexus. It is plain, though, that reconquest remained in his mind and, as I have argued, his chosen instrument, for loosening the Turkish grip, was the First Crusade, backed up by his own (somewhat diminished) forces. The capture and garrisoning of the principal cities of the Aegean coastlands and Maeander valley (together with the extrusion of Turks from nearby islands), marked a first stage in the reconquest of Asia Minor. An opportunity to build on the success of the First Crusade came with the arrival of a third wave of westerners eager to reach the Holy Land, inspired by the news of Jerusalem's capture and another round of *jihad* preaching by papal emissaries in France.

These volunteers for holy war came from Lombardy and south Germany as well as France. Well organized in regional forces under the command of great nobles, they made their way to Constantinople, the Lombards arriving first at the end of February 1101 and being shipped across the Bosporus to Nikomedia in late April. The French and Germans joined them at Nikomedia in early June. The arrangements were the same as in 1097—any Byzantine territory recovered was to be handed over, while the Byzantines would provide advice, logistic help, and some troops. It looks very much as if Alexios hoped to use this massive gathering of western troops to continue the process of reasserting control over the Anatolian plateau. That at any rate is what is suggested by their actions, which were directed at both Danishmends and Seljuks. The first army to leave, that of the Lombards, pushed out across the Anatolian plateau to Ankyra, which it captured, and marched on east, with Neokaisareia deep in Danishmend territory to the north-east as its objective. The Lombards had learned (presumably from the Byzantines) that Bohemond was emprisoned there after being captured by the Danishmends in 1100. A second army, led by William of Nevers, followed in their tracks as far as Ankyra, where it turned south to attack Ikonion, the Seljuk capital. The third and largest army (French and German) followed the route of the First Crusade diagonally across the plateau to Ikonion. All three thrusts ended in disaster. Each crusading army was harassed and worn down by the Turks, before being trapped and destroyed.[53] While the strategic decisions, responsible for the debacle, were those of the great nobles leading the armies, emboldened by the achievements of the First Crusade, it is likely that Alexios did nothing to discourage them, contrary to a claim to that effect made by Anna Komnene writing long after the events.[54] Indeed one may suspect that he had a hand in devising the plan for what looks a grand three-pronged offensive.

Whatever may have been the case, there was only one lesson to be drawn from the bloody *dénouement* of the 1101 campaigns. It was perilous in the extreme to venture out onto the Anatolian plateau and seek to break the power of the Turks by direct attack on their centres of power. In future, the only feasible approach must be indirect and gradual—a slow, step-by-step encroachment from the peripheral mountains onto Turkish territory in the interior plateau. That does indeed seem to have been the policy of Alexios in the second half of his reign and of his two successors, John II and Manuel I. The reassertion of Byzantine authority over Asia Minor remained a long-term aim. But a slow, unglamorous process of gradual strangulation of plateau powers (in effect the application of offensive guerrilla strategy to whole regions rather than single cities, as in the tenth century) could not and did not retain a high priority at all times. Crises rose on other frontiers, which had to be dealt with, and there was the perennial problem of relations with Latin Christendom after the Antioch debacle. It was vital to court, or at least to avoid antagonizing, the principal non-Norman powers which could affect Byzantium, namely the German empire, the papacy, and the Italian maritime republics. This inevitably complicated the task of imposing Byzantium's will on the refractory Normans in the Middle East, a task to which Alexios and both his successors accorded the highest priority for long periods.

Resentment at Bohemond's unilateral abandonment of the agreement made by the Crusaders was the primary driver of this policy. Alexios had done

[53] Tyerman, *New History*, 170–5. [54] *Alexias*, xi.8.2.

everything a rational man could to help the Crusade. But Bohemond, disregarding his commitment, backed by an oath of fealty, to hand over former Byzantine territory (and fending off counter-claims by other Crusade leaders), had seized Antioch as his personal property (which his nephew Tancred ruled during his captivity [1101–3] and after his subsequent departure to the west [1105]).[55] Circumstances in the Middle East were propitious. The power of both neigbouring Muslim empires was receding. After the defeat of al-Afdal in 1099, Fatimid forces fell back on their southern stronghold of Ascalon, and could do no more than launch counterattacks by land and sea as the Crusaders consolidated their hold on the coast and interior of Palestine and Syria (1101–18). As for the Seljuks, the army sent in by Sultan Muhammad Tapar against Antioch in response to an embassy from Alexios in December 1110/January 1111 achieved little because of opposition from local Muslim lordships, and suffered a crushing defeat at the hands of the regent of Antioch at the battle of Sarmin in September 1115. It was the greater local lordships, based on the principal cities of the northern Levant (Mosul, Aleppo, and Damascus), which now dominated the hinterlands of the four states eventually established by the Crusaders (centred on Antioch, Edessa, Tripoli, and Jerusalem). Byzantium was left as the only great (though diminished) peripheral power which could intervene militarily and diplomatically.[56]

The first moves against Bohemond were made in 1099 and 1100. An attempt was made to blockade him by sea. The defences of Cyprus were strengthened. The powerful fortresses of Seleukeia (a former theme capital) and Korykos were seized, which between them commanded the western approaches to Cilicia and the main maritime route to northern Syria passing between Cyprus and the mainland. Laodikeia, captured in 1098 and held by the Byzantines until 1103, formed a third major base from which Byzantine ships could intercept western fleets. In the event, despite the arrival of substantial reinforcements, the Byzantine navy was unable to defeat the fleets from Pisa and Genoa coming to Bohemond's aid, and despite an alliance with Raymond of Toulouse who was besieging Tripoli, whatever gains Byzantium made (especially at a moment of Norman weakness in 1104) were soon lost along with Laodikeia (1106).[57] Alexios' attention

[55] Tyerman, *New History*, 148–9.

[56] M. Brett, *The Fatimid Empire* (Edinburgh, 2017), 233–7, 240–5; Beihammer, *Muslim–Turkish Anatolia*, 361–3; Tyerman, *New History*, 178–82, 185–7, 189–91, 196–8, 200–6.

[57] Beihammer, *Muslim–Turkish Anatolia*, 323–6; Harris, *Byzantium and the Crusades*, 82–3.

was drawn elsewhere from 1105, first to southern Italy (to which Bohemond returned that year) and Dalmatia where Bohemond's second invasion in 1107–8 ended in failure (guerrilla harassment and encirclement forced him to accept a humiliating peace), and second to Asia Minor to fend off Turkish attacks on the western coastlands (1109, 1111) and Bithynia (1113, 1116).[58]

Relatively little progress was made in the strategy of incremental territorial encroachment on the Turks of Anatolia. But Alexios took steps to tighten Byzantium's hold on peripheral regions, (1) by strengthening the fortifications of key centres on the south coast (the regional capital, Attaleia, and several ports), and (2) by maintaining strong garrisons in strategic cities in the west (Akroinion, Philadelphia, Pergamon, Adramyttion, and others).[59] His final campaign, in autumn 1116, when he ventured onto the plateau as far as Philomelion, reasserted Byzantine authority over the eastern approaches to the Aegean coastlands and ended with his evacuating the loyalist population of the Philomelion region to safe Byzantine territory.[60]

Alexios' son and successor, John II (1118–43, see Figure 5.3), pressed on with Alexios' policy of gradually tightening the squeeze on the Turks of Anatolia and, simultaneously, striving to bring Cilicia and the principality of Antioch under effective Byzantine control. There were inevitably distractions. John had to fight two defensive wars in the north, the first short and sharp against a Cuman–Pecheneg horde which, under pressure from the Rus, withdrew south of the Danube (defeated at Berroia in April 1122), the second longer, with fluctuating fortunes, against the Hungarians in 1127–9. There was also trouble from the refractory Serbs of Raška (1123, 1125, 1129).[61] Direct military action (1123, 1129) was backed up by a programme of castle-building to south-east and north-east, by deportation and resettlement of Raškans in Bithynia (1123), and by the installation of Pechenegs in the western Balkans.[62] Finally there was a breakdown in relations with the Venetians, when, at his accession, John did not renew the privileges granted by Alexios. The Venetian response was delayed—until the departure of a large fleet of 70 ships under the Doge's command to Outremer (the Crusaders' states in the Levant) in 1122. There was trouble on the outward voyage, at Corfu

[58] Stephenson, *Byzantium's Balkan Frontier*, 179–83; Beihammer, *Muslim–Turkish Anatolia*, 364–72.

[59] Beihammer, *Muslim–Turkish Anatolia*, 326–7, 363–6.

[60] Beihammer, *Muslim–Turkish Anatolia*, 372–3. It is impossible to say whether or not Anna Komnene was right to allege that Alexios' original plan was to march on Ikonion (*Alexias*, xv.5.3–4).

[61] Lau, *John II Komnenos*, 102–9, 120–3, 140–58.

[62] Lau, *John II Komnenos*, 112–16, 158–68.

**Figure 5.3** Hagia Sophia. Mosaic of Virgin and Child, flanked by John II Komnenos (1118–43) and his Hungarian wife, Piroska/Irene.
*Source*: Wikimedia/Mariano Jiménez.

where the fleet wintered, and open hostility when it set off home after the fall of Tyre to the Crusaders in July 1124. Rhodes, Methone, and Samos were raided that autumn; Lesbos, Andros, and probably Lemnos early in 1125 from Chios which had suffered much from the fleet during the winter. After more offensive strikes, prompted by news of the burning of the Venetian quarter in Constantinople, against Kephalonia and Corfu which guarded the maritime approaches to Greece, John yielded in 1126, making peace and renewing the Venetian privileges.[63]

As for Anatolia, John was able to make two crucial gains in successive campaigns against the Seljuks of Rum before being forced to turn his attention north and west. Each campaign was targeted on a city commanding north–south and west–east routes, first Laodikeia (captured 1119), then Sozopolis and a number of strongholds in the hinterland of Attaleia in 1120.[64] He encountered relatively little resistance, because of a gathering political crisis in the sultanate of Rum—Kilij Arslan's second son and successor, Shahanshah, had been overthrown and executed by his brother

[63] Lau, *John II Komnenos*, 116–19, 124–7, 134–8.
[64] Beihammer, *Muslim–Turkish Anatolia*, 376; Lau, *John II Komnenos*, 93–8.

Mas'ud (probably because of the agreement he reached with Alexios in 1116), and Mas'ud would be ousted in turn by a third brother, 'Arab in 1124. John was only able to follow up these early successes against the Turks, when he was free of entanglements elsewhere, after a year (1130) spent in Constantinople, taking stock, planning, and coping with the flight of his brother and principal lieutenant, Isaac, to the Danishmends. This gave added urgency to what was his prime task, confrontation with the rising power of the Danishmend ruler, Gumushtekin, who was extending his authority from his core territory in eastern Anatolia (between Sebasteia and Cappadocia), (1) east over Melitene, ousting Toghril, a fifth son of Kilij Arslan, (2) north over Pontus where he received the submission of the Byzantine governor, and (3) south over Cilicia, where he defeated and killed Bohemond II ruler of Antioch in 1129 and forced the leading Armenian potentate, the Rupenid, Leon I, to pay tribute in 1131.[65]

John devoted the second half of his reign to the east, seeking to pen in the Danishmend Turks to their core territory in eastern Anatolia and to raise Byzantium's standing in Outremer. He saw it as his duty to take charge of military operations in the northern Levant and to extend the conquests made by the Crusaders, to the east and south of Antioch, thus belatedly fulfilling the commitment made by Alexios in 1097–8. After a year of preparations spent strengthening his base of operations in Bithynia (Lopadion) and, presumably, conducting military exercises (like Heraclius in 622), John set off in 1132 for Kastamon, the Komnenians' home city, in Paphlagonia. Kastamon was besieged and taken, the surrounding territory was cleared of Turkmen raiders, and the army pushed on to the Halys and beyond, taking booty and prisoners. However, the triumph celebrated in 1133 was premature. Gumushtekin recovered Kastamon and John fell ill. It was only after Gumushtekin's death in September 1133 and the resulting divisions between his sons that John returned to the field and targeted Gangra, well to the south of Kastamon on the northern edge of the plateau. With the capture of both cities (Kastamon capitulated, Gangra surrendered after a siege), John gained two useful advanced bases from which to apply increased pressure on the core territory of the Danishmends. This was not the end of Byzantine–Danishmend fighting, which continued when John turned his attention to Cilicia and Antioch.[66]

[65] C. Cahen, *The Formation of Turkey: The Seljukid Sultanate of Rum, Eleventh to Fourteenth Century* (London, 2001), 11–19.

[66] Lau, *John II Komnenos*, 170–91.

John prepared the way with a flurry of diplomatic activity in 1135–7, which resulted in a grand alliance of Byzantium, the papacy, the German empire, and the Italian maritime republics, to secure his position against the Normans of southern Italy and Sicily. The Cilician campaign in 1137 was remarkably successful: John imposed Byzantine authority, installing garrisons in key strongholds—Tarsos which surrendered after a show of force, Adana and Mopsouestia which followed suit, and Anazarbos which was besieged and captured. Marching across the Amanos mountains, he laid on another demonstration involving light infantry and artillery before the walls of Antioch. Raymond of Poitiers, who had married Constance daughter of Bohemond II, fended off a siege, by acknowledging Byzantine suzerainty. He became the emperor's client, swearing an oath of fealty and giving the emperor a right of entry into the city, in return for an undertaking by the emperor to lead a campaign the following year against the key Muslim centres in northern Syria—Aleppo, Shayzar, Hama, and Homs. On the eve of winter (spent in Cilicia), John marched north to drive off a raiding Danishmend army which attacked Maraş (Germanikeia) and a foray raiding Cilicia, and sealed his control of Cilicia by capturing Leon I's mountain redoubts at Geben and Vahka.[67]

The 1138 campaign ended triumphantly with John staging a victory parade in Antioch. But the returns for the effort put in by the Byzantines in conjunction with Antiochene and Edessan forces were meagre. Aleppo, under its *atabeg* Zengi, held out, as did Shayzar. The only gains were three fortresses and tribute from the ruler of Shayzar. John was not even able to station troops in Antioch (a proposal which led to rioting). With the news of the death of the German emperor Lothar and the unravelling of his western alliance, John marched back to Constantinople along the route of his outward march, sending a raiding foray against Ikonion.[68] The next few years were spent countering Danishmend raids on Bithynia and Cilicia (spring 1139); imposing direct imperial authority on Pontus (1139–40); strengthening the defences of the Aegean coastlands, Pontus, and the south coast; and preparing (1141) for a second Syrian campaign.[69] This was scheduled for 1143, after a march in 1142 through Christian-held territory as far as Edessa, in the course of which Turkish raiders were driven away from Sozopolis and Lake Beyşehir (west of Ikonion) was brought under Byzantine control. The circumstances were propitious with the death of

[67] Lau, *John II Komnenos*, 193–229.
[68] Lau, *John II Komnenos*, 229–46.
[69] Lau, *John II Komnenos*, 247–55, 273–90.

Muhammad, the Danishmend emir, in 1142 and the outbreak of civil war between his three sons and his Seljuk son-in-law Mas'ud. This smooth display of Byzantine hegemony was then marred when John's request for Antioch to be handed over was refused point-blank. The army then withdrew west to winter once again in Cilicia, and, after John's unexpected death in spring 1143, marched swiftly back to Constantinople to secure the succession of his fourth son and designated heir, Manuel.[70]

John seems to have pursued his two prime aims in the east—encirclement of the dominant Turkish power on the plateau, and extension of Byzantine authority over Cilicia and northern Syria—with equal vigour. Conciliation of the Armenian church helped cement his hold over Cilicia, while willingness to take a lead in campaigning against the Muslims in northern Syria gained him kudos among the Latins and shifted the balance between suzerain and client in favour of the former. But the chief military effort of his reign was directed against the Turks. He was determined to extend the Byzantine zone of control around the edges of the plateau, as he showed in a late attempt to take Neokaisareia (1140) and his venture into the region of the Pisidian lakes (1142). His equally decisive intervention late in 1137 to maintain the integrity of the county of Edessa and repel the Danishmend attack on Maraş may indicate that he viewed these south-eastern territories as part of the circumvallation of the Anatolian plateau.

## 5.4 Komnenian foreign policy II (1143–80)

Manuel Komnenos had proved himself as a military commander before he came to power, and repeatedly took charge of operations in the field during his reign. He was also that rare thing, an emperor who believed in a hierarchy of earthly rulers; not the neat, tiered system envisaged by some Byzantinists, but something looser, a sort of feudal system in the ideological sphere. The high points of his reign were carefully choreographed scenes in which other rulers did obeisance or were publicly shown to be his clients.[71] He strove to head what he viewed as a family of princes—hence the many years of open rivalry for pre-eminence with the German empire and the importance he attached to negotiations for recognition as emperor by the

[70] Lau, *John II Komnenos*, 258–71.

[71] J. Harris, *Byzantium and the Crusades* (2nd edn, London, 2014), 27–30, 99, 101–2, 113–14, 115–16; P. Magdalino, *The Empire of Manuel I Komnenos, 1143–1180* (Cambridge, 1993), 56, 76–7.

pope.[72] Hence too his determination to assert Byzantine power wherever possible—in the north by forcing the Hungarians into notional dependency, in the east by striving throughout his reign to bring the rulers of the increasingly beleaguered crusader states into his clientage and his willingness to take a leading part in (vain) counteroffensives, and in the west by cultivating notable factions in Italian cities (including Rome).[73] He acted as the arbiter of earthly affairs, raising up first one, then another rival Serb leader, nominating the ruler of Hungary, arranging marriage alliances (the most notable that of his 8-year-old son Alexios to Agnes, 8-year-old daughter of Louis VII) to create a web of familial connections, and shifting his patronage (in the form of commercial privileges) between Italian maritime cities (from Venice to Pisa and Genoa in 1171).[74] He was, in effect, creating, at least in his own mind, a political system transcending east and west, in which the Byzantine emperor held the balance of power, and from which he could draw resources for whatever was his principal project at the time.

There was a cost, a heavy cost—neglect of the vital interests of Byzantium in its near abroad, Asia Minor, Cilicia, and northern Syria. After aborting John's projected campaign against Aleppo in 1143, Manuel returned to the Levant only once, for a brief display of Byzantine might in 1159. Two events gave him no choice. Reynald of Chatillon, ruler of Antioch as Constance's husband since 1153, and Toros, son of Leon I, had joined forces to launch a devastating raid on Cyprus in 1156, Toros then going on to rout a Byzantine force commanded by Manuel's cousin Andronikos at Mamistra in 1158. Manuel hurried out in winter 1158–9. The expedition was a notable success in ideological terms. Toros and Reynald were both to do obeisance in humiliating ceremonies. Baldwin, King of Jerusalem, met Manuel whose niece he had married, and at the end of their talks in Cilicia appeared seated on a lower throne in a public display of an unequal relationship. They both moved on to Antioch, where Manuel's entry was carefully staged as an imperial triumph. These ceremonial acts were followed by the issue of an ultimatum to Nureddin, Zengi's successor as ruler of Aleppo. He was to return conquered Antiochene territory and the county of Edessa together with Christian prisoners-of-war, or face attack by the combined forces of Manuel and Baldwin. In the event, the threat proved empty. Manuel halted the campaign early on, accepted the truce proposed by Nureddin (involving

[72] Magdalino, *Manuel I Komnenos*, 83–90.
[73] Magdalino, *Manuel I Komnenos*, 71–5, 80–1, 83–5.
[74] Magdalino, *Manuel I Komnenos*, 56, 79, 80–1, 93–5, 100–2.

the return of some prisoners), and hurried back to Constantinople, cutting directly across the plateau.[75]

As for the two Turkish states established on the Anatolian plateau, Manuel proved remarkably complaisant. He did not continue his father's policy of increasing pressure and gradual encirclement. Apart from a punitive expedition against Ikonion in 1145 in retaliation for frontier violations, and an outbreak of fighting in 1159 following Manuel's march across Seljuk territory, peace prevailed. It was formalized by treaties in 1147 (with Mas'ud) and 1161 (with Kilij Arslan II). Kilij Arslan was seeking Byzantine aid against his Danishmend rival, who had the backing of Nureddin. He came to Constantinople, where Manuel turned his visit into another occasion for the display of imperial munificence and might. After eighty days of lavish entertainment, he left with a promise of subsidies, in return for which he committed himself to serving the emperor, as a client (like the king of Jerusalem). This agreement held good until 1174, when, on the death of Nureddin, Kilij Arslan seized the towns and fortresses of the Danishmend emirate, from Neokaisareia in the north to Cappadocia in the south. If only Manuel had sought to play off the two Turkish states against each other as he did the German empire and Norman Sicily in the 1160s, if only he had been concerned to chip away at Seljuk territory in the first instance, he would not have been faced with a single, threatening Turkish power in control of the whole interior of Asia Minor.[76]

But Manuel was no more a free agent throughout his reign than his father or grandfather had been. Serious threats from without demanded his attention in the early years of his reign, followed by the perennial problem of Serb dissidence. The first of the threats from without was the Second Crusade, which was called by the pope in response to the news of the fall of Edessa to Zengi in December 1144. This time two kings, the most powerful rulers in Latin Christendom, took personal charge of two armies and marched to Constantinople. There was trouble with the Germans, commanded by the Emperor Conrad III, who arrived first, in September 1047, but it did not lead to serious dissension between the emperors, who were already connected by marriage (Conrad's sister-in-law and adopted daughter, Bertha of Sulzbach, had married Manuel in 1146). Later, the kindness shown to Conrad when he was taken ill and brought back to Constantinople tightened the bonds between them. The Germans were ferried across the

[75] Harris, *Byzantium and the Crusades*, 112–16; Magdalino, *Manuel I Komnenos*, 66–71, 74.
[76] Harris, *Byzantium and the Crusades*, 107; Magdalino, *Manuel I Komnenos*, 76–8, 95.

Bosporus before the arrival of Louis VII and the French on 4 October. These crusaders fared better than their predecessors had in 1101. The Germans were mauled in an early encounter with the Turks, but then joined forces with the French, skirted Seljuk territory and crossed the Taurus to reach Attaleia in January 1148, from where they were taken by ship to Antioch.[77] The more serious threat came, as might have been expected, from the Normans. Roger II, king of Sicily, dispatched an expeditionary force in autumn 1147 to take advantage of Byzantium's preoccupation with the crusade. Corfu was occupied. Greece was attacked. Athens, Thebes, and Corinth were sacked.[78]

Manuel had no choice but to respond with an offensive of his own. He set off for the west with the land forces in 1148, only to be distracted by trouble on the Danube (a Cuman attack). When the anti-Norman campaign was resumed in 1149, the first target was Corfu, which held out into the summer. Manuel himself then took part of the army for punitive action against the refractory Serbs of Raška. The rest of the army was placed under the command of John Axouch, an experienced general, with instructions to cross the Adriatic and use Ancona as a base from which to cultivate support in Italy against the Normans. It took several years for Manuel to suppress the Serb rising which was backed by Hungary and had been incited by the Normans precisely to divert Manuel from his planned invasion of Italy. The Serbs finally submitted in 1154 and accepted Manuel's preferred ruler (Uros). The Hungarians, without Norman support following the death of Roger II in February 1154, followed suit and made peace in spring 1155.[79]

It was now that Manuel made the first of two fateful decisions, to press on with an Italian campaign with the aim of gaining control of the Apulian seaboard, and, in the longer run, of recovering more of Byzantium's former territories in the south. The campaign of 1155–6, while initially successful (Bari was taken along with other coastal cities and turned into the centre of operations), ended in a crushing defeat at Brindisi (May 1156).[80] Rather than deterring Manuel from intervening in Italian affairs, this simply made him resort to diplomacy instead of force and, from 1158 when he made peace with Roger's successor William I, to turn his attention elsewhere in the peninsula. Thenceforth his aim was to boost Byzantine prestige and

[77] Harris, *Byzantium and the Crusades*, 102–6.

[78] Magdalino, *Manuel I Komnenos*, 51.

[79] Magdalino, *Manuel I Komnenos*, 53–6; Stephenson, *Byzantium's Balkan Frontier*, 229–37, 245–7.

[80] Magdalino, *Manuel I Komnenos*, 56–61.

extend Byzantine influence in the north. From 1160, when relations between the two empires deteriorated on the death of Bertha and the accession of Frederick Barbarossa, Manuel was engaging in an open but doomed competition for hegemony with Germany which continued to 1174.[81]

The second fateful decision taken by Manuel in the 1160s, was to interfere in Hungarian internal affairs. He clearly viewed Hungary as part of the Byzantine sphere of influence, a crucial part as it lay between Byzantium and the German empire. The king must, if possible, become a Byzantine client, who could be relied on not only to keep the peace but also to ensure that Hungary acted as a buffer zone. This eventually led to the outbreak of war in 1164, and large-scale fighting over four years. The Hungarians were the aggressors, initially with Czech, German, and Rus backing, and fought to seize and hold the region of Sirmium and northern Dalmatia. Manuel was in personal command of defensive operation until 1167 when a decisive victory in a pitched battle, won by Andronikos Konstosphanos, secured Byzantine control of both regions. Finally, in 1172, Bela, Manuel's candidate, was brought from Constantinople and installed as king. Manuel's long-term goal had been achieved.[82]

During these many years of involvement in the north and west, Byzantium's interests were not completely neglected in Outremer. Amalric, Baldwin III's successor as king of Jerusalem, was courted. A joint attack was made on Damietta in Egypt in 1169, the Byzantine contribution being naval. As for Byzantine land forces, they did not reappear in the Levant, indeed took no action against any Muslim power, until 1173 when Manuel deterred Kilij Arslan from allying with Nureddin by leading an army up towards the plateau via Philadelphia.[83] A year later, after the death of Nureddin and the incorporation of the Danishmend emirate into the sultanate of Rum, the military balance was shifting in favour of the Seljuks. Manuel resolved to take action, resuming, after a gap of over thirty years, John's policy of attacking key towns (Amaseia and Neokaisareia both of which held out), and building or rebuilding aggressively positioned fortified bases (Dorylaion in the north-west, and Soublaion in the south, near Sozopolis).[84] He then prepared for what he termed a holy war of reconquest, mobilizing a large army, with Serb, Hungarian, and Outremer contingents, for a direct assault on Ikonion. He rejected peace terms offered by the sultan. He was evidently

[81] Magdalino, *Manuel I Komnenos*, 61, 83–95.
[82] Magdalino, *Manuel I Komnenos*, 78–83.
[83] Magdalino, *Manuel I Komnenos*, 72–6.
[84] Magdalino, *Manuel I Komnenos*, 95–8.

confident of success, as was also shown by his reliance on a wagon-borne siege train, which greatly restricted his freedom of manoeuvre. He was allowed to advance across the plateau to within striking distance of Ikonion before the Turks attacked, at Myriokephalon, a day's march from Ikonion. There the armed forces of Byzantium and the emperor who had sought to bestride the Mediterranean world suffered a humiliating defeat. The death toll was very high. The plunder was extensive. Manuel himself was nearly captured. It was a disaster, even more serious than defeat at Manzikert. It punctured the imperial pretensions of Manuel. It could not be disguised, however hard Byzantine propagandists sought to do so. Within a very few years, with Manuel's death in 1180, the delicate edifice of imperial power which he had constructed began to fall to pieces.[85]

Manuel overreached himself. That phenomenon which pervades human history, wishful thinking, is to be found in much of his foreign policy, above all towards the west. He reached out for the *simulacrum* rather than the substance of imperial power. He constructed what we might term a *theatre state* operating in an international arena. He may have believed that ties of clientage would eventually thicken into more effective links, that he might, in due course, use them to extract more and more resources and fighting manpower from his clients. The trouble, though, was that Byzantium was not a rising power, increasingly capable of turning influence into authority, clients into agents, but an aged one which was striving, sometimes successfully, sometimes not, to regain a pre-eminent position in the Middle East, eastern Europe, and the Mediterranean. If there was to be a change in the balance of power, it was all too likely to be in favour of the client.

## 5.5 Komnenian Byzantium

Much reduced though Byzantium was after the loss of the Asia Minor interior and of southern Italy, and committed as it was to fighting all manner of adversaries on different fronts through the reigns of Alexios, John, and Manuel Komnenos, it was able to bear the fiscal burden without signs of obvious strain after the initial years of crisis. There was no repetition of the eleventh-century debasement of the gold coinage. The *hyperpyron*, the gold

[85] Magdalino, *Manuel I Komnenos*, 96–100. Key text: *Nicetae Choniatae historia*, ed. J.-L. van Dieten, CFHB 11, 2 vols. (Berlin, 1975), 177–91, trans. H. J. Magoulias, *O City of Byzantium, Annals of Niketas Choniates* (Detroit, 1984).

coin (of 20.5 carats) anchoring the monetary system introduced by Alexios in 1092, maintained its value until the 1180s, in contrast to its electrum and billon fractions. This points to fiscal health (the gold coinage being the chief medium for payment of taxes), and substantial growth in market exchange, met by increased minting of increasingly fiduciary fractional coins. There is then solid numismatic evidence for economic growth and abundant or relatively abundant resources on which the state could draw.[86]

Direct evidence of economic growth is provided by archaeological survey, monastic archives, and written texts. Population growth manifested in the proliferation of rural settlements is best documented for Laconia: the town of Sparta, where there was much new building and reconstruction, was surrounded by an expanding halo of settlements, which reached a post-Roman peak in the Komnenian period (67 settlements and another 49 sites with evidence of agricultural activity); estates (owned presumably by town notables) spread outwards, villages edged closer to the town, and new clusters of farmhouses appeared. Intensive survey elsewhere in Greece confirms this picture—for example, the density of pottery found in the territory of Thebes peaked from the middle of the twelfth century to the middle of the thirteenth, testifying to a network of villages and nucleated hamlets spreading over lowland and hilltop sites. So too does documentary evidence from Macedonia, showing, as it does, an upward demographic curve and the role of estate owners in promoting land clearance and improvement.[87]

Manufacturing output of such commodities as can be tracked—principally wine, olive oil, fine tableware, and silk—rose markedly in the twelfth century. Wine from central Greece was traded throughout the empire and exported north to the Black Sea and beyond, to the Levant and to the west. The prosperity of Laconia is explicable in part by the widespread demand for its olive oil, which could be produced as a cash crop.[88] Development of new forms of decoration for tableware—notably Sgraffito Ware, which betrays the influence of Islamic potters—accompanied a growth of output from the two main centres (Constantinople and Corinth) and several other towns (see Figure 5.4.a, b, and c).[89] Silk cloth production had developed on a large scale outside Constantinople, the chief centres being Thebes, Corinth, and

[86] Laiou & Morrisson, *Byzantine Economy*, 151–3.

[87] P. Armstrong, 'Greece in the Eleventh Century', in Howard-Johnston, *Social Change in Town and Country*, 133–56, at 136–40; Laiou & Morrisson, *Byzantine Economy*, 91–3.

[88] Armstrong, 'Greece', 146–8, 150.

[89] Laiou & Morrisson, *Byzantine Economy*, 115–21; Armstrong, 'Greece', 134, 153–4.

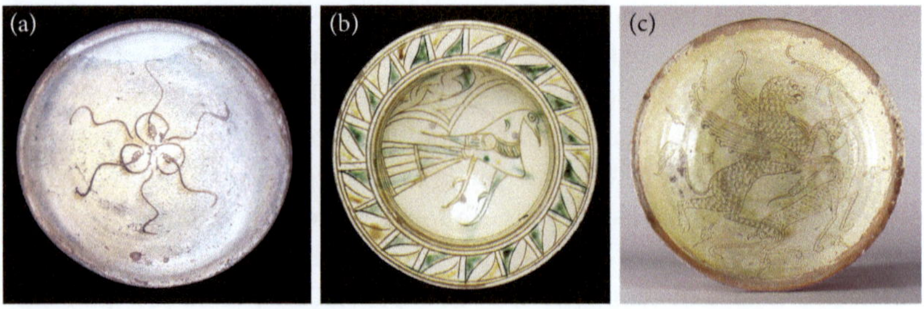


**Figure 5.4** Three glazed dishes: (a) bowl with marine creatures (incised sgraffito, from the Kastellorizo shipwreck); (b) bowl with bird (brown and green sgraffito, from the port of al-Mina, at the mouth of the Orontes river); (c) bowl with griffin attacking doe (fine sgraffito, said to have been found in the Sea of Marmara). New types of fine glazed ceramics were manufactured in the twelfth and thirteenth centuries. They were shipped overseas in large quantities.
*Source*: (a) Ephorate of Antiquities of the Dodecanese; (b) Victoria and Albert Museum; (c) Dumbarton Oaks.

Athens, all three raided for their coveted silk-workers by Roger II of Sicily.[90] There would undoubtedly have been increasing exchange of these and other commodities within Byzantium because of increasing demand. But there was an extra stimulus to commercial exchange—the presence in numerous regional centres of Italian merchants who were operating in a Mediterranean-wide arena in an era of substantial commercial growth.[91]

The effects of economic growth were more pronounced in town than country. The urban notables (*archontes*), who could be seen asserting themselves in one or two beleaguered Anatolian cities in the later eleventh century, came more to fore. They were the owners of the estates which spread in the territory of Sparta and which became more profitable with increasing trade in agricultural produce. If, as many notables probably did, they involved themselves directly in commercial transactions, their wealth and local power would have grown substantially, and with it a sense of corporate solidarity. It would still take several generations before they were able to emancipate themselves ideologically from the notion of Roman, top-down government, from acceptance of the enveloping power of the state, to evolve into something akin to leaders of ancient *poleis*. As for the country, there is a near-consensus among Byzantinists that the process of social change identified and fought by tenth-century emperors continued, perhaps

[90] Laiou & Morrisson, *Byzantine Economy*, 125–30; Armstrong, 'Greece', 148–51.
[91] Laiou & Morrisson, *Byzantine Economy*, 136–9; Howard-Johnston, *Byzantium*, 146–58.

accelerated, in the twelfth century. There is, however, no clear evidence—outside the atypical hinterland of Mount Athos—of peasant villagers' succumbing to the power of local landowners and being transformed into tenants in large numbers. I suspect that village leaders grew more assertive in improved economic conditions and that local town notables could make little headway without the help of provincial officialdom, on which the real *powerful* of the tenth century had relied.[92]

The economic upsurge of provincial towns in the Komnenian age was undoubtedly replicated at Constantinople. As much the largest city in the empire, with the imperial court and the upper echelons of the government in residence, it dominated the economy and remained the prime commercial centre, despite the rise of some provincial cities under Venetian sponsorship. Income from government service, from land, from real estate in the city, and from trade flowed in and supported an elite with many gradations. The presence of permanent Italian trading colonies acted as an additional stimulus, ensuring that the city remained an integral part of the larger Mediterranean economy, with its two poles in Alexandria and Venice.[93] There were two principal effects: first the increasing importance of the mercantile interest, which became very evident in the troubled last years of the twelfth century; second the multiplication of households with substantial disposable wealth to bestow on the intelligentsia. The twelfth century was the heyday of literary patronage, with some fifty to sixty households ready to host *theatra* (soirées) at which *rhetors* performed. With these additions to the main source of patronage (the imperial court), writers, poets, and intellectuals grew in numbers, as did their output (dominated by rhetorical texts).[94]

Despite a crackdown on free thinking in the Komnenian age—manifest in the show trials of John Italos and Eustratios of Nikaia, leading intellectuals in Alexios' reign, one lay, one clerical—and a sustained campaign to upgrade the education of leading clergy and thus enhance the defences of orthodoxy, star performers introduced colour into a literary scene prone to conformism and sycophancy.[95] The greatest star was Theodore Prodromos,

[92] Howard-Johnston, *Byzantium*, 252–60.

[93] M. F. Hendy, 'Byzantium, 1081–1204: An Economic Reappraisal', *Transactions of the Royal Historical* Society, ser.5, 20 (1970), 31–52, at 39–41, 45–52; Angold, *Byzantine Empire*, 276–80.

[94] Cheynet, *Pouvoir et contestations*, 444–5; Magdalino, *Manuel I Komnenos*, 335–56.

[95] Magdalino, *Manuel I Komnenos*, 368, 382–5, 389–92; B. Flusin, 'L'enseignement et la culture écrite', in J.-C. Cheynet, ed., *Le monde byzantin*, II *L'empire byzantin (641–1204)* (Paris, 2006), 341–68, at 363–4.

a professional wordsmith who relied on patronage for a living. There were numerous others whose ambition was to perform at court and to eulogize the reigning emperor, in poetry and sometimes baroque, almost impenetrable prose. Several were churchmen who ended their careers in important sees—notably Michael Italikos who taught philosophy and rhetoric, and the classical scholar Eustathios of Thessalonike.[96] There were significant advances in learning: commentaries on classical texts by Eustathios and John Tzetzes; systematic collections of canon law by John Zonaras and Theodore Balsamon; two new theological compendia—an up-do-date survey of heresies, the *Dogmatic Panoply* of Euthymios Zigabenos, and the *Sacred Arsenal*, edited by Andronikos Kamateros. This last text presented records of two theological debates conducted by Manuel with Latin and Armenian churchmen, together with supporting patristic citations.[97] But the most striking innovations were in fiction—the *Timarion*, a satire on contemporary life inspired by Lucian; novels of thwarted love, travel and adventure based on Hellenistic models; and the *Digenis Akrites*, a tale of love and war, a hybrid of epic and romance, rooted in the realities of the eastern frontier in the ninth century, transmitted orally and written down early in the twelfth century.[98]

Apart from senior bishops who were conscious of something akin to exile in their provincial sees and whose chief contribution to literature took the form of letters to fellow-*littérateurs* in the capital, the literary and scholarly worlds were confined to the capital. In cultural terms, Byzantium could be classified as a city-state, one with a huge hinterland. This was an inevitable consequence of the centralization of power inherited from the dark age. While they did tours of duty in the provinces, senior members of the apparatus of government (apart from the episcopate) resided in Constantinople. The factor of greatest influence on their fortunes was not the growing wealth of the city but the tentacular expansion of the imperial family and its affinity into all aspects of government. Talent was not repressed. There were high-flyers who flourished under all three reigns, but efforts were made to integrate them into the ruling nexus of families through marriage. The object was to keep key posts, above all high command, in absolutely trustworthy hands. The upwardly mobile families who profited

[96] Magdalino, *Manuel I Komnenos*, 323, 333, 340–2, 418–34, 439–41; Flusin, 'L'enseignement et la culture écrite', 364–6.

[97] Magdalino, *Manuel I Komnenos*, 290–7, 328–9, 348–51, 359–60, 367–8, 398–406, 409–11, Flusin, 'L'enseignement et la culture écrite', 365–6.

[98] Magdalino, *Manuel I Komnenos*, 395–6; Angold, *Byzantine Empire*, 248–52.

most from imperial patronage included several—the Angeloi, Batatzai, Palaiologoi, and Kantakouzenoi—who would, before long, reach out for supreme power, as well as others who achieved new prominence, such as the Konstephanoi, Kamateroi, and Petraliphai.[99]

Of the two traditional dominant aristocratic groupings, those from the interior of Anatolia sank steadily into relative obscurity, forced by the loss of their lands in the east to scrabble for estates in the islands and Balkan provinces. The Adrianople grouping was unaffected, indeed gained in importance, and was courted by the Komnenos-Doukas affinity in Alexios' reign. The main beneficiaries were the Bryennioi, Batatzai, and Branai. Below this high aristocratic stratum, there was a basic stability in the staffing of the bureaucracy.[100] At the imperial apex too, there was remarkable stability after Alexios faced off a second military conspiracy, led by Michael Anemas, around 1100/1. There was no serious threat to his rule or to those of his two successors from outside the dynasty. Ructions within the ruling family—the mooted rebellion and subsequent flight of John's brother Isaac to the Sultanate of Rum in 1130, and the volatile behaviour of Isaac's son Andronikos who rebelled twice in the reign of Manuel, the second time taking refuge successively in Antioch, Jerusalem, and Turkish Koloneia—did not spawn serious domestic opposition.[101] All this was to change after Manuel's death in 1180, but for the moment, for all the grandstanding of Manuel and despite the terrible setback of Myriokephalon, the edifice of the Byzantine state seemed to be fixed on firm foundations.

## 5.6 Collapse, 1180–1204

Manuel died on 24 September 1180. He had taken precautions to secure the succession of his designated heir, his eleven-year-old son Alexios by his second wife, Maria of Antioch. Apart from establishing a regency council (his widow, the patriarch, and senior relatives), he involved foreign rulers in guaranteeing young Alexios' rights. This must have seemed an obvious recourse for an emperor who presided over earthly affairs. But, with his

[99] P. Frankopan, 'Kinship and the Distribution of Power in Komnenian Byzantium', *EHR* 122 (2007), 1–34; Angold, *Byzantine Empire*, 241–4; Cheynet, *Pouvoir et contestations*, 280–6, 413–16.

[100] Cheynet, *Pouvoir et contestations*, 100–1, 237–41, 370–2, 374–5.

[101] Cheynet, *Pouvoir et contestations*, 105–9, 413–16, 420–1; Angold, *Byzantine Empire*, 252–5.

own disappearance and Byzantine prestige somewhat dimmed, he was, in effect, licensing powerful neighbours—the king of Hungary, the sultan of Rum, the prince of Antioch, the king of Jerusalem—to intervene in Byzantine internal affairs.[102]

All too soon those internal affairs were in turmoil as a serious split developed between the young dowager empress and her chief ally (and lover) the Protosebastos Alexios Komnenos, nephew of Manuel, on the one hand, and Manuel's daughter Maria Porphyrogenita, married to Renier of Montferrat (member of the most powerful family in northern Italy), on the other. The Protosebastos relied on the higher echelons of the bureaucracy and guards regiments from east and west (*tagmata*) to sustain his rule. The confrontation reached a first crisis in February 1181, with the unmasking of a conspiracy in favour of the Porphyrogenita, involving senior members of the imperial family and its affinity. There followed a period of continuing agitation in the city against the Protosebastos' government, culminating in open insurrections on 10 April and at the beginning of May. Maria and Renier were allowed to go free, while their supporters were emprisoned. These were simply the first two of numerous political crises which were to mark the following two decades and were to hamstring Byzantium's response to the gathering threats from without and within.[103]

The next challenge to the Protosebastos and the dowager empress came from outside the city, from Manuel's cousin, Andronikos Komnenos, an impetuous, deceitful, and unprincipled adventurer and philanderer, who had long coveted the throne. He had been reconciled with Manuel not long before his death, and had been put in charge of Paphlagonia. It was from Paphlagonia that he watched events unfold in Constantinople. He refrained from intervening when the Porphyrogenita, whom he supported, lost the struggle for power, delaying his move west until early spring 1182. He met little resistance and, once the commander of the fleet changed sides, was able to cross the Bosporus and enter the city, preceded by his Paphlagonian troops in May 1182.[104]

This was the start of a reign of terror (modest by modern standards but quite enough to cow opponents). His first targets were the Latins in Constantinople, who were known to have supported the Protosebastos' government. His soldiers initiated a pogrom, rapidly joined by the anti-Latin

[102] Cheynet, *Pouvoir et contestations*, 427.
[103] Cheynet, *Pouvoir et contestations*, 110–11, 427–8, Angold, *Byzantine Empire*, 295–6.
[104] Angold, *Byzantine Empire*, 252–5, 296; Cheynet, *Pouvoir et contestations*, 111–12, 428.

elements in the city's population. It was a case of mob violence, heightened by religious antipathy, leading to wholesale massacre. Andronikos' position was strengthened, but at the cost of a final, ultimately fatal souring of Byzantine relations with the west, especially the Venetians. At the apex of the political system, something similar occurred. Andronikos turned on generals who might be able to rouse their men against him, and, above all, on his many opponents in the ruling nexus of families, purging and blinding them. He promoted a culture of informing, by threatening relatives of a conspirator with the same punishment if they did not report him. He sought to buttress his rule by appealing to the humbler elements in Byzantine society—pandering to the mob in Constantinople, and presenting himself in the provinces as the friend of the peasantry, by cracking down on corruption and forbidding large landowners from alienating land to each other.[105]

His victims included the Porphyrogenita, her husband, the dowager empress, and the young Alexios II. They were disposed of discreetly, opening the way for Andronikos to marry Alexios' young bride (Agnes of France) and to be crowned emperor in September 1183. Such opposition as there was in the provinces, centred on Philadelphia, Nikaia, Prusa, and Lopadion, was suppressed without difficulty. Andronikos' position, though, began to weaken in the capital. He was increasingly isolated, within a close circle of advisers and agents. He would lash out against suspected opponents and inflict cruel punishments. The news of his cruelty seeped out along with what was taken to be contempt for the people of the city. The decisive blow was struck by the Normans of Sicily. They produced a pretender claiming to be Alexios II, and attacked in force in June 1185, taking Dyrrachion which put up no resistance and, after a siege, Thessalonike. From Thessalonike they planned to march on Constantinople. Andronikos tried to shore up his position by arresting Isaac Angelos, thought to be the leader of the residual aristocratic opposition. Isaac escaped, took refuge in St Sophia, and appealed to the people for help. At this the city rose up and proclaimed Isaac emperor (12 September 1185). Andronikos was caught trying to flee to the Rus. Mutilated and publicly vilified, he died a miserable death in the hippodrome. In the meantime the Norman threat was removed by a swift counterattack by a scratch force led by Alexios Branas, one of Andronikos' appointees, an Adrianopolitan grandee who had married a great-niece of Manuel. He surprised and defeated an advance force of Normans at Mosynopolis in Thrace. Pushing on he won a decisive victory over a second

[105] Angold, *Byzantine Empire*, 296–9, 301–3; Cheynet, *Pouvoir et contestations*, 428–34.

force commanding the Strymon valley and advanced on Thessalonike, which the Normans abandoned.[106]

The Normans, perennial enemies of Byzantium, had taken advantage of the political turmoil. While they withdrew eventually from Dalmatia (after 1186), their presence had helped prise loose the Serbs of Raška, who began to assert themselves there and, within a few years, further afield in the Balkans. The two powerful, neighbouring rulers who had guaranteed Alexios II's rights also reacted to news of his death. Relations cooled with the Sultan of Rum, Kilij Arslan II (1156–92), who did nothing to stop Turkmen raids, nominally in support of more pretenders claiming to be Alexios II. More damaging was the action taken by Bela of Hungary: he annexed Dalmatia and the Sirmium region (both former Hungarian possessions) on the news of Manuel's death; after Andronikos' seizure of power, he invaded the central Balkans in 1182, perhaps at the instigation of the dowager empress, and gained control of the strategic corridor running down the Morava valley to Naissos and thence over the mountains to Serdike. In so doing he stirred up the Vlachs and Bulgars, who were in any case resentful of Byzantine taxes.[107]

By the expedient of marrying Bela's daughter Margaret, Isaac received back the Serdike–middle Danube corridor as her dowry. Dissident Vlachs and Bulgars in the mountainous hinterland of Anchialos were harder to deal with, despite the apparent success of a first campaign under Isaac's personal command in spring 1186. The generals who took over later that year failed to press on with effective counter-insurgency operations in and around the Haemus. The first, Isaac's uncle, the Sebastokrator John Angelos, was content to attack the rebels when they ventured into open country; the second, Isaac's brother-in-law, Caesar John Kantakouzenos, who replaced him when he was accused of treason, was defeated in the Haemus. A fatal pause then ensued, because of the rebellion of Alexios Branas who, despite an earlier coup attempt, had been given command of the expeditionary force. It was only after his attack on the capital, backed by the Adrianopolitan aristocratic nexus, had been fended off and his supporters had been conciliated with promises of amnesty that Isaac could return to the fray, in autumn

[106] Angold, *Byzantine Empire*, 299–301; Cheynet, *Pouvoir et contestations*, 113, 115, 118, 119, 429–30; Stephenson, *Byzantium's Balkan Frontier*, 284–8.

[107] Angold, *Byzantine Empire*, 307–8; Stephenson, *Byzantium's Balkan Frontier*, 281–3, 288–9, 295.

1187 and spring 1188. He achieved very little, not least because the rebels now had Cuman support.[108]

Byzantium's decline was all too evident by 1189. There was a malign process at work, a reciprocating action of internal troubles and predation from without.[109] Andronikos exploited a continuing crisis at the centre to seize power, only for foreign predators (Normans) to undermine his position fatally and for others (Vlachs and Bulgars) to expose his successor Isaac II to Alexios Branas' coup attempt. It was a process which would continue to weaken Byzantium over the next fifteen years, leading to a steady contraction of its Balkan resource-base as regions were lopped off by Serb, Vlach, and Bulgar insurgents, and to a fraying of the imperial centre's authority over the provinces. The top-down governmental system inherited from the Roman empire finally began to break down, over seven hundred years after the disaggregation of the western empire. Cyprus was the first to break free under Isaac Komnenos, a great-nephew of Manuel, who took control of the island in 1184. It was followed in 1188 by the strategically placed city of Philadelphia, inland from Ephesos, where a local aristocrat, Theodore Mangaphas, declared independence in spring 1188 and held out until 1190.[110]

The hapless Isaac's troubles worsened in 1189, with the appearance of Frederick Barbarossa at the head of a German crusading army in the Balkans. Ill feeling was generated by the imperial posturing of Isaac and harassment on the ground. Byzantium's prestige sank ever lower in the west, especially after Barbarossa's army (having been ferried across the Dardanelles) marched across Anatolia, swatting off Turkish attacks and capturing Ikonion. Two other armies, French and English, had also been mobilized, in response to the pope's call after the fall of Jerusalem to Saladin in 1187, but they sailed straight to Outremer, arriving at Acre in April and June respectively. The English fleet had made a detour to Cyprus, where they defeated Isaac Komnenos and took control of the island.[111]

Meanwhile, the Byzantine position was deteriorating in the Balkans, where Isaac concentrated on the war against Vlachs and Bulgars, fighting to keep control of the principal coastal cities north of the Haemus and to

[108] Angold, *Byzantine Empire*, 304–6; Stephenson, *Byzantium's Balkan Frontier*, 283–4, 288–94; Cheynet, *Pouvoir et contestations*, 121–3, 437–9.

[109] *Cf.* A. Simpson, 'Perceptions and Interpretations of the Late Twelfth Century in Modern Historiography', in A. Simpson, ed., *Byzantium, 1180–1204: 'The Sad Quarter of a Century'?* (Athens, 2015), 13–34.

[110] Cheynet, *Pouvoir et contestations*, 116–17, 123, 454–5.

[111] Harris, *Byzantium and the Crusades*, 141–7, 151–4.

defend the Thracian plain from depredation. In order to do so, he recognized the *de facto* independence of the Serbs, by marrying his niece Eudokia to the son of the *veliki zupan* Stefan Nemanja in 1192. Fortunes were mixed in the war. Isaac suffered a crushing defeat while returning through the Haemus mountains in 1190, but was more successful when he stayed on the defensive, based at Philippopolis, in autumn 1191. A dispute late in 1192 between the brothers Peter and Asen, leaders of the Vlachs and Bulgars, left the latter as the prime target of Byzantine operations. They were going well in spring 1193 until one of the two generals, a young cousin of Isaac's, Constantine Angelos, rebelled. He marched on Constantinople, only to be halted at Adrianople and handed over to the second general, Basil Batatzes. That allowed the Vlachs and Bulgars, with their Cuman allies, to attack Philippopolis, Serdike, and Adrianople. Worse followed in 1194 when, despite troop transfers from Asia Minor, the combined armies were defeated near Arkadiopolis, and in 1195 when a planned counteroffensive was aborted with the deposition and blinding of Isaac by his brother Alexios Angelos. Vlach–Bulgar raiders took control of the Strymon region.[112]

Alexios III Angelos' rule was sustained by the army, the Adrianopolitan aristocracy, and supporters in his and his brother's close family. He was thus secure, although not well regarded in Constantinople. But it was in his reign that Byzantium lost the old core territories of the Bulgars north of the Haemus. Even when the rivalry between the two capitals of the nascent Bulgar state escalated, after the murder of Asen at Trnovo in 1196 and the armed intervention of Peter from Preslav, Byzantine forces did not intervene. The soldiers refused to cross the mountains to relieve Trnovo. Nor was there any sort of counterattack when Ivanko, Asen's successor, came over to the Byzantine side. He was simply assigned defensive duties at Philippopolis. Then came a decisive step in the break-up of Byzantium's Balkan hegemony. Dobromir, a leading Vlach with lands around Strumica, asserted his independence and began raiding districts between the Strymon and Vardar rivers. Two short ventures into the field by Alexios in spring and autumn 1197 achieved little, leaving him little choice but to sue for peace and recognize Dobromir's mini-principality. Two years later Ivanko rebelled, defeated the army sent against him and extended his authority to the Aegean coast. Alexios achieved his only significant success, the recovery

[112] Stephenson, *Byzantium's Balkan Frontier*, 300–5.

of central Thrace, by duplicity—he seized and executed Ivanko by luring him with the offer of a peace treaty.[113]

Byzantium's authority was now confined to the open plains of Thrace and neighbouring territory as far as the Strymon. North of Thrace, the Haemus mountains and the lower Danube plains were controlled by Kalojan, Peter's son and heir, with whom Alexios had to make peace in 1202 after the loss of the last coastal strongholds held by Byzantium in 1201. To the west, beyond Dobromir's mini-principality, lay Macedonia, over which the Serbs had extended their authority and in the far north-west their core territories of Diokleia and Raška. Alexios' regime was thoroughly discredited but continued to cling to power, despite riots in the capital, two serious coup attempts, and provincial secessions (Mylasa under Michael Komnenos Doukas around 1200, Hellas under Leo Sgouros 1201–2, and the Smoleanoi under Spyridonakes at the end of 1201).[114] Byzantine prestige had sunk very low—so low that Stefan Nemanja's son and successor, another Stefan, had no compunction about discarding his Byzantine wife in 1198. Yet more humiliating was the Byzantine response to a sudden demand at Christmas 1196 for a substantial cash contribution to a crusade planned by the German emperor Henry VI (1190–7), who controlled the kingdom of Sicily through his wife. The mere threat of invasion had Alexios scrabbling around for 1,000 pounds of gold, going so far as to desecrate imperial tombs for their valuables. He was able to keep the sum he raised (7,000 pounds of silver and a smaller amount of gold), when the threat of attack was dissipated with the withdrawal of the German fleet from Acre on the news of Henry's death (28 September 1197).[115]

## 5.7 Fourth Crusade

The final death-dealing blow was struck by two formidable external predators, invited to intervene by yet another claimant to the throne, one with the best possible credentials as the son of the deposed and blinded Isaac II. Young Alexios Angelos managed to slip away from the army in Thrace

[113] Cheynet, *Pouvoir et contestations*, 440–4; Stephenson, Byzantium's Balkan Frontier, 305–8.

[114] Cheynet, *Pouvoir et contestations*, 135–9, 444–6, 455–6; Stephenson, *Byzantium's Balkan Frontier*, 308–10.

[115] Stephenson, *Byzantium's Balkan Frontier*, 308–9; Harris, *Byzantium and the Crusades*, 159–60.

and to board a Pisan ship which took him to Ancona. From early autumn 1201 when he arrived in Italy, he set about appealing for help. He was rebuffed by the new young pope, Innocent III, a high-minded cleric who sought to spread the crusading spirit of self-sacrifice throughout Christendom and who had been striving to assemble a new crusade to follow up Henry VI's. Innocent III would not countenance an attack on fellow-Christians, even if it would bring about a union of the churches and a substantial subvention for his crusade. Alexios had more success at Verona, when he broached the subject of the restoration of his father in a message to the leaders of a crusade who had recently (in April) concluded a treaty with Venice for the transport of a large army to the east. By Christmas he was at the court of Philip of Swabia, Henry VI's brother, married to his (Alexios') sister Eirene. There he met Boniface de Montferrat, elected commander of the crusade in August, and seems to have gained his support, since Boniface later championed his cause.[116]

Under the terms of their agreement with Venice, the great magnates from France north of the Loire, Champagne, and Flanders, who were organizing the crusade, undertook to bring 33,500 soldiers to Venice. For their part, the Venetians would build the necessary horse-transports and troop carriers, and would commit their main fleet of 50 galleys as escorts. They were to be paid 85,000 marks in instalments. The crusaders duly arrived in Venice in summer 1202, but their numbers were far short of those envisaged in the treaty—a mere 12,000 men whose combined contributions fell 34,000 marks short of the agreed sum. The balance between crusaders and their shippers now shifted decisively in the favour of the latter, a development fraught with significance. The aged doge, Enrico Dandolo, took the cross in a carefully staged ceremony, and proposed a temporary moratorium on the debt (to be recouped from the proceeds of victory), on condition that the crusaders helped the Venetians capture Zara, a former possession, on the Dalmatian coast. This occasioned the first of several debates in the crusading army, acting as a *parlement*, about the acceptability of deviations from the central purpose of the crusade, namely an attack on the Nile Delta followed by a march on Jerusalem. The crusade leaders swung the debate in favour of the Venetians (but at the cost of defections). The longest and most difficult of these debates took place after the fall of Zara, at the end of

[116] Harris, *Byzantium and the Crusades*, 163.

December 1202, when a delegation from Philip of Swabia arrived with the pretender Alexios Angelos.[117]

Alexios made a tempting (but unrealistic) offer to obtain the crusade's backing for his installation on the Byzantine throne, which would entail a longer diversion to Constantinople. Apart from church union, long demanded by the papacy, he would provide 10,000 Byzantine troops, provisions, and 200,000 silver marks for the crusade proper, and would second 500 cavalry to boost crusader forces in Outremer. Innocent III made his opposition plain, but did allow hostile action against Christians *in extremis* (interpreted by the crusaders as a serious shortage of provisions). Backed by their paid soldiers and Venice, the Crusade leaders prevailed and the fleet left Zara for Constantinople in April 2003, reaching the Bosporus on 24 June. In early July they crossed the straits, established a bridgehead at Galata and broke into the Golden Horn. An amphibious attack on 17 July was repelled, but with extensive fire damage in the city—at which Alexios III fled and senior officials released the blind Isaac II and declared him emperor. The crusaders demanded that he accept the compact agreed at Zara—namely church union and provision of funds for the crusade—and the coronation of Alexios as co-emperor.[118]

Alexios IV was crowned on 1 August 1203. He paid out 100,000 marks to Venice, which covered the crusaders' debts. His position in the city, however, was very weak, without any base in the bureaucratic establishment. He could only stay in power with the support of the predatory outsiders whom he had brought with him. That required more financial outlay—a promise to subsidize the crusaders for a year from the expiry of the Venetian treaty at Michaelmas 1203, in effect to underwrite the cost of the delayed crusade in 1204. When this was agreed after another debate in the army, he left the city with an escort of western magnates (including Boniface) on a progress through Thrace. Things went from bad to worse while he was away: a second devastating fire was started in the course of a violent confrontation outside the sea-walls; Latins in the city fled across the Golden Horn to the crusader camp; to pay the crusaders, the new government raised money by every possible means, including the ransacking of churches for bullion; eventually opposition to these exactions spilled over into riots, after Alexios' return in November. Relations deteriorated in December. An anti-western faction grew in strength, led by Alexios IV's son-in-law, Alexios Doukas,

[117] Tyerman, *New History*, 502–8, 510–16, 525–31.
[118] Tyerman, *New History*, 531–3, 538–47; Harris, *Byzantium and the Crusades*, 163–8.

known as Mourzouphlos. The Venetian fleet was attacked by fire-ships (1 January). An armed sortie was made a week later by Alexios Mourzouphlos. Finally, Alexios IV was dethroned on 27 January, being replaced first by Nicholas Kannovos (put in by the higher clergy) and then by Alexios Mourzouphlos, whose coup had general backing in the city.[119]

The murder of Alexios IV, probably on 8 February, signalled the collapse of relations with the crusaders. The city's markets were closed to them, precipitating a serious threat to their supplies. The new government was belligerently anti-Latin and prepared for battle. The crusaders had little choice but to attack. The clergy with them justified this, on the grounds that Byzantines were deviant Christians and their new ruler was a regicide. A first assault was made on 9 April, a second on the 13th when the walls were breached (see Figure 5.5). The besiegers pressed on into the city encountering relatively little resistance, slaughtering all whom they met, looting, and starting a third great fire. There followed three days of systematic despoiling of the city, in the course of which churches, houses, and palaces were ransacked for treasure and the relics collected over centuries which had helped keep the city safe. With its fall, the westerners took control of the eastern empire, now reduced to Thrace, Greece, the coastal fringes of Asia Minor, and the Aegean and Ionian islands. A new emperor was elected, Baldwin of Flanders. A new patriarch was appointed, a Venetian. The empire was carved up. The Venetians took control of a much enlarged commercial quarter in Constantinople, from which they expelled the Genoese and Pisans; a series of ports running from the Adriatic round the Peloponnese to the Sea of Marmara; and all the Ionian and almost all the Aegean islands. The new emperor was assigned a rump of the rump empire—Thrace and north-west Asia Minor together with Lesbos, Chios, and Samos. Boniface of Montferrat received Thessalonike, Macedonia, and Thessaly. The rest was distributed as imperial fiefs.[120]

Religious and temperamental antipathies which had deepened through the eleventh and twelfth centuries meant that much of the population would resent rule by westerners. But there were only three pockets of active resistance—around Nikaia and Smyrna in Asia Minor, in Pontos centred on Trebizond, and around Arta in Epiros.[121] They were the only surviving fragments of Manuel's Byzantium, which had seemed to bestride the eastern

[119] Tyerman, *New History*, 547–9; Harris, *Byzantium and the Crusades*, 168–71.
[120] Tyerman, *New History*, 549–55; Harris, *Byzantium and the Crusades*, 171–5, 177–9.
[121] Harris, *Byzantium and the Crusades*, 179–80.

**Figure 5.5** Storming of Constantinople by the Fourth Crusade, 1204 (Tintoretto, 1580).
*Source*: Alamy.

and western Mediterranean. All the rest had been lost for a variety of reasons. First, *chance*—the chance that a rogue member of the ruling dynasty managed to seize power in 1182 and cause mayhem (though the purges and brutal punishments were far outdone by Justinian II during his second reign, 705–11); the chance that Isaac Angelos happened to be in hiding in St Sophia when the crowd rose up against Andronikos Komnenos and that he was thoroughly unsuited to ruling at a time of gathering crisis (for all the military successes conjured up by court rhetors); and the chance that sibling rivalry would determine the next change of emperor and that Alexios III would be even less competent than his brother.[122] Second, and

[122] Angold, *Byzantine Empire*, 311–15.

much more important, the gradual erosion of central authority as the system of government inherited from antiquity was subjected to increasing pressure from the localities. The Balkans were particularly susceptible, since much of the north was governed indirectly, power being delegated to leaders of the localities. Third was myopia on the part of members of the governing elite, looking to further their own interests at the expense of the common good. The Vlach and Bulgar rebellion gained momentum when three Byzantine operations had to be suspended because of coups, two attempted, one successful. Finally, there was the array of predatory powers ready to attack—Serbs, Vlachs and Bulgars, Turks, Venetians, and crusaders. Under their combined pressure, the end came swiftly, in April 1204.

*Byzantium in a Changing World*. James Howard-Johnston, Oxford University Press.
 DOI: 10.1093/9780191999093.003.0006

# 6
# Last Centuries

The sack of Constantinople, the looting of its treasures, and the partition of its diminished territory did not annihilate the idea of Byzantium. The Christian east Romans who had inherited the core of their culture from classical Greece did not suddenly loosen their grasp on so deep-embedded an identity. Even before the new Latin empire faltered, as it did in the face of Bulgar attack in 1205 and 1207, the Emperor Baldwin I being captured and Boniface of Montferrat being killed, fragments of the defunct empire began to bestir themselves. Three stable successor states had emerged by 1210, the smallest in Pontos around Trebizond, founded by David Komnenos;[1] another rather larger in the far west, built up by Michael Komnenos Doukas in Epiros behind the Pindos mountains; and a third in a vulnerable position, caught between the Turks and the capital of the Latin empire, in Bithynia. There the Despot Theodore Laskaris, son-in-law and designated heir of Alexios III, set about organizing resistance to the Latins from Nikaia.

These three Byzantine statelets would be competing with each other, as well as struggling against established and newly established regional powers—besides Turks, Bulgars, Serbs, and Latins (in Thrace, Macedonia, and Greece). They would have to manoeuvre and fight for advantage, in what can be viewed, from the perspective of the Mediterranean, as a medium-sized political arena. It was overlooked by the greater and lesser powers of the west, who retained the ability to intervene by land or by sea—not only those already familiar (the German empire, the kingdom of Sicily, and the Italian maritime cities) but also rising dynasties in France and Spain. As in the twelfth century, the papacy would play a crucial part, given its ability to rouse crusading enthusiasm and its determination to protect the Latin empire.[2] From another perspective, that of the Middle East and the near-limitless expanses of Asia, the arena of combat where Byzantine fought

[1] The so-called empire of Trebizond remained entirely independent of the empire recreated by the Laskarids. Hence it does not feature in the following narrative. It survived until 1461.

[2] N. G. Chrissis, *Crusading in Frankish Greece: A Study in Byzantine-Western Relations and Attitudes, 1204–1282* (Turnhout, 2012) for papal efforts to drum up support for the Latin empire, which tailed off after 1241.

Byzantine was of little more than parochial interest. It was a small world subject in the thirteenth and fourteenth centuries to sudden, dramatic shocks from without.

Each shock had immediate and long-lasting consequences. First came the irruption into the Middle East of the greatest transcontinental power of Eurasia to emerge before the modern age. The Mongols shattered the *status quo* throughout Asia in the 1240s. Two of the four stable great powers which they established were to lower over the Middle East and eastern Europe for several centuries, the Ilkhans of Persia and the Golden Horde in the steppes north of the Caspian and Black Seas. In the far west they reduced the Seljuk sultanate of Rum to tributary status after the battle of Köse Dağı (12 June 1243), and before long caused it to splinter (from the 1260s).[3] The Nikaian statelet may have profited in the short term from the sudden weakening of its principal rival in Asia Minor, but it came under increasing pressure as more Turks were driven west from the 1250s, especially after the Mongols' merciless suppression of the Turkish revolt of 1277–9.[4] Worse was to follow when one of the Turkish splinter groups in Asia, led by the Ottoman dynasty, began to build up its power in the hinterland of Bithynia around the year 1300 and, within forty years, established its hegemony over north-western Asia Minor.[5]

The second shock was of an entirely different order—a worldwide pandemic. The Black Death arrived in summer 1347, carried on Genoese ships from the Crimea across the Mediterranean to Egypt, the Levant, north Africa, Sicily, Italy, Spain, and continental Europe. Byzantium was not spared. It was too integrated into Black Sea and Mediterranean trade networks to escape, but there is surprisingly little written testimony about its impact. The best evidence, both textual and archaeological, relates to Cyprus, lost to Byzantium since 1191, which suffered badly because of its central role in trade with Egypt and the Levant. We may perhaps conjecture that in Byzantium the plague did not mutate into its ultra-infectious pneumonic form as it did later in transalpine Europe. Mortality rose significantly, but not as far as 40–50 per cent. Population growth, which reached a plateau around 1300, went into reverse, but there is no evidence of wholesale

[3] For a detailed and authoritative account, see D. Korobeinikov, *Byzantium and the Turks in the Thirteenth Century* (Oxford, 2014), 170–216, summarized in D. A. Korobeinikov, 'Raiders and Neighbours: The Turks (1040–1304),' *CH Byz.Emp.*, 692–727, at 719–23.

[4] Korobeinikov, 'Raiders and Neighbours', 723–6, summarizing *idem*, *Byzantium and the Turks*, 217–36, 251–6.

[5] C. Foss, *The Beginnings of the Ottoman Empire* (Oxford, 2022), 231–43.

depopulation or urban decline. Nor does it seem that the steady encroachment of Turks and Serbs on the three remaining pockets of Byzantine power (around Constantinople, around Thessalonike, and in the Peloponnese) was even temporarily halted.[6]

The effects of the third great shock were entirely beneficial. Renewed Mongol campaigning in the Middle East under Timur struck a devastating blow against the rising Ottoman power at the battle of Ankara (1402). Byzantium was released from tributary status and recovered substantial territory. A reprieve of some twenty years was obtained, before a fateful decision to intervene in a succession dispute triggered a resumption of the Ottoman advance.[7]

The history of Byzantium in its last centuries was thus far from a straightforward story of decline. Contingencies of all sorts—from the character of individual emperors to changing circumstances—determined the course of events. There was a period of revival in the decades immediately following the fall of Constantinople when two of the rival statelets were able to feed on the decaying Latin empire, and one of slow weakening during the reign of Andronikos II Palaiologos (1282–1328). By the beginning of the fourteenth century Byzantium's own resources were so limited that it became little more than the plaything of outside powers.[8] Torn apart by civil wars, divided between those in the governing elite who acknowledged a new world order and were ready to become Ottoman clients and those who looked to the west for support and were ready to accept papal supremacy, the trajectory was a downward one, which might be halted or even reversed, but would then resume, until the long-deferred end came in 1453.

## 6.1 Nikaian empire, 1204–61

Theodore Laskaris, Alexios III Angelos' son-in-law and designated heir, like many other high-ranking figures, managed to escape from Constantinople and make his way to Asia Minor, in his case to Nikaia. From there he

[6] D. M. Nicol, *The Last Centuries of Byzantium, 1261–1453* (2nd edn, Cambridge, 1993), 216–19; A. E. Laiou, 'The Palaiologoi and the World around them', *CH Byz.Emp.*, 803–33, at 817–18, 824, 829–30; T. Papacostas, 'Manuscript Notes and the Black Death in Rural Cyprus', in T. Shawcross & I. Toth, eds., *Reading in the Byzantine Empire and Beyond* (Cambridge, 2018), 133–54.

[7] Necipoğlu, *Byzantium between the Ottomans and the Latins*, 18–21, 24–35.

[8] Harris, *Byzantium and the Crusades*, 122–6, 130–1; Laiou, 'Palaiologoi', 810–11.

succeeded in extending his authority gradually over the swathe of Byzantine territory still independent of the Turks, in the fertile Marmara and Aegean coastlands of Asia Minor.[9]

He owed his success almost entirely to the Bulgars in Europe and the Turks in Asia Minor. It was the Bulgar threat which forced the Latin emperor to transfer his forces to Europe in 1205, thus preventing them from following up their victory over Theodore's forces at Adramyttion (19 March). It was the victory of the Bulgar ruler, Kalojan, at Adrianople in April which ensured that several years would pass before Latin forces launched an offensive against the nascent Nikaian mini-empire in 1211–12.[10] Yet more important was the agreement he made with exiled Kay-Khusro I in August 1204, to back the latter's restoration to the sultanate. Once back in power, Kay-Khusro reciprocated by agreeing a military alliance at the end of March 1205. Seljuk troops then helped Theodore to extend his authority in Bithynia (to Prusa and over lands occupied by the Latins the previous winter) and, as important, to begin the fight to eliminate the Komnenoi of Trebizond as serious contenders for the empire. They attacked the Pontos in 1205, thus preventing the Grand Komnenos Alexios I from going to the aid of his brother David in Paphlagonia. David Komnenos' army was defeated by Theodore at Nikomedia in late summer.[11]

There were other rivals to contend with, Byzantine aristocrats who controlled other localities—Theodore Mangaphas at Philadelphia, Savvas Asidenos at Sampson (ancient Priene) overlooking the lower Maeander plain, Nikephoros Kontostephanos further up the Maeander valley, and Manuel Maurozomes at its head. They all submitted to Theodore in the course of 1205, in Maurozomes' case only after two bouts of warfare in May and late summer. As Kay-Khusro's father-in-law, Maurozomes alone retained a degree of independence at Laodikeia and Chonai, which were incorporated only notionally into Theodore's state. Theodore's claim to preeminence in western Asia Minor was made manifest when he was proclaimed emperor in 1205 and crowned three years later by a new patriarch elected in Nikaia by a duly constituted synod.[12] There remained one task before the claim could be justified—the Komnenoi must be defeated and

[9] M. Angold, *A Byzantine Government in Exile: Government and Society under the Laskarids of Nicaea (1204–1261)* (Oxford, 1975), 9–14, 97–100.

[10] Angold, *Byzantine Government in Exile*, 12.

[11] Korobeinikov, *Byzantium and the Turks*, 134–8, 147–8.

[12] Angold, *Byzantine Government in Exile*, 13; Korobeinikov, *Byzantium and the Turks*, 134, 137–43.

forced to disgorge Paphlagonia. But before that could happen, the Nikaian state had to surmount a great crisis in 1210–12.

The ultimate cause of the crisis was the arrival of the deposed emperor, Alexios III Angelos, at Attaleia around 1210. He had left Epiros, where he had been living after being ransomed from Boniface of Montferrat—surely with encouragement from the Despot, Theodore's other main rival. Kay-Khusro I, Alexios III's son-in-law, decided to give him his support, declaring Theodore to be a usurper. He went so far as to ally with the Latin emperor Henry I. In 1211 he marched down the Maeander valley and besieged Antioch-on-the-Maeander. Theodore countered, fought a hard battle nearby (probably on 17 June) and prevailed after Kay-Khusro was killed (supposedly in a duel with Theodore). Alexios was captured and forced to abdicate. Theodore was recognized as emperor by Kay-Khusro's son and successor, Kay-Kawus I, reciprocating by sending rich gifts as well as alms to be distributed at Kay-Khusro's funeral. The alliance was resumed.[13]

But the crisis was not over. The Latin Emperor Henry I invaded Nikaian territory in July 1211. He won two victories in Bithynia in July and October over such forces as Theodore could put into the field after the heavy losses inflicted by the Turks. He then marched south as far Nymphaion, inland from Smyrna. It was only after Nikaian resistance stiffened in spring 1212 and a minor victory was won near Pegai, that a truce was signed (followed by a full treaty in December 1214). From 1213 Theodore and Kay-Kawus were free to plan an operation against the Komnenoi. It took place in 1214 and resulted in the conquest and partition of the long, thin coastal strip of Paphlagonia, the Byzantine share running from the Sangarios river to Amastris. Theodore's position was now relatively secure, buttressed by his marriage to the daughter of Leon I, king of Armenian Cilicia, in December 1214. He thereby obtained a potential ally against the Seljuks, should they again become hostile.[14]

Nikaian–Seljuk relations did, in fact, remain good for decades to come, with one exception early in the reign of Theodore I's successor, his son-in-law John III Batatzes (1222–54). In 1225 fighting broke out, when the Sultan Kay-Qubad was making a concerted effort to strengthen his position vis-à-vis all his neighbours. He was probably encouraged by five brothers who had gained asylum after a failed rebellion against John III. There was also the not insignificant factor of the absence of the main Nikaian army in

[13] Korobeinikov, *Byzantium and the Turks*, 148–50, 154–6.
[14] Korobeinikov, *Byzantium and the Turks*, 150–4.

Europe 1224–5. The Seljuks attacked some unspecified fortresses, but then came off worse in the border warfare which followed (to 1229). A new peace treaty was signed in 1232, the Seljuks being eager to secure their western frontier as they became aware of the growing Mongol threat in the east.[15]

Peace, guaranteed peace, with the Seljuks was also vital for the Nikaians, if they were to compete effectively with their Epirote rivals in Europe, who had managed to defeat and capture the new Latin emperor as he marched across Epiros in 1216. They had been powerless to intervene when the Epirotes launched a successful offensive in 1218, against the Latins in Thessaly and the Bulgars in Macedonia, which culminated in the encirclement and capture of Thessalonike in 1224. They could only do so after routing the Latins in Asia Minor that same year and compelling them to evacuate their remaining territory, except for an enclave opposite Constantinople.[16] Their first venture in 1225 failed—they had to withdraw the forces sent against Adrianople because of Kay-Qubad's attack.[17] Subsequent ventures were more successful, that of 1235 in alliance with the Bulgars resulting in the conquest of southern Thrace as far as the Maritsa river, that of 1242 in the conquest of the Aegean coastlands as far the Strymon river and the subordination of the Epirote emperor in Thessalonike who accepted the title of despot.[18] A brief hiatus followed, while John Batatzes took stock of the situation in Asia Minor after the Mongol victory over the Seljuks at Köse Dağı (26 June 1243). His policy, which was followed by his son and successor Theodore II Laskaris (1254–9), was to avoid entanglements in the east, and to rely on diplomacy to shore up the sultanate of Rum, and, if possible, to establish good relations with the Mongols. It was a remarkably successful policy which led to a treaty between Theodore II and Hülegü in 1257 and a marriage alliance seven years later.[19]

The Nikaians were free to concentrate on their rivalry with the Epirotes and to extend their territory in Europe. In 1246 they took advantage of the weakening of Bulgaria after the death of John Asen (1241) to annex Bulgar territories in Macedonia and, with the aid of the leading citizens, to take Thessalonike. A preemptive attack on Epirus in 1252 which resulted in the conquest of the fertile inland basins of Macedonia beyond the Vardar river strengthened their position. Finally, with the recovery of the Rhodope

[15] Korobeinikov, *Byzantium and the Turks*, 156–9, 172–6.
[16] Nicol, *Last Centuries*, 12–13, 20–2.
[17] Korobeinikov, *Byzantium and the Turks*, 157–8.
[18] Angold, *Byzantine Government in Exile*, 23, 279; Nicol, *Last Centuries*, 26.
[19] Korobeinikov, *Byzantium and the Turks*, 177–82, 184–92, 197–9, 203–6.

mountains in 1256, which had been seized by the Bulgars on hearing the news of John Batatzes' death (late 1254), the Nikaian Balkan provinces were reasonably secure behind defensible frontiers. Efforts were also made to knit together the ruling houses and aristocracies of Nikaia and Epiros through marriage alliances, the most important being between a granddaughter of John Batatzes and the eldest son of Michael Komnenos Doukas, ruler of Epirus, which was celebrated in Thessalonike in 1256.[20]

The Nikaian empire was thoroughly Byzantine, not simply in its outward trappings but in its institutions and social order. Supreme power was vested in a legitimate emperor (the designated heir of Alexios III, and his designated heirs), who governed in association with the same aristocratic families as the Angeloi. There was naturally some turn-over, some great families disappearing, others appearing, in a system which was not so ossified as to preclude the rise of new men, members of local aristocratic families. But the core of the governing elite consisted of the old Komnenian aristocracy, which, though a hereditary aristocracy in reality, did not hold hereditary titles and hereditary offices. The crown's power was undoubtedly enhanced, as had happened at the start of the Komnenian period, by its ability to bestow estates on favoured families.[21]

It was a stratified social order, as it had been under the Komnenoi and Angeloi, headed by the imperial family and its affines. There were clear gradations between aristocrats with extensive estates and with expectations of office on one hand and pronoiars in the country (owing military service in exchange for government land grants) and notables in the towns on the other, between both the latter and village leaders, between village leaders and the peasantry in general. It is impossible to say whether the balance between large landowners with dependent tenants and peasant proprietors had shifted radically in favour of the former, but it is unlikely that there was much difference in the living standards of tenantry and independent peasantry.[22]

The state loomed as large as ever it had, with a fiscal ability to reach down and tap the resources of individual households. In essence the administrative structure remained the same as it had been under the Komnenoi,

[20] Angold, *Byzantine Government in Exile*, 24–6, 280–2.

[21] Angold, *Byzantine Government in Exile*, 67–71; Korobeinikov, *Byzantium and the Turks*, 58–68.

[22] Angold, *Byzantine Government in Exile*, 123–7, 129–32, 214–20, 260–4, 267–9.

just operating on a much smaller scale. The Vestiarion remained in charge of finance, in association with ministries (*sekreta*) covering different heads of expenditure. It was responsible for conducting surveys, assessing individual liabilities, keeping records, and raising and storing the state's revenue. The only function outsourced (to provincial officials and tax-farmers) was collection.[23] The provincial system in Asia Minor was a lineal descendant of that set-up in the first age of crisis, in the seventh and eighth centuries. Mainland provinces, small compared to their dark-age predecessors, were called themes, some with familiar names (Paphlagonia, Thrakesion), and were governed, as they had been under the Komnenoi, by dukes. Many Aegean islands were independent administrative units. The European provinces differed in two important respects: (1) they were in effect occupied territories, with garrisons at strategic points and governors (*kephalai*) performing primarily military functions, overseen in the case of Macedonia by a viceroy at Thessalonike; and (2) many of the towns had rights and customs guaranteed by imperial golden bulls. Little is known of the justice system apart from the use of what was in essence Roman law. Above the provincial level, the high courts of Constantinople disappeared, being replaced by the imperial court (or Senate) acting in a judicial capacity.[24]

The trappings of empire were carefully preserved—a court stratified according to rank and office (increasingly merged), and elaborate ceremonial directed by the Protovestiarios, one of the highest-ranking officials. Once the Aegean coastlands were secure, the capital was transferred by John Batatzes from Nikaia to Nymphaion inland from Smyrna, with the Vestiarion based to the north at Magnesia.[25] The gap between imperial show and military reality was greater than ever before. The armies put into the field were very small by comparison to Byzantium in its heyday—some 6,000 men by the end of the Nikaian period, including many foreign mercenaries, chiefly Latin but also Cuman. Cuman refugees from the Mongols had been welcomed from Bulgaria and resettled in the Balkans and Asia Minor. But the show mattered, never more so than in 1257 when Mongol ambassadors, who had been purposely brought by a circuitous and difficult route, were received with a military parade and a magnificent audience with the emperor and the full court hierarchy. Thereafter Nikaian emperors could pose virtually as equals of the great conqueror Hülegü, their cordial

[23] Angold, *Byzantine Government in Exile*, 204–14, 221–36, as modified by Korobeinikov, *Byzantium and the Turks*, 69–74.

[24] Angold, *Byzantine Government in Exile*, 152–3, 166–74, 243–96.

[25] Angold, *Byzantine Government in Exile*, 63–5, 205–6.

relations eventually culminating in a marriage alliance between the two ruling families.[26]

The strong state was to remain a defining characteristic of Byzantium almost to the last. There was no weakening of public authority even as the landed aristocracy consolidated its power. Government remained a collaborative enterprise, the fortunes of the state and the great landowners rising and falling in tandem in the fourteenth and early fifteenth centuries.[27]

The achievements of Nikaian emperors in recreating a mini-empire in Asia Minor, stabilizing the frontier with the Turks, and conquering large swathes of the southern Balkans were crowned by two victorious campaigns. The first dealt once and for all with the rival claims of the despots of Epiros. The Epirotes had gone on the offensive in 1257, targeting Thessalonike, and had gained two valuable allies in Manfred ruler of Sicily and William of Villehardouin ruler of Achaia. But a Nikaian counteroffensive exploited tensions between Byzantines and Latins and won a decisive victory in Macedonia, in the Pelagonian plain, towards the end of July 1259. The Despot Michael took refuge on Kephalonia and the despotate ceased to exist for a few months. The next Nikaian target was Constantinople itself. The necessary naval force for an attack was acquired on the signing of a treaty at Nymphaion (13 March 1261) with the Genoese, who, in return for taking over all the Venetian concessions and gaining access to the Black Sea, were to provide the Nikaians with fifty ships. In the event Genoese aid was not needed, as a small Nikaian force operating in Thrace managed to capture the great city when it was denuded of defenders on 25 July 1261. The ultimate aim of the exiled empire was achieved. Byzantine emperors would once again hold court in the city refounded by Constantine, and would seek to manage the affairs of the Mediterranean and Middle East.[28]

The principal beneficiary of these successes was Michael Palaiologos, member of a prestigious Komnenian family, who seized power after the death of Theodore II in 1258. His relations with both John III and Theodore II had been volatile. He twice fell from favour and was emprisoned. The cause of his first fall in 1253 was suspicion that he was in treasonable contact with the Epirotes from his command in Thessaly. He was tried but not convicted. Under pressure from the military, John Batatzes freed him and

[26] Angold, *Byzantine Government in Exile*, 187–92; Korobeinikov, *Byzantium and the Turks*, 74–9, 198–9.

[27] R. Estangüi Gómez, *Byzance face aux Ottomans: Exercise du pouvoir et contrôle du territoire sous les derniers Paléologues (milieu XIVe– milieu XVe siècle)* (Paris, 2014).

[28] Nicol, *Last Centuries*, 27–8, 31–7.

appointed him Grand Constable in command of the Latin mercenaries. He came under suspicion again from Theodore II Laskaris in 1256, and went over to the Seljuks before he could be arrested. Welcomed and put in charge of the Greek troops in the Seljuk army, he fought the Mongols that autumn at the battle of Sultanhanı, another comprehensive Mongol victory. When he returned to Nikaia (via Kastamonu), he was posted to Europe after swearing loyalty to the Laskarids, but again fell under suspicion and was emprisoned in 1258, only to be freed on the death of Theodore II at the end of August.[29]

Over the following months he conducted a slow-moving coup. The first step was to dispose of George Mouzalon, the regent appointed by Theodore to govern during the minority of his son John (aged eight). Despite his unpopularity as the most favoured of the new men appointed to high office by Theodore, George was confirmed as regent by a general assembly of the aristocracy (i.e. the Senate), but, within little more than a week, at the beginning of September, he was assassinated by Latin mercenaries during the memorial service for Theodore. The choice of a new regent fell to the Senate, which, at a new meeting, preferred Michael to the candidate favoured by the Laskarid family, and gave him the title of Grand Duke. The election was subject to confirmation by the Patriarch Arsenios, and the resident bishops at Nikaia who formed the patriarchal synod. A third meeting of the Senate was held on 13 November 1258 at Magnesia, which was attended by the patriarchal synod and representatives of the military, under the presidency of the patriarch. Michael was confirmed as regent, and, despite opposition from the Laskarid faction, was made *basileopator* and despot, with the unanimous support of the army and a majority of the aristocracy and clergy (including the patriarch).[30]

The next step was taken on new year's day 1259, with the reluctant acquiescence of the patriarch, when Michael was raised up on a shield (in the old Roman manner) and acclaimed emperor at Nymphaion, after exchanging oaths with the young John Laskaris. The patriarch had insisted on this and on oaths of allegiance to both emperors from the magnates (with an additional oath to defend one of them against conspiracy by the other). His prime concern was to guarantee the young co-emperor's rights. When it came to the coronation at Nikaia, Michael applied intense pressure on the

[29] Nicol, *Last Centuries*, 29–31; Angold, *Byzantine Government in Exile*, 167–8; Korobeinikov, *Byzantium and the Turks*, 192–3.

[30] Angold, *Byzantine Government in Exile*, 80–8.

patriarch to have himself crowned first, something finally authorized by an episcopal tome. After the ceremony, in which his young co-emperor was crowned with a special headdress rather than the crown, Michael took him off to Nymphaion. Arsenios' reaction was to withdraw to a monastery and to refuse to carry out his duties, which resulted, at the emperor's insistence, in his deposition by the synod, and a split in the church and the court. At the death of his unpopular successor early in 1261, Michael allowed the synod to reinstate Arsenios, who was installed in St Sophia in September 1261 and crowned Michael for the second time.[31]

This was not the end of the matter. The patriarch was outraged when Michael took the final step in his usurpation, by having young John Laskaris blinded on Christmas Day 1261 and emprisoned thereafter in a fortress in Asia Minor. Arsenios excommunicated Michael and did not relent, despite Michael's prayers for forgiveness. Finally, in 1264, Michael had him forcibly evicted and sent into exile. His successor too was bullied into resigning. It was only on 2 February 1267 that the Patriarch Joseph, Arsenios' successor's successor, received the emperor back into the church.[32]

The successes achieved by Michael Palaiologos in 1259–61 were offset by his alienation of much of the episcopate and many monks in Asia Minor at his treatment of Arsenios, not to mention his brutal pushing aside of his Laskarid co-emperor, contrary to his sworn oath. A hard core of dissident clergy remained loyal to Arsenios, denying the legitimacy of Arsenios' successors and hostile to an emperor who dealt so autocratically with the church. The laity in Asia Minor were equally shocked when the news of the blinding leaked out. Among them too a party of Laskarid loyalists gathered strength, not least from the sense that Asia Minor was being neglected as resources were directed into the restoration of imperial government at Constantinople.[33]

Two tears had been made in the fabric of the state, one between church and state, the other between the economic core of the revived empire in Asia Minor and the authorities in the capital. Both would grow in the course of the reigns of Michael and his son Andronikos II, culminating in open religious warfare over relations with the papacy and a serious weakening in the resolve of aristocracy and people in Asia Minor in the face of Turkish attacks.

[31] Angold, *Byzantine Government in Exile*, 88–91.
[32] Angold, *Byzantine Government in Exile*, 91–2; Nicol, *Last Centuries*, 48–9.
[33] Nicol, *Last Centuries*, 44–6.

## 6.2 Struggle for survival, 1261–1321

The entry of Michael VIII Palaiologos into Constantinople in August 1261 marked the restoration of the Byzantine empire. Government could once again be exercised from the great city at the junction of Europe and Asia. Its territory was much reduced compared to that in its early eleventh-century heyday, after the depredations of Turks, Bulgars, Serbs, and Latins. The Palaiologan empire was a rump of the rump of the east Roman empire, with a long, vulnerable frontage both in Asia Minor and in the Balkans.

The key strongholds commanding the approaches to the fertile Marmara and Aegean coastlands of Asia Minor from the interior plateau were in Turkish hands—fortified cities such as Dorylaion, Kotyaion, Akroinion, and Laodikeia. The coastlands, which extended in the north into Paphlagonia on the Black Sea and in the south to Caria had thus been stripped of their outer defences, leaving the hills and river valleys running west and north-west open to infiltration by Turkmen tribal confederations. Whatever fortifications might be put up—say along the Sangarios river and around Nikaia in the north, around Philadelphia and in the Maeander valley in the south—these coastlands would be indefensible against large-scale invasion by organized forces. This territory on the western fringe of Asia Minor constituted the major resource-base of the empire: (1) Bithynia with its chief centres (Nikaia, Nikomedia, Prusa, Lopadion); (2) the northern Aegean coastlands from the Hellespont down to the Hermos river with the ancient cities of Lampsakos, Adramyttion, Pergamon, Phokaia, Smyrna, Magnesia, and Sardis; and (3) the Kayster and Maeander valleys with cities such as Ephesos, Miletos, Tralles, Nyssa, and Antioch.[34] It could only be secured by hyperactive diplomacy, reaching into the Turkish world of the interior of Asia Minor and beyond to the great power, centred on Tabriz, of the Mongol Ilkhans. Military action could only play a subsidiary role, pushing back local infiltrators.

The narrower northern and southern coastlands had much stronger natural defences, the Pontic mountains and the Taurus, but, apart from the western half of Paphlagonia, both were lost to Michael VIII, a pocket kingdom under the Grand Komnenoi holding Trebizond and adjoining strips of coastland, Turks in control of the southern coastlands around Attaleia.

The position was better in the Balkans. The whole of Thrace up to the steep southern slope of the Haemus range, not just the Thracian approaches

[34] Korobeinikov, *Byzantium and the Turks*, 217–19.

to Constantinople, was in Byzantine hands, along with key coastal cities further north, Anchialos and Mesembria. Bulgaria, brought within the sphere of influence of the Golden Horde, was confined to its core early medieval territory. The Rhodope mountains formed a natural bastion guarding eastern Macedonia. Western Macedonia had been conquered in the Nikaian period, with the frontier pushed out beyond the Vardar and up over the southern upland basins of the interior to include Edessa, Kastoria, Ochrid, Prilep, and Skopje (ancient Scupi). Control of Thessalonike in the south helped shore up Byzantine authority, in what was, in essence, a broad salient pushing west toward Epiros, with Serbia to the north and Latin Greece to the south beyond Olympos and neighbouring mountains. The only relatively open sector of the frontier was on the north side of the salient, facing Serbia, which ran across the forested hills and open plains of Macedonia.[35]

The restored empire would be a major player in Balkan politics, able to hold its own with these neighbouring powers over the next few decades. A first gain was made very early, when William of Villehardouin, captured at the battle of Pelagonia in 1259, was ransomed in 1262. In return for his release, he ceded various fortresses in the Peloponnese, including Mistra and Monemvasia. Thereafter Michael VIII made opportunistic attacks on his neighbours, first in 1264 on Epiros which ceded Ioannina and on William of Villehardouin, when he reneged on his deal after receiving papal permission to do. There were other Byzantine strikes south and west in 1274, on Thessaly and Dyrrachion, but these were part of a larger struggle.[36] For the ousting of the last Latin emperor, Baldwin II, was taken ill by the west, not only in Italy and Sicily but further afield in Spain and France. Michael VIII and his son and successor, Andronikos II, had to be on guard against the danger of a revanchist expedition to reinstate the Latin empire. Such expeditions would have the enthusiastic support of the papacy, despite its vociferous opposition to the diversion of the Fourth Crusade against Constantinople. Minor differences in doctrine and rite between Catholics and Orthodox were now taken to justify armed action against the Orthodox.

All manner of defensive measures were taken: first and foremost, naval shipbuilding to create a fleet, which would enable Byzantium to negotiate on more equal terms with the Italian maritime republics; second, new treaties with the Genoese (1267) who were allowed to establish a trading colony

[35] Angold, *Byzantine Government in Exile*, 279–83.
[36] Nicol, *Last Centuries*, 46–8, 58–9.

at Galata, across the Golden Horn from Constantinople, and with the Venetians (1268); third and most important, a full range of diplomatic activity, extending from high-level contacts to subversion and reaching far afield across the Mediterranean, which was designed to break up anti-Byzantine coalitions. *In extremis* Michael was even ready to bend in terms of faith.

Michael VIII Palaiologos had no choice but to focus his attention on the west for most of his reign. Baldwin II escaped to Sicily, to the court of Manfred Hohenstaufen who had inherited his father's hostility to Byzantium, and then made his way to the papal Curia, at which the new pope, Urban IV, proclaimed a crusade in 1261 directed against Constantinople. The response was poor, with the exception of Manfred, who, as the son-in-law of the despot of Epiros and with forward bases in Albania and northern Greece, was well placed to take action. But, like his father Frederick II, he was at odds with the papacy and had been excommunicated. Faced with this fissure in the west, Michael began in June 1262 to vamp the pope, indicating that he was ready to remove the schism and restore the unity of the church. Serious negotiations took place in 1263–4, involving four Franciscan monks and a Greek Catholic bishop from southern Italy, and resulted in a proposal from the emperor that a church council be convened.[37]

With the death of Pope Urban IV in October 1264, the proposal was not followed up. Instead, another initiative of Urban's was pursued by his successor, Clement IV. With papal backing Charles of Anjou, brother of the king of France, Louis IX, attacked, defeated, and killed Manfred at Benevento in 1266. The papacy now had a protector rather than an enemy in southern Italy and Sicily, and proceeded to form a coalition of Baldwin II, Charles of Anjou, and William of Villehardouin, sealed by marriage alliances between the parties (the treaty of Viterbo in May 1267). Instead of the church council he had suggested, Michael was told that the Greek church must submit on the pope's terms. Although the threat was not immediate—Charles of Anjou had offered 2,000 knights for a crusade, but only in 1273 or 1274—it was plain. The attack would come by land along the Via Egnatia. Charles had gained control of Dyrrachion, at its western end, in 1271, and the submission of the Albanians in its hinterland who acknowledged him as their king. In addition both Serbia and Bulgaria supported him. Michael had no choice but to yield to the papacy's demands.[38]

[37] Nicol, *Last Centuries*, 48–9.

[38] Nicol, *Last Centuries*, 49–52.

The years following the treaty of Viterbo were spent in increasingly difficult negotiations with a succession of popes. Even the relatively placatory pope Gregory X, elected in September 1271 after a three-year hiatus, insisted on Byzantium's submission before the legates he invited could attend the general council at Lyons he had announced for 1274. Cornered, Michael did his best to browbeat the church into accepting union, even if it was only lip service. The opposition, clerical and lay, gathered way, rallying around Patriarch Joseph. The Arsenite faction joined in, as did several members of the imperial family. Michael's campaign had one success, when John Bekkos, the intellectual who had led the opposition before being imprisoned, was won over to the view that Catholics shared the essentials of the faith and should not be classified as heretics. On release, he became the mouthpiece for the unionists and won over a minority of the clergy. The patriarch was pushed aside, confined to a monastery, and some bishops were persuaded to draft a general profession of Catholic faith, for presentation to the council, along with a more detailed profession from Michael and his heir, Andronikos. The two documents were taken by legates to the Council of Lyons. Latin translations were read out and an oath of loyalty to Rome and acceptance of the Catholic creed was sworn on the emperor's behalf by the lay legate, the Grand Logothete George Akropolites at the formal celebration of the reunion of the church on 6 July 1274.[39]

This was not the end of the crisis, just a temporary easing. Michael made immediate use of it to attack Thessaly, held by the staunch anti-unionist brother of the despot of Epiros (a failure—the army was defeated), and to re-establish control over the islands of the Aegean with his fleet and the aid of client westerners (initially successful). He also launched an offensive against Charles' bridgehead in Albania, from the fortress of Berat, commanding the key pass from the east. For two years from 1274 the Angevin garrisons remained on the defensive, while Charles was preoccupied elsewhere. There was no question, though, of Charles' abandoning his plan, especially as he had married his daughter to Philip, son of Baldwin II, and had thus become father-in-law of the claimant to the Latin empire. Michael's prime task was to persuade successive popes, who were increasingly sceptical of Byzantium's conversion to Catholicism, of his good faith. This involved a solemn public proclamation of the union at a synod of clergy and laity in winter 1276, and a ceremony in the Blachernai palace in April

[39] Nicol, *Last Centuries*, 52–7.

1277 at which Michael and Andronikos swore to recognize the supremacy of Rome and the Roman creed.[40]

But solid evidence was not forthcoming in the form of unequivocal professions of faith from the patriarch and from the clergy individually. Michael prevaricated, stressing the strength of the opposition, reporting the tough measures he was taking against it, and sending a general declaration of submission, signed and sealed, from a synod held in 1279.[41] Meanwhile the threat from Charles of Anjou was growing as he shipped troops and supplies across the Adriatic to Albania, ready for an attack on the empire, whenever the prohibition issued by Pope Nicholas III (elected in November 1277) might lapse, as it did at his death in August 1280. That autumn Charles launched his long-delayed offensive, involving some 8,000 troops under the command of Hugues le Rouseau de Sully, a Burgundian knight. The first objective was the fortresss of Berat. The siege lasted several months until the arrival of a relief army in spring 1281 and the capture of Hugues by some Turkish mercenaries. The news caused dismay in the Angevin army, which turned and fled to the coast. Far from being disheartened, Charles now shifted his attention from land to sea, and signed a treaty with Venice on 3 July 1281 at Orvieto, the residence of the new French pope, Martin IV, who authorized the use of force against the Byzantines. The Venetians, aggrieved at the privileges of the Genoese, agreed to transport a force of 8,000 cavalry and to supply an escort of forty warships. The date of the expedition was fixed for spring 1283.[42]

The outlook for Byzantium was made grimmer by the support given by other Balkan powers to Charles. The despot of Epiros signed a treaty. His brother in Thessaly was sympathetic. The Morea had passed to Charles on the death of William of Villehardouin in 1278. Bulgaria declared itself an ally, while Serbia took action, invading Byzantine Macedonia and capturing Skopje in 1282. Michael countered with a remarkable feat of diplomatic outreach (1) to the steppes of Ukraine (the Golden Horde was to keep a careful watch on the Bulgars), (2) to Hungary (deterred from joining the Serbs), (3) to Egypt (for a loan of ships for the defence of Constantinople), and (4) to Aragon. Peter III of Aragon was his prime target, since he had a large fleet and was eager to avenge the death of his father-in-law Manfred. It is impossible to know what inducements were offered to persuade him to intervene, given the secrecy shrouding the negotiations. But there were channels of

[40] Nicol, *Last Centuries*, 58–62.
[41] Nicol, *Last Centuries*, 62–5.
[42] Nicol, *Last Centuries*, 65–7.

communication available, not least Peter's chancellor and secretary, John of Procida, one of several refugees from Angevin Sicily. Hand in hand with open and covert diplomacy, a campaign of subversion was launched in Sicily. Nothing is known about the process, but large sums must have changed hands. For it was extraordinarily successful, resulting in a popular uprising in the capital, Palermo, on 30 March 1282, the massacre of the French in the city, and the spread of unrest throughout the island. Charles' own invasion fleet, assembled in the harbour of Messina, was destroyed. Then, in August, Peter of Aragon arrived and expelled the French.[43]

There would be no danger of large-scale attack from the west for twenty years, while the Angevin kingdom of Naples and Aragonese Sicily were at war. That was the good part of the legacy of Michael VIII. The bad part was the bitter animosities in the church created by the drive for union and high-handed treatment of the clergy. Michael died in December 1282, at the start of an expedition against John Doukas, ruler of Thessaly. His son and heir, Andronikos II, was a very different character—gentle, of a scholarly disposition, contemplative, ill-equipped to face the buffeting he would get from rival church factions. He immediately renounced his father's unionist policy and proclaimed the restoration of Orthodoxy. He was then carried along by the strong anti-unionist current, (1) deposing John Bekkos (to whom he was close) from the patriarchate and restoring Joseph, and (2) yielding to pressure for prominent unionists to be brought to trial, beginning with John Bekkos. Synod after synod was convened at which feelings ran high and the old hostility between Arsenites and the supporters of Joseph flared up. The compromise figure chosen to succeed Joseph, who died in 1283, a distinguished scholar, Gregory II, did his best to appease the Arsenites, but managed to create more dissension when, in a formal condemnation of John Bekkos, he went into detail about the Procession of the Holy Spirit (the chief theological issue dividing Orthodox and Catholics). He was driven from office and succeeded by Athanasios (patriarch 1289–93, 1303–9), a holy man, plucked out of seclusion, an uncompromising puritan who sought to upgrade moral standards. He created yet more turbulence in the church and lay society. The troubles only ended when the Arsenite party, weakened by the loss of much of Byzantine Asia Minor, compromised and agreed to reunite with the rest of the church in 1310.[44]

[43] Nicol, *Last Centuries*, 67–71.

[44] Nicol, *Last Centuries*, 93–106.

There were still problems to be dealt with in the Balkans in the early years of Andronikos' reign. The main threat came from the Serbs. Two major military strikes were organized, the first in 1282 (to make them desist from encroaching on Byzantine Macedonia) by a force of 4,000 Nogaj Mongols summoned from the Golden Horde, the second in 1297 by Byzantine forces in response to the loss of Dyrrachion. Hostilities ended in 1299 when Andronikos agreed to marry his five-year-old daughter Simonis to the Serb king, Stefan Uroš II Milutin, providing as her dowry the territory in Macedonia gained by the Serbs. That peace lasted until Milutin's death in 1321. The Epirotes represented a lesser threat, but were targets of Byzantine attack in 1283 when the *sebastokrator* John Doukas of Thessaly was allied with the Serbs (the naval and military expedition was a failure, partly because of malaria) and in 1293 after Epiros had entered an alliance with Charles II, Angevin king of Naples (the Epirotes held out against Byzantines by land and Genoese by sea, with the aid of the Prince of Achaia, Florent of Hainault, an Angevin vassal). Far to the south, a new partition of the Peloponnese, recognizing Byzantine gains, was agreed by Florent in a seven-year peace treaty signed in 1289.[45]

From the start of his reign, Andronikos realised that he must cut back on expenditure, after the massive military and diplomatic efforts of Michael VIII. His most notable cut affected the navy. *It was disbanded*, reliance instead being placed on the Genoese, now more than ever an integral part of the state. The last recorded action of the navy was the attack by eighty ships on Demetrias as part of the 1283 offensive against Thessaly. The voluntary axing of a fleet was a quite extraordinary imperial act.[46] The navy, built up in the seventh century, had played a vital part in the survival of Byzantium in the face of the Arab onslaught. Later it helped Byzantium project its power west over the whole Mediterranean, as well as protecting the Aegean and all its islands from predators. It had enabled Byzantium to launch attacks on Bulgaria from the Black Sea and the Danube. It had fended off the Rus in their early expansionist phase. Combined operations were launched against the great islands of the Mediterranean in the era of revival—Crete, Cyprus, Sicily. It was at all times essential to the security of the state, given the vulnerability of the capital to attack by sea.

[45] Nicol, *Last Centuries*, 114–21; A. E. Laiou, *Constantinople and the Latins: The Foreign Policy of Andronicus II, 1282–1328* (Cambridge, MA, 1972), 30, 38–41, 93–100; J. V. A. Fine Jr, *The Late Medieval Balkans: A Critical Survey from the Late Twelfth Century to the Ottoman Conquest* (Ann Arbor, MI, 1987), 219–20, 222–3.

[46] Laiou, *Constantinople and the Latins*, 74–6.

Without a navy Byzantium was at the mercy of western maritime powers, as was shown in the 1290s, when Venice began to encroach on the Genoese commercial sphere in the east. Byzantium could only look on as a powerless spectator as the two great maritime cities went to war (1293–9) and as Venetian fleets penetrated into the Golden Horn (1296, 1297, and 1302). When peace was finally made, in 1302, it was on Venetian terms.[47]

The greatest problem facing Andronikos was Turkish pressure on what remained of Byzantine Asia Minor. Without strong natural defences, he relied above all on the Ilkhanids (the Mongols of Iran) to keep the Turks in check, despite the danger that turbulence among the five Turkmen confederations in Asia Minor, occasioned by Ilkhanid intervention, might trigger more Turkmen to migrate west and require military countermeasures from the Byzantines.[48]

There were four serious crises between 1260 and 1302. The first was induced by Mehmed-bey, leader of the Denizli Turkmen, who controlled extensive territory, from the southern coastlands around Attaleia and Alania to the southern sector of the Byzantine frontier, including Laodikeia. Michael VIII led punitive campaigns against them, winning two victories in 1260 and 1261 in the Maeander region. But it was a Mongol force, dispatched by the Ilkhan Hülegü in 1262, after Mehmed-bey refused to visit the Mongol court, which, in conjunction with the Seljuks of Rum, inflicted the decisive defeat in 1262, killed Mehmed-bey himself and drove his Turkmen out of the southern coastlands. But the confederation was not destroyed, and, under the leadership of Ali-bey, Mehmed's son, pushed down the Maeander valley past Tralles to the coast where they captured Strobilos. This thrust seems to have been a show of force designed to extract concessions from the Byzantines, namely a grant of winter grazing lands (*kislak*) in the Maeander valley to replace those lost in the south. This was agreed by Michael's brother, the Despot John in 1264.[49]

These Turkmen occupied a broad frontier zone (*uj*) from the interior plateau to the Aegean coast, which straddled the frontier hills and lapped around several notable cities (Ikonion and Laodikeia foremost among them). They were under Seljuk suzerainty and co-existed peacefully with villagers and townsmen in the Maeander valley.[50] This stable *modus vivendi*

[47] Nicol, *Last Centuries*, 107–8, 110–12; Laiou, *Constantinople and the Latins*, 101–14.
[48] Korobeinikov, *Byzantium and the Turks*, 233–4.
[49] Korobeinikov, *Byzantium and the Turks*, 223–7, 245–6.
[50] Korobeinikov, *Byzantium and the Turks*, 228–33.

was brought to an abrupt end in 1277, when the Mamluk Sultan Baibars I invaded Asia Minor, defeated the Mongols near Elbistan in the Anti-Taurus basin, and marched to Kayseri where he was proclaimed Sultan of Rum (April 1277). He withdrew to Damascus (where he died in June) at the approach of the main Mongol army commanded by the Ilkhan Abaqa. Baibars' appearance had threatened Mongol control of Asia Minor indirectly as well as directly. For it galvanized the Turkmen into action. One confederation, centred on Karaman, was already in revolt. Their leader now brought in two others to form a powerful rebel coalition, which took control of the southern march of the sultanate of Rum, from Sivrihisar to Konya, under a sultan (Cimri) of their creation. Faced with this widespread Turkmen insurrection, the Ilkhan sent another army into Asia Minor, this time under his brother Qongqurtay, which, again in conjunction with a Seljuk force, defeated the rebel coalition, killed the leader of the Karaman Turkmen, and pursued Cimri as he fled west towards the Byzantine borderlands. He was defeated and flayed alive on 30 May 1279 some distance east of the *uj* of the Denizli Turkmen, who had remained neutral. It was then the turn of the Denizli Turkmen to be attacked, by the Seljuk wazir, their lands devastated and their leader, Ali-bey, executed.[51]

The devastation of much of the frontier zone east of Byzantine territory in the course of the repression of the Turkmen revolt and the associated turbulence among the Turkmen led to wholesale change in western Asia Minor. In the north, two Turkmen confederations pressed against the Byzantine frontier, taking over much of western Paphlagonia and raiding Bithynia. There were raids in the centre which reached the Cayster river. In the south a new amalgam was formed out of the remnants of the Menteşe and Denizli Turkmen, which conquered the territory to the south of the Maeander. Michael VIII reacted swiftly, himself taking charge of the defence of Bithynia in 1280–2, and sending his son Andronikos to stabilize the situation in the south. Andronikos fought a battle, attacked the environs of Laodikeia, and rebuilt Tralles (captured during the great 1277–9 rebellion) only for it to fall again in 1284. Michael shored up the defences on both banks of the Sangarios river in the north, while, in the south, Andronikos boosted the population of Ephesos and Anaia with resettled Cretan refugees. Later, after Michael's death, Andronikos continued his defensive work in Bithynia in 1283–4, along the lower Sangarios and on the coast between Lampsakos and Adramyttion.[52]

[51] Korobeinikov, *Byzantium and the Turks*, 252–4.

[52] Korobeinikov, *Byzantium and the Turks*, 234, 246–50, 253–7, 259–60.

More rebellions by the Turkmen of Germiyan and Karaman on the western marches of the sultanate of Rum in the years 1286–91 prompted another Ilkhan intervention in force (the third) in late October 1291. The new Ilkhan Geikhatu, who knew the sultanate well, ravaged the lands of Karaman and Esref Turkmen (the former twice), captured Laodikeia, massacred its inhabitants and devastated the lands of the Menteşe Turkmen in little more than two months (late November 1291–late January 1292). Seljuk authority and administration were destroyed from Konya to the Byzantine frontier. The Turkmen confederations were blasted to pieces. In consequence there was renewed raiding across the Byzantine frontier. The prime target seems to have been the theme of Neokastra behind the central section of the frontier (in winter 1292–3).[53]

The Byzantine response was prompt and effective. Andronikos himself was in Bithynia. He seems to have been doing his best to assuage any sense of estrangement between the Asia Minor provinces and the capital, by paying long visits to Nikaia and Lopadion, the two principal centres in Bithynia (1290–1), and spending two years (1291–3) in the old Nikaian capital of Nymphaion.[54] He appointed two generals to take charge of the defence of Neokastra (Libadarios) and the region immediately to the south between the Cayster and Maeander rivers (Alexios Philanthropenos, a nephew). Alexios proved very successful in campaigns which took him south from Gallipoli (where he landed in March 1293) to the Maeander valley. He defeated both the Germiyan and Menteşe Turkmen in 1294, in battles fought south of Philadelphia and in the Maeander valley. He went on, in 1295, to reimpose Byzantine authority on the lower Maeander region and to recapture Miletos. But then something went wrong. Alexios fell under suspicion, perhaps for not forwarding enough of the spoils gathered by his troops to Andronikos, perhaps because of enduring antagonism among the people and soldiers in Asia Minor towards the imperial authorities in Constantinople, but most probably because his troops' pay was intermittent. With his rebellion in November 1295 (swiftly quelled when his troops were bribed by Libadarios), and the disintegration of his army, the effort to hold on to western Asia Minor was fatally undermined. A later attempt to reconstitute a local army, entrusted to another imperial relative, John

[53] Korobeinikov, *Byzantium and the Turks*, 261–4.

[54] Laiou, *Constantinople and the Latins*, 76–9; Korobeinikov, *Byzantium and the Turks*, 260–1.

Tarchaneiotes, failed. The rich provinces lying between the hills and coast were all too vulnerable when the fourth crisis broke in 1298–9.[55]

This time it was the Mongol governor of Asia Minor, Sulemis, who rebelled late in 1298 and attracted a large number of Turkmen to his cause. The rebellion spread through northern Anatolia from Eskişehir to Sivas and beyond. He defeated and killed two other Mongol commanders in the sultanate, before facing a large army sent by the Ilkhan and being defeated near Erzincan in late April 1299. He was able to escape to Mamluk territory, and returned in the summer with Mamluk backing, seeking to raise up the Turkmen of the western borderlands of the sultanate. He thus succeeded in stirring up the Turkmen world adjoining Byzantine territory, both directly himself and indirectly through the devastation wrought by the pursuing Mongol army which captured him at Ankara. This marked the final stage in the break-up of the old Turkmen confederations and the emergence of new smaller groupings, foremost among them in the north the Turks of Osman, founder of the Ottoman dynasty.[56]

The predictable consequence was an increase in the range and frequency of Turkish raids on what remained of Byzantine Asia Minor, along the whole length of the frontier, in 1300 and 1301. Andronikos sent what troops he had, placing them under the command of his son and co-emperor Michael IX and Mouzalon governor of Bithynia, supplemented with a large force of Alans. The Alans, who originated from either the Don steppes or the north Caucasus, had been resettled in Bulgaria by the Golden Horde. Whether or not their migration on to Byzantine territory was authorized by the Golden Horde is not known. Both generals' operations in 1302 ended in disaster. Michael IX was dissuaded by his generals from engaging the Turks when he reached Magnesia, and was then deserted by some of his Byzantine soldiers and all of his Alans. He had to take refuge in Pergamon, only returning to Constantinople at the beginning of 1304. The population of Magnesia fled likewise, first to Adramyttion and thence to Lampsakos. The Turks were able to occupy land on the north bank of the Maeander up to the Hermos river. In Bithynia Mouzalon did fight but was decisively defeated by Osman's Turks on 27 July 1302 at the battle of Bapheus near Nikomedia. At this much of the population of eastern Bithynia fled west,

[55] Laiou, *Constantinople and the Latins*, 80–4, 87–9; Korobeinikov, *Byzantium and the Turks*, 264–71.

[56] Korobeinikov, *Byzantium and the Turks*, 271–3.

leaving the main cities (Nikaia, Nikomedia, Prusa) surrounded by Turks and only a narrow strip along the coast safe in Byzantine hands.[57]

There were ominous developments in the west. First, a single, powerful claimant to the Latin empire emerged—the brother of the king of France (Philip IV), Charles of Valois, who married Catherine of Courtenay, the nominal Latin empress, in 1301. In the fateful year 1302, he was sent with 4,000 troops to southern Italy, at the papacy's request, to help the Angevins of Naples against the Aragonese of Sicily. His imperial claim was recognized but he must first expel Frederick III, brother of James II of Aragon, from Sicily. In the event he greatly strengthened his position without fighting, renewing the Treaty of Viterbo with Charles II of Naples in March, brokering the Peace of Caltabelotta in August between Naples and Sicily, and receiving a promise of help for his expedition east from Frederick III.[58] Second, with the end of fighting in Sicily, a 6,500/8,000 strong force of mainly Catalan soldiers, led by Roger de Flor, was no longer needed there. Roger de Flor offered his services to Andronikos. For Andronikos Roger was a *deus ex machina*, who would fight the Turks and reverse Byzantine losses in Asia Minor. His Catalan Company was a medieval analogue to the Germanic warbands which roamed the western Roman empire at the end of antiquity, but it would cause much more mayhem.[59]

The Catalans arrived at Constantinople in September 1303 on Genoese ships, were bivouacked for the winter on the Kyzikos peninsula on the far side of the Sea of Marmara, and then conducted a successful campaign against the Turks. They fought several major battles, the first to secure their winter-quarters in November 1303, the other three in the course of operations in spring and early summer 1304 in the central zone. In the course of their sinuous march, first south to the region of Pergamon, then inland (south-east) to Philadelphia, then west to Nymphaion, Magnesia, and Ephesos, they cleared out the Turks from the plains of the Hermos and lower Maeander, thus relieving the cities from Turkish pressure.[60] The campaign was halted in August, when Andronikos recalled them ostensibly for operations in Thrace with his son, Michael IX, his real reason being their depredations and demands for money. They had plundered Philadelphia,

[57] Laiou, *Constantinople and the Latins*, 89–92; Korobeinikov, *Byzantium and the Turks*, 273–4.

[58] Laiou, *Constantinople and the Latins*, 128–31.

[59] Laiou, *Constantinople and the Latins*, 131–4.

[60] Korobeinikov, *Byzantium and the Turks*, 285–7.

Pyrgos, and Ephesos, had besieged Magnesia when it resisted, and had raided the islands of Chios, Lesbos, and Lemnos.[61]

The Catalans crossed to Gallipoli, where they were joined by another Catalan force from Sicily, which had been invited east by Roger with the consent of Frederick III and James II. These Aragonese rulers were thinking of using them to attack Constantinople, and sent out, with papal permission, an advance force of 13 galleys in spring 1305, to be followed by a large expedition later in the year. At the same time tensions were growing with the Catalans. There was a dispute over money in the autumn and some raiding of Thrace. Then they began to fortify the Gallipoli peninsula and to stockpile foodstuffs. Relations were, eventually, patched up. Roger agreed to go back to Asia Minor with 3,000 men, in return for the title of Caesar and authority over Asia Minor. But first he paid a visit to Michael IX who was preparing to resume operations against the Bulgars. There Roger was assassinated, on the night of 30 April 1305. Freed of any obligations to the emperor, the Catalans thenceforth made war on Byzantium.[62] Military action was no longer subordinated to a diplomatic end, the extraction of concessions (political, territorial, or financial), but was now undertaken in its own right, to cause harm and to provide the Catalans with the necessities of life. With a secure base in an easily defended peninsula, they could roam at will over Thrace, as they did later in Macedonia from a second redoubt on the Kassandreia peninsula.[63] Their numbers were smaller than the Germanic groupings which had moved with their wagon trains through Roman provinces in late antiquity, and they were not accompanied by their families. Hence they could be accommodated on peninsulae, rather than the large regions (Epirus, Aquitaine, Spain, North Africa) required by Germanic peoples in the late fourth and fifth centuries.

Andronikos issued a formal appeal for Genoese help in late spring 1305. The Genoese responded by seconding ships from the fleets which they sent each year to the Black Sea for operations against the Catalans. A success of theirs in 1305 at the end of May was swiftly negated when Michael IX was defeated as he advanced on Gallipoli on 10 July. This left Thrace easy prey to the Catalans, who roamed at will, gathering supplies and besieging important towns (Raidestos 1305, Adrianople 1306, Vizye 1307). Andronikos resorted to the desperate expedient of starving them out, instructing the

[61] Laiou, *Constantinople and the Latins*, 136–7.
[62] Laiou, *Constantinople and the Latins*, 137–47.
[63] Laiou, *Constantinople and the Latins*, 209.

villagers to refrain from cultivating their fields in October 1306. It was a dangerous gamble, but it worked—the Catalans left for Macedonia in early summer 1307, but, in an ominous development, shifted their allegiance from Frederick III to Charles of Valois, western claimant to the empire, who had obtained the vital papal approval for an expedition east and an undertaking from Venice to provide the necessary naval transports.[64]

The position of Byzantium was parlous. Turks led by Osman (Ottomans) were encroaching on Bithynia, seizing four strongholds in 1304. Ephesos fell in 1305 to a Turkmen warleader after the departure of the Catalans. The rump of Bithynia rose up late in 1306 at the tax demands of the centre. It was only the dispatch of a 30,000-strong army by the Ilkhan Oljeitu, in response to a Byzantine appeal, which prevented Osman from pressing his siege of Nikaia to a conclusion in 1307, and forced him back to his core land, the mountainous territory to the east of Bursa.[65] In the Balkans the Bulgars joined forces with the Catalans in 1305 and occupied Mesembria and Anchialos. The Catalans were attacking Thessalonike. Charles of Valois was planning his expedition and courting both the Serbs and dissidents in Constantinople.[66]

But from 1308 the balance began to shift. There was growing tension between Charles of Valois and the Venetians over money. Thessalonike resisted land and sea attack. A competent Byzantine general, Chandrenos, launched guerrilla attacks on the Catalans from the city, and continued to do so after they left Macedonia for Thessaly. He also defeated a powerful Turkish warband which had broken away from the Catalans and taken refuge in Serbia. Finally, in autumn 1309, the French commander of the Catalans, Thibaut, was forced out and the Catalans threw off their vassalage to Charles of Valois. After two years' campaigning in Thessaly (1309–10), the second on behalf of Walter of Brienne, Duke of Athens, they turned on him when he dismissed all but a few from his service in spring 1311, defeated the Frankish forces of Athens and Achaia in Boeotia, and settled in Athens, whence they continued to attack Byzantine possessions by land and sea. Far removed from Constantinople, they no longer posed a mortal threat. Nor did Charles of Valois despite the proclamation of a crusade by the Council of Vienne (December 1312), despite a surge of crusading fervour in France

[64] Laiou, *Constantinople and the Latins*, 153–7, 162–4, 166–73, 181–3, 200–7.

[65] Laiou, *Constantinople and the Latins*, 174; Korobeinikov, *Byzantium and the Turks*, 211–12, 284–5; Foss, *Beginnings*, 137, 144–5, 163–71.

[66] Laiou, *Constantinople and the Latins*, 170–1 (Bulgars), 208–20 (Catalans, CP, Serbs).

and a renewed alliance with Naples brought about by the marriage of his daughter by Catherine de Courtenay to Philip of Taranto, son of Charles II of Naples. The necessary funds were not forthcoming, especially from the king of France, and before long (from 1314) both France and the papacy were distracted by internal troubles.[67]

Andronikos was able to repair relations with Venice, Aragon, Serbia and Bulgaria in the decade following the Catalans' seizure of Athens. A small but efficient army was built up. Gains were made in Epiros, Thessaly, and the Peloponnese. At home the Arsenite schism had been finally brought to an end in 1310. The most powerful of the Turkish warbands which had been operating in the Balkans, in alliance with the Catalans, was finally defeated in 1313 by a joint Byzantine, Serb, and Genoese army. Most of the Turks were massacred before they could cross back to Asia Minor. A new self-reliance was induced into the towns of Thrace and Macedonia in the years when they were threatened by the Catalans—something paralleled at this time in such cities in Asia Minor (notably Philadelphia, Nikaia, Nikomedia, Prusa) as maintained their loyalty to the empire despite a surrounding sea of Turks. In the more distant reaches of the empire—the reconquered parts of Epiros, Thessaly, and the Peloponnese—town notables were granted delegated authority by the centre.[68]

It looked as if stability had at last returned to what remained of the empire.

## 6.3 Dissolution, 1321–71

Fourteenth-century Byzantium was one of four medium-sized states competing for hegemony in the Balkans.[69] Its core territories, the rump of the Komnenian rump of the empire in its early eleventh-century heyday, were Thrace, Macedonia, and Thessaly. In addition there were outlying possessions in Asia Minor (a few isolated enclaves), Epiros, and the Peloponnese. Centrifugal forces were strong, as power leaked from the centre and individual towns acquired increasing autonomy. The classical Greek *polis* which had been submerged beneath monarchical power since the rise of Macedonia in the second half of the fourth century BC was reasserting itself.

[67] Laiou, *Constantinople and the Latins*, 220–7, 231–2, 237–42, 249–50.
[68] Laiou, *Constantinople and the Latins*, 190–3, 212, 227–9, 232–3, 244–7.
[69] The other three were Bulgaria, Serbia, and the Ottomans.

What remained of the empire was now, in many respects, a collection of city-states, subject to a greater or lesser extent to the authority of the emperor or of those to whom he delegated authority, in particular the Despots of Thessalonike and the Morea.

There are two ways of looking at the Balkans. The first and more common approach is to look in from outside.[70] The prospect is daunting—a quintessentially fragmented and fractious region, criss-crossed by mountain chains, a land broken up by nature into a multitude of greater and lesser polities centred on one or more plains within a highland landscape. The natural political unit is smallest in its southern protrusion, mainland Greece and the Peloponnese, and on the western, Dalmatian coast. In the east by contrast two extensive plains, the lower Danube valley and Thrace, provide massive arable bases for state-construction. The Balkans, on this view, was a large refractory region, a *terre d'insolence*, a region of endemic conflict into which outside powers would intervene at their peril.

Only the greatest of external predators could hope to extend effective authority over the Balkan interior. The Romans pushed in from the Dalmatian coast in the west and up the Danube and its major western tributaries (Sava and Drava) from the east, driving two major arterial roads through the broken country, one diagonal from Viminacium via Naissus and Serdica to Byzantium, the other lateral from Dyrrachion via Thessalonike to Byzantium. The medieval Hungarian kingdom was, by comparison, a feeble power threatening the Balkans from the north. The much-feared predators threatening the Danube plain from the north-east were the nomads of the Pontic steppes, of whom the Bulgars were the most successful, establishing a stable state centred on the Dobruja within defensible natural frontiers in the second half of the seventh century. After more than holding their own against Byzantium for several generations, as we have seen, they extended their authority west and south in the middle decades of the ninth century. Their distant and more powerful successors were the Mongols of the Golden Horde, who preferred to exercise indirect rather than direct control of the lands south of the Danube, and limited their interventions to isolated military forays.

The most welcoming approach to the Balkan interior was that from the east, from the great plain of Thrace transected by the Maritsa river. First, though, the invader had to cross the Bosporus or the Dardanelles. The Persians did so in massive force in their vain attempt to subdue the Greeks

[70] Obolensky, *Byzantine Commonwealth*, 5–24; Whitby, *Emperor Maurice*, 59–66.

in 480–79 BC. Fourteenth-century Byzantium faced a very different threat, from the various Turkish emirates established in the Marmara and Aegean coastlands of Asia Minor.[71] Just as Turkmen raiders had preceded the advance of ordered Turkish powers westward across Asia Minor in the second half of the eleventh century, so too predatory bands of Turks who percolated across in the early fourteenth century and raided Thrace at times of trouble opened the way for more systematic operations by the most powerful of the Asia Minor Turks, the Bithynian emirate of the Ottomans.

The alternative to this external approach is to look out from the interior, from Macedonia, the natural power-centre of the Balkans.[72] Sheltered by the formidable Dinaric chain from the Adriatic and by the Haemus and Rhodope mountains from the Thracian and the Danube plains, it stretched from the upper course of the Morava river in the north to the Aliakmon and lower Vardar in the south. A superficial glance might lead one to suppose that it was an upland region, thinly populated and given over primarily to stock-raising. This is far, far from the truth. The landscape may have been dominated by forested hills, but, lurking among them, lay many fertile alluvial basins. The most notable, because the largest, were Metohija and Kosovo Polje in the north, and, towards the south, Pelagonia straddling the modern Greek–North Macedonian border, Ovče Polje (east of the Vardar valley), and the plain of Thessalonike. There were many others with their own central places such as Ochrid, Kastoria, Skopje, Strumica, and Berroia/Verria. Macedonia had a chequerboard landscape akin to that of Iran and central Asia, but on a smaller scale and divided by well-watered hills covered with oak and beech rather than arid mountains, salt desert, and steppe. In aggregate the enclosed plains of Macedonia constituted a massive resource-base, from which the kings of Macedon were able not only to dominate the Balkans but to conquer much of the world in the late fourth century BC.

The Serbs were the distant successors of the Macedonians. The development of some sort of ethnic consciousness is well documented for the twelfth century. Armed resistance to Byzantium centred on the highlands of Diokleia/Zeta inland from Kotor, and on lowland Raška immediately to the east, comprising the large plain of Kosovo and the upper valley of the Ibar river. A century on, as the Nikaian emperors were extending their authority

[71] P. Lindner, 'Anatolia, 1300–1451', in K. Fleet, ed., *Cambridge History of Turkey*, I *Byzantium to Turkey 1071–1453* (Cambridge, 2009), 102–37, at 110–13.

[72] Hammond, *History of Macedonia*, I, 3–12.

over Thrace and much of Macedonia in the 1250s, the discovery of silver mines transformed Serb fortunes. Colonies of Saxon miners were invited to extract the ores (gold, lead, copper, and iron as well as silver). Merchants from Kotor and Dubrovnik came inland and established their own colonies which took over the management of the mines. The consequences were increased trade, general economic growth, and a massive boost to the crown's income. Uroš (1243–76) acquired the wherewithal to hire mercenaries (notably Alans brought west by the Golden Horde) and through them to assert his authority over the perennially refractory nobles of the kingdom. The new mineral wealth also enabled successive rulers to found monasteries and build elegant churches with fine decorative schemes, unrivalled within the Orthodox world.[73]

In the longer run, the wealth generated by the mines gave added impulse to the expansionist drive of Serbia, as well as helping the king to hold his own against his powerful northern neighbour, Hungary, and Byzantium's nomad allies, the Nogaj Mongols. It was under Uroš' younger son, Milutin, who took over the throne and the central lands from his older brother, Dragutin in 1282, that the Serbs began to push south and south-east into Byzantine Macedonia. That was the front where territorial gains were easier to come by than in the mountainous west where Zachloumia/Hum (to the north) and Albania (to the south) were Serbia's immediate neigbours. Any push northward was barred by Dragutin's two appanages, one Serbian in the north-west (granted in 1282), the other a strip of Hungarian land bordering Serbia (Mačva, granted in 1284 by the king, his father-in-law). It was assuredly the nobles who brought Milutin to power, as a ruler who would make war on their weakest neighbour, Byzantium. This at any rate is what he did on gaining the throne. He immediately joined Charles of Anjou's coalition and invaded Byzantine territory, pushing across the Sar mountains to take the Skopje basin. After facing and repulsing an attack by the Nogaj Mongols in alliance with Byzantium, he resumed the offensive in 1283, dispatching two armies to range over Byzantine Macedonia, one to the east, to the Strymon valley and beyond to the sea at Christoupolis, the other south to take Kičevo and Debar.[74]

[73] Obolensky, *Byzantine Commonwealth*, 247–52; Fine, *Later Medieval Balkans*, 199–204; S. Ćurčić, *Architecture in the Balkans from Diocletian to Suleyman the Magnificent* (New Haven, 2010), 486–505, 652–82.

[74] Fine, *Later Medieval Balkans*, 217–19.

A war of raid and counter-raid continued through the 1280s and 1290s, during which the Serbs probably extended and consolidated their conquests. As for operations on a large scale, Milutin turned his attention to the north, where major campaigns were launched against Braničevo (1291, jointly with Dragutin) and Vidin (1292), and to the west where he invaded northern Albania and captured Dyrrachion (1296). After the repulse of a major Byzantine attack in 1297, Milutin, increasingly at odds with Dragutin, proved amenable to Byzantine peace proposals. Eventually a treaty was negotiated, sealed by Milutin's marriage to five-year-old Simonis, granddaughter of Andronikos II. Serbia's annexations in Macedonia were recognized, under the guise of the bride's dowry. Their extent was defined by the fortresses retained by Byzantium—Ochrid and Prilep in the south, Prosek, Stip, and Strumica in the south-east. This first outward push had netted a substantial part of Byzantine Macedonia, and left what remained all too vulnerable if the peace were to be broken.[75]

As for Byzantium, the new era of stability did not last long. Division, political, social, and religious, prevailed through much of the fourteenth century. Rival claimants to the throne fought each other. With the revival of the *polis* came internecine conflict (*stasis*) between the elite and the main body of the citizenry. Finally, there was a revival of internal doctrinal conflict at the intellectual apex of society. External predators, principally Turks and Serbs, were able to make extraordinary advances and feed off the weakening body politic of Byzantium.

The first of three civil wars grew out of a family quarrel after the death of Michael IX, Andronikos IIs' son (a more than competent general). Michael's son, Andronikos III (crowned co-emperor in 1316, aged 19), and a coterie of young supporters, exploiting resentment at high taxation, rebelled and forced the old emperor to agree to a formal partition of the empire (June 1321). But he fought back, caught his grandson with a pincer attack in Thrace and reduced him to junior ruler of a united empire (July 1322). Both parties looked to foreign allies for support, grandson to Bulgars (and Nogaj Mongols), grandfather to Serbs, when relations between the two of them deteriorated in 1327. When it came to open conflict, Andronikos III's allies (including Venetians) helped him capture Constantinople (May 1328). Stefan Dečanski, who had seized power in Serbia (January 1322), took no action to support his ally Andronikos II, but began to extend Serb authority

[75] Fine, *Later Medieval Balkans*, 219–23.

down the Vardar valley and south towards Ochrid (besieged in 1329). Serbia's position grew much stronger after a decisive victory over Andronikos III's Bulgar allies at Velbužd (Kjustendil) in 1330.[76]

The Ottomans too profited from the civil war. They shifted their capital to Bursa (ancient Prusa) when it surrendered in April 1326, and, after a final feeble Byzantine intervention (halted at Pelekanon, June 1329), received the surrenders of Nikaia (1331) and Nikomedia (1337). The only way to contain the Ottomans thereafter was to pay them tribute (to secure the remaining Byzantine enclaves in Asia Minor, in particular Philadelphia) and to cultivate the rival Turkish *beyliks* to the south, Saruhan (Lydia) and Aydin (the rest of the Aegean coastlands except for Caria). Umur, bey of Aydin, was Byzantium's chief ally from late 1325 to 1345. An alliance with Turks was essential if Byzantium was to counter the growing power of Serbs in the Balkans.[77]

There was something ineluctable, though, about the expansion of the Serbs once Stefan Dušan had deposed Dečanski in 1331. He was backed by the nobles as a ruler who would be committed to the policy of aggression against Byzantium, hence as one who would provide them with office and land in annexed territories. He did indeed concentrate on extending his authority over Macedonia, despite distractions in the west (rebellion in Zeta 1332) and in the north (low-level warfare with Hungary 1334–46) and the south-west (assertion of authority over local chieftains in northern Albania, and, temporarily, over Dyrrachion, 1336–7). He conquered Byzantine Macedonia in two stages, taking advantage of internal conflicts. The rebellion of Syrgiannes, a member of the coterie around Andronikos III, late in 1333, was exploited by a brief offensive push south and south-east, which culminated in the siege of Thessalonike. By August 1334, when peace was negotiated, several major centres were in Serb hands—Ochrid, Prilep, and Strumica, which surrendered, Kastoria which was captured, as well as Siderokastron, Cemren, and Prosek.[78]

Just as in Andronikos II's reign a series of crises (weathered with difficulty), first in Asia Minor, then in the Balkans, had been followed by a brief interlude of calm (1313–21), so too his grandson Andronikos III, from his seizure of sole power in 1328, had to cope with a succession of problems but managed, by the late 1330s, to stabilize the situation in the east and restore Byzantine authority over Thessaly and Epirus.

[76] Laiou, *Constantinople and the Latins*, 284–99; Fine, *Late Medieval Balkans*, 270–3.

[77] Nicol, *Last Centuries*, 169–75; C. Imber, *The Ottoman Empire 1300–1481* (Istanbul, 1990), 19–21.

[78] Fine, *Late Medieval Balkans*, 286–90.

But Andronikos' premature death, in 1341, triggered a second serious civil war, which pitched John Kantakouzenos, the leading figure in his government, against the dowager empress, the patriarch, and another member of the late emperor's circle, Alexios Apokaukos. This provided Dušan, in the guise of Kantakouzenos' ally, with the pretext for a second sustained offensive. Kantakouzenos, accompanied by 2,000 troops, took refuge in Serbia in 1342, after his rivals' coup in Constantinople. While Dušan welcomed him at Priština, he soon took action on his own behalf, making a series of gains—Edessa/Vodena (1342), Kastoria (again), and Hlerin/Florina (1343); Serres, Kavalla, and Drama (1345). It was the Ottoman leader, Orkhan (he replaced Umur of Aydin as Kantakouzenos' chief Turkish ally from 1345), rather than Dušan, who helped Kantakouzenos re-enter Constantinople and reach a settlement with the patriarch and empress in February 1347. His main rival was now Dušan, who had been crowned emperor (of the Serbs and Greeks) in Skopje at Easter 1346. His pretensions to imperial rule gained more substance when, exploiting the disorganization caused by the Black Death, he took control of Epiros (1347) and Thessaly (1348).[79]

John Kantakouzenos took control of the government in early February, 1347, a little over five years after being proclaimed emperor at Didymoteichos in Thrace. He was the second intellectual to occupy the throne (after Andronikos II), and was later, in retirement, to take command of history. It was agreed that he would rule jointly with John V, Andronikos III's fifteen-year-old son, for the first ten years as senior emperor. The future looked bleak, with Macedonia lost to the Serbs and Thrace much ravaged by various Turkish marauders (from the early 1330s). Byzantium itself was riven by social strife in provincial towns and cities, where the traditional leadership of the notables (now largely landowners who no longer lived in the country) was challenged from below, by the middling classes and the people at large. The first semi-revolutionary uprising in Adrianople was soon followed elsewhere, most notably in Thessalonike where the so-called Zealots remained in power for ten years (1341–50).[80] At the same time, a fierce theological dispute broke out in the church, between believers in the powers and limitations of human reason, able to bring intellectual illumination but not to encompass the divine essence, and those (Hesychasts, led by Gregory

[79] Nicol, *Last Centuries*, 185–208; Fine, *Late Medieval Balkans*, 292–4, 296–8, 300–10, 320–1.

[80] Nicol, *Last Centuries*, 191–5; M. Kiel, 'The Incorporation of the Balkans into the Ottoman Empire, 1353–1453', in Fleet, *Cambridge History of Turkey*, I, 138–91, at 144.

Palamas) who argued that divine energies irradiated the material world and that it was possible, with grace, to achieve direct knowledge of God. It lasted for over thirty years from the 1330s, gaining in intensity after the victory of John Kantakouzenos in the 1341–7 civil war and from the involvement of Athos monks, who, in carefully induced trances, found themselves bathed in divine light. This mattered at a time when the Orthodox needed to stand firm against the papacy. It also revived the long-dormant but central theological issue of the relationship of the divine to the human which had bedevilled Christology in late antiquity.[81]

The only significant success of Kantakouzenos' short reign (1347–54) was the ousting of the Zealot regime in Thessalonike and the reintegration of the city in the empire, achieved with the help of a Turkish pirate fleet and a renegade Serb officer (1350). Two attacks on the Serbs failed: in 1348 the allied Ottoman army halted at Christoupolis, on the border of Macedonia, and set about gathering plunder, rather than aiding the emperor's son Matthew; an opportunistic attack by Kantakouzenos himself in 1350 was stopped at Servia, and his gains were soon lost. The Genoese were alienated and posed a grave threat to the capital (1348–52). The Ottomans steadily improved their position by judicious interventions, first on the side of the Genoese against the Venetians (early 1352), then backing each party in turn in the third civil war (1352–6) between the Kantakouzenoi (father and son Matthew) and John V Palaiologos. An act of God in March 1354, taking the form of an earthquake which shook the Gallipoli peninsula and caused the population to flee, enabled them to establish a bridgehead on the peninsula, through which to funnel the troops needed to consolidate their hold on the northern shore of the Sea of Marmara.[82]

The battle fought at Demotika in winter 1352–3 which ended in a crushing Ottoman victory over the Serbs and Bulgars backing John V marked the end of any practical imperial designs on the part of the Serbs. Their great conquering ruler was still on the throne, could still afford to fund large mercenary forces, but the dynamic process of expansion which had brought the Serbs to the edge of Thrace, within striking distance of Constantinople, had been brought to a halt. No longer could Serbian nobles look forward with confidence to future conquests, to the sharing of plunder and land with

[81] Nicol, *Last Centuries*, 210–15; N. Siniossoglou, *Radical Platonism in Byzantium: Illumination and Utopia in Gemistos Plethon* (Cambridge, 2011), 93–113; N. Russell, 'The Hesychast Controversy', in A. Kaldellis & N. Siniossoglou, eds., *The Cambridge Intellectual History of Byzantium* (Cambridge, 2017), 494–508.

[82] Nicol, *Last Centuries*, 215–42; Fine, *Late Medieval Balkans*, 322–5.

Dušan. Dušan's prestige, as vital as the wealth which funded the royal army, was diminished. That of his son Uroš would plunge down, encouraging regional leaders to consolidate their power at the expense of the crown.

The grim prospect facing John V after his clandestine entry into Constantinople and Kantakouzenos' abdication (4 December 1354) was that of steady Ottoman encroachment on what was left of Byzantine territory.[83] That is indeed what happened. Despite the temporary loss of Gallipoli (1366–77), the Ottomans were able to harness the Turkish forces from other Anatolian emirates already established in Thrace to their cause and, step by step, to extend their authority north and west over the Balkans. Between 1359 and 1369 they gained control of the whole Maritsa valley, as they took each of its chief cities in turn—Didymoteichos, Philippopolis, and Adrianople. They sealed their dominant position by defeating the Serb rulers of southern Macedonia, Uglješa and his brother Vukašin, on the Maritsa on 26 September 1371. The Serb empire, which had broken apart into some six independent component parts (Zeta, the core lands with northern Macedonia, southern Macedonia, Thessaly, Epiros, and Albania), was now at the Ottomans' mercy.[84]

John V was a virtually powerless onlooker. Byzantium, consisting now of three isolated fragments of the empire—the capital city and eastern Thrace, Thessalonike and environs, and the Morea—was indefensible. It would be engulfed before long by Turks. There was no choice but to appease them, and to reach out to nearer and distant Christian powers for help. All John could do was to turn himself into a peripatetic ruler, going in person to negotiate with foreign rulers—in 1357 to Orkhan (after ransoming his son who had been captured by Greek pirates from Phokaia); in 1366, in the middle of winter, to the king of Hungary (an unsuccessful venture, which ended with the Bulgars' barring his way home at Vidin for several months); and finally to Rome in 1369, where he formally accepted the tenets of the Catholic church and did obeisance to the pope (he was again detained on his way home, at Venice). For the grand, divinely appointed supreme earthly ruler to travel to other courts was degrading enough. To be held twice against his will, until outsiders intervened (Count Amadeo of Savoy who attacked Bulgaria with his fleet in October 1366, his younger son

[83] Nicol, *Last Centuries*, 242–50; Fine, *Late Medieval Balkans*, 325–7.

[84] Nicol, *Last Centuries*, 261–3, 265–6, 273–5; Fine, *Late Medieval Balkans*, 345–53, 357–66, 370–80; Imber, *Ottoman Empire*, 26, 29.

Manuel who brought the money he owed Venice in the middle of winter 1370–1) was utterly shameful.[85]

Worse still, John's conversion to Catholicism augured badly for the future, opening up a division between those ready to modify their faith in the hope of western help and those prepared, in the last resort, to submit to the Turks. The only ray of hope came from the recovery of Gallipoli in 1366 by the small expeditionary force which Amadeo of Savoy had brought from the west. If only opposition to the western church could be quelled and a larger crusading force assembled, Byzantium might yet survive.

## 6.4 Last decades

The Ottomans had been but one among several splinter groupings of Turks left in Asia Minor after the Mongol destruction of the Seljuk sultanate of Rum in 1243. Their rise was slow and laborious, as first they gained control over the highlands overlooking Bithynia, then, from around 1300, with a pause extending from 1307 (caused by a crushing defeat at the hands of the Mongols) to the middle 1320s, they began pushing down into Byzantine territory in the Bithynian plain and clawing their way to regional hegemony in western Asia Minor.[86]

They were able to take the lead in warfare against the Byzantines, and to use their prestige as *ghazi* warriors to strengthen their position vis-à-vis rival emirates in the Aegean coastlands. But the *jihad* which they were conducting was far removed from that of twentieth- and twenty-first century jihadists. Theirs was a tolerant, inclusive holy war, like that fought by the Arabs in the seventh century. The aim was not to force-feed their subjects with Islam but to extend the authority of a Muslim power as widely as possible, drawing Christians and recent converts as well as Muslim volunteers and dervish holy men into the imperial enterprise. It was to prove extraordinarily effective against the Byzantines and other Christian powers in the Balkans.[87]

Their expansion steadily gathered momentum, especially after their seizure in 1354 of Gallipoli, gateway to the rich plains of Thrace, Macedonia,

85 Nicol, *Last Centuries*, 256–73, 276–7; Imber, *Ottoman Empire*, 25–6.

86 C. Foss, *The Beginnings of the Ottoman Empire* (Oxford, 2022).

87 D. Kastritsis, 'Conquest and Political Legitimation in the Early Ottoman Empire', in J. Harris, C. Holmes, & E. Russell, eds. *Byzantines, Latins, and Turks in the Eastern Mediterranean World after 1150* (Oxford, 2012), 221–45, at 221–34.

and the Danube valley. Predatory Ottoman forces were able to extend their activities and, within half a century, to subjugate most of what was left of the Byzantine Balkans outside the Peloponnese and to cut short the rise of Serbia to regional predominance. Religious tolerance, respect for the rights of those who submitted voluntarily, and a well-advertised commitment to justice for all not only undermined the resistance of Byzantine elites but encouraged some (notably John VI Kantakouzenos) to appeal to them for military assistance at times of civil conflict.[88]

Byzantium in its last century of existence in three isolated enclaves was riven by dissension, political, religious, and social. Civil war in the fourteenth century caused a fatal weakening, exploited to the full by rival powers, principally Serbs and Ottomans. The religious division ran deep, especially in the two great cities, between those whose prime concern was to preserve the true, ancestral faith and retain God's favour and those who looked to the only quarter, the Latin West, from which effective military and naval help might come to fend off the Ottomans. Worse, though, was the division between the humble classes—those of modest means (the *metrioi*) and the poor—and the governing classes, which continued to affect Thessalonike, and the division between the administration in the Morea and the local landowners. All three Byzantine enclaves were plainly doomed as the fourteenth century drew towards a close.[89]

The tale of those last decades is a gloomy one of ineluctable decline. But there were shafts of light. The higher echelons of society in Constantinople and Thessalonike—the *archontes* (notables) comprising aristocrats, who had turned to trade to sustain their fortunes, and the commercial elite—established ramifying connections with the trading cities of the West.[90] That fundamental trait of the ancient city-state, a commitment to commercial enterprise, once more came to the fore. Equally striking was the role played by the intelligentsia in Palaiologan Byzantium. Literati had always been highly regarded after the easing of the dark age struggle for survival, especially in the eleventh century. But they played a more prominent part in government, in court life, and in relations with the outside world in the

[88] Kastritsis, 'Conquest and Political Legitimation', 234–8; Necipoğlu, *Byzantium between the Ottomans and the Latins*, 26–7.

[89] Necipoğlu, *Byzantium between the Ottomans and the Latins*, 41–3, 47–55, 69–74, 76–82, 194–8, 209–20, 231–2, 236–40, 259–67.

[90] Constantinople: T. Kiousopoulou, *Emperor or Manager: Power and Political Ideology in Byzantium before 1453* (Geneva, 2011), 27–38, 55–64, 168. Thessalonike: Necipoğlu, *Byzantium between the Ottomans and the Latins*, 74–6, 81–2, 192–4, 204–5.

last centuries, as well as sustaining Byzantium's tradition of classical scholarship. The rollcall is impressive. Two distinguished scholars served for long periods as chief ministers, Theodore Metochites (1270–1332), under Andronikos II (see Figure 6.1a and b), and Demetrios Kydones (*c*.1324–*c*.1397), a formidable advocate of ecclesiastical union, under John V. Two exercised supreme power: John VI Kantakouzenos who wrote, *inter alia*, a massive history of his own time, and Manuel II, who prided himself on his mastery of rhetoric and theology (he wrote up his disputations with Muslim and Catholic clerics). Other notable members of the intelligentsia were Manuel Chrysoloras (Manuel II's roving ambassador in the west, a fine classical scholar who taught Greek in Italy), Bessarion (staunch upholder of the union who became a cardinal), Laonikos Chalkokondyles (historian who looked above all to Herodotus as a model), and the humanist Gemistos Plethon who took his inspiration from Plato and recommended a complete restructuring of society in the Morea.[91]

The last Palaiologan emperors took what measures they could to bolster their defences.[92] Most striking were their travels to seek military aid from fellow-Christians in the north and west—which were to culminate in the prolonged visit of Manuel II to the court of Charles VI in France (June 1400–November 1402), with a brief trip across the Channel to the court of Henry IV (October–December 1400).[93] For the physical defence of the remaining fragments of the empire, they relied on the formidable late-antique walls of Constantinople and Thessalonike (as well as the chain which could be laid out on pontoons to bar access to the Golden Horn). Their fighting manpower was very limited. The navy, which had been recreated by John VI Kantakouzenos, could deploy no more than ten warships, leaving Byzantium reliant on Venice for defence of its coasts.

[91] S. Runciman, *The Last Byzantine Renaissance* (Cambridge, 1970), 61–84; Wilson, *Scholars of Byzantium*, 256–64 (Metochites); J. R. Ryder, *The Career and Writings of Demetrius Kydones: A Study of Fourteenth-Century Byzantine Politics, Religion and Society* (Leiden, 2010); L. Neville, *Guide to Byzantine Historical Writing* (Cambridge, 2018), 266–72 (Kantakouzenos); S. Celik, *Manuel II Palaiologos (1350–1425): A Byzantine Emperor in a Time of Tumult* (Cambridge, 2021), 138–57, 234–44, 288–97; L. Thorn-Wickert, *Manuel Chrysoloras (ca.1350–1415): Eine Biographie des byzantinischen Intellektuellen vor dem Hintergrund der hellenistischen Studien in der italienischen Renaissance* (Bonn, 2006); A. Akısık-Karakullukçu, 'A Question of Audience: Laonikos Chalkokondyles' Hellenism', *BZ* 112 (2019), 1–29; M. Malone-Lee, *Cardinal Bessarion: Most Latin of Greeks, Most Greek of Latins* (Abingdon, 2024); V. Hladký, *The Philosophy of Gemistos Plethon: Platonism in Late Byzantium, between Hellenism and Christianity* (Farnham, 2014).

[92] J. Harris, *The End of Byzantium* (New Haven, 2010), 75–8.

[93] C. J. Hillsdale, *Byzantine Art and Diplomacy in an Age of Decline* (Cambridge, 2014), 221–7.

**Figure 6.1** Chora Church (Kariye Camii): (a) interior of parecclesion; (b) fresco of Anastasis. Theodore Metochites (1270–1332), a distinguished scholar and powerful minister, funded the restoration of the building *c*.1310–17 and its decoration with mosaics and frescoes.

*Source*: (a) David Hendrix; (b) Bridgeman.

It was not unreasonable for anti-unionists to put their greatest hope in the supernatural—in the two patron saints of the great cities, the Mother of God and St Demetrios—and in a divine response to the faith of the Orthodox channelled down through hundreds of small, bejewelled places of cosmic power on earth.

But the onward march of the Ottomans was inexorable. Adrianople became their main Balkan base from its capture in 1369. From western Thrace (firmly controlled by 1370), Murad I (1362–89) extended his authority over Bulgaria (in the 1370s and again in 1388), over southern Macedonia including Thessalonike (1383–7), and over the key centre in Epiros, Ioannina (by 1385/6). Bayezid I (1389–1402) consolidated the Ottoman position, gaining control of the whole of Serbia (1393), after a decisive victory, marred by the death of Murad, in Kosovo (1389), and annexing Bulgaria after a failed rebellion (1393). He also conquered Thessaly (1393–5), and gained control of the lower Danube after defeating a Hungarian-led crusade at Nikopolis (1396). Even more important politically was the formal submission in 1371 of the Serb princes who had not fought on the Maritsa, and, a year later, of the emperor. John V was facing brute reality, when, for all his claim to superordinate status, he had been become a minor, local ruler in an Ottoman world. This was made all too evident when his son and successor, Manuel II (1391–1428) was summoned, along with other Balkan vassals (his brother Theodore, Despot of the Morea, his nephew and co-emperor John, and the two leading Serb princes), to attend on Bayezid in Serres in winter 1393–4. The following year, when Manuel ignored a second summons, Ottoman forces were deployed against Constantinople, initiating an eight-year blockade, and the first of several attacks was made on the Morea.[94]

Murad and Bayezid were able to call on their vassals as well as a reserve of troops in the Balkans for service in Asia Minor. This gave them a decisive advantage against the rival emirates in Asia Minor, save for Karaman in the interior. By a mixture of force and diplomacy, Murad was able to push east, south, and south-east, taking (1) Ankyra, (2) much of Germiyan (including Kotyaion), (3) Hamid to the south of Germiyan, and, after (4) a successful campaign against Karaman which was forced to cede Beyşehir, (5) the small emirate of Tekke on the south coast around Antalya. He thus gained a belt of territory behind the emirates of the Aegean coastlands. It fell to Bayezid

[94] Imber, *Ottoman Empire*, 30–6, 42–52; Nicol, *Last Centuries*, 284–308, 312–13; Tyerman, *New History*, 852–8.

to complete the Ottoman conquest of the western emirates (Saruhan, Aydin, Menteşe) as well as Byzantium's last significant outpost in Asia Minor, Philadelphia. Thereafter he targeted his eastern neighbours, first the emir of Sivas (Sebasteia) in summer–autumn 1391 (Manuel II served on this campaign), later, in 1397, the emir of Karaman, who had attacked and captured the governor-general of Asia Minor. Ikonion was stormed, the emir was executed and Karaman was incorporated into the nascent Ottoman empire. The emir of Sivas was targeted again in 1398 after his seizure of Amaseia. Amaseia was recovered. The ruler of Samsun (Amisos) was replaced with Sisman, son of the last Bulgarian tsar. Sivas was captured followed by Melitene, northern outpost of the Mamluks of Egypt. The whole of Asia Minor, from the Aegean to the Euphrates, was now in Ottoman hands.[95]

Around the year 1400, the Ottomans had recreated something akin to the Byzantine empire in its eleventh-century heyday. They were in command of Asia Minor and almost all the Balkans. Their only rival in the Middle East was Mamluk Egypt. In the Balkans, serious resistance was limited to the far south-west (the highlands of Albania and Epiros behind the Adriatic coast), and from Hungary and Wallachia beyond the Danube. Byzantium no longer played any significant part in regional affairs: Constantinople was holding out under blockade, food supplies being ferried in by sea, but would not be able to resist a massive assault; Thessalonike had been lost in 1387; the only substantial bloc of territory in the Peloponnese had been thoroughly devastated and prepared for occupation. At sea the Ottomans were raiding widely in the Aegean and building up their naval strength.[96]

Then came an intervention, not divine, not from above, but from the great power built up by Timur in western Eurasia. This revived Mongol empire, centred on Samarkand, which encompassed Afghanistan, northern India, Iran, and Azerbaijan, came into contact with the Ottoman empire at its north-east extremity. There the defeated emir of Sivas and his neighbour the emir of Erzincan appealed for help to Timur. He responded in summer 1400 by marching to Sivas, which he took. It may be that he was less interested in the nascent Ottoman power than the Mamluks of Egypt. For it was into their sphere of influence in Syria that he intruded in 1401, defeating a Mamluk army and plundering the chief cities before attacking and sacking Baghdad.

[95] Imber, *Ottoman Empire*, 26–8, 37–42.
[96] Imber, *Ottoman Empire*, 49–51; Harris, *End of Byzantium*, 5–7, 10–11.

Instead of appeasing Timur, Bayezid attacked Erzincan and received two of Timur's victims, the fugitive Caliph and the ruler of Azerbaijan who had been stripped of his lands. Timur set off from his winter quarters in the Caucasus in spring or early summer 1402 to crush the Ottomans, taking the powerful fortress of Kamacha on his way to Ankyra. The decisive battle was fought nearby on 28 July. The Ottoman army was routed. Bayezid and two of his sons were taken prisoner. Timur then divided his army into five raiding corps to maximize the plunder and tribute gained, mainly from the Marmara and Aegean coastlands. He only withdrew in summer 1403, once the Ottoman empire in Asia Minor had been reduced to a small emirate in the north-west and the emirs of Saruhan, Aydin, Menteşe, Germiyan, and Karaman had regained their independence and recovered the lands annexed by Bayezid.[97]

Worse was to follow, as Bayezid's sons fought each other for supreme power. This internecine warfare (1403–13) which pitted Mehmed against Isa, Suleyman against Musa, and Mehmed against Musa left the nascent empire vulnerable to external predators—the emirate of Karaman, Byzantium, Serbia, and Venice.[98] Suleyman realized that he needed to secure the Ottoman base in Europe if he was to re-impose Ottoman authority in Asia Minor. He had to appease and neutralize his weaker Christian adversaries, Byzantium and Serbia, and to reach a mutually acceptable arrangement with Venice. He opened negotiations with Venice soon after escaping from Timur across the Bosporus. Within a few months he signed the treaty of Gallipoli (January or February 1403) with the Manuel II's co-emperor John VII (Manuel had not yet returned); representatives of Venice, Genoa, and Rhodes; and the leading Serb prince, Stefan Lazarevich, who had escaped after the battle like Suleyman. Major concessions were made to Byzantium: Thessalonike, Athos, the islands of Skiathos, Skopelos, and Skyros (off the coast of central Greece), and a long strip of Black Sea coast from Constantinople to Mesembria or Varna were handed over; the annual tribute paid to Bayezid was cancelled; and, something to turn Byzantine heads, the new sultan offered himself to be the emperor's son. The other parties, not so centrally placed as the Byzantines, seem to have received no more than an agreement to maintain the status quo. This meant that the small lordships established in the Peloponnese, the Aegean, and the Adriatic were temporarily free to pursue their own interests, as was Stefan

[97] Imber, *Ottoman Empire*, 52–6.

[98] Imber, *Ottoman Empire*, 64–73.

Lazarevich, who, after facing and putting down a serious rebellion by his nephew, George Brankovich, moved his capital north, well away from Ottoman territory, to Belgrade.[99]

Manuel could now be viewed as the arbiter of Balkan affairs and benevolent patron of the sultan, *in theory*. When Suleyman decided to deal with Musa, who had built up his power in the eastern Balkans (1410), Manuel had him and his troops ferried across the Bosporus. After Suleyman's defeat and death (February 1411), Manuel similarly provided the ships for each of the three expeditionary forces which Mehmed led against Musa in 1412 and 1413, on the understanding that Mehmed would keep the peace with Byzantium. His army reinforced with troops from Elbistan in the Anti-Taurus, with the Serbs of Stefan Lazarevich and George Brankovich, and with Byzantine troops from Thessalonike, Mehmed routed Musa near Sofia in July 1413. He then renewed the treaty with Byzantium, with two additional cessions of territory—part of Thessaly and the Marmara coast.[100]

In practice Manuel was trapped, as his possessions were surrounded by Ottoman lands. All he could do was manage what he had, make appointments, go on tours of inspection, and cultivate Latin Christendom. He visited the Morea twice: in 1408 to deliver a funeral oration on his brother Theodore, and to appoint his small son Theodore as the new Despot; in 1414 he provided the peninsula with a forward line of defence across the isthmus of Corinth, the Hexamilion built on Justinianic foundations, and helped put down a peasant revolt against landlords.[101] Mehmed (1413–21) observed the treaty. He was fully occupied otherwise, fighting the emirates of Karaman and Aydin in Asia Minor, fending off rebellions in Asia and Europe in 1416, and resuming the outward raiding activity by sea and land which gave the nascent Ottoman empire its dynamic thrust, the targets being Negroponte, Bosnia, Wallachia, and Albania. The only serious reverse came in the Straits in 1416, when the main Ottoman fleet was sunk by the Venetians.[102]

When Mehmed died, Manuel once again intervened in the civil war which broke out, but this time he backed the wrong party—Mehmed's brother Mustafa against his son Murad II (1421–51). Murad responded with attacks on Constantinople and Thessalonike (1422), and, after disposing of a second rival (another Mustafa, his brother) and threatening to invade the

[99] Imber, *Ottoman Empire*, 56–9; Fine, *Late Medieval Balkans*, 500–3; Harris, *End of Byzantium*, 22–6, 35–7.
[100] Imber, *Ottoman Empire*, 66–73, 76; Harris, *End of Byzantium*, 80–6.
[101] Nicol, *Last Centuries*, 324–9; Celik, *Manuel II*, 297–8, 310–14.
[102] Imber, *Ottoman Empire*, 75–90; Harris, *End of Byzantium*, 86–90.

Morea (1423), secured a new treaty on better terms (February 1424)—Byzantium was once again made tributary and was stripped of the coastal cities on the Black Sea (except for Mesembria) and the Strymon valley. Manuel's co-emperor John VIII, the effective ruler after Manuel's stroke in late 1422, went on another demeaning year-long tour (1423–4) to Venice, northern Italy (Milan and Mantua) and Hungary to ask for help. The Venetians were allowed to take over Thessalonike (September 1423). Once again the Byzantine emperor was penned into his Constantinopolitan enclave, while the sultan could set about extending his dominions in both Asia and Europe, annexing Aydin, Menteşe, and Germiyan (mid to late 1420s), capturing Thessalonike (1430), subjecting Ioannina and Arta in Epiros (1430), responding to an Albanian rising with a campaign of terror (1433), subjecting Serbia (1435), and defeating Karaman (1437). The only Byzantine gains were made in the Morea, where Clarentza and Patras were captured by 1430.[103]

John VIII (sole emperor 1425–48), a powerless bystander as the Ottoman empire steadily expanded, continued to look to the Latin west (see Figure 6.2a). He regarded church union as the only feasible way of

**Figure 6.2** Portraits of John VIII Palaiologos and Mehmed the Conqueror: (a) medal with profile bust of John VIII Palaiologos (1425–48), by Antonio Pisanello (1395–1455); (b) Sultan Mehmed II, 1480. Gentile Bellini (active about 1460; died 1507). Oil, originally on wood, transferred to canvas, 69.9 × 52.1 cm. Layard Bequest, 1916.

*Source*: (a) Metropolitan Museum of Art, New York; (b) © National Gallery, London.

[103] Imber, *Ottoman Empire*, 91–116; Harris, *End of Byzantium*, 92–6, 106–26.

obtaining naval and military help on the scale needed. He took the initiative in 1430 with an embassy to Rome, proposing that a council be held to resolve the schism. Pope Eugenius IV (1431–47) summoned a council to Basel in 1431. The main issue which preoccupied the delegates for the next seven years was that of supreme authority in the church—was it vested in bishops assembled at councils or in the papacy? Three Byzantine delegates arrived in 1434 at the council's invitation, and were caught up in the controversy. Both parties, conciliarist and papal, sought to win Byzantine support for their cause. Embassies were exchanged with Constantinople, it being agreed by both parties that the question of the schism should go before a church council.[104]

The Byzantines opted for the pope's invitation to a council to be held at Ferrara. Their large delegation, headed by emperor and patriarch, sailed to Italy on Venetian ships hired by the pope, arriving in Venice in early February 1438. The delegation included leading Byzantine intellectuals such as Bessarion, Isidore (Bishop of Kiev from 1436), Mark Eugenikos (Bishop of Ephesos, a staunch anti-unionist), Gemistos Plethon, and his friend George Scholarios (lawyer, philosopher, and theologian, who knew Latin well). There were also representatives of the three eastern patriarchs. This made it a true ecumenical council. Proceedings began in Ferrara on 9 April 1438 and ended in Florence on Sunday 5 July 1439, when the final document was signed (including a compromise formula about the *filioque*). Only one Byzantine bishop demurred (Eugenikos). The union was publicly celebrated the following day. A fortnight later most of the delegation left, followed by the emperor. The voyage home was hampered by bad weather. The emperor reached Constantinople in February 1440.[105]

There was much opposition to the union. Some of the signatories publicly repudiated their action. Mark Eugenikos led a propaganda campaign. The emperor's brother Demetrios, despot of Byzantium's Black Sea enclave of Mesembria, rebelled and attacked Constantinople with Turkish help in summer 1442 (he was captured). The divisions in clergy and laity ran deep. Whether or not the whole enterprise had been worthwhile depended upon the success of the pope in rousing a crusade. It was very late, though. The Ottomans were in firm control of western Asia Minor and all the Balkan peninsula except for northern Albania and the Byzantine enclaves. Both

[104] Harris, *End of Byzantium*, 127–33.

[105] Nicol, *Last Centuries*, 352–9; Harris, *End of Byzantium*, 134–7, 142–7; M. Angold, *The Fall of Constantinople to the Ottomans* (Harlow, 2012), 30–2.

Constantinople and the Morea were at their mercy whenever they might choose to concentrate their forces against them.[106]

The crusading army, when it formed up in summer 1443, consisted largely of troops from the Christian kingdoms most threatened by the Ottomans—Hungary in coalition with Poland (the two were united under Ladislas III of Poland), and Serb rebels. Only the fleet, consisting of Venetian and Burgundian galleys, came from the west. A first campaign late in 1443 was successful: the army marched south-east from Belgrade towards the capital of Ottoman Rumelia at Adrianople, defeated a defending army at Niš, captured Sofia, but then turned back at the onset of a very severe winter. In February Ladislas agreed a truce with Murad, but then broke it on being informed that the fleet from the west had arrived off the Morea in July and was planning to link up with his troops. The fleet, however, did very little after reaching the Straits in September, failing to stop Murad crossing the Bosporus with a large army. He trapped the Christian army (without the Serbs, who were keeping to the truce) at Varna on the Black Sea coast. The battle which followed was hard fought, with heavy casualties on both sides (including the papal representative and Ladislas III), ending in an Ottoman victory. Apart from a raid up the Danube by the Burgundian component of the fleet in conjunction with a Wallachian force in 1445, and a Hungarian attempt to link up with Albanian insurgents in 1448, which ended in defeat (at Kosovo), there was no further attempt to shake Ottoman rule in the Balkans.[107]

In Murad II's last years the Ottomans continued to push outward against Wallachia, Epiros, Albania, the Morea (invaded by two armies in 1446), and Aegean islands, especially Negroponte. The accession of Mehmed II on 18 February 1451 marked a change of policy (see Figure 6.2b). Constantinople at last became the Ottomans' prime target.[108] Their other adversaries—Serbia, Hungary, and the emirate of Karaman—were neutralized with new treaties. A great fortress, Rumeli Hisar, was built between March and August 1452 on the European shore of the Bosporus, at its narrowest point, opposite an Asian counterpart. The Bosporus was now under Ottoman control. An army was dispatched to ravage the Morea that autumn, to prevent any interference from the two despots. A new fleet of large and small galleys was built at Gallipoli.

[106] Harris, *End of Byzantium*, 156–8, 162–4.

[107] Imber, *Ottoman Empire*, 120–1, 129–36, 139–41; Tyerman, *New History*, 862–3; Harris, *End of Byzantium*, 147–54.

[108] Angold, *Fall of Constantinople*, 145–8.

A large army was mobilized in spring 1453, comprising the regular troops serving in the Balkans and Asia Minor, supplemented by a Serbian contingent and *ghazi* warriors summoned for the long-unfulfilled aim of the original Arab *jihad*. The siege train included many pieces of artillery.[109]

The manpower available for the defence of the city was very limited. This is emphasized by one eyewitness who puts it as low as 5,000, including Genoese and Venetian volunteers (a clear underestimate).[110] Much would depend on the formidable land walls and the chain used to block the entrance to the Golden Horn (see Figure 6.3a and b). The emperor in charge was Constantine XI, who had only gained the throne after a struggle with his brothers—he had been crowned in Mistra on 6 January 1449, some three months after his father's death, and had entered Constantinople on 12 March. The much reduced population of the city remained deeply divided over the union with Rome. The concelebration of the liturgy which was to seal it was delayed until the last—to 12 December 1452. But when the siege began on 5 April 1453, the people buried their differences and resisted stoutly.[111]

That was the day the besieging army came within sight of the city, before closing in two days later. The fleet arrived a week after the army. The artillery then began its bombardment—far more damaging than the traditional stone-throwers in use since the late sixth century. Gunpowder had reached western Eurasia and the Ottomans had many cannons, including one monstrous weapon. This made a first breach by the central St Romanos Gate on 21 April, which the defenders repaired with barrels full of earth and stones. A second breach was made in the sea defences on the 22nd, when Ottoman light galleys were manhandled on greased rollers overland, behind Galata, from the Bosporus to the Golden Horn. The defence of the weak sea walls now rested on the Venetian ships in the harbour. An attempt to set fire to the Turkish galleys failed, but they were kept to their anchorage on the north side of the Golden Horn.[112]

The bombardment continued day and night, pounding the minds of the defenders as well as the land walls. The first major assault was made with battering rams at night on 7 May, followed by a second on a larger scale, again by night, on a different sector on the 12th. Both were repelled. A new breach, larger than the first, in the walls by the St Romanos Gate was being repaired on the night of 16 May, when the defenders discovered that a mine

[109] Imber, *Ottoman Empire*, 141–9; Harris, *End of Byzantium*, 166–8, 181–6.

[110] The actual figure was a little over 10,000: Angold, *Fall of Constantinople*, 5–6.

[111] Nicol, *Last Centuries*, 369–81; Necipoğlu, *Byzantium between the Ottomans and the Latins*, 220–5; Harris, *End of Byzantium*, 186–97.

[112] Imber, *Ottoman Empire*, 151–4; Harris, *End of Byzantium*, 197–201.

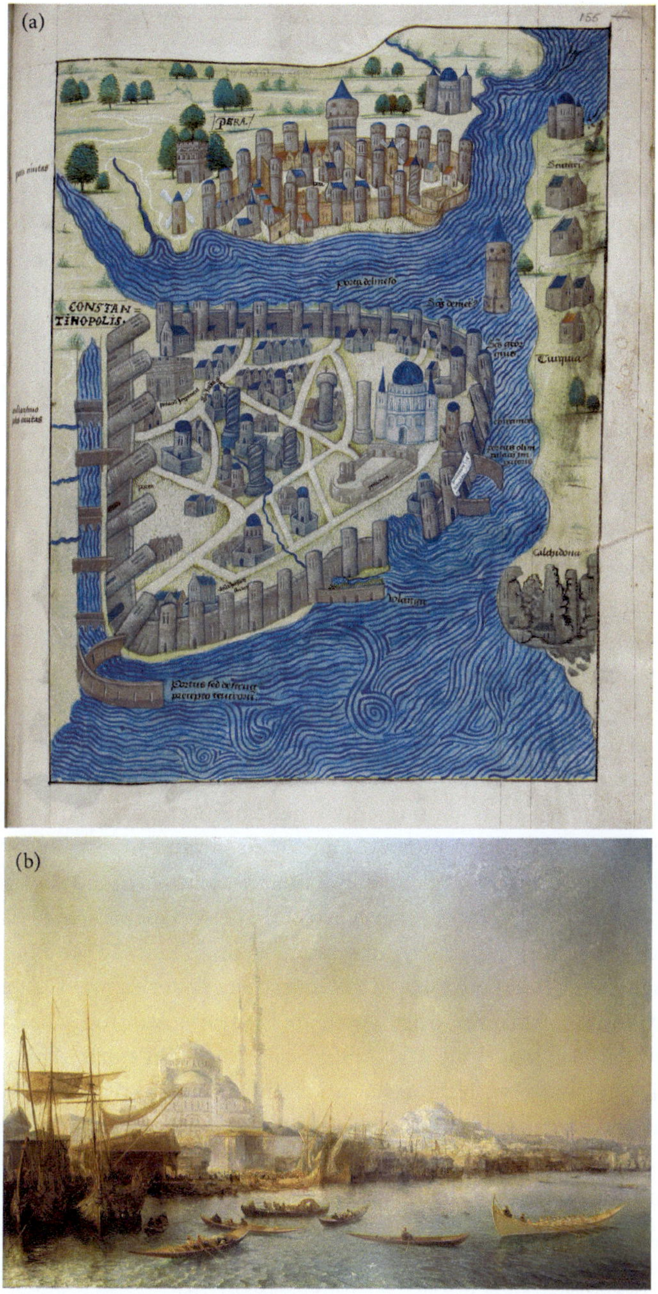


**Figure 6.3** Two panoramas: (a) panorama of Constantinople (from the *Liber Insularum Cycladum* of Cristoforo Buondelmonti [*c*.1385–*c*.1430], in ms. Arundel 93, fol. 155 [*c*.1485]); (b) view of Constantinople and Golden Horn, 1840 (Théodore Gudin [1802–80]).

*Source*: Bridgeman.

had been dug under the wall. It was the first of five to be found and neutralized over the following nine days. Psychological attacks preceded the final assault—a naval feint against the boom (21st), intensified bombardment (24th), numerous fires and loud shouting (to midnight on the 26th, on to dawn on the 27th, up to midnight on the 28th). To the sound of trumpets, during the day on the 28th, the whole besieging army was drawn up and scaling ladders were made ready. Finally, before dawn on the 29th, the general assault began. The defenders, far outnumbered and worn down, had no chance. The crucial breakthrough came at the breach made by the great cannon at the St Romanos Gate. The defenders who survived broke and fled. Constantine XI was one of the many dead.[113]

For the second time Constantinople had fallen to armed assault. This time there would be no revival. There was no Anatolian or Balkan redoubt to which to retreat. The Morea was very far from being a redoubt. The mini-Byzantine state on the Black Sea, centred on Trebizond, ruled by the so-called Grand Komnenoi, had been but a minor player in the affairs of north-east Asia Minor and the Caucasus, quite independent of the Nikaian and Constantinopolitan state. Both would be snuffed out by the Ottomans, in 1460 and 1461 respectively.[114]

Byzantium was annihilated with the loss of its last substantial possession, its capital city. Soon its monuments would be overshadowed by the fine buildings erected by the Ottomans, above all mosques designed by Sinan which hold, in the lightest of embraces, huge volumes of air, in such marked contrast to the small, sombre, bejewelled churches of Palaiologan Byzantium. Mehmed II's sixteenth-century successors, Selim I (1512–20) and Suleyman the Magnificent (1520–66) would resume the conquering ways of past sultans, extending their authority north to Hungary, east to Transcaucasia, south to Syria, Egypt, Iraq, and Arabia, and west over north Africa. Their authority, enhanced with the assumption of the caliphal title, was projected over the Mediterranean and the oceanic world beyond the Middle East by their naval power. They became a world power, feared in Iran and south-east Asia, feared and admired in Europe.[115]

*Byzantium in a Changing World*. James Howard-Johnston, Oxford University Press.
 DOI: 10.1093/9780191999093.003.0007

[113] Imber, *Ottoman Empire*, 154–7; Harris, *End of Byzantium*, 201–6.
[114] Nicol, *Last Centuries*, 394–409.
[115] Ćurčić, *Architecture in the Balkans*, 732–48; N. Malcolm, *Useful Enemies: Islam and the Ottoman Empire in Western Political Thought, 1450–1750* (Oxford, 2019), 131–58.

# Bibliography

## Sources

*Acts of the Lateran Synod*: R. Price, P. Booth, & C. Cubitt, *The Acts of the Lateran Synod of 649*, TTH 61 (Liverpool, 2014).

Al-Tabari: *Annales quos scripsit Abu Djafar Mohammed ibn Djarir at-Tabari*, II.3, ed. I. Guidi, D. H. Müller & M. J. de Goeje (Leiden, 1885–9), 1418 (AH 102)—1718 (AH 123), trans. D. S. Powers, *The History of al-Tabari*, 24 *The Empire in Transition* (Albany, NY, 1989), K. Y. Blankinship, *The History of al-Tabari*, 25 *The End of Expansion* (Albany, NY, 1989), and C. Hillenbrand, *History of al-Tabari*, 26 *The Waning of the Umayyad Caliphate* (Albany, NY, 1989).

*Annae Comnenae Alexias*, ed. D. R. Reinsch & A. Kambylis, CFHB 40, 2 vols (Berlin, 2001), trans. E. R. A. Sewter, rev. P. Frankopan, *The Alexiad* (London, 2009).

Anon., *Taktika*, ed. & trans. G. T. Dennis, *Three Byzantine Military Treatises*, CFHB 25 (Washington, DC, 1985), 246–335.

*Basilicorum libri LX*, ed. H. J. Scheltema, D. Holwerda & N. Van der Wal, 17 vols (Groningen, 1945–88)—digital ed. B. H. Stolte & T. E. van Bochow (Leiden, 2017).

*Book of the Eparch*: *Das Eparchenbuch Leons des Weisen*, ed. & trans. J. Koder, CFHB 33 (Vienna, 1991).

Christopher of Mytilene: F. Bernard & C. Livanos, ed. & trans., *The Poems of Christopher of Mytilene and John Mauropous* (Cambridge, MA, 2018).

*Chronographiae quae Theophanis continuati nomine fertur Libri I–IV*, ed. & trans. M. Featherstone & J. Signes Codoñer, CFHB 53 (Berlin, 2013).

*Chronographiae quae Theophanis Continuati nomine fertur liber quo Vita Basilii Imperatoris amplectitur*, ed. & trans. I. Ševčenko, CFHB 42 (Berlin, 2011).

*Constantini Manassis Breviarium chronicum*, ed. O. Lampsides, CFHB 36, 2 vols (Athens, 1996), trans. L. Yuretich, *The Chronicle of Constantine Manasses*, TTB 6 (Liverpool, 2018).

Constantin VII Porphyrogénète, *Le livre des cérémonies*, ed. & trans. G. Dagron, B. Flusin, D. Feissel & M. Stavrou, 5 vols (Paris, 2020).

*Constantini Porphyrogeniti tres tractatus de expeditionibus militaribus imperatoris*, ed. & trans. J. F. Haldon, CFHB 28 (Vienna, 1990).

Constantinus Porphyrogenitus, *De administrando imperio*, ed. Gy. Moravcsik, trans. R. J. H. Jenkins, CFHB 1 (Washington, DC, 1967), with commentary in vol. II, ed. R. J. H. Jenkins (London 1962) and in Konstantin Bagrjanorodny, *Ob Uprovlenii Imperij*, ed. G. G. Litavrin & A. P. Novosel'tsev (Moscow, 1989).

*Digenis Akritis*, ed. & trans. E. Jeffreys (Cambridge, 1998).

Fredegar: J. M. Wallace-Hadrill, ed. & trans., *The Fourth Book of the Chronicle of Fredegar with its Continuations* (London, 1960).

*Geoponica*: ed. & trans. E. Lelli et al., *L'agricoltura antica. I 'Geoponica' di Cassiano Basso*, (Soveria Mannelli, 2010).

*Ioannis Malalae chronographia*, ed. J. Thurn, CFHB 35 (Berlin, 2000), trans. E. Jeffreys, M. Jeffreys & R. Scott, *The Chronicle of John Malalas*, Byzantina Australiensia 4 (Melbourne, 1986).

*Ioannis Scylitzae Synopsis historiarum*, ed. H. Thurn, CFHB 5 (Berlin, 1973), trans. B. Flusin & J.-C. Cheynet, *Jean Skylitzès, Empereurs de Constantinople* (Paris, 2003).

John Geometres: E. M. van Opstall, ed. & trans., *Jean Géomètre, Poèmes en hexamètres et en distique élégiaques* (Leiden, 2008).

Kekaumenos: G. G. Litavrin, ed., *Sovety i rasskazy Kekavmena: sochinenie vizantijskogo polkovodtsa XI v.* (Moscow, 1972).

Legislation of tenth-century emperors: N. Svoronos, ed., *Les novelles des empereurs macédoniens concernant la terre et les stratiotes* (Athens, 1994), trans. E. McGeer, *The Land Legislation of the Macedonian Emperors* (Toronto, 2000).

*Léon Choerosphaktès, magistre, proconsul et patrice; biographie-correspondance*, ed. & trans. G. Kolias (Athens, 1939).

*Leonis Diaconi Caloënsis Historiae libri decem*, ed. C. B. Hase (Bonn, 1828), trans. A.-M. Talbot & D. F. Sullivan, *The* History *of Leo the Deacon: Byzantine Military Expansion in the Tenth Century* (Washington, DC, 2005).

*Leonis VI Tactica*, ed. & trans. G. T. Dennis, *The Taktika of Leo VI*, CFHB 49 (Washington, DC, 2010).

*Liudprandi Antapodosis*, ed. J. Becker, *Scriptores rerum Gemanicarum in usum scholarum* (Hanover–Leipzig, 1915).

Malchus, ed. & trans. R. C. Blockley, *The Fragmentary Classicising Historians of the Later Roman Empire: Eunapius, Olympiodorus, Priscus and Malchus*, 2 vols (Liverpool, 1981–3), II, 401–62.

Matthew of Edessa, *Zhamanakagrut'iwn*, ed. M. Melik-Adamian & N. Ter-Mik'ayelian (Etchmiadzin, 1898), trans. A. E. Dostourian, *Armenia and the Crusades, Tenth to Twelfth Centuries: The Chronicle of Matthew of Edessa* (Lanham, Maryland, 1993).

*Mauricii Strategicon*, ed. G. T. Dennis, CFHB 17 (Vienna, 1981), trans. G. T. Dennis, *Maurice's Strategikon: Handbook of Byzantine Military Strategy* (Philadelphia, 1984).

Michael Attaleiates: I. Pérez Martín, ed., *Miguel Attaleiates, Historia* (Madrid, 2002), trans. A. Kaldellis & D. Krallis, *The History: Michael Attaleiates* (Cambridge, MA, 2012).

*Michaeli Pselli Chronographia*, ed. D. R. Reinsch, Millennium-Studien 51 (Berlin, 2014), trans. E. R. A. Sewter, *Fourteen Byzantine Rulers: The Chronographia of Michael Psellos* (Harmondsworth, 1966).

*Miracula S. Demetrii*: P. Lemerle, *Les plus anciens recueils des miracles de saint Démétrius*, 2 vols (Paris, 1979–81).

*Nicephori Bryennii historiarum libri quattuor*, ed. & trans. P. Gautier, CFHB 9 (Brussels, 1975).

*Nicetae Choniatae historia*, ed. J.-L. van Dieten, CFHB 11, 2 vols (Berlin, 1975), trans. H. J. Magoulias, *O City of Byzantium, Annals of Niketas Choniates* (Detroit, 1984).

*Nicolai I Constantinopolitani Patriarchae epistolae*, ed. & trans. R. J. H. Jenkins & L. G. Westerink, CFHB 6 (Washington, DC, 1973).

Nikephoros Ouranos, *Taktika*, cc.62–5, ed. & trans. E. McGeer, *Sowing the Dragon's Teeth: Byzantine Warfare in the Tenth Century*, DO Studies 33 (Washington, DC, 1995), 134–63.

Nikephoros Phokas, *Praecepta militaria*, ed. & trans. E. McGeer, *Sowing the Dragon's Teeth: Byzantine Warfare in the Tenth Century*, DO Studies 33 (Washington, DC, 1995), 12–59.

*Nikephoros Patriarch of Constantinople Short History*, ed. & trans. C. Mango, CFHB 13 (Washington, DC, 1990).

*Novels of Justinian*: D. Miller & P. Sarris, *The Novels of Justinian*, 2 vols (Cambridge, 2018).

*Patmut'iwn Sebeosi* (Erevan, 1979), ed. G. V. Abgaryan, trans. R. W. Thomson, in R. W. Thomson & J. Howard-Johnston, *The Armenian History Attributed to Sebeos*, TTH 31 (Liverpool, 1999).

Paulus diaconus: L. Bethmann & G. Waitz, eds, *Pauli historia Langobardorum*, MGH, Scriptores rerum Langobardicarum et Italicarum saec. VI–IX (Hanover, 1878), trans. F. Bougard, *Paul Diacre Histoire des Lombards* (Turnhout, 1994).

*Peira*: D. R. Simon & D. R. Reinsch, *Die Peira: Ein juristisches Lehrbuch des 11. Jahrhunderts aus Konstantinopel—Text, Übersetzung, Kommentar, Glossar*, 2 vols (Berlin, 2023).

Philotheus, *Cletorologium*, ed. & trans. N. Oikonomidès, *Les listes de préséance byzantines des IXe et Xe siècles* (Paris, 1972), 80–235.

Procopius, *Anecdota*, ed. & trans. H. B. Dewing (Cambridge, MA, 1935).

*Risalat ibn Fadlan*, ed. S. Dahhan (Damascus, 1959), trans. P. Lunde & C. Stone, *Ibn Fadlan and the Land of Darkness: Arab Travellers in the Far North* (London, 2012).

Step'anos Taronec'i Asołik, *Patmut'iwn tiezerakan*, ed. S. Malxaseanc' (St Petersburg, 1885), trans. T. Greenwood, *The Universal History of Step'anos Tarōnec'i* (Oxford, 2017).

*Symeonis Magistri et Logothetae Chronicon*, ed. S. Wahlgren CFHB 44.1, (Berlin, 2006), trans. S. Wahlgren, *The Chronicle of the Logothete*, TTB 7 (Liverpool, 2019).

*Théodore Daphnopatès, Correspondance*, ed. & trans. J. Darrouzès & L. G. Westerink (Paris, 1978).

*Theophanis chronographia*, ed. C. de Boor, 2 vols. (Leipzig, 1883-5), trans. C. Mango & R. Scott, *The Chronicle of Theophanes Confessor: Byzantine and Near Eastern History AD 284–813* (Oxford, 1997).

Theophanes continuatus, ed. I. Bekker (Bonn, 1836).

*Traité sur la guérilla*: H. Dagron & H. Mihăescu, ed. & trans., *Le traité sur la guérilla (De velitatione) de l'empereur Nicéphore Phocas (963–969)* (Paris, 1986).

## Modern Works

Abulafia, D. *The Western Mediterranean Kingdoms 1200–1500: The Struggle for Dominion* (London, 1997).

Ahrweiler, H. *L'idéologie politique de l'empire byzantin* (Paris, 1975).

Akısık-Karakullukçu, A. 'A Question of Audience: Laonikos Chalkokondyles' Hellenism', *BZ* 112 (2019), 1–29.

Alchermes, J. D. 'Art and Architecture in the Age of Justinian', in M. Maas, ed., *Cambridge Companion to the Age of Justinian* (Cambridge, 2005), 343–75.

Allen, P. *Sophronius of Jerusalem and Seventh-Century Heresy* (Oxford, 2009).

Allen, P. & Neil, B. *Maximus Confessor and his Companions: Documents from Exile* (Oxford, 2002).

Angold, M. *A Byzantine Government in Exile: Government and Society under the Laskarids of Nicaea (1204–1261)* (Oxford, 1975).

Angold, M. *The Byzantine Empire, 1025–1204: A Political History* (2nd edn, London, 1997).

Angold, M. *The Fall of Constantinople to the Ottomans* (Harlow, 2012).

Antonopoulou, T. 'Emperor Leo VI the Wise and the "First Byzantine Humanism": On the Quest for Renovation and Cultural Synthesis', in B. Flusin & J.-C. Cheynet, eds, *Autour du* Premier humanisme byzantin *& des* Cinq études sur le XIe siècle, *quarante ans après Paul Lemerle*, *TM* 21.2 (2017), 187–233.

Armstrong, P. 'Greece in the Eleventh Century', in J. Howard-Johnston, ed., *Social Change in Town and Country in Eleventh-Century Byzantium* (Oxford, 2020), 133–56.

Bakay, K. 'Hungary', in T. Reuter, ed., *New CMH* III *c.900–c.1024* (Cambridge, 1999), 536–52.

Baloup, D. & Josserand, P., eds, *Regards croisés sur la guerre sainte: guerre, religion et idéologie dans l'espace méditerranéen latin (XI–XIIIe siècle)* (Toulouse, 2020).

Banaji, J. *Exploring the Economy of Late Antiquity: Selected Essays* (Cambridge, 2016).

Baynes, N. H. *Byzantine Studies and Other Essays* (London, 1955).

Beihammer, A. D. *Byzantium and the Emergence of Muslim-Turkish Anatolia, ca.1040–1130* (London, 2017).

Berend, N. 'Hungary in the Eleventh and Twelfth Centuries', in D. Luscombe & J. Riley-Smith, eds, *New CMH* IV *c.1024–c.1198*, pt.2 (Cambridge, 2004), 304–16.
Bernard, F. *Writing and Reading Byzantine Secular Poetry, 1025–1081* (Oxford, 2014).
Bessard, F. *Caliphs and Merchants: Cities and Economies of Power in the Near East (700–950)* (Oxford, 2020).
Bianquis, T., Guichard, P. & Tillier, M., eds, *Les débuts du monde musulman VIIe–Xe siècles: De Muhammad aux dynasties autonomes* (Paris, 2012).
Bisson, T. N. 'The Feudal Revolution', *PP* 142 (1994), 6–42.
Blockley, R. C. *East Roman Foreign Policy: Formation and Conduct from Diocletian to Anastasius* (Leeds, 1992).
Bonifay, M. 'The Distribution of African Pottery under the Roman Empire: Evidence versus Interpretation', in A. Wilson & A. Bowman, eds, *Trade, Commerce, and the State in the Roman World* (Oxford, 2017), 327–51.
Bonner, M. *Jihad in Islamic History: Doctrines and Practice* (Princeton, NJ, 2006).
Booth, P. 'The Muslim Conquest of Egypt Reconsidered', in C. Zuckerman, ed., *Constructing the Seventh Century, TM* 17 (2013), 639–70.
Börm, H. & Wiesehöfer, J., eds, *Commutatio et contentio—Studies in the Late Roman, Sasanian and Early Islamic Near East: In Memory of Zeev Rubin* (Düsseldorf, 2010).
Borrut, A. *Entre mémoire et pouvoir: L'espace syrien sous les derniers Omeyyades et les premiers Abbassides* (Leiden, 2011).
Bourin, M., Martin, J.-M., & Menant, F., eds, *L'anthroponymie document de l'histoire sociale des mondes méditerranéens médiévaux*, Collection de l'École française de Rome 226 (1996).
Bowman, A. K., Garnsey, P., & Cameron, A., eds, *CAH* XII *The Crisis of Empire, AD 193–337* (Cambridge, 2005).
Brett, M. *The Fatimid Empire* (Edinburgh, 2017).
Brown, P. *The World of Late Antiquity: From Marcus Aurelius to Muhammad* (London, 1971).
Brown, P. *Society and the Holy in Late Antiquity* (London, 1982).
Brown, P. *Power and Persuasion in Late Antiquity: Towards a Christian Europe* (Madison WI, 1992).
Brown, P. *Authority and the Sacred: Aspects of the Christianisation of the Roman World* (Cambridge, 1995).
Brown, P. 'The World of Late Antiquity Revisited', with comments by G. W. Bowersock et al., *Symbolae Osloenses*, 72 (1997), 5–90.
Brown, P. R. L. 'A Dark-Age Crisis: Aspects of the Iconoclast Controversy', *EHR* 346 (1973), 1–34, repr. in P. Brown, *Society and the Holy in Late Antiquity* (London, 1982), 251–301.
Brown, T. S. 'Byzantine Italy, c.680–c.876', in R. McKitterick, ed., *New CMH* II *c.700–c.900* (Cambridge, 1995), 320–48.
Browning, R. *Medieval and Modern Greek* (London, 1969).
Brubaker, L., ed., *Byzantium in the Ninth Century: Dead or Alive?* (Aldershot, 1998).
Brubaker, L. & Haldon, J. *Byzantium in the Iconoclast Era (ca.680–850): The Sources—An Annotated Survey* (Aldershot, 2001).
Brubaker, L. & Haldon, J. *Byzantium in the Iconoclast Era, c.680–850: A History* (Cambridge, 2011).
Cahen, C. *The Formation of Turkey: The Seljukid Sultanate of Rum, Eleventh to Fourteenth Century* (London, 2001).
A. Cameron, *Procopius and the Sixth Century* (London, 1985).
Campbell, J. K. *Honour, Family and Patronage: A Study of Institutions and Moral Values in a Greek Mountain Community* (Oxford, 1964).

Canard, M. *Byzance et les Arabes,* II *La dynastie Macédonienne (867–959), 2 Extraits des sources arabes* (Brussels, 1950).
Canard, M. *Histoire de la dynastie des H'amdanides de Jazîra et de Syrie* (Paris, 1953).
Canard, M. 'La prise de Heraclée', *Byz.* 32 (1962), 345–79.
Caseau, B. & Huebner, S. R., eds, *Inheritance, Law and Religions in the Ancient and Medieval Worlds* (Paris, 2014).
Celik, S. *Manuel II Palaiologos (1350–1425): A Byzantine Emperor in a Time of Tumult* (Cambridge, 2021).
Cheynet, J.-C. *Pouvoir et contestations à Byzance (963–1210)* (Paris, 1990).
Cheynet, J.-C. 'L'anthroponymie aristocratique à Byzance', in M. Bourin, J.-M. Martin, & F. Menant, eds, *L'anthroponymie document de l'histoire sociale des mondes méditerranéens médiévaux,* Collection de l'École française de Rome 226 (1996), 267–94.
Cheynet, J.-C. 'Théophile, Théophobe et les Perses', in *He Byzantine Mikra Asia* (Athens, 1998), 39–50.
Cheynet, J.-C. 'L'aristocratie byzantine (VIIIe–XIIIe siècle)', *Journal des Savants* (July–December 2000), 281–322, trans. in J.-C. Cheynet, *The Byzantine Aristocracy and its Military Function* (Aldershot, 2006), no. I.
Cheynet, J.-C., ed., *Le monde byzantin,* II *L'empire byzantin (641–1204)* (Paris, 2006).
Cheynet, J.-C. *The Byzantine Aristocracy and its Military Function* (Aldershot, 2006).
Cheynet, J.-C. *La société byzantine: L'apport des sceaux,* 2 vols (Paris, 2008).
Cheynet, J.-C. 'L'administration provinciale dans la correspondance de Michel Psellos', in M. D. Lauxtermann & M. Whittow, eds, *Byzantium in the Eleventh Century: Being in Between* (Abingdon, 2017), 45–59.
Cheynet, J.-C. 'La guerre sainte à Byzance au Moyen Âge: un malentendu', in D. Baloup & P. Josserand, eds, *Regards croisés sur la guerre sainte: guerre, religion et idéologie dans l'espace méditerranéen latin (XI–XIIIe siècle)* (Toulouse, 2020), 13–32.
Cheynet, J.-C. 'Transformations in Byzantine Society in the Eleventh Century, Particularly in Constantinople', in J. Howard-Johnston, ed., *Social Change in Town and Country in Eleventh-Century Byzantium* (Oxford, 2020), 16–43.
Chrissis, N. G. *Crusading in Frankish Greece: A Study in Byzantine–Western Relations and Attitudes, 1204–1282* (Turnhout, 2012).
Christie, N. *The Lombards: The Ancient Longobards* (Oxford, 1995).
Corbier, M. 'Coinage and Taxation: The State's Point of View, A.D. 193–337', *CAH* XII (Cambridge, 2005), 327–92.
Cormack, R. *Byzantine Art* (Oxford, 2000).
Cosentino, S. 'Byzantine Sardinia between West and East: Features of a Regional Culture', *Millennium,* 1 (2004), 329–67.
Costambeys, M., Innes, M., & MacLean, S. *The Carolingian World* (Cambridge, 2011).
Crone, P. *The Nativist Prophets of Early Islamic Iran: Rural Revolt and Local Zoroastrianism* (Cambridge, 2012).
Crow, J. 'The Infrastructure of a Great City: Earth, Walls and Water in Late Antique Constantinople', in L. Lavan, E. Zanini, & A. Sarantis, eds, *Technology in Transition AD 300–650* (Leiden, 2007), 251–85.
Ćurčić, S. *Architecture in the Balkans from Diocletian to Suleyman the Magnificent* (New Haven, CT, 2010).
Curta, F. *Southeastern Europe in the Middle Ages 500–1250* (Cambridge, 2006).
Dagron, G. 'Byzance et le modèle islamique au Xe siècle. À propos des Constitutions tactiques de l'empereur Léon VI', *Comptes rendus de l'Académie des Inscriptions et Belles-Lettres,* 127.2 (1983), 219–43.
Daley, B. E. *God Visible: Patristic Christology Reconsidered* (Oxford, 2018).

Daryaee, T. *Sasanian Persia: The Rise and Fall of an Empire* (London, 2010).
Dauge, Y. A. *Le barbare: recherches sur la conception romaine de la barbarie et de la civilisation* (Brussels, 1981).
Delouis, O., Métivier, S., & Pagès, P., eds, *Le saint, le moine et le paysan: Mélanges d'histoire byzantine offerts à Michel Kaplan* (Paris, 2016).
Demus, O. *Byzantine Mosaic Decoration: Aspects of Monumental Art in Byzantium* (London, 1948).
de Planhol, X. *Les fondements géographiques de l'histoire de l'Islam* (Paris, 1968).
Destephen, S., Dumézil, B., & Inglebert, H., eds, *Le prince chrétien de Constantin aux royautés barbares (IVe–VIIIe siècles), TM* 22.2 (2018).
Dignas, B., & Winter, E. *Rome and Persia in Late Antiquity: Neighbours and Rivals* (Cambridge, 2007).
Dodds, E. R. *Pagan and Christian in an Age of Anxiety: Some Aspects of Religious Experience from Marcus Aurelius to Constantine* (Cambridge, 1965).
Doimi de Frankopan Šubić, P. *The Foreign Policy of the Emperor Alexios I Komnenos (1081–c.1100)* (DPhil, Oxford, 1998).
Drocourt, N. & Kolditz, S., eds, *A Companion to Byzantium and the West, 900–1204* (Leiden, 2022).
Ducellier, A. 'Balkan Powers: Albania, Serbia and Bulgaria (1200–1300)', in J. Shepard, ed., *Cambridge History of the Byzantine Empire, c. 500–1492* (Cambridge, 2008), 779–802.
Elton, H. 'Military Forces', in P. Salin, H. Van Wees, & M. Whitby, eds, *The Cambridge History of Greek and Roman Warfare*, 2 vols (Cambridge, 2007), II, 270–309.
Estangüi Gómez, R. *Byzance face aux Ottomans: Exercise du pouvoir et contrôle du territoire sous les derniers Paléologues (milieu XIVe– milieu XVe siècle)* (Paris, 2014).
Exarchos, L. 'Komnenoi and Staufer: Ambition and Confrontation', in N. Drocourt & S. Kolditz, eds, *A Companion to Byzantium and the West, 900–1204* (Leiden, 2022), 215–46.
Fine Jr., J. V. A. *The Late Medieval Balkans: A Critical Survey from the Late Twelfth Century to the Ottoman Conquest* (Ann Arbor, Michigan, 1987).
Fleet, K., ed., *Cambridge History of Turkey*, I *Byzantium to Turkey 1071–1453* (Cambridge, 2009).
Flusin, B. 'L'enseignement et la culture écrite', in J.-C. Cheynet, ed., *Le monde byzantin*, II *L'empire byzantin (641–1204)* (Paris, 2006), 341–68.
Flusin, B., & Cheynet, J.-C., eds, *Autour du* Premier humanisme byzantin *& des* Cinq études sur le XIe siècle, *quarante ans après Paul Lemerle, TM* 21.2 (2017).
Forrest, S. J. *Destroying the 'Brazen Wall': Byzantium and the Umayyad Caliphate in the First Reign of Justinian II, 685–695* (MPhil, Oxford, 2018).
Foss, C. *The Beginnings of the Ottoman Empire* (Oxford, 2022).
Foy, D. 'An Overview of the Circulation of Glass in Antiquity', in A. Wilson & A. Bowman, eds, *Trade, Commerce, and the State in the Roman World* (Oxford, 2017), 265–99.
France, J. *Victory in the East: A Military History of the First Crusade* (Cambridge, 1994).
Franklin, S., & Shepard, J. *The Emergence of Rus 750–1200* (London, 1996).
Frankopan, P. 'Byzantine Trade Privileges to Venice in the Eleventh Century: The Chrysobull of 1092', *Journal of Medieval History*, 30 (2004), 135–60.
Frankopan, P. 'Kinship and the Distribution of Power in Komnenian Byzantium', *EHR* 122 (2007), 1–34.
Frankopan, P. *The First Crusade: The Call from the East* (London, 2012).
Freeman, P., & Kennedy, D., eds, *The Defence of the Roman and Byzantine East*, BAR Int. Ser. 297 (Oxford, 1986).
French, D. H. & Lightfoot, C. S., eds, *The Eastern Frontier of the Roman Empire*, BAR Int. Ser. 553 (Oxford, 1989).

Fried, J. 'The Frankish Kingdoms, 817–911: The East and Middle Kingdoms', in R. McKitterick, ed., *New CMH* II *ca.700–ca.900* (Cambridge, 1995), 142–68.
Garrood, W. 'The Byzantine Conquest of Cilicia and the Hamdanids of Aleppo, 959–965', *Anatolian Studies*, 58 (2008), 127–40.
Gasparri, S. 'The Formation of an Early Medieval Community: Venice between Provincial and Urban Identity', in V. West-Harling, ed., *Three Empires, Three Cities: Identity, Material Culture and Legitimacy in Venice, Ravenna and Rome, 750–1000* (Turnhout, 2015), 35–50.
Golden, P. B. 'The Peoples of the South Russian Steppes', in D. Sinor, ed., *Cambridge History of Early Inner Asia* (Cambridge, 1990), 261–5.
Golden, P. B., Ben-Shammai, H., & Róna-Tas, A., eds, *The World of the Khazars: New Perspectives*, Handbook of Oriental Studies 17 (Leiden, 2007).
Golden, P. B. 'Khazar Studies: Achievements and Perspectives', in P. B. Golden, H. Ben-Shammai, & A. Róna-Tas, eds, *The World of the Khazars: New Perspectives*, Handbook of Oriental Studies 17 (Leiden, 2007), 7–57.
Goodwin, T., ed., *Arab-Byzantine Coinage and History* (London, 2012).
Gordon, M. S. *The Breaking of a Thousand Swords: A History of the Turkish Military of Samarra (A.H. 200–275/815–889 C.E.)* (Albany, NY, 2001).
Gouma-Peterson, T., ed., *Anna Komnene and her Times* (New York, 2000).
Gray, E. W. 'The Roman Eastern *Limes* from Constantine to Justinian: Perspectives and Problems', *Proceedings of the African Classical Associations*, 12 (1973), 24–40.
Gray, P. T. R. 'The Legacy of Chalcedon: Christological Problems and Their Significance', in M. Maas, ed., *Cambridge Companion to the Age of Justinian* (Cambridge, 2005), 215–38.
Greatrex, G. 'Nika Riot: A Reasssessment', *JHS* 117 (1997), 60–86.
Greatrex, G. *Rome and Persia at War, 502–532* (Leeds, 1998).
Greatrex, G., & Lieu, S. N. C., eds, *The Roman Eastern Frontier and the Persian Wars, Part II AD 363–630: A Narrative Sourcebook* (London, 2002).
Greenwood, T. 'Failure of a Mission? Photius and the Armenian Church', *Le Muséon*, 119 (2006), 123–67.
Gutas, D. *Greek Thought, Arab Culture: The Graeco-Arabic Translation Movement in Baghdad and Early Abbasid Society (2nd–4th/8th–10th Centuries)* (London, 1998).
Gyselen, R., ed., *Sasanian Persia and the Tabarestan Archive*, Res Orientales 27 (Bures-sur-Yvette, 2019).
Haarer, F. K. *Anastasius I: Politics and Empire in the Late Roman World* (Leeds, 2006).
Haldon, J. F., & Kennedy, H. 'The Arab Byzantine Frontier in the Eighth and Ninth Centuries: Military Organization and Society in the Borderlands', *Zbornik Radova Viz. Inst.*, 19 (1980), 79–116.
Hall, E. *Inventing the Barbarian: Greek Self-Definition through Tragedy* (Oxford, 1991).
Hammond, N. G. L. *A History of Macedonia*, 3 vols (Oxford, 1972–88).
Harper, K. *The Fate of Rome: Climate, Disease and the End of an Empire* (Princeton, NJ, 2017).
Harris, J. *The End of Byzantium* (New Haven, CT, 2010).
Harris, J. *Byzantium and the Crusades* (2nd edn, London, 2014).
Harris, J., Holmes, C., & Russell, E., eds, *Byzantines, Latins, and Turks in the Eastern Mediterranean World after 1150* (Oxford, 2012).
Hattersley-Smith, K. *Byzantine Public Architecture between the Fourth and Early Eleventh Centuries AD, with Special Reference to the Towns of Byzantine Macedonia* (Thessaloniki, 1996).
Heather, P. J. *Goths and Romans 332–489* (Oxford, 1991).

Heather, P. 'New Men for New Constantines? Creating an Imperial Elite in the Eastern Mediterranean', in P. Magdalino, ed., *New Constantines: The Rhythm of Imperial Renewal in Byzantium, 4th–13th Centuries* (Aldershot, 1994).

Heather, P. *The Fall of Rome: A New History* (London, 2005).

Heather, P. *Empires and Barbarians: Migration, Development and the Birth of Europe* (London, 2009).

Heather, P. *Rome Resurgent: War and Empire in the Age of Justinian* (Oxford, 2018).

Hedeager, L. *Iron Age Myth and Materiality: An Archaeology of Scandinavia AD 400–1000* (London, 2011).

Hendy, M. F. 'Byzantium, 1081–1204: An Economic Reappraisal', *Transactions of the Royal Historical Society*, ser. 5, 20 (1970), 31–52.

Herzig, E., & Stewart, S., eds, *Early Islamic Iran*, The Idea of Iran 5 (London, 2012).

Hillenbrand, C. *Turkish Myth and Muslim Symbol: The Battle of Manzikert* (Edinburgh, 2007).

Hillsdale, C. J. *Byzantine Art and Diplomacy in an Age of Decline* (Cambridge, 2014).

Hladký, V. *The Philosophy of Gemistos Plethon: Platonism in Late Byzantium, between Hellenism and Christianity* (Farnham, 2014).

Hodges, R., & Whitehouse, D., rev. C. Morrisson, J. Lefort, & J.-P. Sodini, *Mahomet, Charlemagne et les origines de l'Europe* (Paris, 1996).

Hogarth, D. G., & Munro, J. A. R. 'Modern and Ancient Roads in Eastern Asia Minor', *Royal Geographical Society, Supplementary Papers*, 3 (1893), 643–739.

Holmes, C. *Basil II and the Governance of Empire (976–1025)* (Oxford, 2005).

Howard-Johnston, J. 'Procopius, Roman Defences North of the Taurus and the New Fortress of Citharizon', in D. H. French & C. S. Lightfoot, eds, *The Eastern Frontier of the Roman Empire*, BAR Int. Ser. 553 (Oxford, 1989), 203–29, repr. in J. Howard-Johnston, *East Rome, Sasanian Persia and the End of Antiquity* (Aldershot, 2006), no. II.

Howard-Johnston, J. 'The Siege of Constantinople in 626', in C. Mango & G. Dagron, eds, Constantinople and its Hinterland (Aldershot, 1995), 131–42, repr. in J. Howard-Johnston, *East Rome, Sasanian Persia and the End of Antiquity: Historiographical and Historical Studies* (Aldershot, 2006), no. VII.

Howard-Johnston, J. 'Anna Komnene and the *Alexiad*', in M. Mullett & D. Smythe, eds, *Alexios I Komnenos* (Belfast, 1996), 260–302.

Howard-Johnston, J. *East Rome, Sasanian Persia and the End of Antiquity: Historiographical and Historical Studies* (Aldershot, 2006).

Howard-Johnston, J. 'A Short Piece of Narrative History: War and Diplomacy in the Balkans, winter 921/2–spring 924', in E. M. Jeffreys, ed., *Byzantine Style, Religion and Civilization: In Honour of Sir Steven Runciman* (Cambridge, 2006), 340–60.

Howard-Johnston, J. 'Byzantine Sources for Khazar History', in P. B. Golden, H. Ben-Shammai & A. Róna-Tas, eds, *The World of the Khazars: New Perspectives*, Handbook of Oriental Studies 17 (Leiden, 2007), 163–93.

Howard-Johnston, J. 'Byzantium, Bulgaria and the Peoples of Ukraine in the 890s', in *Materialy po Arkheologii i Etnografii Tavrii*, 7 (Simferopol, 2008), 342–56.

Howard-Johnston, J. 'The Sasanians' Strategic Dilemma', in H. Börm & J. Wiesehöfer, eds, *Commutatio et contentio—Studies in the Late Roman, Sasanian and Early Islamic Near East: In Memory of Zeev Rubin* (Düsseldorf, 2010), 37–70.

Howard-Johnston, J. *Witnesses to a World Crisis: Historians and Histories of the Middle East in the Seventh Century* (Oxford, 2010).

Howard-Johnston, J. 'Military Infrastructure in the Roman Provinces North and South of the Armenian Taurus in Late Antiquity', in A. Sarantis & N. Christie, eds, *War and Warfare in Late Antiquity*, 2 vols (Leiden, 2013), II, 853–91.

Howard-Johnston, J. *Historical Writing in Byzantium*, Kieler Felix-Jacoby Vorlesungen (Heidelberg, 2014).

Howard-Johnston, J. 'Partitive Inheritance in Principle and Practice in Eleventh-Century Byzantium', in B. Caseau & S. R. Huebner, eds, *Inheritance, Law and Religions in the Ancient and Medieval Worlds* (Paris, 2014), 259–71.

Howard-Johnston, J. 'Theophanes on the Recent Past: The Crisis of 782 and its Antecedents', in M. Jankowiak & F. Montinaro, eds, *Studies in Theophanes*, *TM* 19 (Paris, 2015), 473–90.

Howard-Johnston, J. 'The India Trade in Late Antiquity', in E. W. Sauer, ed., *Sasanian Persia: Between Rome and the Steppes of Eurasia* (Edinburgh, 2017), 284–304.

Howard-Johnston, J. 'World War in Eurasia at the End of Antiquity', in R. Gyselen, ed., *Sasanian Persia and the Tabarestan Archive*, Res Orientales 27 (Bures-sur-Yvette, 2019), 9–28.

Howard-Johnston, J., ed., *Social Change in Town and Country in Eleventh-Century Byzantium* (Oxford, 2020).

Howard-Johnston, J. 'Bilingual Reading, the *Alexiad* and the *Gesta Roberti Wiscardi*', in T. Shawcross & I. Toth, eds, *Reading in the Byzantine Empire and Beyond* (Cambridge, 2021), 467–98.

Howard-Johnston, J. *The Last Great War of Antiquity* (Oxford, 2021).

Howard-Johnston, J. 'The Coming of the Arabs to Iran', *Sasanian Studies*, 1 (2022), 99–126.

Howard-Johnston, J. *Byzantium: Economy, Society, Institutions 600–1100* (Oxford, 2024).

Howard-Johnston J., & Hayward, P. A., eds, *The Cult of Saints in Late Antiquity and the Early Middle Ages: Essays on the Contribution of Peter Brown* (Oxford, 1999).

Howard-Johnston, J. D., ed., *Byzantium and the West c.850–c.1200*, *Byz. Forsch.* 13 (1988).

Humfress, C. 'Law and Legal Practice in the Age of Justinian', in M. Maas, ed., *Cambridge Companion to the Age of Justinian* (Cambridge, 2005), 161–84.

Humfress, C. *Orthodoxy and the Courts in Late Antiquity* (Oxford, 2007).

Humphreys, M. T. G. *Law, Power, and Imperial Ideology in the Iconoclast Era c.680–850* (Oxford, 2015).

Imber, C. *The Ottoman Empire 1300–1481* (Istanbul, 1990).

Jackson Bonner, M. R. *Three Neglected Sources of Sasanian History in the Reign of Khusraw Anushirvan*, Studia Iranica, cahier 46 (Paris, 2011).

Jankowiak, M. *Essai d'histoire politique du monothélisme à partir de la correspondance entre les empereurs byzantins, les patriarches de Constantinople et les papes* (PhD, Paris–Warsaw, 2009).

Jankowiak, M. '*Notitia* I and the Impact of the Arab Invasions on Asia Minor', *Millennium* 10 (2013), 435–61.

Jankowiak, M. 'The First Arab Siege of Constantinople', in C. Zuckerman, ed., *Constructing the Seventh Century*, *TM* 17 (2013), 435–59.

Jankowiak, M., & Montinaro, F., eds, *Studies in Theophanes*, *TM* 19 (Paris, 2015).

Jeffreys, E., Haldon J., & Cormack, R., eds, *The Oxford Handbook of Byzantine Studies* (Oxford, 2008).

Jeffreys, E. M. 'Nikephoros Brennios Reconsidered', in V. N. Vlysidou, ed., *The Empire in Crisis? Byzantium in the Eleventh Century (1025–1081)* (Athens, 2003), 201–14.

Jeffreys, E. M., ed., *Byzantine Style, Religion and Civilization: In Honour of Sir Steven Runciman* (Cambridge, 2006).

Jeffreys, M. 'Psellos' Network of Non-Military Administrators', in M. Jeffreys & M. D. Lauxtermann, eds, *The Letters of Psellos: Cultural Networks and Historical Realities* (Oxford, 2017), 435–41.

Jeffreys, M., & Lauxtermann, M. D., eds, *The Letters of Psellos: Cultural Networks and Historical Realities* (Oxford, 2017).

Jenkins, R. J. H. 'The Classical Background to the *Scriptores post Theophanem*', *DOP* 8 (1954), 11–30.

Johns, J. *Arabic Administration in Norman Sicily: The Royal Diwan* (Cambridge, 2002).

Jones, A. H. M. *The Later Roman Empire 284–602*, 3 vols (Oxford, 1964).

Kaldellis, A. 'Did Ioannes I Tzimiskes Campaign in the East in 974?', *Byz.* 84 (2014), 235–40.

Kaldellis, A. *Rivers of Gold, Streams of Blood: The Rise and Fall of Byzantium, 955 AD to the First Crusade* (New York, 2019).

Kaldellis, A., & Siniossoglou, N., eds, *The Cambridge Intellectual History of Byzantium* (Cambridge, 2017).

Kastritsis, D. 'Conquest and Political Legitimation in the Early Ottoman Empire', in J. Harris, C. Holmes, & E. Russell, eds *Byzantines, Latins, and Turks in the Eastern Mediterranean World after 1150* (Oxford, 2012), 221–45.

Kennedy, H. *The Great Arab Conquests: How the Spread of Islam Changed the World We Live in* (London, 2007).

Kennedy, H. *Muslim Spain and Portugal: A Political History of al-Andalus* (London, 2014).

Kennedy, H. *The Prophet and the Age of the Caliphates: The Islamic Near East from the Sixth to the Eleventh Century* (3rd edn, London, 2016).

Kiel, M. 'The Incorporation of the Balkans into the Ottoman Empire, 1353–1453', in K. Fleet, ed., *Cambridge History of Turkey*, I *Byzantium to Turkey 1071–1453* (Cambridge, 2009), 138–91.

Kim, H. J. *The Huns* (London, 2016).

Kingsley, S., & Decker, M., eds, *Economy and Exchange in the East Mediterranean during Late Antiquity* (Oxford, 2001).

Kiousopoulou, T. *Emperor or Manager: Power and Political Ideology in Byzantium before 1453* (Geneva, 2011).

Kislinger, E. 'Byzantinische Flotten in der venezianischen Lagune 806–810/811: Zu chronologisch-inhaltlicher Manipulation in der Annales regni Francorum', *Millenium*, 17 (2020), 303–22.

Koltsida-Makre, I. 'The Representation of the Cross on Byzantine Lead Seals', *Studies in Byzantine Sigillography*, 4 (1995), 43–51.

Kominko, M. *The World of Kosmas: Illustrated Byzantine Codices of the Christian Topography* (Cambridge, 2013).

Korobeinikov, D. A. 'Raiders and Neighbours: The Turks (1040–1304),' in J. Shepard, ed., *Cambridge History of the Byzantine Empire, c.500–1492* (Cambridge, 2008), 692–727.

Korobeinikov, D. *Byzantium and the Turks in the Thirteenth Century* (Oxford, 2014).

Krallis, D. *Michael Attaleiates and the Politics of Imperial Decline in Eleventh-Century Byzantium* (Tempe, AZ, 2012).

Laiou, A. E. *Constantinople and the Latins: The Foreign Policy of Andronicus II, 1282–1328* (Cambridge, MA, 1972).

Laiou, A. E. 'The Palaiologoi and the World around them', in J. Shepard, ed., *Cambridge History of the Byzantine Empire, c. 500–1492* (Cambridge, 2008), 803–33.

Laiou, A. E., & Morrisson, C. *The Byzantine Economy* (Cambridge, 2007).

Lau, M. *The Emperor John II Komnenos: Rebuilding New Rome 1118–1143* (Oxford, 2023).

Lauxtermann, M. D., & Whittow, M., eds, *Byzantium in the Eleventh Century: Being in Between* (Abingdon, 2017).

Lavan, L., Zanini, E., & Sarantis, A., eds, *Technology in Transition AD 300–650* (Leiden, 2007).

Lemerle, P. 'L'histoire des Pauliciens d'Asie Mineure d'après les sources grecques', *TM* 5 (1973), 1–144.

Lemerle, P. *Le premier humanisme byzantin: notes et remarques sur enseignement et culture à Byzance des origines au Xe siècle* (Paris, 1971).

Lemerle, P. *Byzantine Humanism: The First Phase* (Canberra, 1986).

Le Patourel, J. *The Norman Empire* (Oxford, 1976).

Leyser, K. 'The Tenth Century in Byzantine–Western Relationships', in D. Baker, ed., *Relations between East and West in the Middle Ages* (Edinburgh, 1973).

Leyser, K. 'Ends and Means in Liudprand of Cremona', in J. D. Howard-Johnston, ed., *Byzantium and the West c.850–c.1200, Byzantinische. Forschungen,* 13 (1988), 119–43.

Liebeschuetz, J. H. W. G. *The Decline and Fall of the Roman City* (Oxford, 2001).

Liebeschuetz, J. H. W. G. 'The Lower Danube Region under Pressure: From Valens to Heraclius', in A. G. Poulter, ed., *The Transition to Late Antiquity on the Danube and Beyond* (Oxford, 2007), 101–34.

Lilie, R.-J. *Die byzantinische Reaktion auf die Ausbreitung der Araber*, Miscellanea Byzantina Monacensia 22 (Munich, 1976).

Lilie, R.-J. *Handel und Politik zwischen dem byzantinischen Reich und den italienischen Kommunen Venedig, Pisa und Genua in der Epoche der Komnenen und der Angeloi (1081–1204)* (Amsterdam, 1984).

Lindner, P. 'Anatolia, 1300–1451', in K. Fleet, ed., *Cambridge History of Turkey*, I *Byzantium to Turkey 1071–1453* (Cambridge, 2009), 102–37.

Little, L. K., ed., *Plague and the End of Antiquity: The Pandemic of 541–750* (Cambridge, 2007).

Ljubarskij, Ja. N. *Mikhail Psell: Lichnost' i tvorchestvo* (Moscow, 1978).

Loud, G. A. *The Age of Robert Guiscard: Southern Italy and the Norman Conquest* (London, 2000).

Luscombe, D., & Riley-Smith, J., eds, *New CMH* IV *c.1024–c.1198*, pt. 2 (Cambridge, 2004).

Maas, M., ed., *Cambridge Companion to the Age of Justinian* (Cambridge, 2005).

Magdalino, P. *Tradition and Transformation in Medieval Byzantium* (Aldershot, 1991), no. XIV ('Hellenism and Nationalism in Byzantium').

Magdalino, P. *The Empire of Manuel I Komnenos, 1143–1180* (Cambridge, 1993).

Magdalino, P., ed., *New Constantines: The Rhythm of Imperial Renewal in Byzantium, 4th–13th Centuries* (Aldershot, 1994).

Magdalino, P. 'The Road to Baghdad in the Thought-World of Ninth-Century Byzantium', in L. Brubaker, ed., *Byzantium in the Ninth Century: Dead or Alive?* (Aldershot, 1998).

Mahé, J.-P. 'Basile II et Byzance vus par Grigor Narekac'i', *TM* 11 (1991), 555–73.

Mahé, A., & Mahé, J.-P. *Histoire de l'Arménie des origines à nos jours* (Paris, 2012).

Mainstone, R. J. *Hagia Sophia: Architecture, Structure and Liturgy of Justinian's Great Church* (London, 1988).

Malcolm, N. *Useful Enemies: Islam and the Ottoman Empire in Western Political Thought, 1450–1750* (Oxford, 2019).

Malone-Lee, M. *Cardinal Bessarion: Most Latin of Greeks, Most Greek of Latins* (Abingdon, 2024).

Mango, C. *Le développement urbain de Constantinople (IVe–VIIe siècles)* (Paris, 1985).

Mango, C. *Byzantine Architecture* (London, 1986).

Mango, C., & Dagron, G., eds, Constantinople and its Hinterland (Aldershot, 1995).

Marrou, R. I. *A History of Education in Antiquity* (London, 1956).

Marsham, A. 'Were there Strategic Considerations in the Seventh-Century Arabian Conquests?', Proceedings of 2017 Tübingen conference on the Battle of Yarmuk (forthcoming).

Martin-Hisard, B. 'Constantinople et les archontes du monde caucasien dans le *Livre des cérémonies*, II, 48', *TM* 13 (2000), 359–530.
Marzano, A., & Métraux, G. P. R., eds, *The Roman Villa in the Mediterranean Basin: Late Republic to Late Empire* (Cambridge, 2018).
Mathews, T. F. *The Art of Byzantium* (London, 1998).
McCabe, A. *A Byzantine Encyclopaedia of Horse Medicine: The Sources, Compilation, and Transmission of the* Hippiatrica (Oxford, 2007).
McCormick, M. 'Byzantium and the West, 700–900', in R. McKitterick, ed., *New CMH* II *c.700–c.900* (Cambridge, 1995), 349–80.
McCormick, M. *Eternal Victory: Triumphal Rulership in Late Antiquity, Byzantium and the Early Medieval West* (Cambridge, 1986).
McGeer, E. *Sowing the Dragon's Teeth: Byzantine Warfare in the Tenth Century*, DO Studies 33 (Washington, DC, 1995).
McKitterick, R., ed., *New CMH* II *c.700–c.900* (Cambridge, 1995).
McLynn, N. 'Imperial Piety in Action: The Theodosians in Church', in S. Destephen, B. Dumézil, & H. Inglebert, eds, *Le prince chrétien de Constantin aux royautés barbares (IVe–VIIIe siècles)*, *TM* 22.2 (2018), 315–39.
Meier, M. *Geschichte der Völkerwanderung: Europa, Asien und Afrika vom 3. bis zum 8. Jahrhundert n. Chr.* (Munich, 2019).
Meyendorff, J. *Imperial Unity and Christian Divisions: The Church 450–680 A.D.* (Crestwood, NY, 1989).
Millar, F. W. *The Roman Near East: 31 BC–AD 337* (Cambridge, MA, 1993).
Mitchell, S. 'The Life of St. Theodatus of Ancyra', *Anatolian Studies*, 32 (1982), 93–113.
Mitchell, S. *A History of the Later Roman Empire, AD 284–641* (Oxford, 2007).
Mitford, T. B. *East of Asia Minor: Rome's Hidden Frontier*, 2 vols (Oxford, 2018).
Morris, R. 'The two Faces of Nikephoros Phokas', *BMGS* 12 (1988), 83–115.
Morris, R. *Monks and Laymen in Byzantium, 843–1118* (Cambridge, 1995).
Morrison, C. 'Revisiter le XIe siècle quarante ans après: expansion et crise', in B. Flusin & J.-C. Cheynet, eds, *Autour du* Premier humanisme byzantin *& des* Cinq études sur le XIe siècle, *quarante ans après Paul Lemerle*, *TM* 21.2 (2017), 611–25.
Moulet, B. *Évêques, pouvoir et société à Byzance (VIII–XIe siècle)* (Paris, 2011).
Müller-Mertens, E. 'The Ottonians as Kings and Emperors', in T. Reuter, ed., *New CMH* III *c.900–c.1024* (Cambridge, 1999), 233–66.
Mullett, M. 'Epistolography', in E. Jeffreys, J. Haldon, & R. Cormack, eds, *The Oxford Handbook of Byzantine Studies* (Oxford, 2008), 882–93.
Mullett, M., & Smythe, D., eds, *Alexios I Komnenos* (Belfast, 1996).
Naval Intelligence Division, Geographical Handbook Series, *Turkey*, 2 vols (Oxford, 1942).
Necipoğlu, N. *Byzantium between the Ottomans and the Latins: Politics and Society in the Late Empire* (Cambridge, 2009).
Nelson, J. L. 'The Frankish Kingdoms, 814–898: The West', in R. McKitterick, ed., *New CMH* II *ca.700–ca.900* (Cambridge, 1995), 110–41.
Nelson, J. L. 'Rulers and Government', in T. Reuter, ed., *New CMH* III *c.900–c.1024* (Cambridge, 1999), 95–129.
Németh, A. *The* Excerpta Constantiniana *and the Byzantine Appropriation of the Past* (Cambridge, 2018).
Neville, L. *Heroes and Romans in Twelfth-century Byzantium: The* Material for History *of Nikephoros Bryennios* (Cambridge, 2012).
Neville, L. *Guide to Byzantine Historical Writing* (Cambridge, 2018).
Nicol, D. M. *The Last Centuries of Byzantium, 1261–1453* (2nd ed., Cambridge, 1993).

Niewöhner, P. 'What Went Wrong? Decline and Ruralization in Eleventh-Century Anatolia: The Archaeological Record', in J. Howard-Johnston, ed., *Social Change in Town and Country in Eleventh-Century Byzantium* (Oxford, 2020), 98–132.

Noyé, G. New Light on the Society of Byzantine Italy', in J. Howard-Johnston, ed., *Social Change in Town and Country in Eleventh-Century Byzantium* (Oxford, 2020), 157–95.

Obolensky, D. *The Byzantine Commonwealth: Eastern Europe 500–1453* (London, 1971).

Oikonomidès, N. *Les listes de préséance byzantines des IXe et Xe siècles* (Paris, 1972).

Omissi, A. *Emperors and Usurpers in the Later Roman Empire: Civil War, Panegyric, and the Construction of Legitimacy* (Oxford, 2018).

Ostrogorsky, G. 'The Byzantine Emperor and the Hierarchical World Order', *Slavonic and East European Review*, 35 (1956–7), 1–14.

Ousterhout, R. *Visualizing Community: Art, Material Culture, and Settlement in Byzantine Cappadocia* (Washington, DC, 2017).

Ousterhout, R. 'Aesthetics and Politics in the Architecture of Justinian', in *Constantinople réelle et imaginaire: Autour de l'oeuvre de Gilbert Dagron, TM* 22.1 (2018), 103–20.

Papacostas, T. 'Manuscript Notes and the Black Death in Rural Cyprus', in T. Shawcross & I. Toth, eds, *Reading in the Byzantine Empire and Beyond* (Cambridge, 2018), 133–54.

Payne, R. 'The Making of Turan: The Fall and Transformation of the Iranian East in Late Antiquity', *Journal of Late Antiquity*, 9 (2016), 4–41.

Peacock, A. C. S. *The Great Seljuk Empire* (Edinburgh, 2015).

Pelikan, J. *Christianity and Classical Culture: The Metamorphosis of Natural Theology in the Christian Encounter with Hellenism* (New Haven, CT, 1993).

Pohl, W. *The Avars: A Steppe Empire in Europe, 567–822* (Ithaca, NY, 2018).

Popović, A. *The Revolt of the African Slaves in Iraq in the 3rd/9th Century* (Princeton, NJ, 1999).

Poulter, A. G., ed., *The Transition to Late Antiquity on the Danube and Beyond* (Oxford, 2007).

Poulter, A. G. 'The Transition to Late Antiquity', in A. G. Poulter, ed., *The Transition to Late Antiquity on the Danube and Beyond* (Oxford, 2007), 1–50.

Prasad, P. *Diplomacy and Foreign Policy in the Personal Reign of Constantine VII Porphyrogennetos (945–959)* (DPhil, Oxford, 2015).

Prigent, V. 'Des pères et des fils: Note de numismatique sicilienne pour servir à l'histoire du règne de Constantin IV', in O. Delouis, S. Métivier, & P. Pagès, eds, *Le saint, le moine et le paysan: Mélanges d'histoire byzantine offerts à Michel Kaplan* (Paris, 2016), 589–616.

Rapp, C. *Holy Bishops in Late Antiquity: The Nature of Christian Leadership in an Age of Transition* (Berkeley–Los Angeles, 2005).

Rapp, C. 'Literary Culture under Justinian', in M. Maas, ed., *Cambridge Companion to the Age of Justinian* (Cambridge, 2005).

Reuter, T., ed., *New CMH* III *c.900–c.1024* (Cambridge, 1999).

Reynolds, P. 'The Supply Networks of the Roman East and West: Interaction, Fragmentation, and the Origins of the Byzantine Economy,' in A. Wilson & A. Bowman, eds, *Trade, Commerce, and the State in the Roman World* (Oxford, 2017), 353–95.

Riedel, M. L. D. *Leo VI and the Transformation of Byzantine Christian Identiy: The Writings of an Unexpected Emperor* (Cambridge, 2018).

Runciman, S. *The Emperor Romanus Lecapenus and his Reign: A Study of Tenth-Century Byzantium* (Cambridge, 1963).

Runciman, S. *The Last Byzantine Renaissance* (Cambridge, 1970).

Russell, N. 'The Hesychast Controversy', in A. Kaldellis & N. Siniossoglou, eds, *The Cambridge Intellectual History of Byzantium* (Cambridge, 2017), 494–508.

Ryder, J. R. *The Career and Writings of Demetrius Kydones: A Study of Fourteenth-Century Byzantine Politics, Religion and Society* (Leiden, 2010).

Salin, P., Van Wees, H., & Whitby, M., eds, *The Cambridge History of Greek and Roman Warfare*, 2 vols (Cambridge, 2007).

Sarantis, A., & Christie, N., eds, *War and Warfare in Late Antiquity*, 2 vols (Leiden, 2013).

Sarantis, A. *Justinian's Balkan Wars: Campaigning, Diplomacy and Development in Illyricum, Thrace and the Northern World A.D. 527–65* (Prenton, 2016).

Sarris, P. 'The Justinianic Plague: Origins and Effects', *Continuity and Change*, 17 (2002), 169–82.

Sarris, P. *Economy and Society in the Age of Justinian* (Cambridge, 2006).

Sarris, P. *Empires of Faith: The Fall of Rome to the Rise of Islam, 500–700* (Oxford, 2011).

Sarris, P. *Justinian: Emperor, Soldier, Saint* (Cambridge, 2023).

Sauer, E. W., ed., *Sasanian Persia: Between Rome and the Steppes of Eurasia* (Edinburgh, 2017).

Sergi, G. 'The Kingdom of Italy', in T. Reuter, ed., *New CMH* III *c.900–c.1024* (Cambridge, 1999), 346–71.

Ševčenko, I. 'Re-reading Constantine Porphyrogenitus', in J. Shepard & S. Franklin, eds, *Byzantine Diplomacy* (Aldershot, 1992), 167–95.

Shawcross, T., & Toth, I., eds, *Reading in the Byzantine Empire and Beyond* (Cambridge, 2021).

Shepard, J. 'Aspects of Byzantine Attitudes and Policy towards the West in the Tenth and Eleventh Centuries', in J. D. Howard-Johnston, ed., *Byzantium and the West c.850–c.1200* (Amsterdam, 1988), 67–118.

Shepard, J. 'Slavs and Bulgars', in R. McKitterick, ed., *New CMH* II *c.700–c.900* (Cambridge, 1995), 228–48.

Shepard, J., ed., *Cambridge History of the Byzantine Empire, c. 500–1492* (Cambridge, 2008).

Signes Codoñer, J. *The Emperor Theophilos and the East, 829–842: Court and Frontier in Byzantium during the Last Phase of Iconoclasm* (Farnham, 2014).

Simpson, A. *Niketas Choniates: A Historiographical Study* (Oxford, 2013).

Simpson, A., ed., *Byzantium, 1180–1204: 'The Sad Quarter of a Century'?* (Athens, 2015).

Simpson, A. 'Perceptions and Interpretations of the Late Twelfth Century in Modern Historiography', in A. Simpson, ed., *Byzantium, 1180–1204: 'The Sad Quarter of a Century'?* (Athens, 2015), 13–34.

Siniossoglou, N. *Radical Platonism in Byzantium: Illumination and Utopia in Gemistos Plethon* (Cambridge, 2011).

Sinor, D., ed., *Cambridge History of Early Inner Asia* (Cambridge, 1990).

Sodini, J.-P. 'The Transformation of Cities in Late Antiquity within the Provinces of Macedonia and Epirus', in A. G. Poulter, ed., *The Transition to Late Antiquity on the Danube and Beyond* (Oxford, 2007), 311–36.

Sophoulis, P. *Byzantium and Bulgaria, 775–831* (Leiden, 2012).

Stephenson, P. *Byzantium's Balkan Frontier: A Political Study of the Northern Balkans, 900–1204* (Cambridge, 2000).

Stephenson, P. 'Balkan Borderlands (1018–1204)', in J. Shepard, ed., *Cambridge History of the Byzantine Empire, c. 500–1492* (Cambridge, 2008), 664–91.

Svoronos, N. G. 'Recherches sur le cadastre byzantin et la fiscalité aux XIe et XIIe siècles: le cadastre de Thèbes', *BCH* 83 (1959), 1–145, 805–25.

Svoronos, N. G. *La Synopsis Major des Basiliques et ses appendices: Recherches sur la tradition juridique à Byzance* (Paris, 1964).

Teall, J. 'The Byzantine Agricultural Tradition', *DOP* 25 (1971), 33–59.

Thorn-Wickert, L. *Manuel Chrysoloras (ca.1350–1415): Eine Biographie des byzantinischen Intellektuellen vor dem Hintergrund der hellenistischen Studien in der italienischen Renaissance* (Bonn, 2006).

Tounta, E. 'Political and Cultural Encounters between Byzantium and the Normans, 11th–12th Centuries', in N. Drocourt & S. Kolditz, eds, *A Companion to Byzantium and the West, 900–1204* (Leiden, 2022), 247–69.

Treadgold, W. *The Byzantine Revival 780–842* (Stanford, 1988).

Treadwell, L. 'Byzantium and Islam in the Late 7th Century: A "Numismatic War of Images"', in T. Goodwin, ed., *Arab-Byzantine Coinage and History* (London, 2012), 145–55.

Treadwell, L. 'The Samanids: The First Islamic Dynasty of Central Asia', in E. Herzig & S. Stewart, eds, *Early Islamic Iran*, The Idea of Iran 5 (London, 2012), 3–15.

Turner, J. P. *Inquisition in Early Islam: The Competition for Political and Religious Authority in the Abbasid Empire* (London, 2013).

Twitchett, D., ed., *Cambridge History of China*, III *Sui and T'ang China* (Cambridge, 1979).

Twitchett, D. 'Hsüan-tsung (reign 712–56)', in D. Twitchett, ed., *Cambridge History of China*, III *Sui and T'ang China* (Cambridge, 1979), 333–463.

Tyerman, C. *A New History of the Crusades* (London, 2007).

Vasiliev, A. A. *Byzance et les Arabes*, I *La dynastie d'Amorium (820–867)*, rev. H. Grégoire & M. Canard (Brussels, 1935)—cited as *BA* I.

Vasiliev, A. A. (rev. M. Canard), *Byzance et les Arabes*, II.1 *La dynastie Macédonienne (867–959)* (Brussels, 1968)—cited as *BA* II.1.

Vlysidou, V. N., ed., *The Empire in Crisis? Byzantium in the Eleventh Century (1025–1081)* (Athens, 2003).

von Falkenhausen, V. *Untersuchungen über die byzantinische Herrschaft in Süditalien vom 9. bis ins 11. Jahrhundert* (Wiesbaden, 1967).

Walker, P. E. 'The "Crusade" of John Tzimisces in the Light of New Arabic Evidence', *Byz.* 47 (1977), 301–27.

Walter, C. *The Warrior Saints in Byzantine Art and Tradition* (Aldershot, 2003).

Wander, S. H. *The Joshua Roll* (Wiesbaden, 2012).

Ward-Perkins, B. *From Classical Antiquity to the Middle Ages: Urban Public Building in Northern and Central Italy AD 300–850* (Oxford, 1984).

Wasserstein, D. J. 'The Khazars and the World of Islam', in P. B. Golden, H. Ben-Shammai & A. Róna-Tas, eds, *The World of the Khazars: New Perspectives*, Handbook of Oriental Studies 17 (Leiden, 2007), 373–86.

Weitzmann, K. *Studies in Classical and Byzantine Manuscript Illumination* (Chicago, 1971), 176–223 ('The Character and Intellectual Origins of the Macedonian Renaissance').

West-Harling, V., ed., *Three Empires, Three Cities: Identity, Material Culture and Legitimacy in Venice, Ravenna and Rome, 750–1000* (Turnhout, 2015).

Wharton, A. J. *Art of Empire—Painting and Architecture on the Byzantine Periphery: A Comparative Study of Four Provinces* (Pennsylvania, 1988).

Whitby, M. 'Procopius and Roman Defences in Upper Mesopotamia', in P. Freeman & D. Kennedy, eds, *The Defence of the Roman and Byzantine East*, BAR Int. Ser. 297 (Oxford, 1986), 717–35.

Whitby, M. *The Emperor Maurice and His Historian: Theophylact Simocatta on Persian and Balkan Warfare* (Oxford, 1988).

Whittow, M. 'Ruling the Late Roman and Early Byzantine City', *PP* 129 (1990), 3–29.

Whittow, M. *The Making of Orthodox Byzantium, 600-1025* (London, 1996).

Wickham, C. *Early Medieval Italy: Central Power and Local Society, 400–1000* (London, 1981).

Wickham, C. *Framing the Middle Ages: Europe and the Mediterranean 400–800* (Oxford, 2005).
Wilkes, J. 'Provinces and Frontiers', *CAH* XII (Cambridge, 2005), 212–68.
Wilson A., & Bowman, A., eds, *Trade, Commerce, and the State in the Roman World* (Oxford, 2017).
Wilson, N. G. *Scholars of Byzantium* (London, 1983).
Wybrew, H. *Orthodox Liturgy: The Development of the Eucharistic Liturgy in the Byzantine Rite* (London, 1989).
Zuckerman, C. 'On the Date of the Khazars' Conversion to Judaism and the Chronology of the Kings of Rus Oleg and Igor', *REB* 53 (1995), 237–70.
Zuckerman, C. 'Khazars and Byzantium—The First Encounter', in P. B. Golden, H. Ben-Shammai, & A. Róna-Tas, eds, *The World of the Khazars: New Perspectives*, Handbook of Oriental Studies 17 (Leiden, 2007), 399–432.
Zuckerman, C., ed., *Constructing the Seventh Century, TM* (2015).

# Index

Since the index has been created to work across multiple formats, indexed terms for which a page range is given (e.g., 52–53, 66–70, etc.) may occasionally appear only on some, but not all of the pages within the range.